RADICAL-IN-CHIEF

BARACK OBAMA AND THE UNTOLD STORY OF AMERICAN SOCIALISM

STANLEY KURTZ

THRESHOLD EDITIONS

New York   London   Toronto   Sydney

Threshold Editions
Division of Simon & Schuster, Inc.
1230 Avenue of the Americas
New York, NY 10020

First Threshold Editions hardcover edition October 2010

THRESHOLD EDITIONS and colophon are trademarks of Simon & Schuster, Inc.

For information about special discounts for bulk purchases, please contact Simon & Schuster Special Sales at 1-866-506-1949 or business@simonandschuster.com.

The Simon & Schuster Speakers Bureau can bring authors to your live event. For more information or to book an event contact the Simon & Schuster Speakers Bureau at 1-866-248-3049 or visit our website at www.simonspeakers.com.

Designed by Elliott Beard

Manufactured in the United States of America

10 9 8 7 6 5 4 3 2 1

Library of Congress Cataloging-in-Publication Data

Kurtz, Stanley.
    Radical-in-chief : Barack Obama and the untold story of American socialism / Stanley Kurtz.—
1st Threshold Editions hardcover ed.
        p.   cm.
    1. Obama, Barack—Political and social views.   2. United States—Politics and government—2009–
3. Illinois—Politics and government—1951–   4. Radicalism—United States.   5. Socialism—
United States.   6. Presidents—United States—Biography.   7. Legislators—Illinois—Biography.
8. Political activists—Illinois—Chicago—Biography.   9. Community organization—Illinois—
Chicago—History—20th century.   10. Chicago (Ill.)—Social conditions—20th century.   I. Title.
    E908.3.K87 2010
    973.932092—dc22
    [B]   2010032032

ISBN 978-1-4391-5508-0
ISBN 978-1-4391-7696-2 (ebook)

CONTENTS

SEVEN

Ayers and the Foundations   261

EIGHT

Jeremiah Wright   299

NINE

State Senate Years   329

TEN

The Obama Administration   355

Conclusion   387

What on Earth
Is a Community Organizer?

Ever since Barack Obama's meteoric rise to the presidency began, Americans have been asking themselves that question. The answer, it turns out, solves the riddle of Obama's political convictions. Community organizing is a largely socialist profession. Particularly at the highest levels, America's community organizers have adopted a deliberately stealthy posture—hiding their socialism behind a "populist" front. These organizers strive to push America toward socialism in unobtrusive, incremental steps, calling themselves "pragmatic problem-solvers" all the while. Barack Obama's colleagues and mentors were some of the smartest and most influential stealth-socialist community organizers in the country. Their strategies of political realignment and social transformation guide the Obama administration to this day.

Although contemporary community organizers deliberately hide their socialism, with a bit of digging, their secrets can be revealed. In neglected archives and long-forgotten issues of obscure journals, the untold story of modern American socialism lives. As the revolutionary hopes of sixties radicals banged up against the hard reality of a popular Reagan presidency, America's socialists turned to a combination of community organizing and local politics to move the country steadily leftward by degrees. These were the socialists who schooled Obama. Their story is his story.

The socialist community organizers who inspired and trained Obama openly embraced American democracy. Although they admired Marx, Lenin, and Mao—along with Obama's idol, Saul Alinsky—in the medium term, at least, these organizers surrendered their revolutionary hopes and abandoned authoritarian ways. Some retained a soft spot for Third World Communist regimes in Cuba and Latin America. And surely the program favored by Obama's organizing mentors could be seen as a subtle—and sometimes not so subtle—assault on traditional American freedoms.

Yet this new stealth socialism, which Obama studied and absorbed as a community organizer in Chicago, became more sophisticated and transformed itself into the policies he is now enacting as president. Over the long term, Obama's plans are designed to ensnare the country in a new socialism, a stealth socialism that masquerades as a traditional American sense of fair play, a soft but pernicious socialism similar to that currently strangling the economies of Europe.

This is Barack Obama's secret. The president has systematically disguised the truth about his socialist convictions, sometimes by directly misrepresenting his past and sometimes by omitting or parceling out damaging information to disguise its real importance. Jeremiah Wright, Bill Ayers, and ACORN—all of Obama's well-known radical ties are entry points into the much larger and still unknown socialist world where Obama's career was nurtured. That is why the president has disguised and withheld the truth about these political partnerships.

The time has come to lift the veil and reveal the untold story of America's Radical-in-Chief and his socialist political world.

CHAPTER 1

The Socialism Puzzle

Late on the afternoon of April 1, 1983, a twenty-one-year-old Barack Obama made his way into the historic Great Hall of Manhattan's Cooper Union to attend a "Socialist Scholars Conference."[1] Within twenty-four hours, his life had transformed. There at that conference Obama discovered his vocation as a community organizer, as well as a political program to guide him throughout his adult life.

When Obama attended that first Socialist Scholars Conference, he was in his senior year at Columbia University, where he'd transferred after two years at Occidental College in Los Angeles. Those Columbia years are more mysterious than any other portion of Obama's history. The *New York Times* calls them a "lost chapter" of the president's life.[2] In 2008, the Obama campaign refused to discuss his days at Columbia, declining either to release transcripts or to name friends.[3]

It's clear that Obama's New York interval was a time of "solitude and isolation." In Obama's telling, when his mother and sister came to visit, they "just made fun of me because I was so monklike. I had tons of books. I read everything. I think that was the period when I grew as much as I have ever grown intellectually."[4] But what exactly was Obama reading during this interlude of personal isolation and internal growth? In what direction was his restless intellect pushing him? New York's annual Socialist Scholars Conferences have a great deal to do with the answer to that question, while also suggesting a reason for Obama's relative silence about his four-year sojourn in New York.

CUDDLY KARL MARX

However isolated Obama may have been during his years at Columbia, politics served as at least a partial antidote to the solitude. Obama followed the campus anti-military movement closely, interviewing activists from two organizations, Arms Race Alternatives and Students Against Militarism, for an article he penned entitled, "Breaking the War Mentality."[5] The piece appeared in the campus newsmagazine, *Sundial,* just three weeks prior to the 1983 Socialist Scholars Conference. In that article, Obama worried that the nuclear freeze movement's narrow focus on blocking the deployment of just a few controversial weapons systems risked playing into the hands of "military-industrial interests," with their "billion dollar erector sets." Pressing the point, Obama wondered whether it might be a mistake to separate disarmament issues from broader social questions. Were nuclear weapons themselves really the problem, or was America's reluctance to control arms merely a symptom of larger economic and political troubles?[6] So while we know that in both his course work and his extracurricular writing at the time,[7] Obama was concentrating on international issues, he clearly hoped to approach those questions from the standpoint of a more sweeping critique of American life.

Systematic criticism of American society is exactly what the 1983 Socialist Scholars Conference promised to provide. Fliers and ads featured caricatures of an almost cuddly-looking Karl Marx reclining on a stack of books. Promotions touted the conference as a meeting "In honor of Karl Marx's centennial (1818–1883)."[8] Not by coincidence was this conference held at New York's Cooper Union. For in the wake of Marx's death a century before, the Great Hall of this venerable private college had been the site of the largest memorial to the giant of socialism anywhere in the world—a matter of pride for American Marxists to this day. Six thousand mourners crowded into the Cooper Union to honor Marx on March 19, 1883, while five thousand additional mourners were turned away.[9]

When the renowned nineteenth-century Cuban journalist and revolutionary José Martí addressed that memorial assembly, he acknowledged the fearsome nature of Marx's task of "setting men in opposition against men." Yet "an outlet must be found for this anger, so that the brutality might cease," said Martí. Then, gesturing toward the large, leaf-garlanded picture of Marx that dominated Cooper Union's Great Hall that day, Martí lauded Marx as an "ardent reformer, uniter of men of different peoples, and tireless, powerful organizer."[10] A century later, the vocation of socialist organizer was alive, well, and still reverberating through Cooper Union's halls.

SOCIALIST ORGANIZERS

The opening remarks of the 1983 Cooper Union Socialist Scholars Conference were delivered by City University of New York (CUNY) professor Frances Fox Piven.[11] Piven served on the National Executive Committee of the Democratic Socialists of America (DSA) in the 1980s, and the conference itself was sponsored by the DSA.[12] Widely recognized as a preeminent theorist, strategist, and historian of community organizing, with a keen sense of the roots of contemporary organizing in America's early communist and socialist movements, Piven was an obvious choice to open the conference. Piven's ties to ACORN (Association of Community Organizations for Reform Now) ran deep, and this conference would provide her with an opportunity to put forward her latest innovation—a voter registration strategy designed to radicalize the Democratic Party and polarize the country along class lines. Piven's strategy would be carried out in collaboration with ACORN, Project Vote, and related organizations over the ensuing decades.[13] Not coincidentally, Obama would soon embark on a lifetime alliance with these very groups. Yet discussion of Piven's latest strategic thinking would await the following morning's panels. To open a conference in honor of Marx's centennial, Piven offered an appropriately expansive reflection on Marx's relevance to the present.

Although there are few easily accessible published accounts of the 1983 Cooper Union Socialist Scholars Conference, it is possible to piece together not only Piven's opening remarks, but what the experience of the larger conference would have been like for Obama and others. Piven's personal papers at the Sophia Smith Collection of Smith College contain a conference brochure, as well as hand-written notes of her opening remarks. The Records of the Democratic Socialists of America at New York University's Tamiment Library contain files on the '83 conference, and various other relevant internal documents. Contemporaneous publications by conference participants in assorted socialist periodicals cast substantial light on the content of many presentations, and microfilm records of the American Marxist *Guardian* newspaper include reportage on the '83 conference. These and other sources make it possible to reconstruct the day that changed Barack Obama's life.

The Marx invoked by Piven in her brief but eloquent opening conference remarks was less the economic theorist or historian than the man whose ideas "helped people around the globe to struggle to *make* history." With Marx's help, said Piven, "common people became historical actors, and *their* history is far from over." "We must stand within the intellectual and political tradition Marx bequeathed," she continued, yet treat it not as a "dead inheritance," but as a "living tradition—the creation of thinking, active people" who shape history inspired by

Marx's ideas, yet continually adjusting and adapting those ideas to "new political conditions." [14]

Anyone familiar with Piven's writings, like her 1977 classic, *Poor People's Movements: Why They Succeed, How They Fail,* with Richard Cloward, will know how seriously she meant those words. [15] Piven's organizing strategies actively, yet never slavishly, draw upon Marx's thought, even as they adapt the Marxist tradition to modern American circumstances. The secret, well understood by leading organizers (Barack Obama included), yet still unknown to the vast majority of Americans, is that contemporary community organizing is largely a socialist enterprise—a novel adaptation of Marxist principles and practices to modern American realities. Marx himself was a great organizer, and America's leading community organizers are Marxists. By calling on common folk to seize and make their own history on the model of Marx—even if in a novel American context—Piven was acknowledging the socialist character of contemporary community organizing.

IS OBAMA A SOCIALIST?

Thus we arrive at the central question. What if Barack Obama's fiercest critics are right? What if the president of the United States is a socialist? The Obama-as-socialist claim is often dismissed as an outrageous exaggeration. After all, socialism calls for collective ownership of the "means of production." Bailouts of General Motors and the banking system, expanded energy regulation, and high government spending notwithstanding, Obama has proposed nothing like a sweeping government takeover of America's entire business system. It's true that government command of the nation's health-care system would encompass up to 16 percent of the economy, yet Obama denies that fully nationalized health care is his goal. [16] Even if his critics are right and Obama quietly favors transition to a government-run "single-payer" plan over the long term, the lion's share of the free-enterprise system would remain intact. Moreover, since many non-socialist liberals favor government-run health care, it seems unfair to label even the most expansive interpretation of Obama's health-care goals as socialist.

Part of the problem here turns on questions of definition. On both the right and the left, socialism can be defined strictly (as total government control of an essentially redistributive economy) or loosely (as any governmentally imposed compromise of pure capitalist principles on behalf of economic equality). If you define socialism strictly, then claims that Obama is a socialist look like overheated slander. Defined more loosely, even left-leaning *Newsweek* can claim that "we are all socialists now," and conservatives can legitimately raise warning flags about the long-term implications for liberty and prosperity of ambitious liberal reforms.[17]

But if it's all a matter of semantics, why bother? Why not just drop the whole "socialism" debate as a sticky, impossible-to-pin-down, emotionally fraught mess? That's how it seemed to me during the 2008 presidential campaign, when I published a long series of investigative articles on Obama's political background and ideology. When the question of Obama's alleged socialism came up in interviews, I'd try to bracket the issue. You can make a good argument that he is, I'd agree, but ultimately I put the socialism issue off as a sticky, irresolvable question of definition.[18] What I did claim in 2008, and what I expected to argue in this book, is that Obama's political convictions are vastly farther to the left than the popular image of a bipartisan, technocratic, and pragmatic Obama acknowledges.

So when I began my post-campaign research for this book, my inclination was to downplay or dismiss evidence of explicit socialism in Obama's background. I thought the socialism issue was an unprovable and unnecessary distraction from the broader question of Obama's ultra-liberal inclinations. I was wrong. Evidence that suggests Obama is a socialist, I am now convinced, is real, important, and profoundly relevant to the present. It took some time to uncover the details of the 1983 Socialist Scholars Conference that I now believe had so formative an influence on Obama's political career. It was earlier, however—when

I discovered programs from the 1984 and 1985 Socialist Scholars Conferences (which I believe Obama also attended)—that I began to change my mind about the Obama-as-socialist issue.[19] I did a double-take when I saw those conference programs dotted with names I'd run across researching Obama's world of community organizing. I was particularly stunned to see that Jeremiah Wright's theological mentor, the eminent black liberation theologian James Cone, had spoken at the 1984 Socialist Scholars Conference.[20] Could Obama have been familiar with the Marxist-inflected theology that inspired Jeremiah Wright well before he moved to Chicago? Could this help explain why Obama chose Wright as his pastor?

SOCIALIST STRATEGY

The more I dug into things, the more the theme of socialism appeared to tie together various aspects of Obama's political life. It quickly became clear that I would not be able to set the issue aside. But what about all those messy definitional questions? I had no choice but to dive in and confront them. I'd have to educate myself in the socialism of the 1980s, and beyond. What I discovered through researching contemporary American socialism changed my way of thinking about Barack Obama, and about much else besides.

Having once taught Marx alongside a series of other thinkers in a university "Great Books" program, I thought I understood at least the basics. After reading history's leading radical, I worked with a fairly strict definition of socialism: full collective control of the means of production. This academic background was yet another reason why the whole Obama-as-socialist question made me uncomfortable.

I thought I knew too much, but in fact I knew too little. My academic interest in Marx had focused on his theories of history and society. I was far less knowledgeable about Marx's strategy and tactics—his vision of how a socialist world would actually come about. The simple answer, of course, is that Marx expected to see capitalism overthrown by a violent socialist revolution. Yet there's a great deal more to it than that. Marx "the organizer" was a subtle fellow. The world's most famous revolutionary was often willing to use democratic means to achieve his ultimate ends. Marx was prepared to compromise his long-term goals in pursuit of short-term gains, particularly when he thought this democratic maneuvering would position the communist movement for more radical breakthroughs in the future. And Marx-the-democrat was sometimes less than fully open about his ultimate goals. He recognized that not only his enemies, but even potential followers could be put off by his most radical plans. So, depending on context, even with workers he aspired to lead in revolution, Marx withheld the full truth of who he was and what he hoped to achieve.[21]

These are the sorts of questions socialists debate amongst themselves. Marx never systematized his strategic or tactical thinking, and various groups of followers interpret his example differently. Some downplay Marx's tactical compromises and focus on the goal of a violent revolution designed to usher in full-scale authoritarian socialism. Others claim that Marx would have happily achieved his revolutionary goals by peaceful democratic means, if he'd thought that would work. These "democratic socialists" add that a peaceful political path to socialism is the only route that makes sense in America's thoroughly democratic context. The most committed democratic socialists even claim to reject authoritarian socialism altogether. Socialism and democracy, they say, are complementary goals.

This is the stuff of never-ending factional dispute among American socialists: Should we socialists eschew capitalist-tainted politics and foment revolution? Or should we openly (or perhaps not so openly) dive into America's electoral system and try to turn its political currents in our own direction? Should we accept only full-scale socialism at-a-blow, or should we settle for a piecemeal transition to a socialist world, even if that risks co-optation by capitalism along the way? In other words, the battle over relatively "strict" and "loose" definitions of socialism is constantly being waged among socialists themselves.

Few Americans understand any of this. More to the point, the bubbling, breathing, living world of American socialism in the decades that followed the upheavals of the sixties is almost totally unknown to us. There are few serious accounts of America's socialist left in the seventies, eighties, and nineties. Yet Barack Obama's political life—and the world of community organizing generally—is intimately bound up with the story of American socialism during those decades. It is a story we'll have to teach ourselves. Because once you understand the socialism that dominated that 1983 conference in New York, the notion of a socialist American president looks less like an absurd exaggeration and more like an all-too-disturbingly real possibility.

PRAGMATIC OBAMA?

Various objections can be raised to this line of argument. On one popular view, for example, President Obama is not an ideologue but a pragmatist. After all, any politician vying for success in a South Chicago district populated by impoverished minority and liberal university voters would have to lean left. On ascending to the presidency, an essentially pragmatic Obama would presumably revert to a moderate, even bipartisan, stance, in keeping with his national constituency.

One problem with the "pragmatist" argument is that Obama actively chose Hyde Park as his adoptive home. In other words, Obama selected one of the most left-leaning districts in the nation as his political base for a reason. And Obama was clearly walking a radical path well before he stepped into Cooper Union's Great Hall. In a famous passage of his memoir, *Dreams from My Father,* Obama speaks of carefully choosing his friends at Occidental College from among the "Marxist professors," "structural feminists," and other radical outsiders. Even in his early college years, Obama was determined "to avoid being mistaken for a sellout." [22]

In February of 2010, John C. Drew, an acquaintance of Obama

around 1980–81, reported that during his time at Occidental College, Obama was a "pure Marxist socialist." According to Drew—himself a Marxist radical in his youth—the young Obama hewed to the "Marxist-Leninist" view that a violent socialist revolution was likely within his lifetime. The job of a proper radical, Obama believed, was to prepare for that event.[23] A couple of months later, in April of 2010, David Remnick's fascinating, thoughtful, and highly sympathetic biography of Obama effectively confirmed Drew's report by revealing that the future president and many of his closest friends at Occidental College were socialists.[24] This collection of evidence from diverse sources regarding Obama's early socialist convictions could be dismissed as proof of nothing more than the passing ideological fling of a young man in college. After studying Obama's life, however, these reports strike me as merely the most visible markers along what is in fact a continuous ideological trail, ranging from the childhood influence of Obama's radical mentor, Frank Marshall Davis, to the Socialist Scholars Conferences of Obama's New York years, to the future president's community organizing days and political career.

No doubt, for many a mature politician of pragmatic bent, the passing fancies of youth just don't matter anymore. Obama is not that type. Everything about his story bespeaks continuity and sincerity of conviction. While *Dreams from My Father* does much to obscure the details of Obama's political beliefs and actions, the larger message of the book is that his progressive political stance is sincerely held. *Dreams* makes it clear, moreover, that progressive politics served as the solution to Obama's personal crisis—the internal struggle forced upon him by his biracial heritage and his father's tragic absence.

In other words, Obama's long-time political convictions are nothing if not deeply and sincerely held. That is virtually the point of *Dreams*. On this score, at least, I believe Obama's self-portrayal to be entirely accurate. Obama is a community organizer who sincerely believes what other community organizers believe. The problem is that community organizers are not forthcoming about the true nature of their beliefs. All too often, they consciously mask a hard-edged socialism in feel-good euphemistic code. The word "pragmatism," moreover, holds a special place of honor in that same deliberately misleading language.[25]

A PASSING INFATUATION?

Another objection to accounts of Obama's radicalism holds that even if the president did have a youthful infatuation with socialism, it was just a passing phase. Yet there are abundant signs of continuity in Obama's political views. In July of 2009, the *New York Times* dusted off the president's twenty-six-year-old *Sundial* essay for a front-page article entitled "Youthful Ideals Shaped Obama Goal of Nuclear Disarmament."[26] Tracing Obama's ideas about nuclear weapons from his undergraduate years to the present, the *Times* concluded that the president's core convictions on this issue—and even some of his specific phrasing—had changed little over time. No doubt there are many politicians whose youthful writings bear little on present policy. In Obama's case, however, the connection is strong.

The profound continuity between Obama's youthful socialism and his adult career has been obscured by the secrecy so common to contemporary socialist endeavor. That secrecy, however, can be breached. Archival research makes it possible to piece together the socialist background of modern community organizing, and also to recover heretofore lost connections between Barack Obama and that hidden socialist world. In particular, investigation reveals significant ties between Obama and the Midwest Academy, arguably the most influential institutional force in community organizing from the seventies through the nineties, and very much a crypto-socialist organization. Nearly every thread of Obama's career runs directly or indirectly through the Midwest Academy, a fact which has gone almost entirely unreported. Along with the Socialist Scholars Conferences of the early eighties, the story of the Midwest Academy will serve as our gateway to a broader understanding of the history of American socialism in the post-sixties era.

DOES OBAMA'S PAST MATTER?

Another objection to revelations of Obama's radicalism is the claim
that his early ties and convictions have no real bearing on his conduct
as president. Now that the campaign is over, this argument goes, the
president's past is effectively off the table and all that really matters is
his conduct in office. Since Obama hasn't appointed William Ayers as
Secretary of Education or proposed a full-scale government takeover
of the economy, there is simply no point in rehashing his past, however
radical it may or may not have been.

There are several problems with this argument. For one thing, the
president actually has appointed a number of controversial radicals,
whose selection can fairly be connected to his own political past.[27] And
consider the most important domestic issue of Obama's presidency:
health care. A critical moment in the health-care debate came in early
August of 2009, when a video montage of contradictory statements
about health reform by President Obama and others went viral.[28] The
video montage opens with a clip of President Obama shooting down
what he calls "illegitimate" claims that a health-care "public option" is
actually a "Trojan horse" for a "single-payer" system. In other words,
the president denies any intention to lever a government-sponsored
health-care plan (which individuals could reject in favor of private insurance) into a total federal takeover of the nation's health-care system.
As we've seen, the president goes so far as to dismiss the "Trojan horse"
argument as unfit for legitimate debate.

Yet just after that clip comes another from 2007, in which candidate Obama refers to a one- to two-decade transition period during
which he hopes his health reforms will undermine private insurance
plans. Then comes a clip of Obama from 2003 in which he forcefully
announces his support of a single-payer health-care system. This is
followed by a clip of Massachusetts congressman Barney Frank saying,
in effect, that the public option really is a Trojan horse for single-payer.
Then follows Illinois congresswoman Jan Schakowsky, proudly agree-

ing with critics of reform that the public option will put the insurance industry out of business. Schakowsky favors a government-run system and plainly wants the private insurance industry to go bust as quickly as possible. Having displayed these "confessions" by Obama, Frank, and Schakowsky, the montage cuts back to a clip of President Obama smoothly claiming that "nobody is talking about some government takeover of health care." Nobody but Frank, Schakowsky, and Obama, anyway.

This video had a devastating impact on public support for the Democrats' health-care plan and played a important part in driving the town hall "Tea Party" protests of August 2009. The administration attempted to rebut the video by dismissing the early footage of Obama as misleading and out of context.[29] Yet the White House never showed—or even tried to show—that a fair and contextual understanding of Obama's pre-2009 views would in fact contradict the upshot of those clips.

One lesson from this dustup is that the pre-presidential history of Barack Obama has already had an enormous impact to our policy debates—and rightly so. We cannot simply dismiss the past and focus only on what the president says and does in the here and now, because almost any policy change—particularly the sort of sweeping reforms advocated by President Obama—opens a vast range of additional possibilities. To a large extent, the outcome of any reform will ultimately depend on where the president wants the country to go over the long term. So the mind of the man who will enforce and propose the laws over a four- to eight-year period has everything to do with what any single reform will someday become—a simple system fix or an opening to radical change. To know the president's mind is to know a great deal.

In the case of health care, the more deeply we delve into the context of Obama's early policy views, the more radical—and sincerely held— they appear to be. While it can theoretically be argued that Obama's initial support for single-payer health care was a pragmatic adjustment to the demands of his left-leaning Hyde Park constituency, evidence suggests the opposite. From his early community organizer days to his time in the Illinois State Senate, Obama worked closely with health-care advocates of broadly socialist conviction.

Obama's key ally during his pro-single-payer state senate days was Quentin Young, a health-care activist and, according to documentary sources, a leading Chicago socialist. One of Young's most important partners in health-care advocacy was John McKnight, an admirer of some of the more radical health and welfare proposals of Sweden's left-leaning social planners. McKnight was an organizing mentor to Obama, and also recommended him for law school. Illinois congresswoman Jan Schakowsky, who so boldly promised a slide down the slippery slope to single-payer on that video, was, according to documentary evidence, an active member of the Chicago-area branch of the Democratic Social-ists of America. Schakowsky also had close ties to the crypto-socialist Midwest Academy (so important to Obama's own career), and to the Academy-run network of community organizations.[30]

Taken in isolation, any one of these political partnerships would not necessarily imply or prove that Obama himself was a socialist. After all, politicians frequently work in coalitions with others whose views they do not entirely share. As we dive more deeply into published and archi-val records, however, a powerful pattern emerges. Obama's ties to the world of community organizing—which he himself portrays as bonds of authentic conviction—seem to flow from a strategy Obama first em-braced at those Socialist Scholars Conferences in New York. Viewed in the full sweep of Obama's political development, his early socialist alliances appear to be products of sincere belief, while his suave reas-surances as president take on an air of pragmatic backpedaling and dissembling. If Obama is pragmatic, it is pragmatism in pursuit of long-term radical goals.

RED-BAITING?

No doubt, this connecting of the empirical dots will give rise to charges of "red-baiting." Too often this word merely invokes the ghosts of the McCarthy era to delegitimate any criticism of the hard left. Yet it is entirely within bounds to criticize socialists for their politics. There's a difference between irresponsible name-calling and responsible reporting. I call for no boycotts of Bernie Sanders supporters (Sanders being the openly socialist senator from Vermont). Nor do I ask HMOs to drop socialist doctors, or film studios to shun socialist writers (although I reserve the right to express my dislike of Hollywood's politics). More important, the American people aren't particularly interested in blacklisting socialists either.

Senator Sanders's socialist views, however, are out in the open. His socialism is liable to informed acceptance or rejection by the voters of Vermont. This is where I think the president falls short. At a minimum, socialist or not, Barack Obama is vastly further to the left than much of the public realizes. Largely through grievous sins of omission, but sometimes through false denials as well, he has systematically misled the American people about the true nature of his views. The degree of subterfuge here goes far beyond the typical prevarication and backtracking found in politicians of national ambition. This much I argued during the 2008 campaign, and expected to repeat in this book. Yet I now believe we can go further.

Evidence clearly indicates that the president of the United States is a socialist. I mean to lay out the evidence and allow the reader to decide if the conclusion is warranted. That Obama was a socialist in college and early adulthood is hard to deny at this point. The real question is whether Obama abandoned his socialist convictions, or like so many of his community organizer colleagues, simply drove them underground.

There is a great deal more at stake here than a simplistic game of pin-the-socialist-tail-on-the-Democratic-donkey. The same sources that confirm the radicalism of Obama's allies Quentin Young and John McKnight also reveal the frightening implications for liberty of even the most well-intended and supposedly "democratic" variations of socialism. Likewise, sources that reveal the socialist background of Congresswoman Schakowsky also illuminate the larger political intentions and strategies of community organizing in modern America. My study of the post-sixties history of American socialism has not only been a personal education, it has also been downright frightening. As American socialism has turned largely invisible (with honorable exceptions like Bernie Sanders), the public has largely forgotten what socialism means and just how dangerous it can be. I hope this book will help to serve as a reminder, not only of socialism's hidden, incremental, and electorally based strategies, but also of precisely how harmful this brand of politics is.

Guilt by association? Everything I've been arguing tells against that charge. I am not talking about neighborly friendships—or merely pragmatic political alliances—between Barack Obama and partners of far more radical conviction. My claim is that Barack Obama himself has long been drawn to socialism, and has worked in close and deep political partnership with a wide array of socialists throughout his career—out of inner conviction. The political romance, moreover, gives no indication of ever having ceased. Under the tutelage of Frank Marshall Davis, a young Obama drank in socialist radicalism. He nurtured this stance in college, then built a mature socialist worldview around the theories and strategies he encountered at the New York Socialist Scholars Conferences of the early eighties. As a community organizer and aspiring politician, Obama lived and worked—by conviction—in the midst of Chicago's largely hidden socialist world, the existence of which had been disclosed to him by those conferences in New York. Obama's rise within Chicago's socialist universe was no accident. The future president's organizing and political careers depended upon his gaining the confidence and support of some of the savviest socialists in the country. Obama could hardly have won their trust without largely sharing their politics. Very little of this immersion in the world of socialism has even been acknowledged, much less repudiated, by the president. It is his secret.

AYERS AND WRIGHT

What then of Bill Ayers and Jeremiah Wright? We can think of these two men and their relationship to Barack Obama on the model of the Willis Tower (formerly Sears Tower) and the John Hancock Center in Chicago's skyline. Approaching Chicago's downtown from a distance, one of these two immense towers will likely be all you see of the city. For a time it may even appear as though these dual landmarks are all there is to Chicago's downtown. On closer approach, however, just below the level of these looming giants, a vast and brilliant line of gleaming sky-scrapers appears. So, too, President Obama's ties to William Ayers and Jeremiah Wright are simply the most obvious indicators of a far more widespread phenomenon. Obama's radical ties are broad and deep—high and wide. What's at stake here—far more than two very large em-barrassments—is an extended, if partially obscured, radical political world. It is a world Obama himself has long been a part of.

In 2008, my attempt to access the archives of an education founda-tion jointly run by William Ayers and Barack Obama helped inject the Ayers issue into the presidential campaign.[31] I also helped uncover the full significance of Obama's ties to ACORN, and reported new infor-mation about Reverend Wright as well.[32] During the Ayers uproar of 2008, the Obama campaign took aggressive steps to discredit me, even attempting to block my appearance on Milt Rosenberg's respected Chicago radio program.[33] Later in the campaign, when I wrote about Obama's still poorly understood links to the ACORN-controlled "New Party," the Obama campaign attacked me again.[34]

Although I'm proud to have had some small part in the 2008 presi-dential campaign, I never felt that either the McCain camp or, certainly, the mainstream press had quite caught the drift of my central argument. Although William Ayers's history as a Weather Underground terrorist is a worthy and important issue in and of itself, it has never been the most important aspect of the Ayers-Obama link. What's particularly significant about Obama's ties with this unrepentant terrorist is less Ayers's terrorism than the lack of repentance. Since coming out of hiding, Ayers has certainly smoothed out his rhetoric. Yet he's never truly abandoned his radical views. So the real problem is that Obama had a political alliance with someone as radical as Ayers *in the present*. And Obama's Ayers tie is only one of a great many other such radical links. That Ayers's terrorist past makes him notorious only helps to shed light on the much broader phenomenon of Obama's hard-left political alliances. That was my argument during the campaign.[35]

Unfortunately, this point got lost in a debate about Ayers's past and Obama's specific knowledge of that history. And although I published extensively on additional ties between Obama and various radical groups right up through election day, the mainstream press effectively circled the wagons and refused to follow up.[36] Of course, the economic crisis gave Obama an enormous boost toward the end of the campaign. Even so, greater public awareness of his all-too-genuinely radical past might have made a difference.

It's past time to bring the president's background into the light of day. I make no claim here to provide a complete account of Barack Obama's past. The influence of Obama's family, his overseas trips, his law school days, and his time in the U.S. Senate all receive relatively limited treatment here, when treated at all. Nor am I interested in Obama's personal life. I've made no attempt to research Obama's personal relationships, his early drug use (long ago overcome), or like matters. I'm interested in Barack Obama's political convictions, not his private life (or, for that matter, the circumstances of his birth). Yet I do claim to bring significant new information to the table. I also provide the historical and intellectual context required to make sense of mysteries new and old about Obama's political convictions. No doubt this material will be sifted, refined, supplemented, and corrected over time. Historians will be researching and debating Obama's past for decades, perhaps centuries, to come. We are only at the beginning of the discovery process. Yet the full truth about Obama's hidden socialist world can only be discovered if the phenomenon itself is brought to the surface. That is what I aim to do.

CHAPTER 2

A Conference for Marx

Why did Barack Obama become a community organizer? Obama's carefully crafted memoir, *Dreams from My Father*, offers several reasons for his choice of this career path in his senior year. When Obama's college friends asked him what a community organizer does, he couldn't answer in detail because he himself didn't know. So "instead I'd pronounce on the need for change. Change in the White House, where Reagan and his minions were carrying on their dirty deeds. Change in the Congress, compliant and corrupt. . . . Change won't come from the top, I would say. Change will come from a mobilized grass roots."[1] So one of Obama's reasons for becoming a community organizer was to help push national politics to the left.

Although not presented as such, this is a sophisticated and somewhat surprising answer. Classically, after all, according to modern community organizing's founder, Saul Alinsky, organizers are supposed to avoid entanglement in electoral politics. In the early eighties, however, the relationship between community organizing and national politics was changing. So perhaps Obama knew something about his newly chosen profession after all.

Obama's second reason for taking up community organizing was more personal. Neither born nor raised in a black home, Obama urgently wanted to be part of an African-American community. Local organizing seemed to Obama a contemporary successor to the great civil rights struggle of the sixties—a movement that generated a deep sense of community among American blacks. So through the shared sacrifice of organizing—the poverty wages, political struggles, and acts of community building—Obama hoped to earn himself a place in an African-American world to which he had previously been a stranger.[2]

There is a hint in *Dreams* of a third and more ambitious reason for becoming an organizer—a synthesis of the other two. Obama hoped that the community he'd help build would reach beyond any single race, to transform America itself, "Because this community I imagined was still in the making, built on the promise that the larger American community, black, white, and brown, could somehow redefine itself—I believed that it might, over time, admit the uniqueness of my own life."[3] So Obama took up organizing to secure his own racial identity, to push national politics to the left, and ultimately to provoke a deeper redefinition of America itself. An America thus re-defined would be a country Obama-the-outsider could at last fully belong to, because it would be an America that he himself had worked to create.

Obama's account adds up to a quick but eloquent description of the vision of community organizing presented at the April 1983 Cooper Union Socialist Scholars Conference. Although Obama presents himself as naive, in fact, he was knowledgeable about socialist theories of community organizing from the start. No doubt community organizing's day-to-day practice was at first a mystery to Obama. Yet he grasped the big picture quickly. Obama's account is precise, believable, and beautifully wrought. His transgressions are sins of omission and misdirection. But, oh, what sins!

Impressive and informative though it is, Obama's story doesn't add up. Everything we know about Obama says that he is deliberate in decision, meticulous in preparation, and an avid reader. Whether we consider the organizer who over-scripted his early confrontations with Chicago authorities, the Project Vote leader bursting with plans and suggestions, or the president who relies on a teleprompter to control his message, Barack Obama does not jump into major decisions or high-risk situations lightly. He studies; he prepares; he deliberates.

Are we to believe that Obama committed himself to a career in community organizing without understanding what it was? "That's what I'll do," exclaims Obama in *Dreams*, "I'll organize black folks. At the grass roots. For change."[4] No doubt, Obama did say something like this to himself. But where was he when he said it, and who gave him the idea to begin with? Obama stayed true to his dream of becoming a community organizer through two years of failed job searches.[5] No mere impulse can explain that. Organizing *was* the solution to Obama's identity crisis, but he would never have realized this—or clung to his hopes so tenaciously—without first researching and exploring his professional goal with all of his characteristic thoroughness. That is precisely what happened.

SENIOR YEAR

When, exactly, did Obama decide to become a community organizer? Obama states very clearly in *Dreams* that it was 1983.[6] Obama describes himself talking about organizing with his college classmates.[7] He also sent out letters in search of an organizing job "in the months leading up to graduation."[8] So Obama must have decided to become a community organizer sometime between January and June of 1983—the latter half of his senior year at Columbia College. What was Obama doing at that time?

Obama's Columbia years appear to be the least known period of his life.[9] Yet we do know something of that time. In his senior year at

Columbia, Obama was "majoring in political science and international relations and writing his thesis on Soviet nuclear disarmament."[10] We also know that Obama's senior thesis advisor, Michael L. Baron, taught a year-long seminar on "international politics and American policy."[11] Obama was reportedly "a very, very active participant" in that seminar, displaying "a broad sense of international politics and international relations."[12] Although Obama did not graduate with honors,[13] he got an A in Baron's course, and years later Baron ended up recommending Obama for law school.[14] We also know that Obama published a passionate and well-researched article on the student anti-war movement in the March 10, 1983, issue of the Columbia campus newsmagazine, *Sundial*.[15]

In short, Obama's core efforts in his senior year were bent toward international issues. This makes perfect sense. Obama's African heritage, his years in Indonesia, and his anthropologist mother would all have given him a special interest in international relations. His thesis, his best course work with his closest faculty connection, and his own extracurricular writing all confirm it. Moving back to Obama's years at Occidental College, we know that, although he had many interests, disarmament was certainly among them. One of his Occidental roommates tells of facing a formidable Obama in a classroom debate on nuclear disarmament.[16] *Dreams,* of course, presents Obama's anti-apartheid activism at Occidental as a formative influence. Also, a 1990 *Boston Globe* piece says that Obama "specialized in international relations at Occidental College."[17] Moving forward, the post-Columbia job Obama took to save money toward his soon-to-be-impoverished organizing career involved helping companies with foreign operations "understand overseas markets."[18]

For all these reasons, it seems probable that Obama was headed for a career in international relations. In any case, his attention was likely taken up with international issues right through the publication of his essay on the student anti-nuclear movement in early March of 1983. So what happened between March and June of 1983 that might have pushed Obama off of the international course he was so clearly on and gotten him exclaiming instead, "That's what I'll do, I'll organize black folks. At the grass roots. For change"? Since Obama was already searching for organizer jobs "in the months leading up to graduation," the most likely moment for Obama's organizing epiphany would have been sometime between early March and mid-April of 1983.

LIKE ICE-SKATING

Once you know what went on there, it's virtually impossible not to conclude that the Cooper Union Socialist Scholars Conference of April 1 and 2, 1983, was Obama's transformational moment. How do we know Obama was there? He tells us so himself, in *Dreams,* although if you blink you'll miss it. Speaking of his New York days, Obama says:

> Political discussions, the kind that at Occidental had once seemed so intense and purposeful, came to take on the flavor of the socialist conferences I sometimes attended at Cooper Union or the African cultural fairs that took place in Harlem and Brooklyn during the summers—a few of the many diversions New York had to offer, like going to a foreign film or ice-skating at Rockefeller Center.[19]

In the course of a sentence, Obama's attendance at socialist conferences is transformed from something intense and consequential into just another urban diversion.

That Obama works to minimize his report is unsurprising. That Obama acknowledges attending socialist conferences at all is more interesting. *Dreams from My Father* was published in 1995, just as Obama was gearing up for his first political campaign. A passing revelation like this would appeal to Hyde Park's influential and knowing socialist constituency, without unduly disturbing others. This may seem to attribute too much calculation to Obama, but his organizing colleagues in Chicago were hyper-conscious about revealing their socialism. Obama may also have worried that records of his attendance at New York's Socialist Scholars Conferences would surface. Why not acknowledge the fact in such a way as to minimize attention and defuse the power of eventual revelation? The socialist conference issue may also help explain why Obama's 2008 campaign consistently refused to name friends from the New York era.[20]

In fact, I have found Obama's name on a DSA (Democratic Socialists of America) mailing list for one of the New York Socialist Scholars Conferences. Although the list is not labeled, analysis of its contents and associated material strongly suggests that Obama pre-registered for the 1984 Socialist Scholars Conference. (For a review of the evidence, see Chapter Three.) This is significant because after the Marx Centennial in 1983, the DSA's annual Socialist Scholars Conferences moved out of the Cooper Union and into the Boro of Manhattan Community College. So although Obama explicitly speaks only of Cooper Union as a conference locale, evidence indicates that he continued attending annual Socialist Scholars Conferences in 1984, and likely 1985 as well. Obama himself speaks of attending socialist "conferences," in the plural, so at a minimum, he would have been present for at least two of the three annual Socialist Scholars Conferences held during his time in New York. And since Cooper Union is the only location Obama specifically mentions, he surely attended the 1983 Marx Centennial Conference. Could Obama have attended a socialist conference or conferences at New York's Cooper Union, but not the Cooper Union Socialist Scholars Conference of April 1983? That is exceedingly unlikely.

I've read through event notices in *New York Democratic Socialist* and *Democratic Left* (the local and national organs, respectively, of the Democratic Socialists of America) for the period when Obama was in New York. I found no notice of any DSA event at the Cooper Union other than the Socialist Scholars Conference of 1983. That event, on the other hand, was advertised widely, not only in *New York Democratic*

Socialist[21] and *Democratic Left*,[22] but in the socialist periodical *In These Times*[23] and in notices found as far afield as *The Stony Brook Press*,[24] a student paper on Long Island's North Shore. The 1984 New York Socialist Scholars Conference likewise had a large notice in *In These Times*,[25] and the 1985 conference had a large ad in *Democratic Left*.[26]

It's evident from the event notices in *New York Democratic Socialist* that by far the majority of New York DSA seminars, panel discussions, and classes on socialism were held at CUNY Graduate Center, where many prominent DSAers were on faculty. There were also events and demonstrations at Columbia University. DSA did sponsor other events—issue forums, awards dinners, and such at various locations in New York City—but I saw no notices for such events scheduled at Cooper Union.

It's very likely that New York DSA held the Socialist Scholars Conference at Cooper Union in 1983, and again at the Borough of Manhattan Community College in 1984 and 1985, because the usual DSA venue of CUNY Graduate Center lacked the space to host a substantial conference. The documentary evidence for Obama's attendance at the 1984 Socialist Scholars Conference (discussed in Chapter Three) certainly suggests that Obama had a particular interest in this conference series.

There was also the specific motivation of conference organizers in 1983 of commemorating Marx's centennial at the Cooper Union, where he had been memorialized after his death. That, along with the shift of the Socialist Scholars Conferences in 1984 to the Borough of Manhattan Community College, points to Cooper Union as a likely one-shot locale, rather than a regular DSA conference venue. Borough of Manhattan Community College was part of the CUNY system, which made it more convenient than Cooper Union for use by an organization whose leading lights were concentrated at CUNY Graduate Center.

Conferences were major events, requiring extensive preparation and significant publicity. Reading through event notices in *Democratic Left*, we find a number of announcements of DSA conferences across the country. The 1983 Socialist Scholars Conference at Cooper Union is announced,[27] but no other conference at Cooper Union is advertised. Had New York's DSA moved out of its usual site for lectures, panel discussions, and public classes in socialism at CUNY Graduate Center for yet another conference at a large venue like Cooper Union, we would surely see publicity on a scale roughly comparable to that for the New York Socialist Scholars Conferences. Yet no such publicity is to be found.

A file of New York DSA internal planning documents for the Socialist Scholars Conference[28] includes a document drawn up just after the successful Cooper Union Socialist Scholars Conference. That document (beginning "The success of the Scholars Conference demonstrates . . .") indicates that the April 1983 Cooper Union Conference was filling a gap in intellectually oriented leftist political events created by the recent decline in an event series run by MARHO, the Mid-Atlantic Radical Historians Organization, out of John Jay College in Manhattan, near Lincoln Center. MARHO had put on leftist conferences and other similar events at John Jay for several years prior to 1983. According to the planning document: "Recently, though, they [MARHO] have lost energy and have ceased to put on frequent events . . . CUNY's Democratic Socialist Clubs and IDS [Institute for Democratic Socialism] should move to fill this vacuum . . . Our events should be held at CUNY Graduate Center in an auditorium that could hold 100+ people."

So the April 1983 Cooper Union Socialist Scholars Conference, held during the middle of the second of Obama's two college school years at Columbia University, was filling a "socialist conference gap" that had spanned much of the time since Obama's arrival in New York. Immediately after the April 1983 Cooper Union conference, socialist lectures and panels at CUNY Graduate Center and full-scale conferences at Borough of Manhattan Community College, CUNY, filled the gap left by the declining leftist event series at John Jay College on Manhattan's Upper West Side. In other words, evidence strongly indicates that Cooper Union was not a regular location for socialist conferences, but was, on the contrary, a onetime venue. It was chosen as a site to attempt to revive the lapsed tradition of Socialist Scholars Conferences because of the Marx centennial, and its success led to a series of smaller socialist speaking events at CUNY Graduate Center, and full-scale socialist conferences at the Borough of Manhattan Community College, CUNY.

Given all this, Obama's reference to "socialist conferences" at Cooper Union surely means that we can reliably place him at the April 1983 Cooper Union Socialist Scholars Conference. From this point on, I will treat Obama's attendance at that conference as established.

Obama's reference to "socialist conferences" at Cooper Union, in the plural, is most likely compressing the 1983 Cooper Unions Socialist Scholars Conference with his attendance at the 1984 (and possibly 1985) Socialist Scholars Conference at the Borough of Manhattan Community College. This sort of literary compression (which Obama owns up to in the introduction to *Dreams from My Father*) allows him to pass swiftly and lightly over an awkward topic.[29]

The topics of community organizing and minority participation in socialist politics were pervasive at the Cooper Union Conference. Some panels focused directly on these themes, yet many others would have touched on them as well. In my account, I'm going to concentrate on a couple of panels that addressed community organizing and minority politics in detail. These also happen to be panels I think Obama was likely to have attended. How, for example, could Obama have resisted a session on the links between race and class—a preoccupation of his? Yet I also plan to show that interest in community organizing and minority coalition-building was by no means confined to one or two Cooper Union panels. On the contrary, these issues were the talk of the 1983 Socialist Scholars Conference. Wherever Obama was, he would have run into excited discussion about his soon-to-be chosen profession of community organizing, and its link to electoral politics. So while I'll venture some educated guesses about Obama's likely pattern of panel attendance, in the end, the details of his movements are less important than the overall thrust of the Marx Centennial Conference itself.

That 1983 Socialist Scholars Conference was more than a commemoration of Marx. According to the program, the Cooper Union conference was explicitly meant to be "a revival of the Socialist Scholars Conferences which did much to revive interest in socialism and Marxism in the academy during the sixties and early seventies."[30] Actually, the annual Socialist Scholars Conferences held in New York from 1965 through 1970 were far more than merely academic events. Those meetings of scholars and activists (with many individuals playing both roles) were clearly "movement" affairs. And although that first series of conferences eventually foundered on the gulf between scholars and activists—and on the conflicting militancies of the black movement, the women's movement, and the lesbian and gay movement—the eighties revival featured a similar blending of scholarship and activism.[31] In the tradition of Marx, whether overtly scholarly or not, the purpose of each panel was not merely to describe the world, but to change it.

Since I'm arguing that the impact of these conferences on Obama was immense, we need to understand them in some depth. At the very center of Obama's secret world, these Socialist Scholars Conferences cannot be properly decoded without knowledge of the history, theory, and political environment that shaped them. Public ignorance of this socialist world is ultimately the most significant barrier to an appreciation of Obama's background. So it's worth considering the tradition that Cooper Union conference revived.

NEVER SPENT A BILLION

In September of 1967, *Barron's National Business and Financial Weekly* (very much a capitalist organ) carried an extended and critical report by Alice Widener on the Third Annual Socialist Scholars

Conference.[32] This was the high point of the sixties conference series, before the worst of the factional infighting set in. Widener's 1967 conference report also serves as a revealing introduction to the revived conference series of the eighties. That's because many of the key characters are the same—although in the sixties their cards were turned up and laid clearly on the table.

After taking some shots at the various Soviet and communist delegates in the house, Widener describes a particularly well-attended panel on "Poverty in America," featuring Michael Harrington. In 1967, Harrington was well on his way to becoming the most influential socialist in America—a modern successor to socialist leaders Eugene Debs and Norman Thomas. Later, in the eighties, Harrington would head the DSA, the sponsor of those revived Socialist Scholars Conferences. Harrington's real claim to fame, however, was *The Other America*, the 1962 book that inspired the "War on Poverty."[33]

After reading an extended review of Harrington's book, and just three days before his own assassination, President Kennedy ordered the organization of a federal War on Poverty. President Johnson carried the plan forward, appointing Sargent Shriver to head the program. Harrington served as a prominent member of Shriver's planning team, the goal of which was to abolish poverty in America.[34] Yet by general consent, the War on Poverty failed, and Harrington spent much of the ensuing years disowning the fiasco.

For Reagan Republicans, Johnson's War on Poverty was a textbook example of government gone wrong. In the conservative view, by generating ever more welfare dependency, government money merely aggravated the very conditions Presidents Kennedy and Johnson had hoped to abolish. For Harrington, on the other hand, the War on Poverty was a flop because it nickeled and dimed a problem that demanded far greater government spending. When Harrington said as much to Sargent Shriver at the time, Shriver shot back, "Well, I don't know about you, Mr. Harrington, but I've never spent a billion dollars before." (Obviously, "billion" was a scarier figure in the sixties.) Many will side with Shriver, but to the socialist Harrington, the real reason the War on Poverty failed was Shriver's refusal to demand far greater government spending.[35] At that 1967 Socialist Scholars panel, Harrington took pains to repudiate the Johnson administration's half-measures, while still arguing for the viability and necessity of government-based solutions.[36]

Notice that Harrington's brand of socialism did not prevent him from working within the system—even signing on with the Democratic Party. One reason the notion of a socialist president seems absurd is the image it generates of a disgruntled outsider pressing for violent revolution. There were plenty of embittered outsiders at the 1967 Socialist Scholars Conference. In fact, violent revolutionaries clearly outnumbered Harrington-style "democratic socialists." Yet precisely because Harrington advocated a socialism that confined itself to strictly democratic and legal means, he had a level of visibility and influence—and panel attendance—few other socialists could match.

Another draw for the crowd at the poverty panel was the knowledge that Harrington was about to be slammed by his radical rivals. Speaking for these not-so-democratic radicals was labor organizer Stanley Aronowitz, who said he was with "a revolutionary action group." Rejecting even an enlarged poverty program as mere "reformism," Aronowitz offered a hard-edged Marxist analysis. "Racism is based on the profit system," said Aronowitz. The police, he continued, are the arm of the ruling class in the ghettos. Speaking in the aftermath of a wave of urban riots, Aronowitz noted that blacks had already led the way by forming anti-police self-defense committees. It remained for Americans to follow their revolutionary example. As for the War on Poverty, Aronowitz continued, only one good thing has come of it: "At least it has given employment to the organizers." At this, Widener reports, "the audience burst into laughter, applause, and cheers." "That's right man," someone called out from the audience, "It gave our organizers some bread."[37] This being 1967, Widener has to explain to her readers that "bread" is slang for money. Unchanged from 1967 to today, however, radical organizers still look to cop some bread from a clueless Uncle Sam.

The extraordinary thing about this session is that, by the end, Harrington actually capitulated to Aronowitz and the rest of his critics. After heated discussion, Harrington said he'd be on board for a violent revolution: "OK," he agreed, "if you think it will work."[38] Doctoral dissertations could be written around that long-forgotten concession. For it reveals that even the greatest modern proponent of purely democratic socialism saw democracy more as a tactic than a principle—merely the most practical route to socialism in the United States. Eventually, the collapse of "the sixties" brought revolutionaries like Aronowitz back to earth—and put Harrington in control of America's socialist movement. Yet this forgotten moment exposes Harrington's underlying radicalism, while also casting doubt on the radicals' latter-day professions of democratic intent.

BURN THE BANKS

Fifteen years later, Stanley Aronowitz, now a sociologist, was a leader within Harrington's Democratic Socialists of America, and (according to DSA records) may well have planned the panels Obama attended at the 1983 Cooper Union Conference.[39] In all that time, the differences between the factions represented by Harrington and Aronowitz had not disappeared. Yet they had moderated, in part because of the emergence of a third alternative between the two extremes—an alternative that had everything to do with community organizing.

The remainder of Widener's riveting description of the 1967 Socialist Scholars Conference focuses on a "Black Power" panel session at which plans were made to lever the next summer's season of urban riots into full-scale revolution. A scheme to burn down twenty American cities was floated, to be followed by "a military struggle in the streets." Unlike Cuba and elsewhere, panelists patiently explained, revolution would actually be easier in modern cities, where a combination of "violence, sabotage, and traffic tie-ups can bring down the system." Widener reports that one of the most militant planners was Ivanhoe

Donaldson, campaign manager to Georgia State House member Julian Bond. (In the eighties, Bond became one of the most prominent politicians affiliated with Harrington's DSA.) As campaign manager to one of the most successful black politicians in the South, Donaldson might be presumed to have been a strictly democratic socialist. To the contrary, Donaldson called on revolutionary forces to leave the ghettos and go downtown to torch the banks. Said Donaldson, "There's a Chase Manhattan Bank at 125th Street in this town. We're trying to get jobs in a bank we ought to destroy." [40]

By 1983, the revolutionary impulse among ostensibly democratic socialists had by no means disappeared, although now it was buried out of sight. At the same time, the democratic tactic had triumphed. In Reagan's America, socialists largely gave up on revolution (at least in the short and medium term) and settled instead on a program of local electoral resistance. A revived tradition of community organizing supplied the key to the new strategy. Now, instead of capitulating to the system by working at a bank—or overthrowing capitalism by burning banks down—socialist organizers developed more subtle techniques. Press banks with demonstrations from the outside to grab hold of the economy from within. Force the banks to work with you—even fund you—as you slowly turn financial institutions into instruments of social redistribution. Then harness the money and energy of these local battles to a new political movement. This still unknown chapter of American socialist history profoundly shaped Barack Obama.

With the sixties background in mind, let's return to the 1983 Cooper Union Marx Centennial Conference. Following Frances Fox Piven's opening remarks (see Chapter One), and two talks on the nuclear freeze movement by European guests, Michael Harrington was introduced to the Great Hall as America's leading socialist. [41] We can piece together the gist of Harrington's address from a 1983 news report, [42] from his broader writings, and from his article, "Standing Up For Marx," published as a cover story in DSA's newsletter, *Democratic Left,* in anticipation of the conference. [43]

MARX THE DEMOCRAT

In his Cooper Union remarks, Harrington repudiated the image of a totalitarian-friendly Marx and insisted instead that freedom and democracy are the essence of socialism. This is the claim of Harrington's larger body of work, which interprets Marx as a misunderstood democrat—misunderstood especially by his own followers, including his close collaborator Friedrich Engels. Harrington goes so far as to claim that Marx himself misunderstood his own best impulses during an early and "immature" ultra-leftist phase.[44] Certainly, this is a dubious reading of Marx. Even some of Harrington's leading admirers reject it.[45] In light of his willingness to shift tactics and embrace revolution in 1967, we can ask if Harrington himself honestly believed that Marx was a democrat.

In a sense, Harrington was sincere. As his thought developed from the sixties through the eighties, Harrington increasingly turned away from classic socialist plans for nationalization of the economy. Instead, he embraced a gradualist program in which workers and community groups would gain control of industries from within, redistributing wealth along the way.[46] For Harrington, union ownership of a company, or reserved seats for community organizations on boards of directors or public utility commissions, *was* democracy and *was* socialism. So even in the event of a violent revolution (which with luck would never be necessary), Harrington believed that community-controlled wealth redistribution would effectively guarantee democracy in a post-revolutionary world. By the eighties, then, Harrington looked less to a socialist central government than to a consortium of unions and community organizations (for example, ACORN in its dealings with banks) to act as guardians of a genuine people's democracy.

Of course, treating community groups like ACORN or its affiliated SEIU union locals as guardians of decentralized "democracy" in a socialized state will strike many as the very opposite of democracy as Americans understand that term. Yet by 1983, Harrington's DSA was embracing this vision of a grassroots-based socialism. This is what Harrington was getting at when he told the assembly at Cooper Union: "We must reject collectivism imposed by elites of any sort upon the working people, but allow for people at the base to take over decisions that affect their lives—that is what Marxism is all about."[47]

Harrington and his DSA colleagues had already moved to put this socialist vision into practice through work with community organizers (and future Obama colleagues) at Chicago's Midwest Academy. But Obama wouldn't have to wait for Chicago. Breakout panels on the second day of the Cooper Union conference would offer a detailed vision of a new, decentralized, community-based brand of socialism.

FREE SPEECH FOR SOCIALISTS

Not only did Harrington's address to the all-conference plenary foreshadow this new socialist vision, so did a preceding plenary speech on European disarmament by Luciana Castellina, Italian Communist Party member and deputy in the European and Italian parliaments. Castellina argued that the nuclear freeze movement should be seen as something more than an effort to block deployment of a few American missiles. For her, the freeze movement portended a broader public effort to dismantle the entire Cold War system of competing American- and Soviet-led blocks. "Peace will not be granted by the bipolar leadership of the world," said Castellina. The solution will come, not "through an agreement reached at the top, but by cutting through this process" via massive mobilization from below.[48]

Castellina's well-received address must have delighted Obama, who only three weeks before had published a piece warning nuclear freeze proponents against targeting their efforts too narrowly. And paralleling Harrington's efforts to shift the focus of socialism away from elites at the top, toward people at the base, Castellina repudiated both Soviet and Western leaders and called mass mobilization from below the real key to large-scale change. The echoes with Obama's phrase, "Change won't come from the top. . . . Change will come from a mobilized grass roots," are clear.

As if to prove Castellina's point, her plenary address was followed by a talk from Jean Pierre Cott, a member of the French Parliament and a former cabinet member. A nominally socialist leader, Cott shocked the crowd by calling for the dismantling of at least some of France's welfare state and a correspondingly increased role for the free market. Cott then issued stinging criticisms of America's nuclear freeze movement, rejecting its unilateral surrender to the Soviet military buildup.[49] "Peace has often been the twin sister of aggression," warned Cott. "If we want to deter the Soviets from doing anything foolish, this does mean the deployment of arms." As Cott endorsed NATO's planned deployment of Pershing 2 and cruise missiles in Europe (the specific targets of the nuclear freeze movement), the crowd exploded into boos and hisses, nearly drowning him out. Cott was left shouting, "Comrades! Let us not kid ourselves!" and pleading for the right to free speech under socialism.[50]

In any case, between Reagan's dominance at home and European leaders like Cott, American socialism was increasingly turning from centrally planned collectivism toward grassroots strategies—with a revitalized community organizing tradition at the center of the program. Crucial to this ambitious new socialist vision of community organizing was a novel connection between organizing and electoral politics. With Carter out and Reagan cutting into volunteer programs like VISTA, government-supplied "bread" for organizers was quickly disappearing.[51] As livelihoods were put at risk, the traditional reluctance to enter electoral politics gave way. Socialist organizers made plans to harness grassroots power to a progressive political movement of national scope.

HAROLD WASHINGTON

In the eighties, Harold Washington's successful insurgent campaign for mayor of Chicago was the most important example of this new socialist strategy. That may seem surprising, since Harold Washington never described himself as a socialist. Yet the progressive coalition that defeated the Chicago machine and lifted Washington into office was the very model of socialist hopes for America's political future. Washington was carried to victory by a popular movement of newly politicized black and Hispanic voters, supplemented by progressive whites. These groups were mobilized by activist Chicago churches (like Jeremiah Wright's Trinity United Church of Christ) and by Chicago's many leftist community organizations.[52] In significant part, this coalition was buttressed behind the scenes by Chicago's powerful but discreet contingent of democratic socialists.

Harold Washington's successful campaign to replace Chicago's Democratic machine with an openly "progressive" governing coalition electrified the socialist world, and forever shaped the political ambitions of Barack Obama. Anyone who reads Obama's *Dreams from My Father* will know how important Harold Washington's example was to Obama during his years in Chicago. More interesting is the fact that the 1983 Cooper Union Socialist Scholars Conference took place virtually on the eve of Washington's final victory. Events in Chicago loomed over the conference and almost surely helped inspire Obama to embrace community organizing. So before plunging into an account of Saturday's panels, we need to look more closely at the Harold Washington phenomenon and what it meant to socialists in 1983.

Harold Washington's close ties to Chicago's socialists reached back to 1977, when he ran a failed campaign against the machine-backed candidate in a special election to replace the elder Mayor Daley (who had died in office). Although Washington did not call himself a socialist and did not completely reject capitalism, his campaign representatives approached several politically skilled and well-connected Chicago socialists for assistance.[53] These socialist operatives were members of the New American Movement (NAM), a organization largely made up of ex-sixties radicals. When it was founded in 1970–71, NAM generally avoided electoral politics, working instead to create a mass-based movement for a socialist revolution. NAM is where anti-Harrington radicals like Stanley Aronowitz gathered after the collapse of the radical SDS (Students for a Democratic Society) in 1969. But as America drifted rightward and hopes for revolution dimmed, a few NAM members began to experiment with left-insurgent politics within the Democratic Party.[54]

When Chicago NAMers entered Washington's 1977 campaign, they learned to their delight that he was receptive to some of their most radical policy recommendations. In fact, Washington offered a number of socialist-friendly ideas on his own (the establishment of a publicly owned municipal bank, for example). NAM members contributed substantially to Washington's position papers and made progress convincing Washington supporters that they could actively work with socialists.[55] That first Washington campaign was a turning point in the decade-long process through which the most radical socialists of the sixties put off their revolutionary plans and adopted a Harrington-like gradualist electoral strategy instead.[56]

The result was the 1982 merger of NAM with Michael Harrington's DSOC (Democratic Socialist Organizing Committee) to form the new, Harrington-led Democratic Socialists of America (DSA). Although tensions between the revolutionary radicals and Harrington's followers continued, most DSAers were committed to electoral politics within the Democratic Party.

Harrington's overall strategy was to force a two-party "realignment" by pulling the Democrats sharply to the left. Harrington expected that this would drive business interests away from the Democrats and into the Republican Party. In theory, however, a flood of newly energized minority and union voters would more than make up for the Democrats' losses. Harrington hoped that once the two parties were polarized along class lines, the working-class-dominated Democrats would embrace socialism as their natural ideology.[57]

Harold Washington's election thrilled America's socialists because it appeared to portend just such a realignment. Washington himself was about as close to socialist as a major American politician could safely be. His victory was powered by a political awakening manifested in a massive voter-registration campaign in Chicago's black community. Chicago's blacks, rather than the city's white middle-class "lakefront liberals," were now spearheading a new progressive movement. Could minority voters be a sleeping giant that, once awakened, would vanquish Reagan and usher in a progressive future?[58]

GIDDY SOCIALISTS

Best of all, following the lead of his 1977 campaign, Washington openly courted and worked with Chicago's socialists. In December of 1982, candidate Washington spoke before Chicago DSA's regular membership meeting, receiving an enthusiastic reception from a crowd more than twice its usual size. DSA members played key roles in the upper echelons of Washington's campaign, and DSAers involved with unions and community organizations helped bring those groups onto the Washington bandwagon. All told, Chicago DSA was probably the most important non-black group to back Washington. By helping to raise his share of white voters to 12 percent, the DSA arguably handed Harold Washington his victory.[59]

During the Washington campaign, *Chicago Socialist*, the newsletter of the Chicago chapter of the DSA, was giddy with excitement. With justice it could claim: "We have established ourselves as a small but important electoral force in the city."[60] This was an extraordinary coup for a group long used to marginality, and still operating only partially in the open. Chicago DSA was not a secret organization. On the other hand, it generally did not openly join in coalitions by, say, having its name printed on the letterhead of groups collectively backing a given candidate or cause. Chicago DSA members tended to influence campaigns as individuals, although in fact their participation was often coordinated by a DSA committee.[61] Harold Washington's willingness to address a regular DSA meeting promised a new world of open recognition and acceptance for Chicago's socialists. What really made Chicago DSA "heads swirl," however, was the prospect that the Washington victory might stand as a model for other cities, and even for a broader leftward realignment of the national Democratic Party.[62]

America's socialists were certainly paying close attention. A simple picture of Harold Washington makes the point. Obama was a voracious reader, especially during his New York years, and almost surely spent plenty of time around the book and magazine display tables at the Cooper Union conference. If Obama had leafed through a copy of DSA's then-current newsletter, he would have seen a full-page ad for the country's most popular socialist magazine, *In These Times*. The ad features a large picture of "Representative Harold Washington," just weeks away from victory in his race for mayor. Beneath the picture is an endorsement from Washington: "*In These Times* . . . provides valuable ammunition in the fight for civil rights and economic justice."[63]

In These Times ran these large Harold Washington picture-ads in leftist publications for the next several months. The striking thing is that openly socialist congressman Ronald Dellums is reduced to a minor blurb at the bottom of the ad. And although Bernie Sanders, the openly socialist mayor of Burlington, Vermont, had won re-election just a month before, he received only a fraction of the news coverage that socialist publications devoted to Washington. Washington was featured in three *In These Times* weekly cover stories between February and April of 1983, with a great deal of coverage in between. The more hard-edged Marxist American *Guardian*, supposedly too radical to put much faith in electoral politics, was also plastered with Washington campaign news for months.

Obama likely saw much of this material. After all, the sort of person who attends socialist conferences is the sort who reads *In These Times*. The Cooper Union gathering featured an all-conference lunch session on socialist periodicals, so if Obama didn't know about *In These Times* before the conference, he likely did after. And given the report that Obama was a revolutionary Marxist-Leninist in 1980 (see Chapters One and Three), it's quite possible that he was also reading the *Guardian*.

The extraordinary thing is that, without actually declaring himself a socialist, Harold Washington beat out more openly radical politicians, literally turning himself into the poster boy for American socialism. It was enough that Washington was virtually socialist himself, willing to work closely with organized socialists, and a possible catalyst to a class-based realignment of the parties. Washington also symbolized the potential of an energized, minority-led progressive coalition to alter the balance of political power in the United States. *In These Times* saw the emotional support for Washington among Chicago's blacks as a reincarnation of the sixties: "It was like Harold was Martin Luther King all over again."[64] Combine this with Washington's willingness to push for tax increases and a redistributionist program, and it's easy to see why *In These Times* and America's socialists were swooning.

A celebratory editorial in the April 20–April 26 issue of *In These Times* captures the optimism—and strategy—of the moment:

> The black community in every city is a natural left constituency. This is true not only for municipal politics but also nationally. . . . In other words, the left, including its socialist wing, can now begin to enter the mainstream of American life along with blacks. For while a fully mobilized black community can provide the solid core of victory, as it did in Chicago, in many places blacks can be successful only in coalition with Hispanics, labor and the left . . . the new reality is that the coalitions, if they come into being at all, will be based on mobilized black communities and, therefore will most likely be led by blacks.[65]

This line of thinking was already being bandied about at the Cooper Union Conference, held less than three weeks before that editorial was written. The buzz in the socialist world in April of 1983 was that blacks would be the leaders of a new socialist-friendly American political movement—a reincarnation of the sixties civil rights struggle, uniting all the races, but this time pushing beyond traditional civil rights toward egalitarian "economic rights." Imagine the effect of this on an alienated and young left-leaning Obama, searching for an identity and career, and yearning to earn himself a bona fide place in America's black community. Here was a path that could transform Obama from odd man out into the center of attention. In Obama's own words, here was a way of "redefining the larger American community" by cobbling together a coalition of "black, white, and brown," a coalition Obama's unique background would fit him to lead. And at Saturday's Cooper Union panels, he'd learn exactly how to go about it.

WHERE WAS OBAMA?

Although it's impossible to know with certainty which panels Obama attended at this and subsequent Socialist Scholars Conferences, we can certainly make informed guesses. Given his interests, for example, it's tough to imagine Obama passing up the early afternoon Cooper Union panel on "Race & Class in Marxism." After all, Obama was in the midst of a painful personal struggle with his own racial identity, and we know from *Dreams* that he was preoccupied with the confluence of race and class. It's easy enough to highlight a number of other panels at the 1983–85 Socialist Scholars Conferences that Obama was likely to have attended. The details of Obama's movements, however, are not the central issue, since the gist of the themes treated in these panels would surely have gotten through to Obama in any case.

In the early- to mid-1980s, renewed interest in a grassroots electoral strategy linked to community organizing, voter registration, and minor-

ity mobilization was widespread in the DSA. Any number of panels
Obama might have attended would have touched on this same strategy.
The grassroots approach was highlighted in the 1983 all-conference
plenary addresses. And as the American Marxist *Guardian* wrote of
the 1984 conference, many of the best discussions at these events took
place in the hallways, between sessions.[66] No doubt Obama would have
heard the buzz about community organizing there as well.

Then there are the books. Internal DSA files show conference organizers making concerted efforts to display panelists' books at literature
tables.[67] We know that Obama was reading voraciously at just this time.
A 2008 piece on Obama in the London *Sunday Times* quotes a friend
and fellow organizer remarking on the large number of books lining
Obama's otherwise spare Chicago apartment in the mid-1980s. Along
with philosophy, history, and black literature, there were also "some
works on revolution."[68] No doubt a good number of Obama's revolutionary books came from the New York Socialist Scholars Conferences.
So Obama could easily have read the work of panelists he missed—or
gone more deeply into the substance of talks that interested him. In
short, while we cannot know Obama's panel attendance with certainty,
considering panels on his favorite topics, all-conference plenary sessions, hallway conversations, a general lunch meeting on socialist journals, and readily available books and other literature, it's possible to
piece together a picture of what Obama learned at these conferences.

SOCIALIST INCUBATOR

A morning panel on "Social Movements" at the 1983 Cooper Union
Conference could easily have introduced Obama to his new vocation.[69]
This panel was largely devoted to community organizing and its ties to
the DSA's electoral strategy. Featuring two "stars," Frances Fox Piven
and Barbara Ehrenreich, the Social Movements panel was probably the
biggest draw of the morning. Certainly, in light of what we know of his

interests, Obama would have been far less attracted to competing panels on sexuality, history, labor, Western Europe, and Eastern Europe.

Peter Dreier is listed as the first speaker at the Social Movements panel. In the years leading up to the Cooper Union conference, Dreier had published a series of pieces on grassroots political strategies in the DSA newsletter, *Democratic Left*, and in *Social Policy*, the journal that serves as the intellectual home base of American community organizing.[70] Like Piven, Dreier was an influential member of the DSA's National Executive Committee (NEC). Dreier now writes frequently for *The Nation*, and has been a major influence on community organizing for decades. In his various writings, Dreier's concern is to deepen the ties between community organizing and electoral politics, and also between community organizing and socialism.

"Socialist Incubators," a 1980 piece in *Social Policy*, lays out the vision of community organizing that informed Dreier's presentation at the Cooper Union Conference.[71] Dreier's strategic goal in that piece is to combine diverse community organizations into a national grassroots movement to "democratize control of major social, economic, and political institutions." A drawing that illustrates the article shows a line of everyday folks walking into a board of directors meeting at a company called "U.S. Motors." In other words, in this socialist utopia, members of unions and grassroots community organizations control America's businesses. Dreier is seeking public control of America's economy, yet means to accomplish it from below—through pressure from leftist community organizations. (Dreier would later serve as a key strategist in ACORN's campaign to pressure banks into funding high-risk mortgages to low-credit customers.)

In Dreier's vision, a grassroots movement for public control from below could gradually overcome American cultural resistance to state-run enterprises. With community organizations leading the way to a more collectively oriented national consciousness, changes like the importation of a Canadian-style government-run health-care system would eventually follow. So in Dreier's view, community organizations are "socialist incubators," slowly pushing their own members—and eventually America itself—toward socialist consciousness.

Ultimately, says Dreier, "socialist incubators must lead to the electoral arena." If community organizations like ACORN, Ralph Nader's Public Interest Research Groups (PIRGs), and campus anti-apartheid activists could unite, with help from socialist advisors, they could catapult radicals in the mold of Berkeley congressman Ronald Dellums into public office. Politicians who thought of themselves as part of this grassroots socialist movement could "provide the legitimacy and staff resources to give national coherence to an otherwise fragmented movement." In short, a synergy between grassroots community organizations and politicians that they themselves had put into office would slowly "incubate" an American rebirth of socialism.

PRECIPITATE A CRISIS

Still bolder aspects of Dreier's strategic vision are laid out in his February 1979 *Social Policy* essay, "The Case for Transitional Reform."[72] This piece, influential within organizing circles but virtually unknown outside, supplies a Marxist framework and a long-term strategy for community organizing. Here Dreier draws on French Marxist theorist Andre Gorz's notion of "transitional reforms," or "non-reformist reforms," to suggest a way of transforming American capitalism into socialism. The central idea, borrowed from Gorz, is to create government programs that only seem to be "reforms" of the capitalist system. Rightly understood, these supposed reforms are so incompatible with capitalism that they gradually precipitate the system's collapse.

Dreier's strategy has two parts. On the one hand, quasi-socialist institutions need to be pre-established in the heart of capitalist society, so as to turn a coming moment of crisis in a socialist direction. These quasi-socialist institutions, of course, would be groups like ACORN, with a significant semi-governmental role via their insertion into the banking system, public utility commissions, business boards of directors, and so forth. The second part of the strategy involves "injecting unmanageable strains into the capitalist system, strains that precipitate an economic and/or political crisis."

Dreier has in mind a "revolution of rising entitlements" that "cannot be abandoned without undermining the legitimacy of the capitalist class." "Proximately," says Dreier, "the process leads to expansion of state activity and budgets, and . . . to fiscal crisis in the public sector. In the longer run, it may give socialist norms an opportunity for extension or at least visibility." So Dreier's plan is to gradually expand government spending until the country nears fiscal collapse. At that point, a public accustomed to its entitlements will presumably turn on its capitalist masters when they propose cutbacks to restore fiscal balance. Dreier fears that this intentionally wrought crisis might actually backfire and produce fascism instead of socialism. That is why he believes it's so important to have a left-wing grassroots movement already in place. Left-wing community organizers will turn the national fiscal crisis in a socialist direction. Dreier seems to think that some revolutionary violence may emerge at this point. Yet his stress is on conditions designed to achieve a gradual transition to socialism.

"The Case for Transitional Reform" appeared in 1979, just two years after Harold Washington's first mayoral campaign began to convince some NAMers that left-insurgent politics within the Democratic Party might be a viable socialist option after all. Dreier's piece marked a similar turning point in the world of community organizing, part of the process whereby radical socialists began to give up on immediate revolutionary hopes and accept "reformist" strategies instead. In the late seventies, and especially in the Reagan-dominated eighties, radical socialists began to turn in force to both electoral politics and community organizing. Dreier caught the spirit of the times by crafting a strategy combining gradualist tactics with a broader Marxist vision for radical social change.

A brief news report on the Social Movements panel makes it clear that Dreier's Cooper Union talk developed themes initially laid out in his "Socialist Incubators" piece—the need to gather local community organizations into broader political coalitions in synergistic relationship with candidates (preferably grassroots organizers themselves) at the state and local levels.[73] Ultimately, said Dreier, this is the way to combat Reaganomics. Dreier's strategy certainly helps make sense of Obama's original definition of community organizing as a response to Reagan's "dirty deeds." Obama's message is Dreier's message: "Change won't come from the top. . . . Change will come from a mobilized grass roots." Dreier may or may not have broached his "crisis strategy" at the Cooper Union panel, but Obama surely learned about it eventually, since Gorz's notion of "non-reformist reforms" is well known among community organizers. In fact, yet another Cooper Union panel could easily have discussed Gorz.

We can read what is probably a reworked version of Dreier's Cooper Union talk in a cover piece he co-published with John Atlas and John Stephens (both also active in the DSA) in the July 23–30, 1983, issue of *The Nation*.[74] This piece, "Progressive Politics in 1984," came to embody the political strategy favored by those DSA members most committed to community organizing. It was reprinted in DSA's internal "discussion bulletin," *Socialist Forum*, and passed around at the 1983 national DSA convention. Obama likely saw the article when it came out in *The Nation*. (Interestingly, when you turn the page to get to the continuation, you're confronted by a large picture of Harold Washington staring out from that omnipresent full-page ad for *In These Times*.)

The piece begins with the story of Doreen Del Banco, a community organizer who won election to the Connecticut State Legislature. Because of Del Banco's connections to left-labor and community groups, "she was able to mobilize a small army of experienced and energetic campaign workers." Del Banco worked with one of the "Citizens Action" groups, part of a loose national coalition of community organizations coordinated through Chicago's Midwest Academy, the crypto-socialist organization that Obama himself would someday develop ties to. In their bylines, the authors of the *Nation* piece made no secret of their active association with the Democratic Socialists of America. It's also of interest that, twenty-five years later, Peter Dreier would serve as an advisor to Obama's 2008 presidential campaign.[75]

The Dreier, Atlas, and Stephens *Nation* piece touched on ACORN and the SEIU and emphasized the role of community organizations and voter registration drives in Harold Washington's Chicago victory. In effect, this piece, which Obama may have heard a trial version of at Cooper Union, foreshadows his entire political career (as does Dreier's "Socialist Incubators," which mentions a number of groups with which Obama developed close ties). Dreier, Atlas, and Stephens call their approach the "party-within-a-party-plan"—a way to use the lever of community organizing to force the Democrats far to the left, thereby sparking a broader class-based realignment of the two parties. Here was a way of placing community organizing at the service of Michael Harrington's ultimate strategic dream.

DISRUPT THE DEMOCRATS

Harold Washington's stunning upset victory in the Chicago Democratic mayoral primary came on February 22, 1983. The Democratic nomination is usually tantamount to election in Chicago, but with the city divided between black and white—machine and independent—the outcome of Washington's general election battle with Republican Bernard Epton was anything but a foregone conclusion. The Cooper Union Conference, held just ten days before the April 12 general election, lay very much in the shadow of Chicago politics.

In the runup to Cooper Union, Peter Dreier used Harold Washington's Chicago primary upset to tout a new voter registration plan designed by fellow community organizing strategist and DSA Executive Committee member Frances Fox Piven. In DSA's internal "discussion bulletin," *Socialist Forum,* Dreier highlighted the importance of a new article by Piven and her longtime collaborator Richard Cloward, "Toward a Class-Based Realignment of American Politics: A Movement Strategy."[76]

Cloward and Piven wanted workers at various government agencies to start registering welfare recipients standing in line to collect their benefits. Pointing out that many DSA members already worked in welfare waiting rooms, legal service offices, and related agencies, Dreier urged full-scale socialist support for Piven's plan. The key to success, said Dreier, would be to combine DSA's electoral strategy with its heavy involvement in community organizing. If socialists could extend the reach of existing grassroots groups to still-unorganized poor and minority communities, and then tie these grassroots groups to registration campaigns on the model of Project Vote, the Harold Washington model might be replicated across the country. This strategy, of course, virtually describes Obama's career path, and was a focus of much of the rest of the Social Movements panel. You can almost hear Obama saying to himself, "That's what I'll do, I'll organize black folks. At the grass roots. For change . . . And for socialism."

Piven herself was on this panel, the thrust of which was optimism about a long-term strategy in which community organizing would combine voter registration and minority mobilization to turn the country left, thereby giving socialism a new lease on life.

As explained in the article Dreier was touting, Cloward and Piven's strategy went well beyond mere voter registration. Their plan was to turbo-charge leftist politics by actively provoking conflict. Cloward and Piven expected that government workers doing effectively political registration work at welfare lines would get into trouble. Government employees registering welfare recipients on government property as a way of fighting Ronald Reagan's budget cuts were sure to be "charged with exploiting their positions and coercing their clients for self-interested and partisan motives." Cloward and Piven actually wanted to provoke this sort of attack. They believed that as soon as attempts were made to rein in politicized welfare workers, their clients would explode in protest, kicking off a massive movement reminiscent of the effort to register southern black voters in the sixties. "Until a registration campaign provokes just this level of conflict," wrote Cloward and Piven, "all is prologue."[77]

So according to Cloward and Piven, voter registration by itself would not be enough to "break the grip of the ruling groups." Capitalists and their tame Democratic Party allies would continue to manipulate the consciousness of poor voters into supporting the current economic system. According to Cloward and Piven, only with the emergence of a massive protest movement on the model of the civil rights and anti-war movements of the sixties would the Democratic Party be "disrupted and transformed."[78] A Democratic Party flooded with poor and minority voters angry about attempts to keep them from the ballot box would kick out moderate politicians and usher in the long-awaited two-party realignment around competing capitalist and working-class poles. The path to an American socialism would then be open.

So when Obama compared his interest in grassroots organizing to the heady days of the civil rights movement, he was right. The socialist organizers at Cooper Union consciously thought of their strategies as attempts to reignite the driving emotions of the sixties.

Frank Reisman, another member of the Social Movements panel, would have delivered to his listeners a treasure house of strategic thinking about community organizing.[79] Reisman edited *Social Policy* and helped to turn that (largely socialist) journal into the most important intellectual voice of community organizing in the country. Dreier's "Socialist Incubators" piece, his article on "non-reformist reforms," Cloward and Piven's voter registration piece, and many other seminal articles on community organizing were published in *Social Policy* from the late seventies through the eighties and beyond. The editor of *Social Policy* could have provided Obama with the keys to the intellectual kingdom of community organizing.

RACE & CLASS IN MARXISM

Given the young Obama's deep personal interest in issues of race, class, and the links between them, the early afternoon panel on "Race & Class in Marxism" would surely have caught his eye. The only truly serious competition with the Race & Class in Marxism panel would have been a session on "State and the Economy." The draw here was less the topic than the fact that Detroit congressman John Conyers was the first speaker.[80] We know that when Obama sent out letters seeking organizer jobs, he also contacted "any black elected official in the country with a progressive agenda."[81] That would certainly have included Conyers, who had a well-established cooperative relationship with the DSA. Although it seems unlikely that Obama would have passed up the entire Race & Class in Marxism panel, it's easy to imagine him dashing over to catch Conyers's talk and then moving back to the session on race and class. (Obviously, we can't know Obama's movements in detail. The point is that the themes we're discussing were conference-wide.)

Although a Conyers presentation on "State and the Economy" might seem far afield of community organizing, that is not necessarily the case. In February 1982 in Detroit, about a year before the Cooper Union Conference, Conyers addressed DSA's first public event after its creation from the merger of DSOC and NAM. Here's how Chicago DSA covered Conyers's 1982 talk in its newsletter:

> Representative Conyers . . . reminded DSA members that "liberal bullshit politics never worked and never will work, and that's why we got Reagan." Conyers urged the organization to emphasize local grassroots development, a strategy many DSA members agree the organization should adopt.[82]

So even if Obama had dashed over to catch Conyers's talk, he might have gotten an earful about grassroots strategies and community organizing.

Back at the Race & Class in Marxism panel, Stanley Aronowitz was holding forth. I'm going to concentrate, however, on talks by Manning Marable and Cornel West.[83] Although Cornel West is the bigger name today, in 1983, West was only beginning his ascent. At the time, Manning Marable was a vice chair of the DSA and "probably the best known black Marxist in the country."[84] That's how West himself described Marable in his review of Marable's 1983 book, *How Capitalism Underdeveloped Black America*. Since this book appeared either just before or shortly after the Cooper Union Conference, and since it constitutes an in-depth discussion of race, class, and Marxism, it's a safe bet that Marable's panel presentation would have conveyed the core ideas of the book, his most ambitious work to date. It also seems likely that Obama would have made a point of eventually reading this book.

The first thing that strikes you about *How Capitalism Underdeveloped Black America* is Marable's deep sense of alienation from the United States. "To be Black and socialist in America is to be a nonconformist," he begins.[85] In his preface, Marable quotes his wife's half-joking comment that, after publication, they'd be forced to flee the country. Marable's half-serious reply: "Our bags are always packed."[86] Marable opens the book by excerpting Frederick Douglass's bitter 1852 rejection of American Fourth of July celebrations, as if nothing had changed in the United States since slavery.[87]

Marable's bitterness flows from his central thesis. While many argue that black poverty is caused by a history of systematic minority exclusion from the American system, Marable claims that the system itself is *designed* to make blacks poor: "America's 'democratic' government and 'free enterprise' system are structured deliberately and specifically to maximize Black oppression."[88] For Marable, racism doesn't contradict the American way. Instead it reveals the oppressive truth of the entire capitalist system.

Although a vice chair of the Democratic Socialists of America, in his writing Marable is far more willing than Michael Harrington to openly repudiate American democratic norms. His model in *How Capital-*

ism Underdeveloped Black America is the influential twentieth-century
African-American author W. E. B. DuBois, whom Marable says was a
life-long socialist, even when DuBois downplayed that socialism for
strictly tactical reasons.[89] For Marable, "no real democracy has ever ex-
isted in the United States."[90] Control of America by white capitalists,
he says, renders the very notion of democracy absurd.[91] While Marable
concedes that Stalinism had its problems, he nonetheless sees the Soviet Union as closer to true democracy than a capitalist United States
will ever be.[92] Black crime is not the fault of the young men who commit it, Marable adds, but of the capitalist system itself.[93] In short, says
Marable, it is impossible to struggle against racism and still remain a
proponent of capitalism.[94] As for American democracy: "Without hesi-
tation, we must explain that a basic social transformation within America's social and economic structures would involve radical changes that
would be viewed as clearly undemocratic by millions of people."[95] In
particular, he says, the rights of any who discriminate against African-
Americans, women, Chicanos, and gays would be restricted.[96]

HOW SOCIALISTS CAN WIN

If Obama did eventually read *How Capitalism Underdeveloped Black
America,* he would surely have been struck by Marable's choice of a
poem by Obama's mentor, Frank Marshall Davis, to open the chapter
on black capitalism.[97] Davis's poem is a bitter jab at efforts by middle-
class blacks to distance themselves from their poverty-stricken roots.
As for blacks who go into politics, says Marable: "The instant that
the Black politician accepts the legitimacy of the State, the rules of the
game, his/her critical faculties are destroyed permanently, and all that
follows are absurdities."[98] Marable argues that between mass incarceration of young black men and Reagan's budget cuts, America is moving toward subtle fascism and de facto genocide of American blacks.[99]
As Marable attacks America, excoriates the prison system, rejects

"middle-classness," and spins out theories of Reagan's genocidal intent, it's tough not to think of Jeremiah Wright, whose sermons touch on all these themes. Wright may or may not have read Marable, but the larger point is that both men were espousing a common hard-left view of the United States.

Given Marable's bitter repudiation of America, you might think he rejects conventional politics altogether. Not so. The intriguing thing about Marable is the way he combines a sweeping and embittered opposition to the entire American system with a far more subtle and patient political strategy. Marable does have qualified praise for a few black politicians, particularly Congressmen Ronald Dellums and John Conyers, whom he describes as "open advocates of democratic socialism."[100] Marable has praise for Harold Washington as well.[101] For Marable, properly calibrated leftist political gradualism in the present promises to undo the entire American system in the future: "The revolt for reforms within the capitalist state today transcends itself dialectically to become a revolution against the racist/capitalist system tomorrow."[102]

Ultimately, then, for all his rejectionist rhetoric, Marable's strategy and tactics bear a striking resemblance to those of Dreier and Piven: "Progressives can gain positions within the state, especially at municipal and state levels, which can help fund and support grass roots interests and indirectly assist in the development of a socialist majority."[103] Like Dreier, Marable even invokes Gorz's notion of "non-reformist reforms," with universal health care as one of his prime examples.[104] In the end, Marable's program echoes what Obama could have heard at the Social Movements panel: Penetrate the legislatures, expand entitlements, restrict capitalism through regulation, and place all of this in synergy with a proto-socialist grassroots movement.

Marable would likely have added something to his panel talk about the Harold Washington phenomenon. We know events in Chicago were on his mind, because Marable had a piece in the *Guardian* just two weeks before the Cooper Union Conference entitled "Many messages

for Marxists from Chicago mayoral race."[105] There Marable says that
Washington's "social democratic" program places him "slightly to the
left of almost every mayor of any U.S. city—with the exception of Berkeley's [openly socialist] Gus Newport." And in comments that could
conceivably have been made at the Cooper Union conference itself, in
an April 6 *Guardian* article, Marable argues for an electoral strategy for
blacks built around "mass-based organizing" of "third world forces."[106]
Once again, we can almost hear Obama saying to himself, "That's what
I'll do, I'll organize black folks. At the grass roots. For change."

A PATH TO REVEREND WRIGHT

Cornel West's talk, while it may have touched lightly on the need for
multi-racial coalitions and grassroots organizing, was important for
another reason. West's panel presentation that day could easily have
been Obama's introduction to the world of black liberation theology.
With multiple chances to hear from West at other Socialist Scholars
Conferences, one or another talk by West likely helped lead Obama to
Reverend Wright.

In 1983, West was a young assistant professor at Union Theological
Seminary. Union was home to James Cone, the founder of black liberation theology, and Jeremiah Wright's theological mentor. West worked
closely with Cone, serving as a bridge between the socialist world and
the black theological community. West and Cone co-taught a seminar at Union Theological Seminary on "Black Theology and Marxist
Thought." Out of that seminar came a 1980 essay by Cone, "The Black
Church and Marxism: What Do They Have to Say to Each Other?"
That piece was issued as a pamphlet by DSA, with an added commentary by Michael Harrington.[107] The same pamphlet was co-published
by the "Black Theology Project," a subdivision of a larger group called
"Theology in the Americas."[108] Theology in the Americas (TIA) and
its Black Theology Project (BTP) subdivision were organizations dedi-

cated to propagating James Cone–style liberation theology.[109] West was a powerful figure within both TIA and BTP, and so was Jeremiah Wright.

The DSA Records at New York's Tamiment Library contain an April 13, 1982, letter from Cornel West to Michael Harrington.[110] Harrington had just met with West and several other black theologians from Union Theological Seminary in an effort to recruit them to the newly formed DSA. Apparently Harrington got a cool reception from many of the Union people, suspicious that DSA would not have the best interest of the black community at heart. West, however, responded positively, enclosing membership dues and telling Harrington of his desire to "legitimate socialist alternatives" in public discourse, while also infusing the African-American church with socialist analysis and ideas. In the letter, West calls himself a "Council Communist," a Marxist tradition flowing out of the work of Rosa Luxemburg, situated halfway between purely democratic socialism, on the one side, and authoritarian Bolshevism, on the other.

West expands on these themes in his first (and still, he says, favorite) book, *Prophesy Deliverance!*[111] The book was published in the fall of 1982, just months before the Cooper Union Conference, so it's a safe bet that West would have laid out the gist of *Prophesy Deliverance!* at the Race & Class in Marxism panel.

The interesting thing about *Prophesy Deliverance!* is that West puts his Marxist points across by way of an extended history of black liberation theology in America. So the doings of James Cone and his affiliated organizations, Theology in the Americas and the Black Theology Project, are a very important part of the book. All this may have been part of West's talk at Cooper Union. In *Prophesy Deliverance!* West portrays black theology as passing through various stages. The current or fourth stage, according to West, is called, "Black Theology of Liberation as Critique of U.S. Capitalism."[112] West mentions Cone's recent work as part of that stage, and also highlights an official 1977 statement by the Black Theology Project. Here's a bit of that BTP manifesto: "Exploitative, profit-oriented capitalism is a way of ordering life fundamentally alien to human value in general, and to black humanity in particular." [113] Online biographies of Jeremiah Wright list him as a BTP board member from 1975 to 1995, so he may well have helped author that 1977 manifesto. [114] Certainly Wright was deeply involved in BTP activities in the mid-1980s. In short, there is every possibility that as early as 1983, at the very moment he decided to become a community organizer, Obama was introduced to a socialist-friendly tradition of black theology whose most important representative in Chicago was Jeremiah Wright. And this would be far from the only opportunity Obama would have had to hear from Cornel West at a Socialist Scholars Conference. In fact, at the 1984 conference, Obama would have had an opportunity to hear from James Cone himself.

The place of community organizing and minority coalition-building in socialist electoral strategies were pervasive concerns of the DSA. Whichever panels Obama attended, whoever he met in the hallways, whatever journals and books he browsed at the literature tables—in one form or another, he would have run into talk about community organizing and the role of African-Americans in socialist politics. A late-afternoon session on "Urban Politics & Policy" would have been another venue in which Obama could have encountered these issues, as would a seemingly unrelated late-afternoon session on "Third World Socialisms," featuring Paulette Pierce, a key member of DSA's African-American Commission. Pierce had a special interest, not only in overseas issues, but also in minority coalition-building in American politics.

Another striking example of the breadth of DSA interest in these issues can be found in an article by Cooper Union conference organizer Bogdan Denitch in the spring 1983 issue of *Social Policy*, entitled "Confronting Coalition Contradictions." [115] Denitch was a close Harrington ally, whose interest was on the opposite end of the DSA spectrum from, say, Manning Marable or Cornel West. Denitch was a proponent of a predominantly "economic" socialism and tended to avoid various forms of identity politics. His special interest was Europe.

Yet in the issue of *Social Policy* that immediately followed the Cooper Union conference, Denitch published an essay on the significance of Harold Washington and minority-led coalitions for socialist politics in America. The point of Denitch's brief *Social Policy* piece is that Harold Washington's Chicago victory points the way to the most effective strategy for uniting a fractious left. The answer, says Denitch, is to build black-led coalitions around economic issues. Denitch could easily have taken up these points at his Cooper Union appearances. As conference organizer, Denitch delivered remarks at the all-conference closing plenary session and spoke at a panel on "Images of Socialism," as well. Clearly, in the spring of 1983, Harold Washington's use of grassroots organizing and black church activism had socialists of all stripes buzzing. So Denitch's piece is yet more evidence that, whether through hallway banter, all-conference plenary sessions, or whatever set of panels he may have attended, Obama would have repeatedly run into the same set of strategic themes at Cooper Union.

HIDING SOCIALISM

Every aspect of Obama's treatment of his career choice in *Dreams from My Father* was an active theme at the 1983 Cooper Union Socialist Scholars Conference. Want to fight the "dirty deeds" of Reagan and his minions? Become a community organizer. Do it well—and do it in a minority community—and you just might become the next Harold Washington, leading a coalition of blacks, whites, and Hispanics ("black, white, and brown") for a socialist "redefinition" of America. Here, in community organizing and its associated proto-socialist political movement, was a rebirth of the sixties struggle for civil rights, yet focused now on economic equality. Through participation in this movement, Obama could earn himself a place in the African-American community, transforming America in the process. Obama says it all in *Dreams*. Only the socialism is omitted. Yet by suppressing the socialist context of his organizing, a deadly serious radical strategy to transform the United States goes missing, buried beneath a heart-rending tale of existential agony and personal redemption.

As for socialism itself, Obama's conservative critics (along with *Newsweek*) seem to have a better handle on the term than anyone else. The idea that America might inadvertently and incrementally fall into socialism is a great deal closer to the strategies of "actual existing socialists" than textbook definitions of economies nationalized at a single revolutionary blow. The reason Americans don't understand this is that the universe of post-sixties socialism has remained largely hidden from public view. Yet this is Obama's world. It's time we got to know it.

CHAPTER 3

From New York to Havana

Tracking down Barack Obama's hidden political convictions and dragging them into the light of day is a task requiring the patience of a detective. We haven't got access to the personal journals Obama kept for years; until some recent cracks in the wall of silence, his former friends and colleagues have been savvy enough to keep quiet; and there is no such thing as a time machine. So clues must be patiently gathered and pieced together, one by one. While the Socialist Scholars Conferences discussed in this chapter provide a tremendously revealing window into the president's hidden past, Obama's energetic and long-standing efforts to shroud his New York years have succeeded in keeping his movements and beliefs during this period difficult to follow.

Yet there are important indicators of what Obama was reading and thinking during this time of intellectual ferment. When juxtaposed with the Socialist Scholars Conferences, these clues will point us in the right direction. Obama was vastly more knowledgeable about the socialist roots of his new profession than he has ever dared let on. Evidence also suggests that Obama was learning not only about socialist community organizing in New York, but about the determination of many organizers to hide their socialist beliefs.

The restless reading of Obama's New York years shaped him profoundly. In Chicago, Obama worked directly with the very best stealth-socialist organizers in the country, some of them the very same people he'd studied and read about years before. That broader picture—as well as the clear evidence that Obama was a socialist during his early college years at Occidental—is what makes the initial clues examined in this chapter so important.

Even our necessarily limited reconstruction of Obama's socialist adventures in New York will suffice to expose the artful dodging Obama engaged in during campaign '08. When it comes to his early knowledge of community organizing and its socialist roots, Obama has long "played dumb." That facade of ignorance cannot survive an investigation of Obama's New York years.

OBAMA IN DSA FILES

Barack Obama's name appears on a large list of names and addresses, in a folder labeled "Socialist Scholars Conference," in the Records of the Democratic Socialists of America (DSA).[1] Analysis of this list and associated materials strongly suggests that Obama pre-registered for the Second Annual Socialist Scholars Conference held on April 19–21, 1984, at the Boro of Manhattan Community College, CUNY, in New York. Recall at the start that Obama himself acknowledges attending "socialist conferences" during his time in New York.[2] Obama's use of the plural means that he likely attended at least two, and perhaps all three of the Socialist Scholars Conferences held in New York between 1983 and 1985.

The list with Obama's name and address is clearly a mailing list, since the names are arranged by zip code, and names without usable addresses have been crossed off the list by hand. The folder containing the mailing list is filled with material that has obviously been used to prepare a program for the 1984 Socialist Scholars Conference—lists of conference speakers from that year, charts of individual panels, and 1984 conference programs as well. There appears to be no material from after 1984 in the folder. A single program for the 1983 conference is present, however, probably as a reference for the 1984 planners.

Subtracting duplicate names, the list totals about one thousand. Since attendance at the 1983 Socialist Scholars Conference was close to fifteen hundred, it seems unlikely that this list simply contains the names of attendees from the 1983 event.[3] We know from material in this folder, and from other parts of the DSA records, that several different conference programs were prepared in 1984.[4] Some, presumably worked up early, had registration forms attached and no appended speakers list. Others had an addendum with information on added panels, while still others, presumably prepared at a late stage, had a full alphabetical list of speakers attached and a more complete list of panels. All of this suggests that the material containing Obama's name was a list of people who had pre-registered for the 1984 conference. These pre-registrants were going to get a mailing of the final, or near-final, conference program, with a full alphabetical list of speakers appended. Material used to produce this program was contained in the folder, along with the mailing list.

Another indicator that the list with Obama's name on it contains attendees of the 1984 conference is that thirty-six people on the list were also speakers at the 1984 conference. Some of these speakers appear to have been late additions to the list of panelists, suggesting that when certain prominent people pre-registered, conference organizers recruited them to participate on a panel.

Obama's address is listed as 339 E. Ninety-fourth Street, #6A, New York, NY 10028. This is an apartment Obama is known to have occupied during much of his time at Columbia.[5] The conference, however, took place in April of 1984, almost a year after Obama's graduation.

One account says that Obama moved out of his college apartment at some point, but doesn't say when.[6] In 2008, the Obama campaign released a list of five residences he occupied in New York, adding that Obama himself had forgotten many details of his movements.[7] A *New York Times* article on Obama's New York years indicates that the New York phone book continued to list the East Ninety-fourth Street apartment as Obama's address, even after he graduated.[8] Obama may also have pre-registered for the 1984 conference early on, before any possible move. In short, despite some ambiguity about Obama's famously mysterious movements in New York, documentary evidence, as well as his own testimony in *Dreams from My Father*, strongly suggests that Obama attended the Second Annual Socialist Scholars Conference, held in April 1984 in New York.

MINORITY RECRUITMENT

Obama's attendance at New York's mid-eighties Socialist Scholars Conferences coincided with a high point in DSA's minority recruitment efforts. Almost as soon as it was formed out of the merger of two smaller groups in 1981–82, DSA started looking to draw in African-American recruits. The rise of the Harold Washington movement in Chicago in 1983 surely added urgency to these efforts. In January of 1982, DSA's board floated the idea of minority quotas on leading committees.[9] A few months later, DSA head Michael Harrington met with the circle of black liberation theologians around James Cone (Jeremiah Wright's theological mentor) and recruited Cornel West (see Chapter Two).

The first DSA national convention, held October 14–16, 1983 (six months after the Cooper Union Socialist Scholars Conference), took several steps to enlarge minority participation. Prior to the convention, DSA leadership sent out letters calling on members to elect particular individuals—including Cornel West—as delegates.[10] The convention then voted to allocate 25 percent of National Executive Committee seats to minorities—three for men and three for women.[11] (DSA had a pre-existing male-female quota system.) The overall effect of these changes was to shift DSA to the left, since minority activists tended to come from more militant backgrounds than Harrington's traditional allies.[12] For example, at the 1983 convention, DSA overcame objections from the more democratic and anti-Soviet sections of the leadership and voted to support the Marxist Sandinista regime in Nicaragua, and other Central American revolutionary movements as well.[13]

The issue of minority recruitment raises some obvious questions. Did Obama ever join the Democratic Socialists of America? Short of this, was he perhaps involved in DSA activities, over and above the Socialist Scholars Conferences? I don't know the answer to these questions. Given the importance of minority recruitment to DSA between 1983 and 1985, it's hard to believe that Obama would not have been aggressively urged—in person at the Socialist Scholars Conferences— to join the DSA. It also seems perfectly possible that Obama might have attended various events sponsored by DSA. New York DSA also sponsored "socialist schools" with classes on a wide variety of political topics, and Obama could have attended such a school.[14] I have no evidence, however, for any Obama involvement with DSA over and above his attendance at Socialist Scholars Conferences.

JESSE JACKSON

Before we plunge into an investigation of Obama's probable doings at the 1984 Socialist Scholars Conference, one more background condition requires discussion. Just as the 1983 Socialist Scholars Conference took place in the shadow of Harold Washington's mayoral campaign, Jesse Jackson's first presidential campaign was very much on the minds of conference participants in 1984. As early as May of 1983, just after Harold Washington's mayoral victory, Jackson broached the idea of a presidential campaign modeled on the Washington phenomenon.[15] In Jackson's words, it was time for America's blacks to "rene-gotiate our relationship with the Democratic Party."[16] Jackson figured that by combining a charismatic campaign with a massive minority registration drive, he could force the Democrats left. Even without his capturing the nomination, the eventual nominee would presumably have to placate Jackson's Rainbow Coalition, or risk defeat at Reagan's hands.

The 1984 Jackson campaign was a seemingly perfect example of the synergy between grassroots organizing, minority coalition-building, and national politics that DSA now hoped to orchestrate. Certainly, many DSAers saw it that way. Manning Marable, the most influen-tial African-American in the organization, viewed Jackson's Rain-bow Coalition as "a new stage of American politics," a de facto leftist "party-in-a-party."[17] Paulette Pierce, a prominent member of DSA's African-American Commission, said that Jackson was "acting out the avowed electoral strategy of DSA," working within the Democrats "to bring together a new progressive majority which could transform the Party."[18]

Even the militant "sectarian" left, usually averse to participation in the two-party system, made an exception in Jackson's case. The near-unanimous conclusion of hyper-radical groups, from the Communist Party to the Communist Workers Party, was that participation in the Jackson campaign would energize their efforts at grassroots organiz-ing.[19] "Although Jackson is not a socialist," said one Chicago radical, "his campaign has contributed to the development of demands outside the usual spectrum set by bourgeois politics."[20] Or, as another hard-leftist put it, Jackson "isn't a socialist, but he questions the divinity of capitalism."[21]

Above all, Jackson's foreign policy views thrilled just about every hard-left faction. It was tough to construe Jackson's statements as any-thing other than outright support for Central America's Marxist rev-olutionaries. "Our foreign policy in Central America is wrong," said Jackson, adding, "We are standing on the wrong side of history."[22] Jackson called on the Reagan administration to withdraw its opposition to the Marxist Sandinista government in Nicaragua: "Successful revolutions in Central America need not threaten U.S. national security."[23] Jackson urged U.S. recognition of Cuba and questioned open-ended U.S. support for Israel. He also called for a 20 percent military spending cut.[24]

The "Marxist-Leninist" (i.e., *not* democratic socialist) American *Guardian* endorsed the Jackson campaign, highlighting its synergy with grassroots organizing efforts. The *Guardian* hoped that Jackson might raise his movement's expectations so high that, once dashed, the Rainbow Coalition would abandon the Democrats and energize an independent quasi-socialist movement of the left.[25] This is exactly what the DSA's "right wing" feared. Harrington and his closest allies were determined to work within the Democratic Party. They were supportive of the newfound synergy between community organizing, minority empowerment, and electoral politics, yet wanted to confine it to the local level. In presidential politics, they worried, openly moving too left, too fast would only split the Democrats and hand the country to Reagan for another four years.[26]

That anti-Jackson stance infuriated black leaders like academic Paulette Pierce, who had cast their lot with the DSA.[27] How could DSA recruit minorities, asked Pierce, if it couldn't choose Jesse Jackson over a moderate Cold Warrior like Walter Mondale? Many—probably most—rank-and-file white DSAers agreed.[28]

So leading up to the April 19–21, 1984, Socialist Scholars Conference, the American left was divided over the Jackson campaign. The vast majority of black socialists, however, stood with Jackson, seeing in him the embodiment of a new grassroots electoral strategy designed to realign (or break) America's two-party system. By April, the Jackson campaign had faltered on the candidate's infamous reference to Jews as "Hymies" and to New York as "Hymietown," followed by Jackson's unconvincing denials and his implications that Jews were trying to discredit him.[29] For the left, however, despite genuine dismay at the

Hymietown controversy, Jackson's magic sparkled throughout. Where was Obama in all this? Chances are he stood with Jackson politically. In any case, we have reason to believe that Obama stood near Jesse Jackson, literally, just three weeks before the 1984 Socialist Scholars Conference. In *Dreams from my Father,* Obama tells of walking through Harlem to hear a speech Jesse Jackson delivered on 125th Street.[30] This reference is probably to the massive March 31 rally Jackson held on 125th Street in Harlem at the height of his 1984 campaign.[31]

MARX AND UNCLE SAM

The theme of the 1984 Socialist Scholars Conference was "The Encounter with America." Programs featured drawings of a burly-looking Uncle Sam and Karl Marx standing side by side and rolling up their sleeves, as if they were about to take on a bunch of evil-doers (presumably corporate types) in a fight.[32] I'm going to concentrate on only one panel at this conference, but will also mention some of the other talks Obama likely encountered.

Obama would have had plenty of opportunities to hear panel talks in 1984 echoing themes introduced at the Cooper Union Conference the year before: grassroots organizing, minority coalition-building, and black-church radicalism. Cornel West presented at two panels in 1984, and we probably have reworked versions of both talks in articles West published in the months following the conference.[33] Obama could also have attended a panel called The Hole in the Electorate, which featured Frances Fox Piven and DSA head Michael Harrington, among others, commenting on Piven's strategy for using minority voter registration to provoke a class-based realignment of the parties. Suffice it to say that all the themes he encountered at the 1983 Cooper Union Conference would have been driven home again in 1984. There is, however, one 1984 conference panel worth discussing in depth, both because Obama would almost certainly have attended it, and because it would have provided a personal introduction of sorts to the father of black liberation theology, James Cone.

DR. KING AND DEMOCRATIC SOCIALISM

Sometime around August–September 1983, DSA issued a pamphlet geared toward recruiting minorities. The pamphlet, featuring a large cover photo of Martin Luther King, Jr., was titled "Reflections on the Legacy," and argued that toward the end of his life, King experienced a political conversion to democratic socialism. The pamphlet featured an essay, "From Reformer to Revolutionary," by King historian David Garrow, with an introduction by Paulette Pierce, a sociology professor and DSA leader who identifies herself in the pamphlet as "a black member of the Democratic Socialists of America."[34] The 1984 Socialist Scholars Conference included a panel on "Dr. King and Democratic Socialism," featuring Garrow, King historian John Ansbro, and James Cone, the founder of black liberation theology and theological mentor to both Cornel West and Jeremiah Wright.[35] Garrow's recruiting pamphlet would have been readily available at the panel and at the conference literature tables. The panel itself surely would have focused on Garrow's claims about King's socialist conversion.

In *Dreams from My Father,* Obama roots his decision to become a community organizer in his desire to carry forward the civil rights crusade of the sixties. Images of struggle from that era, says Obama, "became a form of prayer for me."[36] We also know that by the time Obama arrived in Chicago for his first organizing job, he had already accumulated substantial personal knowledge of the history of King and his movement.[37] So it's tough to imagine Obama passing up a panel called Dr. King and Democratic Socialism—or failing to read the associated pamphlet.

Paulette Pierce was a key figure in efforts to bring DSA around to formal support of Jesse Jackson's presidential campaign. Pierce's 1983 introduction to Garrow's essay is an extraordinary document. High-lighting King's alleged late-life transformation "from a reformer into a revolutionary," Pierce stresses King's eventual abandonment of his belief in America. At first, says Pierce, King may have had an "abid-ing faith in America" and in "the fundamental justness of American institutions."[38] Yet by the end, Pierce notes, King came to believe that " 'America is much, much sicker than I realized.' "[39] This recognition prompted King to argue that " 'The whole structure of American life must be changed.' "[40] According to Pierce, King became convinced that "private ownership and control of the means of production con-tradicted his Christian beliefs."[41] By the end of his life, claims Pierce, King was "clearly on his way to openly embracing a democratic social-ist position."[42]

Garrow's historical essay is remarkable for its focus, not only on King's alleged socialism, but on his attempts at community organizing . . . in Chicago. Garrow recounts the story of King's failed efforts during the Chicago Freedom Movement, begun in late 1965. Despite six months of effort, King's attempts to organize Chicago's poor black citizens into "enduring self-directed groups" collapsed.[43]

King's organizing failure in Chicago, says Garrow, turned him against capitalism and transformed him from a reformer into a "revolu-tionary." Garrow quotes the later King actually opposing integration of a sort: "Let us not think of our movement as one that seeks to integrate the Negro into all existing values of American society."[44] According to Garrow, by the end of his life, King had come to believe that the eco-nomic structure and system of values that sustained American capital-ism would have to go.

Garrow's stress on community organizing in this essay is no fluke. In June of 1985, Garrow was invited to address a DSA National Execu-tive Committee meeting. There Garrow highlighted the importance of King's largely unsung local organizing efforts in the South. According to Garrow, media focus on spectacular demonstrations notwithstand-ing, grassroots organizing was the true key to King's success.[45] Gar-row's work suggests that when Obama speaks of community organizing as a kind of modern successor to King's civil rights movement, he has some historical basis for the claim. Garrow's DSA pamphlet also suggests that when Obama links his own struggle for change to the legacy of Dr. King, he may have socialism in mind—even if most Americans do not hear it that way.

Did Martin Luther King, Jr., really become a democratic socialist toward the end of his life? King does seem to have turned leftward in his later years. Whether he went so far as to privately embrace socialism is less clear. In any case, for our purposes, whether King converted to socialism toward the end of his life is less important than the fact that many in Obama's world believe that King did.

FROM JAMES CONE TO JEREMIAH WRIGHT

How did panelist James Cone respond to Garrow's notion of a late-life socialist conversion by Dr. King? Cone was likely sympathetic to the idea of a radical left turn, yet noncommittal on the specific question of King's socialism. That, at least, is Cone's position in his published work, where he appears a bit uncomfortable with the controversy, given accusations of communist or socialist connections made by King's opponents at the height of the civil rights struggle.[46]

The deeper problem is that, while Cone is deeply sympathetic to Marxism, he worries that when it comes to race, even Marxists might not be radical enough. We saw in Chapter Two that Cone published a pamphlet through DSA called "The Black Church and Marxism: What Do They Have to Say to Each Other?"[47] That pamphlet included a commentary by DSA head Michael Harrington. In his pamphlet, Cone expresses strong sympathy for Marxism, without openly or explicitly signing on as a socialist. It's a safe bet that, at the King panel, Cone's DSA pamphlet would have been touted alongside of Garrow's. It also seems very likely that Obama would have read both pamphlets (and would have done so even if he had missed the panel itself).

In his DSA pamphlet, Cone challenges Marxists from the point of view of black liberation theology. Marxists, Cone says, "have to be open to . . . asking whether fascism is inherent in the very nature and structure of western civilization." [48] Despite his doubts about Western civilization (of which Marxist theory is a part), Cone agrees that black churchpeople need to be open to the need for a "total reconstruction of society along the lines of Democratic Socialism." [49] Capitalism, agrees Cone, is "a system which offers no hope for the masses of blacks." [50]

Again, given Obama's voracious reading habits during his New York period ("I had tons of books. I read everything."), [51] and given his curiosity about all things black—and socialist—it's hard to believe that he would have overlooked Cone's pamphlet. Obama almost certainly knew about Cone through panel appearances by Cornel West, and by Cone himself, at the Socialist Scholars Conferences. So when Obama learned that Jeremiah Wright was a leading follower of James Cone's black liberation theology, he would have understood exactly what Wright was talking about. In fact, Obama would almost certainly have recounted for Wright his experiences with James Cone and Cornel West at the Socialist Scholars Conferences. In short, Obama would have understood Wright's radicalism, as Wright would have grasped Obama's. Surely, then, the socialist-friendly attitudes of Cone, West, and their circle would have provided an immediate foundation for a bond between Obama and Wright. None of the other black preachers Obama encountered could have boasted of a comparable relationship to Cone, West, or the socialist-friendly Black Theology Project. Here, then, is a powerful explanation for Obama's choice of Wright as his pastor.

JACKSON, CONE, AND WRIGHT IN CUBA

In June of 1984, two months after the Second Annual Socialist Scholars Conference, Democratic presidential candidate Jesse Jackson visited Fidel Castro's Cuba at the same time a delegation from the Black Theology Project (BTP) was in the country. The BTP delegation included James Cone and Jeremiah Wright.[52] Although Cornel West was unable to attend, a paper he wrote for the occasion was read in his absence.[53] It was almost as though a panel from the Socialist Scholars Conference had reconvened in Havana, with Reverend Wright as an added attraction. The occasion of BTP's visit was an ecumenical theological seminar and memorial celebration in honor of Martin Luther King, Jr.[54]

At one point in his Cuban visit, Jesse Jackson ended a speech at the University of Havana by leading the crowd in chants of "Long live President Castro! Long live Martin Luther King! Long live Che Guevara!" In the pages of the liberal *New Republic*, Glen C. Loury, then a professor of public policy at Harvard's Kennedy School of Government, condemned Jackson's "clear suggestion that Martin Luther King's movement and Che Guevara's movement are on the same moral and political plane." Added Loury: "Such cavalier use of King's moral legacy will only squander it."[55] Loury doesn't seem to consider the possibility that Jackson's equation of King and Che might have been a well-thought-out comparison, rather than a careless attempt to please his hosts. The more we learn about the Jackson-BTP adventure in Cuba, the more deliberate Jackson's chants appear to be.

For the most part, the American press ignored Jackson's troubling cheerleading, as well as the presence of the BTP delegation alongside him during much of his visit. It wasn't until President Reagan addressed a Hispanic audience and reminded them of Jackson's chants that any attention was paid to the disturbing aspects of Jackson's trip. Then, in a November 2, 1984, *Wall Street Journal* op-ed piece, Diego A. Abich revealed at least a part of the story behind the Jackson-BTP adventure in Cuba.[56]

According to Abich, the Cuban government took extraordinary steps to make certain that Jackson's visit coincided with that of the BTP delegation. BTP's ecumenical hosts in Cuba were not the conservative religious traditionalists so disfavored by Castro, but instead a Marxist theological group controlled by the Cuban government. In fact the seminars held by BTP's "ecumenical" hosts took place in facilities controlled by Cuba's intelligence agency, DGI. (DGI, Abich adds, worked under the direction of the Soviet KGB.) Along with initial soundings among Cone's circle at Union Theological Seminary in the early months of 1984, says Abich, a Cuban "evangelical" operative approached Jeremiah Wright about organizing a Martin Luther King memorial conference, while Wright was on a March 1984 visit to the Marxist Sandinista regime in Nicaragua. Abich then explains how Castro turned the joint Jackson-BTP visit into a major event, milking it for propaganda worldwide, while counting on BTP to sow political discontent in America. Although Abich speaks of "Mr. Castro's manipulation of Rev. Jackson and other black religious leaders," manipulation was not the issue.

A study of the Black Theology Project's records of this trip makes it clear that these visiting American theologians had every intention of assisting the Cuban Revolution. Far from being manipulated, BTP was eager to help Castro, and eager to stoke discontent with America's social system. A copy of Abich's op-ed piece can be found in BTP's files, so the organization clearly knew it stood accused of allowing itself to be manipulated by Castro.[57] Yet a BTP delegation returned to Cuba in 1986, this time led by Reverend Wright.[58] Obviously, if BTP had felt deceived or manipulated by their Cuban hosts after reading Abich's account, they would never have returned.

The October 1984 Bulletin of the Black Theology Project carries an extended account of the joint Jackson-BTP Cuba trip, written by noted black liberation theologian Gayraud Wilmore.[59] Wilmore's account was republished in Jeremiah Wright's church newsletter, "Trinity Trumpet," along with pictures of Wright and Jackson together in Havana.[60] Wilmore makes it clear that BTP's delegation was delighted to encounter Marxist clerics who equated religious liberation with the success of the Cuban Revolution. The BTP delegation was also perfectly aware of the fact that many of the ecumenical scholar-clerics who hosted them were also "activists" in the Cuban Communist

Party. The BTP delegation was present at a service memorializing Dr. King when Jesse Jackson entered the church alongside President Castro himself. This was the first time in twenty-five years that Castro had crossed the threshold of an evangelical church, and according to Wilmore, "the excitement was almost more than either visitors or hosts could bear."[61] The sight of Fidel Castro and Jesse Jackson standing side by side in a Cuban evangelical church was a liberation theologian's dream come true.

REVEREND WRIGHT RETURNS TO CUBA

According to Wilmore, in his remarks at this service, Jackson asked Cubans to "hold on" and patiently wait for "deliverance from the animosity and blockade of the Reagan administration." "By the power of a liberating God and the determination of all fair-minded and progressive Americans," added Jackson, there was reason to hope for relief.[62] Wilmore then praises Jackson for having "had the audacity to link his political fortunes with a radical theological perspective within the U.S. Black Church that calls for serious dialogue between Christians and Marxists and solidarity in struggle with the people of Cuba and Central America."[63] Wilmore concludes: "Blacks in the United States need the example of the effective abolition of racism and poverty that Cuba represents."[64]

In short, rather than having been manipulated by Cuban intelligence and the Cuban Communist Party, the Black Theology Project was positively eager to do everything in its power to assist the Cuban Revolution, seeing in Cuban socialism a model for America in general, and American blacks in particular.

Two years later, in July of 1986, BTP returned to Cuba, with Reverend Wright leading a delegation to the Second Dr. Martin Luther King, Jr., Theological Meeting. According to an article in *Granma* (the official organ of the Cuban Communist Party), "Reverend Jeremiah Wright, a close associate of U.S. political and religious leader Jesse Jackson, spoke on behalf of the people of the United States, and especially the black population." [65] Wright, *Granma* continues, "denounced" racial discrimination in the United States and explained the role of the black Church in American history. [66] There followed an address by Brazilian liberation theologian Frei Betto, who defended Marxism as the key to proper Christian theology.

Records of the Black Theology Project indicate that Reverend Wright was a board member during this 1986 trip. [67] A speakers biography posted on the Internet in conjunction with an appearance by Wright at a 2003 Corinthian Baptist Church event lists him as a member of the BTP board of directors from 1975 through 1995. [68] The Black Theology Project and its parent organization Theology in the Americas (TIA) appear to have been only minimally active after the mid-eighties. Yet BTP-TIA records indicate that Wright took charge of TIA sometime around the late eighties. [69]

Obama had connected with Wright by 1987, just a year after Wright's second trip to Cuba. Wright had no compunctions about headlining Wilmore's long and obviously radical account of BTP's Cuba venture—with pictures—in Trinity Trumpet. Is it conceivable, then, that Wright could have failed to regale Obama himself with tales of these trips—particularly after learning of Obama's encounter with James Cone and Cornel West at those Socialist Scholars Conferences in New York? Given that Wright took over leadership of Theology in the Americas in the late eighties, and continued to serve on the Black Theology Project board through 1995, is it conceivable that Obama would never have heard of Wright's involvement in these organizations? In November of 2009, a video surfaced of Wright addressing the sixtieth anniversary gala for the Marxist journal *Monthly Review*. [70] In that address, Wright stresses the importance of his links to the Black Theology Project—and his ties to Cuba. Considering how free Wright is with this information—indeed how positively proud he is of his trips to Cuba—it is easy to imagine how eagerly Wright would have recounted the tale of it all to Obama.

Does this "likelihood" reach the level of "beyond a reasonable doubt"? I think it does. Ultimately, of course, that is for the reader to decide. But don't decide just yet. Wait for Chapter Eight.

OBAMA'S WORDS

Barack Obama's own statements about his New York years are consistent with the notion that he was a socialist at the time. If these were the only bits of evidence available, it would be a mistake to make too much of Obama's few remarks on this mysterious period in his life. Yet juxtaposing Obama's account of his time in New York with his attendance at Socialist Scholars Conferences reveals a pattern. There is also clear evidence that Obama was a "pure Marxist socialist" during his time at Occidental College (see below). While Obama's college socialism could be dismissed as a passing phase, the evidence from his post-college years in New York suggests continuity of belief.

After graduation, Obama worked for Business International Corporation, a company that produced research reports on global business conditions for overseas companies. His goal was to pay off student loans and save up money for the low-wage organizer jobs to come. In his sympathetic biography, *Obama: From Promise to Power,* published during the runup to the 2008 campaign, *Chicago Tribune* reporter David Mendell quotes Obama explaining that this job gave him an education in "the coldness of capitalism."[71] In *Dreams from My Father*, Obama says the job made him feel "like a spy behind enemy lines."[72] The author of these remarks might easily be taken for an enemy of capitalism. When Obama writes, in *Dreams*, of "the almost mathematical precision with which America's race and class problems joined," it could be interpreted as just a passing remark.[73] On the other hand, Obama's observation echoes widespread Marxist views of race in America (see Chapter Two).

When Obama's mother and half-sister visited him in the summer after his first year at Columbia, he pressed them repeatedly with lectures on "the politics of the dispossessed," even turning on his anthropologist mother:

> I instructed my mother on the various ways that foreign donors and international development organizations like the one she was working for bred dependence in the Third World.[74]

Obama's imperious lectures alarmed his half-sister, Maya, who started wondering if her half-brother's ideological intensity would turn him into "one of those freaks you see on the streets around here."[75] Most readers will concentrate on Obama's struggle to mature and reconcile with his family. Knowledgeable leftists, however, will identify Obama's swipe at his mother as a reference to the "dependency theory" popular among Marxist students of the Third World at the time.

Dependency theory holds that modern multinational corporations and development agencies are little more than updated versions of the looting and plundering colonialists of old. The idea that international businesses are in any way improving conditions in the Third World is anathema to dependency theorists. On the contrary, dependency theory explains the social and economic problems of Third World nations as products of capitalist exploitation. Internal social and cultural factors in these nations don't really matter, the theory goes. What counts are the evils of international capitalism.[76] Obama's lecture would certainly have been a swipe at his liberal anthropologist mother, who had spent a lifetime trying to trace the cultural roots of economic behavior in Indonesia. Reverend Wright's many sermons on Africa, I should add, could easily be summarized as variations on the themes of dependency theory.

NYPIRG

For approximately three months, from about late February through late May of 1985, Barack Obama worked as an organizer for the New York branch of Ralph Nader's Public Interest Research Group (NYPIRG).[77] This was his first true job as a community organizer, and his last position before decamping to Chicago. What made Obama accept a job with NYPIRG? He had dreamed of organizing since 1983, of course. Yet there is more to the matter than that.

NYPIRG was a bona fide part of the grassroots movement Obama hoped to join. There are powerful connections between Ralph Nader's PIRGs and groups like DSA, Richard Cloward and Frances Fox Piven's voter registration organization, Human SERVE, and the network of "Citizen Action" groups managed by Chicago's Midwest Academy.[78] Much of this is described in what is generally agreed to be the best account of the community organizing movement of the late seventies, Harry Boyte's 1980 book, *The Backyard Revolution: Understanding the New Citizen Movement.*[79]

According to Boyte, Ralph Nader's shift from strictly legislative tactics toward citizen organizing in the seventies was a major catalyst of the "new populism" (i.e., the late-seventies national upsurge in community organizing).[80] In fact, it was the Brooklyn office of NYPIRG in 1976 that began one of the first campaigns to pressure banks into loosening credit standards for mortgages in high-risk neighborhoods (i.e., "subprime lending").[81] According to Boyte, for the first decade of his consumer crusade, Nader concentrated on righting corporate wrongs and kept his conventionally liberal political views to himself. Over time, however, Nader became convinced that it wasn't enough to fight isolated corporate abuses. Ultimately, says Boyte, a radicalized Nader decided that the very "structure of power and the distribution of wealth in America" would need to be transformed.

So in the late seventies, a more ideological Nader began to collaborate with other radical community organizations. For public purposes, however, Nader's PIRGs continued to soft-pedal leftist ideology and kept their focus on concrete issues alone (e.g., environmental laws and various forms of corporate regulation). As Boyte puts it: "Nader seemingly had a clear understanding of the enormity of the corporate enemy's power. It appears in retrospect that his specificity about issues was always partly tactical."[82] Here Boyte spots a stealth leftism in Nader's tactics. To summarize Boyte's account, Nader wants to radically transform America's capitalist system. Yet Nader prefers to avoid openly leftist rhetoric, focusing attention instead on concrete reforms that might someday, quietly and gradually, add up to a major transformation of society.

Is it fair to saddle a young Obama with this sort of motive for organizing with NYPIRG? Yes, it is. That's because Obama had almost certainly read Boyte's work. There's even a chance that Boyte's writings brought Obama to NYPIRG in the first place. So it's of interest that Boyte, a first-rank theorist of community organizing, was for years a leader in America's major socialist organizations. Boyte is perhaps the most important advocate of "stealth socialism" in community organizing, and in politics generally. Boyte wouldn't describe himself this way, but his opponents (within socialism) call him a stealth socialist—with justice, in my view.

An in-depth 2008 investigative article for the environmental magazine *Plenty* quotes a student who worked with Obama at CCNY saying: "He read widely, and would hold forth about different theories and models of organizing."[83] The same point is made in more detail by Eileen Hershenov, who hired and supervised Obama for NYPIRG. Says Hershenov: "I have a distinct memory of having several conversations with Barack during that short period about different models of organizing. A number of books were appearing by former organizers with groups like the Southern Christian Leadership Conference (SCLC), and we talked about the pros and cons of these organizing strategies."[84] Harry Boyte worked as a community organizer for the SCLC.

SOCIALIST ORGANIZERS

What books by former community organizers were appearing around 1985? Robert Fisher's *Let the People Decide: Neighborhood Organizing in America*—still probably the best, and best-known, history of community organizing—appeared in 1984.[85] *Community Is Possible: Repairing America's Roots,* Harry Boyte's followup to *The Backyard Revolution,* also appeared in 1984.[86] Juxtaposing Boyte's two books with Fisher's would have put Obama in an excellent position to "hold forth about different theories and models of organizing."[87] The overall argument of Fisher's book is that organizers need to be more open about their radical politics. Boyte represents the opposite view. Although Boyte doesn't overtly say that it's best for organizers to hide their socialism, his work includes sympathetic descriptions of things like Nader's "tactical" focus on concrete issues—despite the radical turn in Nader's own beliefs. Obama had reason to know that, despite the tactical silence of Boyte's own books, Boyte himself was a socialist. So the clash between Fisher's case for organizer openness and Boyte's argument for discretion would surely have made an impression on Obama.

Precisely because Boyte and Fisher were authoritative commentators on community organizing in the mid-eighties, their work has much to teach us about Obama's profession. In *Let the People Decide*, Fisher immediately lets the socialist cat out of the bag. Fisher opens the book with the story of his early organizer days in Cambridgeport, a mixed student and working-class Boston suburb sandwiched between Harvard and MIT. In the early seventies, Fisher organized for the Cambridgeport Homeowners and Tenants Association (CHTA), which followed the classic tactics of Saul Alinsky. "Unlike new left radicals of the early 1960's," says Fisher, "the organizers in CHTA consciously downplayed their radical sentiments and rarely sought to clarify their ideology. . . . In fact, we consciously sought to get beyond the barrier that radical ideology and rhetoric seemed to foster between activists and workers in the 1960's."[88] Unfortunately for these organizers, their stealth tactics failed. Cambridgeport's working-class citizens avoided the group, and CHTA remained an overwhelmingly student-run enterprise. (No doubt Cambridgeport's residents were familiar with the leftist politics of activist students, even without being told.)

Facing failure, one faction of CHTA organizers decided that the root of their problem was Alinskyite stealth: "They emphasized that a militant, avowedly socialist ideology—a clearly stated view of how the capitalist system works and why working people needed to join together to oppose it—was lacking. CHTA needed a clear and correct 'line' to offer working people; then residents would get involved and devote more time and energy to building a multi-racial working-class organization."[89] This, Fisher says, was the argument of the communist faction of organizers. (The word "communist" is Fisher's.) The communists were opposed by democratic-socialist organizers, who agreed to be more ideologically honest, yet objected to the communists' authoritarian insistence on imposing a single "correct" ideological line on CHTA's members.[90]

In the end, this split between Marxist-Leninist and democratic-socialist community organizers effectively killed CHTA. Oddly, however, Fisher takes the fiasco as a lesson that organizers need to be more open about their politics. In fact, community organizing developed in precisely the opposite direction. The communists soon discovered that dictating a "correct" ideological line to American workers only drives them away. By the late seventies and eighties, communism was on the decline among organizers and democratic socialism was the more common position. Given widespread American antipathy to socialism, however, the pressures on organizers to keep their political views quiet were immense. Increasingly, in the world of organizing, Boyte's stealth solution came to dominate.

STEALTH SOCIALISM

Saul Alinsky, the founder of modern community organizing, had already built stealth into the profession.[91] Alinksy told organizers to downplay their own ideologies and instead use the public's concrete grievances to stoke change. Boyte defended this approach, but also went further. His innovation was to propose applying Alinskyite stealth, not merely to community organizing, but to socialism itself.

Over time, Boyte seems to have decided that even Michael Harrington's non-revolutionary form of socialism would be rejected by the vast majority of Americans. So Boyte formed a "communitarian caucus" within Harrington's Democratic Socialists of America (DSA). The communitarians wanted to use the language and ethos of traditional American communities—including religious language—to promote a "populist" version of socialism. Portraying heartless corporations as enemies of traditional communities, thought Boyte, was the only way to build a quasi-socialist mass movement in the United States. Socialists could quietly help direct such a movement, Boyte believed, but openly highlighting socialist ideology would only drive converts away.

In effect, Boyte was calling on DSA to drop its public professions of socialism and start referring to itself as "communitarian" instead. That was too much for DSA to accept. Without at least some level of public socialist affirmation, most DSAers worried that socialism itself would eventually disappear. Boyte's opponents also argued that secret socialism would not remain secret forever: "We can call ourselves 'communitarians,' but the word will get out. Better to be out of the closet; humble, yet proud."[92]

If Boyte failed to convince DSA to package itself as "communitarian" rather than socialist, Boyte's stealthy ways certainly became the dominant mode within community organizing itself. In fact, Boyte was a close associate of the leaders of the Midwest Academy, arguably the most important de facto socialist "front group" in American organizing, and a group with close ties to Barack and Michelle Obama.

The Third Annual Socialist Scholars Conference, held in New York on April 4, 5, and 6, 1985, included a panel called, "The New Populism: Left Potential, Right Danger." The panel was sponsored by the journal *Social Policy*, the intellectual center of American community organizing. Boyte spoke at this session.

We know that in the spring of 1985, Obama was poring over books on community organizing, grappling especially with work by a former organizer for the SCLC. This is surely Boyte, and it seems very likely that Obama would have availed himself of an opportunity to see Boyte at the April 1985 Socialist Scholars Conference. Whether Martin Luther King, Jr., became a late-life convert to socialism is debatable. Boyte, however, had organized for Dr. King, had written the definitive book on contemporary community organizing, and was himself a socialist. How could Obama resist?

S. M. Miller, a professor of sociology and economics at Boston University, was another member of the New Populism panel, and we can find a piece by Miller that clearly came from a panel where he criticized Boyte.[93] Quite possibly, Obama himself heard Miller deliver this criticism directly to Boyte in 1985:

> The left agenda is more profound and more disturbing than it is usually wise to tell those whom radical activists wish to help organize, at least at the beginning. This situation leads organizers not infrequently to be in the situation of keeping back, if not disguising, some of their ultimate objectives. . . . This raises issues of manipulation. . . . Such organizers are not fully representing themselves to others.[94]

Obama spent years in the company of some of the top stealth organizers in the country. Is he perhaps practicing their stealth techniques in his current stint as Organizer-in-Chief of the United States of America?

OBAMA'S DEFENSE

To review, we can reliably place Obama at the 1983 Cooper Union Socialist Scholars Conference, and at least one other such conference—on Obama's own testimony in *Dreams from My Father*. Documentary evidence strongly suggests that Obama attended the 1984 Socialist Scholars Conference, and Obama's interest in theories of community organizing would have given him a strong incentive to attend the 1985 Socialist Scholars Conference as well. We can't be certain of which panels Obama attended at these various conclaves, although it is possible to make informed guesses. While any single reconstruction of Obama's movements at these conferences may be mistaken, the larger pattern is clear. Obama's attendance at various Socialist Scholars Conferences between 1983 and 1985 would have given him an in-depth introduction to the socialist background of community organizing, and would have connected him to socialist-friendly sectors of the black church, ultimately leading him to Jeremiah Wright. We also know from testimony by Obama's colleagues at NYPIRG that he had read widely on competing theories of community organizing, which itself would have taught him much about the socialist background of his chosen profession.

None of this is consistent with the image of Obama as naive about community organizing until well after he moved to Chicago. In March of 2007, *New Republic* reporter Ryan Lizza published a long and thoughtful article on Obama's organizing career.[95] Although Lizza had engaged Obama in "several conversations about his work as an organizer," here is how Lizza began the piece: "In 1985, Barack Obama traveled halfway across the country to take a job that he didn't fully understand. But, while he knew little about his new vocation—community organizer—it still had a romantic ring, at least to his 24-year-old ears." Compare Lizza's account—completely consistent with Obama's depiction of himself in *Dreams*—with the recollections of Obama's NYPIRG colleague: "He read widely, and would hold forth about different theories and models of organizing." Obama's attempt to obfuscate his knowledge of organizing's socialist underpinnings is at the root of the discrepancy between Lizza's account and the testimony of Obama's colleague.

During the 2008 campaign, *Time* magazine asked Obama about his references in *Dreams* to "socialist conferences" and radical thinkers like Franz Fanon. According to *Time*, Obama replied that "this was in the Reagan years and he was also reading works by conservative giants like Milton Friedman and Friedrich Hayek. He browsed among the ideologues but never bought in, he said. 'I was always suspicious of dogma and the excesses of the left and the right.' "[96] So this is Obama's stance on the matter of the Socialist Scholars Conferences. He sampled ideologies of the left and the right, but finally rejected both. Obama's answer is both evasive and adept. Ultimately, the effectiveness of his dodge depends upon public ignorance of community organizing, socialism, and the connections between them.

The most popular annual convention for conservative activists is called CPAC (Conservative Political Action Conference, pronounced C-Pack). Imagine a presidential candidate who attended CPAC conferences throughout his youth, then spent years as an activist in various conservative organizations, before finally becoming a politician with the most conservative voting record in the United States Senate. (Obama had the most liberal Senate record.)[97] Instead of campaigning openly as a conservative (like, say, Ronald Reagan), he claims to be a pragmatist who rejects ideologies of the left and right. Questioned by the press about his youthful conference attendance, he denies being a conservative and insists that during those same years he had also made a point of reading Karl Marx and Michael Harrington. This would not be a persuasive reply.

Many intellectually active conservatives read leftist thinkers. It's certainly a good idea to know something about a wide variety of political views, and Obama deserves credit for studying conservatives as well as Marxists. Yet that does nothing to negate the significance of Obama's lifetime pursuit of a political vocation and strategy outlined at those early Socialist Scholars Conferences. Given the powerful evidence that Obama was a committed socialist during his pre–New York years at Occidental, not to mention his presence at two—and quite possibly three—socialist conclaves, the notion that Obama was simply a curious outsider "browsing" at these conferences is strained past the breaking point. The obvious problems with Obama's reply can be suppressed because Americans have no idea what community organizing is, or how it connects to those Socialist Scholars Conferences—and because the socialism of so many of Obama's organizing colleagues has been intentionally hidden from view. My job is to lift the veil.

EARLY BACKGROUND

Although New York's Socialist Scholars Conferences provided Obama with his calling, they were not by a long shot the future president's first encounter with socialism. Obama's childhood mentor, the prominent poet and journalist Frank Marhsall Davis, had once been a member of the Communist Party. While some darkly hinted in 2008 that Davis may have secretly brought Obama into the party, that is exceedingly unlikely. Davis's one-time party membership was an endless source of trouble. He did all he could to keep it a secret. On the other hand, Davis remained boldly and proudly radical till the end. The issue of party membership aside, he stayed sympathetic to socialism and would surely have communicated this to Obama. It's evident from Obama's memoir that he took Davis's warnings about "selling out" in college to heart. That's what propelled Obama into Occidental College's socialist circles.[98]

OCCIDENTAL

In February of 2010, an acquaintance from Obama's Occidental College years, John C. Drew, let it be publicly known that he had encountered Obama on a couple of occasions around 1980 and 1981, at which time, according to Drew, the future president was a "pure Marxist socialist." Drew himself had been a revolutionary Marxist while at Occidental, but in 1980 was back visiting his girlfriend (who was still a student at Occidental) after having spent some time away at graduate school. In the early eighties, Drew still accepted Marx's analysis of society, yet had increasingly come to see the Marxist vision of a violent, class-based revolution as an unrealistic hope. According to Drew, Obama energetically argued against this deviation from Marxist-Leninist orthodoxy, insisting that a true socialist revolution in the United States was well worth hoping and fighting for. After their debate, Drew concluded that Obama had a "hard Marxist-Leninist point of view."[99]

Today, Drew is a Republican, which for some might bring his testimony into question. Yet in April of 2010, two months after Drew's revelation, David Remnick's rich, useful, and friendly biography of Obama added considerably to our knowledge of the president's socialist convictions and alliances during his time at Occidental.

In Obama's sophomore year, Remnick reports, he shared an apartment with a Pakistani student named Mohammed Hasan Chandoo. Along with Chandoo, Obama was close to another Pakistani student named Wahid Hamid. Remnick explains that Chandoo and Hamid, among others, helped "ignite" Obama politically. Chandoo was "a socialist, a Marxist," and freely admits today that these were his beliefs at the time. Hamid reluctantly confesses to having been a socialist, while trying to distinguish socialism from strict Marxism. Hamid also describes Obama as sharing the political convictions of their leftist circle.[100]

Remnick makes an effort to soften the impact of these revelations: "To slap an ideological tag on Chandoo and Hamid, let alone Obama, is not only unfair, it also credits them with thinking far more program-matically than they did."[101] In Drew's account, however, Obama at this time was very programmatic indeed—boldly and thoughtfully defend-ing the classic hard-Marxist revolutionary line against Drew's critique. Drew's account is very specific—and based on his recollections of an extended ideological debate with Obama. In contrast, Remnick's at-tempts to mitigate the impact of his own revelations are fuzzier and less convincing.

According to Remnick, during the 2008 presidential campaign and afterward, "Hamid and Chandoo were wary of talking to the press, lest they say something that could be used against themselves or, worse, against Obama."[102] This is a significant admission. I've suggested that Obama's relative silence about his New York years, as well as his reluc-tance to name friends from this time, stemmed from a desire to hide his socialist past. Remnick's revelations about the silence of Chandoo and Hamid confirm this. Even after he left Occidental, Obama stayed in touch with his South Asian friends. Do they know more about Obama's socialism in New York than they were prepared to say—even to a friendly source like Remnick? The willingness of Chandoo and Hamid to open up to Remnick about their own and Obama's social-ism appears to be a post-election effort to disclose potentially explo-sive information to a sympathetic source in the least damaging manner possible—lest it come out later, uncontrolled.

Obama's beguiling account of his Occidental years in *Dreams* high-lights what might be called his public debut—a speech he delivered to a campus anti-apartheid rally in early 1981.[103] It's apparent from Rem-nick's report that this rally was organized by Obama and his Marxist friends.[104] Remnick notes the central role of Occidental's Democratic Socialist Alliance in planning the anti-apartheid action.[105] He also ex-plains that Obama occasionally attended meetings of the handful of groups involved in planning the demonstration, including meetings of the Democratic Socialist Alliance.[106] Although Remnick makes every effort to downplay the significance of all this, the plain meaning of what

he reveals is that Obama was active in Occidental's Democratic Socialist Alliance—helping to plan its actions, periodically attending meetings, and serving as a close ally of its top leaders.

It's apparent, then, that Obama's presence at New York's Socialist
Scholars Conferences several years later was not mere intellectual graz-
ing, but instead the logical extension of his socialist convictions and
activities at Occidental. During the 2008 campaign, Obama mocked
John McCain's attacks with a clever quip: "By the end of the week, he'll
be accusing me of being a secret communist because I shared my toys
in kindergarten. I shared my peanut butter and jelly sandwich." [107] This
was an effective jab, but also, I think, a way of attempting to deflect potentially damaging revelations to come.

Although John Drew's account of Obama's college Marxism attracted some notice on the Web, the story never really took off. No
doubt this was because Obama had already confessed to making
friends with Marxist professors at Occidental, and because the whole
episode could be dismissed as a passing enthusiasm of youth. For the
same reason, Remnick's controlled revelations two months later had little noticeable impact. Yet Obama's discovery of his organizer vocation
at the Cooper Union Socialist Scholars Conference of 1983 suggests
that Obama's clearly established socialist interlude at Occidental
in 1980–81 was more significant than it might at first appear. From
Obama's tutelage under Frank Marshall Davis, to his revolutionary
Marxism at Occidental College, to his life-shaping experience at New
York's Socialist Scholars Conferences, and beyond, there is a powerful
thread of ideological continuity. It is socialism in one form or another
that unites the various phases of Obama's political life.

Accounts of Obama's college socialism from Drew and Remnick
also expose Obama's characteristic tactic of defusing potentially damaging revelations with partial and misleading confessions. Obama's
confession in *Dreams* that he made friends with Marxist professors at
Occidental "to avoid being mistaken for a sellout" has caused him some
grief over the years, but not nearly as much harm as the full truth would

have done. We now know that Obama wasn't just "hanging out" with Marxist professors. He was fully and enthusiastically on their side.

OBAMA'S FATHER

What about Obama's socialist father? I've put off discussion of Barack Obama Senior's socialism, partly because it has already been treated in depth by Obama's critics and admirers, but also because it's difficult to say exactly how much Obama knew about his father's beliefs, and when he found out.[108] In 1965, Obama Sr, published an article in the *East Africa Journal* entitled "Problems Facing Our Socialism." The article was a leftist critique of the economic policy favored by Obama Sr.'s own political sponsor. "Problems Facing Our Socialism" called for land redistribution, progressive taxation, regulation, and a decreased privatization in Obama's native Kenya. Given that this article was published just four years after Barack Jr.'s birth, and considering that Obama's parents habitually discussed politics and international development with their friends at the University of Hawaii, it seems certain that Obama's mother would have known of her husband's socialist views. The question is: What did she tell her son, and when?

By his own account, Obama deeply idealized his absent father, packing into his image "all the attributes I sought in myself, the attributes of Martin and Malcolm, DuBois and Mandela."[109] In his mind's ear, Obama often heard his father's stern and righteous injunction: "You do not work hard enough, Barry. You must help in your people's struggle. Wake up, black man!"[110] If young Obama knew that socialism was central to his father's conception of the black man's struggle—as it in fact was—he would surely have felt drawn to aid in the socialist struggle.

Obama did know that his father was a figure in the government of Kenya,[111] so his curiosity about his father's political views would likely have been strong. It was at Occidental that Obama stopped using his casual, boyish, and Americanized nickname "Barry" and adopted his given name "Barack" instead. Caroline Boss, in Remnick's words, "a friend of Obama's and one of the main leftist political leaders at Occidental," explains this shift to "Barack" as a way of connecting to his father.[112] Could it be that in college, an increasingly socialist Obama discovered that, across continents and oceans, a shared ideology might bind him more deeply to the father he never knew?

It's clear by now that a powerful cord of ideological continuity stretches from Obama's early experiences with the ex-Communist (but still strongly socialist) Frank Marshall Davis, through his time as a socialist at Occidental College, to his life-changing attendance at Socialist Scholars Conferences in New York. During his late youth and early adulthood, Obama was a socialist. The future president was ushered into this ideology by early mentors, college friends, and his own intellectual explorations as an adult. Having fully entered the socialist world, the question remains: Did Obama ever leave it?

CHAPTER 4

Obama's Organizing: The Hidden Story

UNO OF CHICAGO

In October 1984, in the midst of his ultimately unsuccessful re-election battle against Democratic challenger Paul Simon, Illinois Republican senator Charles Percy was cornered and forced to hide in a ladies' restroom by about a hundred protesters from a group called UNO (United Neighborhood Organization) of Chicago. By trapping Percy in the women's bathroom, UNO of Chicago successfully disrupted his live appearance on a black radio station, thereby punishing him for his refusal to appear at an UNO forum (which Percy believed had been stacked against him through UNO's collaboration with Simon). Since UNO's largely Mexican membership included a substantial group of "undocumented" workers, there is every likelihood that a large number of illegal aliens were among that crowd running hardball Alinskyite tactics on a U.S. senator.

In those days, UNO's organizers used to gather at a bar after confrontations like this to laugh about how they'd humiliated one or another public official. There must have been heavy toasting that night.[1]

Concealed Connection

What has this to do with Barack Obama? Quite a lot, actually. Obama's account of his Chicago community organizing days in *Dreams from My Father* leaves out a great deal. While any autobiography is bound to be selective, Obama appears to have gone out of his way in *Dreams* to minimize and disguise his involvement with some particularly controversial groups. Above all, Obama has worked to conceal his close ties to UNO of Chicago, a kind of Mexican-American counterpart to the highly confrontational community group ACORN. Recovering Obama's hidden ties to Chicago UNO opens up a new way of looking at his experience as a community organizer. The UNO connection also helps make sense of the ties between Obama and Bill Ayers, Jeremiah Wright, ACORN, and the world of left-leaning foundations that stands behind modern community organizing. Finally, an understanding of Obama's work with UNO helps to puncture the carefully cultivated image of a young organizer averse to Saul Alinsky's most confrontational tactics. In this chapter, then, I reconstruct and reconsider Obama's three initial years of community organizing in Chicago (from June of 1985 to May/June of 1988), focusing particularly on what he has chosen not to tell us about this formative period of his political life.

Obama worked closely with UNO of Chicago. In fact, Obama's own organization, the Developing Communities Project (DCP) might best be thought of as an extension of UNO's network beyond Chicago's Mexican-American neighborhoods and into the black community. Greg Galluzzo, one of Obama's early organizing mentors, founded the United Neighborhood Organization of Chicago, along with his wife,

Mary Gonzales, in 1980.[2] Galluzzo is known today as the head of the Gamaliel Foundation, an influential network of neighborhood organizations to which Obama has long been tied. What's been forgotten—and what Obama has hidden in his memoir, *Dreams from My Father*—is that the Gamaliel Foundation network grew out of the controversial and confrontational group, UNO of Chicago.

Obama was first hired in 1985 by an organizer named Jerry Kellman. Galluzzo had brought Kellman into UNO of Chicago in 1982, and three years later, in 1985, the two were attempting to extend their network's reach beyond the Mexican-American sections of Chicago. With Galluzzo's support, Kellman's plan was to organize neighborhoods filled with recently laid-off steel workers, in South Chicago, nearby suburbs, and sections of northwestern Indiana around Gary. Obama was hired to handle the black neighborhoods of South Chicago, and Kellman brought in an old organizing buddy from Texas, Mike Kruglik, to help with the project. Thus, Kellman and Kruglik became Obama's first organizing mentors. About a year into Obama's time in Chicago, Galluzzo and Kellman decided that the most efficient way to handle their new territory was to divide it up into three distinct segments. Kellman would take Gary, Kruglik the suburbs, and Obama South Chicago. At that point, with Kellman out in Gary, Galluzzo took over the job of supervising Obama, consulting with him on a weekly basis.[3]

Missing Mentor

Obama obscures all this in *Dreams* by creating a single composite organizing mentor named "Marty Kaufman." Significantly, with the exception of family and a few public figures, Obama has changed the names of most of the characters in *Dreams*.[4] This alleged protection of privacy raises the obvious question of why. Why, for example, is Frank Marshall Davis referred to only as "Frank"? Davis died in 1987, some years before *Dreams* was composed, so it couldn't have been a question of his privacy. Davis was also a public figure. In failing to supply Frank's full name was Obama protecting himself from Davis's communist past? By contrast, Jeremiah Wright's real name *is* used in *Dreams*. Yet it's not clear that Wright was more of a public figure at the time than Obama's organizing mentors. So why disguise their identities?

Obama has either left Galluzzo out of *Dreams* altogether or combined Galluzzo's character with Jerry Kellman under the name Marty Kaufman.[5] Obama biographer David Remnick says that "for the most part" Jerry Kellman is "Marty."[6] Obama acknowledges creating composite characters in his introduction to *Dreams*, and in 2004 that procedure raised eyebrows among some in the press.[7] By disguising the characters in *Dreams*, Obama made it impossible for reporters to interview or trace the background of figures from his past.

Today, few remember that Greg Galluzzo was once the head of the most aggressive and controversial community organization in Chicago. UNO broke its connection with Galluzzo and Gonzales in 1988, and since that time, the organization's tactics and worldview have mellowed considerably.[8] When Obama published *Dreams* in 1995, however, some in Chicago might have recalled Galluzzo's early history with UNO. Having it known back then that Greg Galluzzo was your organizing mentor would have been a bit like calling yourself a protégé of ACORN founder Wade Rathke today. This may explain why Obama omitted Galluzzo's role, or folded him into the character of "Marty Kaufman." Even with an alias, it would have been tough to introduce a character based on Galluzzo without mentioning his background as head of a predominantly Mexican-American community organization, and that would have been traceable to UNO.

Only if you already know what to look for can you find fleeting indications in *Dreams* of Obama's ties to UNO. While running off a litany of groups that "Marty" had worked with, Obama includes "Mexicans in Chicago."[9] Obama also notes that, in the final months before law school, "We held a series of joint meetings with Mexicans in the Southeast Side to craft a common environmental strategy for the region."[10] As with his treatment of the Cooper Union Socialist Scholars Conference, this sort of opaque mention allows Obama to claim that he *did* write about UNO, when in fact he disguised it.

A 2008 *Newsday* piece on Obama's organizing days helps to penetrate the mystery. This article tracks down some of Obama's old organizing colleagues by way of exploring charges that, contrary to his claims of working to bridge different ethnic groups, Obama organized exclusively with blacks.[11] To defend Obama, an organizer named Phil Mullins explained that Obama held " 'weekly brainstorming sessions' with his Latino counterparts and worked closely with them on several important projects." *Newsday* also quotes Galluzzo's wife and UNO co-founder, Mary Gonzales, explaining that Obama was an important part of UNO's plans "to connect neighborhoods." Gonzales and Mullins were the second and third ranking officials, respectively, in UNO during much of Obama's time in Chicago.[12] We also learn from a 2008 interview with Kellman that Obama "would hold or attend meetings with other organizers and activists" at a McDonald's in the Pullman neighborhood "two or more times a week."[13] Pullman lies between Obama's DCP territory in Roseland and UNO's Southeast Chicago branch.

In short, Obama appears to have held joint strategy sessions weekly (or more often) with UNO organizers. As we'll see, he acted jointly with UNO as well. Obama's original organizing mentor, Jerry Kellman, worked for Greg Galluzzo and Mary Gonzales at UNO in the years immediately preceding his hiring of Obama. UNO's co-founder, Galluzzo, was Obama's organizing mentor during at least some of the "direct action" ventures detailed in *Dreams from My Father*, and Obama's Developing Communities Project might fairly be thought of as an extension of the UNO network into the black community. Understanding UNO opens up a critically important window on Obama's hidden world. After seeing what's inside, it's hard not to conclude that Obama has been deliberately trying to block our gaze.

Hispanics in Chicago

By 1980, when UNO was founded, Chicago's Hispanic community was divided into distinct and sometimes antagonistic groups. Mexicans were not only different from Puerto Ricans, but were sharply divided among themselves. The older group was made up of highly assimilated second- and third-generation middle-class Mexican-Americans. These ethnic Mexicans were often war veterans and very patriotic. Their saw their own success as proof that America's system worked. These Mexican-Americans believed that immigrants should quickly master English and looked askance at bilingual education.[14]

In contrast, the larger number of unassimilated recent immigrants lived in large barrios with little or no command of English and only the most limited contact with American culture. UNO of Chicago largely appealed to these recent immigrants. In effect, UNO was an alliance between left-leaning, multiculturalist, often white, organizers, on one hand, and a new generation of assimilation-resistant immigrants, on the other. Many UNO members spoke only Spanish, so English-speaking UNO organizers and visiting politicians frequently required translators even to communicate with the membership.[15]

About 90 percent of UNO's constituency in the eighties was Mexican-American, and a sizeable percentage of those were illegal immigrants. UNO of Chicago's Pilsen branch, for example, was in a neighborhood where half the population was "undocumented." This was reflected in UNO's membership.[16] In fact, since UNO's tactics and goals tended to put off middle-class Mexican-Americans, it's possible that some branches of UNO were majority illegal.

Holding a vision of universal human rights that trumped American citizenship, UNO's leftist organizers had no problem with the group's illegal-heavy membership—even though UNO often demanded substantial expenditures of taxpayer dollars.[17] Nor did UNO's organizers have illusions about their membership being representative, even of Chicago's Mexican-American community. Privately, UNO's leaders saw themselves as speaking for perhaps 5 to 8 percent of neighborhood residents.[18] Yet UNO's coffers quickly overflowed with grants from Chicago's progressive foundations, eager to support an Alinsky-style organization of Hispanics.[19] So through UNO, a small, radical, well-funded, yet unrepresentative group led by "progressive" and often white organizers, quite possibly with a higher proportion of illegal residents than the surrounding Mexican-American community, quickly accumulated substantial political power in Chicago. For a time, UNO sponsored voter registration drives, the results of which it touted to politicians in a bid to impress them with the organization's leverage. When UNO leaders discovered that the sheer number of illegals in their membership was limiting registration results, however, the voter drives were quietly discontinued.[20] Much of UNO's energy went into pressuring public officials to relax their enforcement of immigration laws.[21]

Crazy Radicals

After its formation by Greg Galluzzo and Mary Gonzales in 1980, one of UNO's first actions was the push for a new elementary school in a Mexican neighborhood. The battle featured a series of confrontational meetings at the state capital and in Chicago. In classic Alinsky fashion, UNO singled out a Latino school-board member who seemed resistant to their plans and besieged his home. The Chicago school board's Hispanic president later decried UNO's unduly "threatening" tactics, but the board surrendered anyway.[22]

UNO wanted more. The organization quickly demanded that the new school be named "Niños Heroes" (Heroic Children), after six teens honored by Mexicans for sacrificing their lives in battle against the United States in 1847. This demand outraged Chicago's long-time Mexican-American residents, many of whom were American veterans. These patriotic Mexican-Americans peppered the school board and city education officials with letters and phone calls opposing the proposed school name, "even calling UNO members a bunch of un-American and crazy radicals." Yet this could not overcome UNO's persistent pressure tactics. In the end, the board conceded to UNO and the school was named Niños Heroes.[23]

UNO's pressure tactics were effective. Following Alinsky's injunction to "pick a target, freeze it, personalize it, and polarize it," UNO settled on then-mayor Jane Byrne's Hispanic health commissioner, Dr. Hugo Muriel, as an "enemy of the community," in an effort to force the construction of a high-quality (but also highly expensive) free health clinic in a Mexican neighborhood. As noted by Wilfredo Cruz, on whose sympathetic study of UNO I am drawing here, singling out a named "enemy" for attack enabled UNO to keep the issue "uncomplicated," and helped stir the membership to anger and action. Hundreds of protesters descended on Dr. Muriel, not only at his office, but also at his home. Ultimately, the city funded the clinic.[24]

In its early years, UNO regularly escalated its attacks on resistant public officials by pursuing them to their homes, or elsewhere. That's how Senator Percy got trapped in the ladies' restroom. UNO's demands frequently involved the construction of multi-million-dollar facilities. Yet when officials tried to explain their budgetary constraints at UNO's public forums, they were met with well-rehearsed choruses of boos.[25] While UNO remained technically non-partisan, it did subtly cooperate with a few sympathetic public officials.[26] Percy was probably right to fear that an appearance alongside Simon at a UNO election forum was a set-up to generate bad publicity. Harold Washington was a strong ally of UNO, and the rest of Chicago's politicians knew enough to stay away from UNO's public forums when they were pitted against Washington.[27]

While Illinois Republican governor James Thompson managed to remain noncommittal in the face of an angry crowd at an UNO public forum, soon after the event he agreed to withdraw his veto on the release of $24 million in state construction funds.[28] UNO victories like this had fiscal consequences. In significant part because of expenditures on facilities demanded by UNO for Chicago City Colleges, Chicago's property tax rate went up in 1986.[29] Today Illinois is in fiscal crisis, in part because governors and state legislators have proved unwilling to say no to well-organized Alinskyite pressure groups like UNO. In this case, of course, many—perhaps even most—of those booing the governor and demanding millions of dollars in state spending were in the country illegally.

Church Takeover

UNO depended for its success on an alliance with local Catholic churches. This was a continuation and development of Alinsky's own church-based organizing techniques. In fact, UNO had a branch in the Back of the Yards neighborhood, where many of the Eastern European Catholic churches originally organized by Alinsky were now populated by Mexicans.[30] Jerry Kellman, Obama's first organizing mentor, was brought into UNO by Greg Galluzzo in 1982 because of his expertise in Alinskyite church-based organizing. So understanding how UNO interacted with local churches yields revealing insights into Obama's experiences, as recounted in *Dreams*.

To say the least, UNO worked closely with churches, training parish priests and influential congregants in Alinskyite tactics, while putting tremendous efforts into church recruitment. It can be argued that UNO's goal was literally to take over local Catholic congregations from within, transforming them into "progressive" political shock troops in the process. That judgment may seem strong, but many UNO-affiliated priests and congregations came to believe that it was true. UNO organizers consciously made use of their local Catholic alliances to deflect criticism of their troubling tactics.[31] Church alliances were also the secret of UNO's ability to rapidly mobilize large numbers of constituents for meetings with politicians.[32]

UNO would literally spend years trying to build up allied churches—even at the short-term expense of its own organizing—all in the hope of gaining de facto control of a church over time.[33] With unions weaker than in Alinsky's day, churches were the most important pre-existing source of organized constituents, and UNO moved to colonize that source.

A mass exodus of white ethnics to the suburbs had left many Chicago Catholic congregations vulnerable to this strategy. Anglo priests faced smaller congregations of relatively impoverished Mexicans, and cultural barriers to further recruitment.[34] Nor could these churches afford to perform their usual charitable services for the community.[35] UNO promised to solve the financial and membership problems of these priests, in return for Alinskyite training and cooperation in UNO's campaigns. Now, instead of traditional Christian charity, there would be leftist politics.[36]

By no means was this solely a UNO-created strategy. Ever since Alinsky's day, there had been a small group of socialist-leaning Catholic clergy who eagerly cooperated with community organizers. In the 1980s, Monsignor John J. Egan, once Alinsky's close ally, was in many ways the dean of Chicago community organizers. Egan's solution to the problems of Chicago's increasingly impoverished urban churches, with their declining population of priests and nuns, was to infuse them with lay organizers on the Alinsky model.[37] UNO was an important part of that plan. But Egan's affection for leftist politics and Alinskyite tactics was not shared by the Church's hierarchy. While Obama often affirms his Catholic connection by expressing admiration for Chicago's Cardinal Joseph Bernardin, Archbishop (eventually Cardinal) Bernardin was noticeably absent at UNO events, as were most other influential Chicago Catholic clergy.[38]

While UNO at first succeeded in drawing local priests into alliance, many members of the clergy and congregations backed out when they learned the extent of political commitment UNO was expecting. UNO even made exploratory efforts at organizing congregants to seize control of church affairs away from parish priests. This backfired, however, and UNO quickly abandoned the strategy. As it became increasingly apparent that UNO was attempting to take effective control of Catholic churches in Mexican neighborhoods, congregations pulled away and UNO's entire church-based strategy was put into question.[39] In response, UNO moved toward school-based organizing as an alternative.[40] As we'll see, school reform became the theme of the latter part of Obama's organizing days.

Reverend Smalls

Knowing what UNO was all about provides a new perspective on Obama's own organizing efforts. Consider one of the best-known scenes in *Dreams from My Father*, where Obama tries to convince a group of black ministers to join forces with his Developing Communities Project. Things look promising until someone Obama calls "Reverend Smalls" crashes the scene with a bigoted attack on the "white money . . . Catholic churches and Jewish organizers" behind Obama's group.[41] The reader is outraged by Smalls's bigotry and crushed for Obama, who has sacrificed everything to find his identity and affirm his values by organizing in a poor black community. So it's easy to overlook the fact that Smalls also rejects the idea of an alliance with Alinskyite organizers because they're "not interested in us. . . . All they want to do is take over. It's all a political thing, and that's not what this group [of ministers] here is about."[42] Once you know what UNO was up to, it's easy to see that Smalls was right to worry about a political takeover.

By producing a beautifully crafted personal memoir, rather than a straightforward political account, Obama manages to divert us from much that is troubling in his organizing ventures. Readers root for Obama to succeed because his tales of community organizing are wrapped around the story of his personal and family struggles. Also, by putting informed and sensible concerns about community organizing into the mouth of a bigot, Obama deflects attention from very real problems with his radical mentors and allies. Yet it wasn't just Reverend Smalls who refused an alliance with Obama's group. Many other ministers were standoffish as well. So a story that arguably ought to have been about hard-left organizers colonizing churches to swell their controversial protest campaigns, instead turns into a tale of Obama boldly standing against a bigot. In *Dreams*, questions of race, religion, and family tragedy often serve to obscure hard-left political scheming.

SECTION TWO

INTERPRETING *DREAMS*

The Harold Washington Archives and Collections (HWAC), housed in the Harold Washington Library Center in Chicago, contain documents that shed considerable light on Barack Obama's three-year stint as a community organizer in Chicago. Some of these previously unexplored documents are letters from Obama and his Developing Communities Project (DCP) to Mayor Washington, or his staff. The Harold Washington Archives also contain quite a few documents reporting on interactions between the mayor's office and UNO of Chicago.

By combining an analysis of these HWAC documents with contemporaneous news reports and other published literature, it is possible to move beyond the account of Obama's organizing days presented in *Dreams*. Using this archival evidence, along with what we've learned about UNO of Chicago, I'll first reconsider the core organizing experiences Obama recounts in *Dreams*: the fight for a job training center and the asbestos protests. Following this, I'll reconstruct some important events that Obama has chosen to downplay or disguise: aggressive actions undertaken in conjunction with UNO of Chicago, an abortive effort to put together a youth counseling network, and Obama's participation in the city-wide battle over school reform.

Ribbon Cutting

In *Dreams*, Obama gets his first big organizing breakthrough when he discovers that the closest city job-training center run by MET (Mayor's Office of Employment and Training) is a forty-five-minute drive away from his Roseland neighborhood—in the ward of Harold Washington's arch-enemy, Chicago machine boss and alderman Edward Vrdolyak. With so many unemployed young people, Roseland obviously needs a job center of its own. So Obama and the members of his Developing Communities Project invite MET director Cynthia Alvarez to a public meeting at the Altgeld Gardens housing project. Pressed by Obama's group to place a MET center in Roseland, Alvarez agrees to establish one within six months.[43] After that, Obama works closely with Rafiq al-Shabazz, a black-nationalist Muslim organizer, to complete a series of "sticky" negotiations with Alvarez.[44]

At last, the center is created and Harold Washington himself comes to cut the ribbon, awing Obama's star-struck followers, and marking Obama's first major organizing success. At the ceremony, the mayor is met, not only by Rafiq, Obama, and various followers, but also by a local state senator and alderman. Most surprising of all, Reverend Smalls, who had once dismissed Obama's group (with its white, Catholic, and Jewish ties), makes an appearance as well. On hearing of Washington's visit, Smalls phoned Obama, who then graciously helped make a place for Smalls at the ribbon cutting.[45] So in *Dreams*, the story of the MET intake center is a happy tale—the first real proof that Obama knows how to organize and unify, and a small but significant sign that community organizing works.

Harold Washington's briefing notes for this event show him scheduled to arrive at the Roseland Community Development Corporation, to be greeted by its director, Salim Al Narriden (already tentatively identified as Rafiq by the *Los Angeles Times* under the spelling Salim Al Nurridin).[46] He is also to be met by "Barac Obama" [*sic*] and two members of Obama's Developing Communities Project, Dan Lee and

Loretta Augustine-Herron, who are already known to be the characters Will and Angela from *Dreams*.[47] Washington is to be joined by Alderman Perry Hutchinson and State Senator Emil Jones (who became Obama's mentor and sponsor years later when Obama entered the Illinois State Senate). Also present is Reverend Davis of St. John Church (Reverend Smalls?). In addition, the mayor is to be greeted by MET head Maria Cerda (Cynthia Alvarez?).[48]

Wasted Jobs Money?

The most interesting thing about the mayor's briefing notes for the ribbon cutting may be what they tell us about the prize itself. The center Obama acquired for his neighborhood was funded in significant part by the federal Job Training Partnership Act (JTPA).[49] While national politicians of both parties have pushed JTPA and similar employment training programs for decades, there is a remarkable amount of agreement among policy experts on both the left and the right that JTPA never worked. Conservative and liberal experts alike dismiss JTPA as an expensive charade that makes politicians appear to be doing something to cure unemployment, when in fact the program achieves next to nothing.[50] In fact, the least successful parts of JTPA were the sections designed to find jobs for disadvantaged young people—exactly what Obama wanted to accomplish.[51]

In *Dreams*, Obama works to get Roseland a cut of the same government largess enjoyed by Alderman Vrdolyak's ward, taking it for granted that the MET center will actually do some good. The mayor's archived briefing notes tell us that at the ribbon cutting Mayor Washington makes the same point, congratulating DCP for nudging his administration into getting Roseland its "fair share" of funding. But what if we're actually talking about a fair share of useless government pork? What if Obama's efforts have less to do with breaking the grip of a racist Chicago machine than extending a wasteful government spoils system even further than it already runs? Even left-leaning policy wonks note that JTPA programs serve primarily as local patronage money, especially for urban Democratic politicians.[52] When the major studies revealing JTPA's failure were issued, legislators simply ignored the findings and renewed the spending anyway.[53] The advantages of divvying up job-training money were simply too great to resist, whether the spending actually worked or not.

This is all the more striking when we recall that Obama's introduction to his colleagues in *Dreams* came at a rally to celebrate the opening of a five-hundred-thousand-dollar computerized job placement program that Marty Kaufman had funded through the Illinois state legislature.[54] By Obama's own account, that job bank was a failure. Months after it was supposed to have started, no one had found work through the program, the computer system was chaotic, and the people who ran it "seemed more concerned with next year's funding cycle" than with fixing the problems.[55] It looks like Obama's own solution to Roseland's employment problem was just another expensive taxpayer-funded fiasco. David Remnick's sympathetic biography of Obama appears to confirm this. Remnick reports that, according to a minister who worked closely with Obama, the MET center closed after three years, with little evidence that it had actually secured employment for trainees in the meantime.[56]

On the other hand, these government handouts were good for something. For years, liberal interest groups and community organizations had used federal job-training money to fund their own highly politicized work. This sort of abuse of federal jobs money was particularly egregious in JTPA's predecessor program, the Comprehensive Employment Training Act (CETA).[57] Probably the most notorious example of CETA abuse was money that went to an avowedly Marxist-Leninist community organizer for the "job" of "keeping an eye on city, county, and state governments and their jiving of the masses."[58]

This politicized use of federal jobs-training money was supposed to have been eliminated by JTPA, which de-funded "public service employment" and restricted spending to "public/private partnerships" instead. In theory, local businesses would highlight occupations where jobs were available, and the unemployed would be trained for these positions. In practice, it didn't work. The real employment problem wasn't lack of specific skills training, but young applicants with poor reading, writing, and math abilities, along with unreliable job attendance and poor punctuality.[59] Nor was politicization entirely eliminated, since sympathetic local officials could always cut community organizers into JTPA's "public/private partnerships."[60] So with the right sort of political pull, community organizers could continue raiding federal job-training money to fund their own hyper-political activities.

Mayor Washington's briefing notes indicate that Chicago's JTPA public/private partnership did have participation from "community based organizations."[61] This may make sense of Obama's long and "sticky" negotiations with the city over the MET center. What exactly was he negotiating? We can only speculate, but one possibility is that those negotiations turned around how much access Obama's DCP and Rafiq's Roseland Community Development Corporation would have to JTPA money. In other words, even if the MET intake center did little or nothing to secure good jobs for South Chicago's unemployed youth, it probably gave both Mayor Washington and Obama's organization what they needed anyway. Obama got a visible victory, and very possibly organizational access to federal money, while Harold Washington got the gratitude of Roseland's voters. From the standpoint of its original purpose, the federal money involved may well have been wasted. But those same federal dollars were the lifeblood of local politicians and community organizers. All of which brings us to the problem of Rafiq.

Militant Partner

Rafiq is the militant black nationalist community organizer Obama partners with to bring the MET center to Roseland. Rafiq is also the exception that proves the rule. He was too directly involved in Obama's MET story to ignore. Alias or not, the real "Rafiq" might someday be identified as Obama's partner in the MET project, at which point it could become clear that Obama had worked in close collaboration with a black nationalist community organizer who apparently favored conspiracy theories and anti-white rhetoric. If even Obama's own DCP followers were put off by Rafiq's wild talk, what would the general public think?

So while Obama has typically chosen to hide his radical ties, in this case he would need to take a different approach. He would have to distance himself from Rafiq's ideology, while minimizing the extent to which his alliance with Rafiq provided concrete support for this militant's efforts.

Obama spends a great deal of time in *Dreams* doing both of these things.[62] I don't mean to suggest that Obama's reflections on Rafiq's black nationalist ideology are insincere. On the contrary, I think they're penetrating and deeply felt. But I am suggesting that *Dreams'* passages on Rafiq were intended not only to convey Obama's well-considered views on race, but also to protect him from the revelation of an explosively radical connection.

What does Obama actually say about the sort of anti-American, anti-white, and anti-Semitic militance symbolized for him by Rafiq? Rafiq's extremism clearly makes Obama uncomfortable. Yet Obama also suggests that a militant black nationalist stance might be acceptable—if it actually delivered a better life for blacks. The problem, says Obama, is that it doesn't. The separatist self-help preached by militant black nationalists still has to play out within the free enterprise system, which Obama argues cannot be so easily circumvented. The real solution, Obama hints, after showing the inescapability of capitalism's constraints, is to "change the rules of power."[63] This is a typical Alinskyite euphemism for phasing out capitalism and ushering socialism in.

When you think about it, Obama is also tacitly revealing here how he understands his work with people like Jeremiah Wright. By his own testimony, Obama is willing to put up with a considerable amount of angry, conspiratorial, and anti-American talk, so long as he thinks it's part and parcel of an effective plan of political action. He may not buy every far-out thing that his organizer-buddies say, but he shares with them a fundamentally socialist perspective on American society.

Rafiq's views were sufficiently wild, and sufficiently traceable, that Obama had to try to separate himself publicly. Yet Obama obviously provided considerable assistance to Rafiq's radical efforts. Obama tries to minimize this by saying that he really didn't want to know the gruesome details of Rafiq's financial interest in the MET center plan.[64] But when Harold Washington began his ribbon cutting at Rafiq's headquarters, the mayor was obviously providing considerable legitimation for Rafiq's program. Obama was responsible for that.

Was Obama really as ignorant of what Rafiq stood to gain out of their joint venture as he portrays himself? Probably not. During the long and sticky MET negotiation process, Obama would likely have needed to be aware of Rafiq's stake. In fact, Obama was probably using Rafiq's Roseland Community Development Corporation to flesh out a JTPA public/private partnership program that the two of them could jointly control. However "ineffective" Obama might have considered Rafiq's militant strategy and over-the-top rhetoric, he was very likely helping to fund and sustain Rafiq's radicalism with taxpayer dollars. Interestingly, a 2007 *Los Angeles Times* piece knocking Obama for denying credit to his fellow organizers ends with a pro-Obama quotation from Salim Al Nurridin, who we now know was the model for Rafiq.[65] You can see how Al Nurridin might have ignored Obama's criticisms in *Dreams* and remembered instead that Obama had shown him the money.

Having said all that, a different interpretation of the Rafiq episode is possible. That's because, in the May 2008 *Los Angeles Times* article where Rafiq's identity was revealed, Salim Al Nurridin denied that he had ever held the black nationalist views Obama attributes to Rafiq in *Dreams*.[66] The truth of this matter is tough to determine with certainty. Al Nurridin is now a part of Chicago's respectable left-activist circles, and these are not environs in which you want to be known for championing racial separation, much less anti-Semitic conspiracy theories. So it's possible that Al Nurridin simply thought it best to deny his earlier views. On the other hand, Rafiq may be another one of Obama's composite characters. It's possible, in other words, that Obama poured some of his other dealings with black nationalists into the character of Rafiq. We may even be dealing with both of these things—a bit of self-protective revisionism by Al Nurridin, as well as some character compression by Obama. Given the potential for embarrassment on all sides, these questions may never be entirely resolved. In any case, however much Al Nurridin himself was or wasn't included in "Rafiq," Obama's reflections on this character likely served the purpose of distancing him from potentially troubling associations, while providing us with a window into his thinking on the black nationalism issue.

Asbestos

The famous asbestos battle in *Dreams* begins when Altgeld Gardens resident Sadie Evans discovers a public notice from the Chicago Housing Authority (CHA) soliciting bids to remove asbestos from the project's management office. Obama's group worries that Altgeld's apartments also contain dangerous asbestos. When Sadie and Obama question Altgeld's manager, Mr. Anderson, he (falsely) tells them that the apartments have been tested and are asbestos free. When Anderson fails to provide proof of such testing, Obama alerts the media and heads downtown with Sadie and other DCP members to confront the Director of CHA. They get the runaround until the media arrive, at which time the director's assistant, Ms. Broadnax, comes out to meet them. DCP members then negotiate a promise from CHA to test for asbestos, and an agreement that the director will attend a DCP-controlled meeting at Altgeld Gardens.

When the day of the meeting arrives, TV crews and seven hundred Altgeld residents show up. The meeting, however, ends in fiasco. The director arrives late, to a restive crowd, and DCP leaders appear unwill-

ing to hand him the microphone when he tries to speak. Unable even
to answer questions from angry residents, the director walks out, followed by a furious crowd, which menacingly surrounds his car before
he manages to speed away. As a matter of publicity, the meeting is a
success. The media cover the imbroglio, and asbestos removal begins.
Yet Obama is mortified by the unruly and uncivil mess the meeting became. To his chagrin, after the fiasco, DCP was criticized by some for
its methods and motives.[67]

The Harold Washington Archives and Collections contain a number of documents that shed light on these events. We have the text of
a Mailgram from Obama's group to CHA director Zirl Smith, copied
with a separate cover letter to Mayor Washington.[68] We also find city
documents on the asbestos issue, including a long internal report recounting events, and transcripts of local news coverage.[69] According to
these documents, Obama and DCP met first with Altgeld manager Walter Williams (Mr. Anderson?), and downtown encountered the CHA
director's executive assistant, Ms. Gaylene Domer (Ms. Broadnax?), on
May 9, 1986. The Mailgram is signed by Mrs. Kallie Smith (Sadie?),
Ms. Cynthia Helt, Mrs. Loretta Augustine, and Mr. Henry Smith.[70]

The news reports on the meeting where CHA director Zirl Smith
was chased to his car are interesting, but the most important untold
part of the asbestos story lies elsewhere. Obama's account of his own
tactics is misleading and incomplete. In *Dreams*, he portrays himself as
a proponent of civil dialogue, appalled by the way the big meeting spun
out of control. The truth is more complicated. Using his accustomed
method of "non-disclosure disclosure," Obama hides his actual tactics
from the reader, while saying just enough to allow him to deny that he
was hiding anything at all.

Polarize and Pin

As Obama tells it in *Dreams*, the key to the collapse of the asbestos
forum was a broken microphone system. With only a single working

microphone left, Obama instructed meeting leaders to hold the mike up to Smith when it was his turn to speak, but not let go of it. The fear was that if Smith got hold of the microphone, he might talk forever, avoiding pointed questions and taking effective control of the meeting away from DCP. When DCP leader "Linda" insisted on a yes-or-no answer from Smith, he said he'd prefer to answer in his own fashion and reached for the mike. Linda refused to hand over the microphone, and Smith walked out, with Altgeld's furious residents chasing behind. Obama says he tried to head all this off by motioning to Linda to ignore his earlier advice and hand Smith the microphone, but he was too far to the rear of the room to be seen.[71]

This account sugar-coats and disguises the actual tactics taught by Greg Galluzzo and his fellow organizers at UNO of Chicago. The broken microphone system may have contributed to the confusion that night, but the real cause of the fiasco was an organizing technique designed from the start to polarize—and even to "fail." Galluzzo's meeting techniques are meant to box political "targets" into yes-or-no responses to demands, thereby creating win-win situations for the group. If the target says yes, the group gets what it wants. If the target says no, outrage at uncooperative officials increases membership and energizes the group. Consider the following description of Galluzzo's techniques by a sympathetic scholar, Rutgers professor of political science Heidi Swarts:

> Meetings or actions with authorities demonstrate power by . . . overturning deferential norms of interaction, insisting that authorities meet them on their turf, and by strictly controlling the agenda and how many minutes an official is allowed to speak. The opponent is polarized by the pinner, the member designated to pin down the official to yes-or-no answers. Activists are trained to push for yes-or-no commitments, knowing that politicians will avoid them if at all possible. Organizations hold rehearsals, and pinners practice their job. Getting a "no" answer is

seen as preferable to "mush" because it will expose the authority
as an opponent in the eyes of hundreds or thousands of people.
Tight control of the proceedings helps avoid being manipulated
by officials, although it can impart an artificial, staged quality to
the proceedings.[72]

According to Swarts, this technique is a gentler version of same polarizing Alinskyite techniques practiced by ACORN. The somewhat toned-
down aggression of Galluzzo's "pinning" method is specially designed
for "congregation-based" community organizing, since religious congregants typically object to ACORN's aggressive civil disobedience.
However, as Swarts notes, church members are often put off by even
these toned-down polarizing tactics.[73]

While Obama does mention attempts by DCP leaders to push both
Cynthia Alvarez and the CHA director into yes-or-no answers, he
makes this look more like natural conversation than the highly coached
and intentionally polarizing technique it in fact is.[74] Moreover, as news
accounts reveal, when Zirl Smith was unable to take the mike, he was
also being drowned out by shouts of "No, No" from the crowd.[75] We
know from UNO that angry chants and collective boos are also coached
and rehearsed by Galluzzo-trained organizers. Zirl Smith hadn't completed asbestos testing at Altgeld Gardens and hadn't yet determined
where the cash-strapped CHA was going to find the money to pay for
a cleanup. A civil meeting would have allowed him to present his side
of the story. But Galluzzo's techniques aren't meant to be civil. They
are consciously designed either to win—or to fail and enrage. Some of
Obama's supporters began to drift away after the angry meeting, suspicious of his methods and motives. As in the case of Reverend Smalls,
Obama in his book puts these (quite reasonable) concerns into the
mouth of an unsympathetic character, "Mrs. Reece," who has a pen-
chant for making unpleasant, racially tinged remarks.[76] Once again,
Obama uses the race issue to screen out legitimate concerns about his
Alinskyite tactics.

Obama's Ambitions

As we saw in Chapter Two, Obama was likely drawn into community organizing in the hope of using it as a springboard to politics. As Obama tells us in *Dreams,* after the MET ribbon-cutting triumph, his fantasy was to take "the leadership [of DCP] downtown to sit down with Harold and discuss the fate of the city." This was not an unrealistic fantasy, since UNO of Chicago co-founders Greg Galluzzo and Mary Gonzales were often in conference with the mayor over UNO's various projects.[77] But to get inside the mayor's office required a delicate balance between pressuring his administration and acting as an ally.[78] The collapse of the meeting with Zirl Smith threatened to turn Obama into an unfriendly troublemaker in the eyes of Harold Washington's administration, and that would have undermined Obama's personal ambitions. That is why, in his memoirs, Obama distorts it.

Here is another area in which Reverend Smalls was right, however bigoted he may have been about other matters. Smalls explained to Obama that he didn't want to work with DCP because, with Harold Washington in office and black churches already well-connected to the mayor, it was counterproductive to embarrass the administration with public protests.[79] By trapping Zirl Smith in a typical Galluzzo-style confrontation, Obama was playing with fire—potentially alienating the very administration he idolized. The microphone problem may have pushed the situation to an extreme, but the organizing technique itself was designed to cause trouble. Also, UNO of Chicago had more scope to pressure the mayor because Latinos were a swing constituency. Harold Washington could pretty much depend on support from African-Americans, whereas Hispanics were split between Washington and the machine. That means Obama had to be particularly careful about alienating city hall. Ultimately, Harold Washington didn't really need Obama to keep the black vote, although he did need UNO to win Hispanics. These political constraints may have had a significant impact on Obama's work.

In any case, Obama's account of the asbestos fiasco, and of his organizing generally, disguises his willingness to use polarizing Alinskyite tactics. He clearly approves of these polarizing tactics, because in the nineties he knowingly funneled foundation money to the organizers who used them. The reason Obama has to disguise the truth about his tactics is that he embodies community organizing's "inside" strategy. Obama has always aspired to be the kind of organizer who works through the electoral system. His job is to use the government to get hardball Alinskyite organizers the laws and money they want, while also providing an appealingly sanitized picture of organizing itself to the public. Obama is the classic organizing good cop. That means he has to obscure his bad-cop roots.

Landfill Confrontation

During the 2008 campaign, press accounts of Obama's early organizing days incorrectly and consistently portrayed him as rejecting Alinskyite hardball. "Mr. Obama shunned Mr. Alinsky's strategy of using confrontation tactics like pressuring public officials and business leaders by picketing their homes," said the *New York Times*.[80] Obama's ubiquitously quoted organizing mentor, Jerry Kellman, said: "Barack was willing to challenge power, but he was very reticent to use any personal confrontation."[81] Obama's friend and U.S. Senate colleague from Illinois, Richard J. Durban, told the *Washington Post*: "If you read Alinsky's teaching, there are times he's confrontational. I have not seen that in Barack."[82] The Associated Press said that despite working with Alinskyite colleagues, Obama "didn't adopt hard-nose tactics."[83] There were also interviews with DCP leader Loretta Augustine-Herron in which she quoted Obama telling followers to be "polite" and "take the high road."[84]

To the contrary, as we have seen, Obama was closely tied to UNO of Chicago, which specialized in just such aggressive tactics. In fact, Obama personally helped plan one of UNO's most confrontational actions of the eighties: a break-in meant to intimidate a coalition of local business and neighborhood leaders into dropping a landfill expansion deal.

We know of Obama's involvement in this demonstration only because his supporters in 2008 felt it necessary to rebut charges that, contrary to his claims of inter-racial healing, he had organized exclusively with blacks. Only then did Obama's former colleagues from UNO of Chicago reveal that he had helped to plan and lead this multi-ethnic demonstration against landfill expansion on Chicago's South Side.[85]

Especially in 1988, when the landfill demonstration took place, UNO was a staff-dominated group.[86] Despite its supposedly democratic structure, with members and their elected leaders making all decisions, UNO was in fact controlled by a small group of paid organizers. Since Obama was meeting weekly with UNO's organizers to plan actions, he was effectively part of the leadership of one of Chicago's most notoriously radical and aggressive community organizations. Obama carefully disguises this in *Dreams*.

Chicago's landfill battle in the eighties was literally and figuratively a mess. The city's South Side had been a dump since the turn of the century, long before the Altgeld Gardens housing development was placed there. The wetlands in this area, with their thick natural clay underlayer, were ideal for landfill. As the city grew, the dumping-grounds expanded, endangering nearby residents. Yet every other location in the city and state resisted becoming the next waste disposal site. Southeast Chicago itself was split on the issue, since dumping polluted the neighborhood, yet also provided the area with desperately needed jobs.[87] No one wants a dump in his backyard, but the city's landfill needs just kept growing. The difference, according to the *Chicago Tribune*, was that, whereas most Illinois anti-landfill activists used "patience and reason," UNO of Chicago's anti-dumping leader, Mary Ellen Montes, favored civil disobedience and tactics that went "to extremes."[88]

Montes led the landfill demonstration Obama helped to plan. The object was to scuttle a deal in which Waste Management Corporation "would spend millions of dollars on community development projects, including job training, scholarships, housing, health care and day care," in return for neighborhood agreement to expanded landfills.[89] Shouting "No deals!" somewhere between eighty and a hundred UNO-DCP protesters marched to a local bank. There they broke into a meeting being conducted by the bank president and local community leaders. The group was exploring the possibility of a deal with Waste Management. The protesters, presumably including Obama, surrounded the meeting table while Montes told the negotiators, "We will fight you every step of the way."[90] After that, the protesters filed out. But of course, the message of intimidation had been sent. Ironically, years later, in 2006, when it was no longer associated with co-founders Galluzzo and Gonzales, UNO of Chicago accepted just such a deal from Waste Management.[91]

Thus, widespread claims during the 2008 campaign that Obama shunned Alinskyite confrontation tactics were wrong. These false claims were abetted by a biased press corps, reluctant to investigate Obama's past, and by his organizing mentors, intent on protecting their protégé's image. Ultimately, however, the sanitized account of this future president's organizing career originated with Obama himself. The only hint in *Dreams* of the break-in is the prettied-up passage where Obama speaks of holding "a series of joint meetings with Mexicans in the Southeast Side to craft a common environmental strategy for the region."[92] As we'll see, the true story of Obama's early organizing days is completely consistent with his efforts to channel foundation funding to his confrontational Alinskyite colleagues in the nineties.

SECTION THREE

SCHOOL REFORM

In *Dreams*, Obama explains that in the spring of 1987, alarmed by the deepening alienation and gang violence of local teens, he drew up a proposal for a youth counseling network.[93] The idea was to provide at-risk teenagers with mentoring and tutorial services, while also drawing parents into a longer-term battle for school reform. Obama reports that he had trouble selling parts of this plan to his membership.[94] The churches on which DCP depended were filled with teachers, principals, and school superintendents, whereas Obama's reformist allies wanted to transfer power over schools away from teachers' unions, handing it instead to community organizations like UNO, ACORN, and DCP. Resistance to this project from his own members angered Obama. So rather than drop the school reform idea, he went out and drummed up support from others—especially an Afro-centric educator Obama calls "Asante Moran," who helped draw up DCP's youth counseling proposal.[95]

The Harold Washington Archives and Collections contain this proposal, which accompanies letters from Obama to the mayor's office asking for support.[96] We also have internal Washington administration comments on Obama's proposal.[97] These documents do a great deal more than reveal the content of Obama's youth counseling program. They also shed considerable light on his emerging political network, including Reverend Jeremiah Wright, Father Michael Pfleger, and John Ayers (colleague and brother of that famously unrepentant terrorist Bill Ayers).

The Reverend Jeremiah Wright and Father Michael Pfleger, the two incendiary preachers who burst onto the national scene during Obama's 2008 campaign, are both on Obama's youth counseling advisory committee. That means Obama had connected with both at least a year before he left Chicago for law school. Quite possibly, Obama turned to both men to counter the reluctance of priests and ministers in Roseland to join in the battle for school reform. School reform was based on the idea of handing control over the education system to local "school councils" that leftist community organizers hoped to control. The schools battle split Chicago between the liberal, middle-class, and heavily minority teachers' unions, on the one hand, and the still more left-leaning community organizations that hoped to gain power, on the other. Since Wright and Pfleger were at the far left end of the political spectrum, they would have favored the reformist forces.

We see, then, that Obama's relationship with Wright and Pfleger was political from the start. There's nothing surprising about this, given his UNO mentors' strategy of building their political power on a series of religious alliances. In fact, if you're an Alinskyite community organizer and you're not thinking of ministers as political allies, you're doing something wrong. So the notion that Obama was drawn to Wright simply to join up with a respectable local church isn't convincing. On the contrary, Obama's plan called for the mayor to confer with him and his advisory board. So Obama looked to Wright and Pfleger to help him in meetings with the mayor.

John Ayers was yet another key player in the city-wide movement for school reform. Through his affiliation with the Commercial Club of Chicago, Ayers represented the business community's interest in the schools. No doubt John's father, Commonwealth Edison CEO and chair Tom Ayers, helped supply his son with credentials in Chicago's business community. Yet business ties notwithstanding, John Ayers was linked to the network of socialist activists that centered on the Midwest Academy. John's brother Bill wouldn't arrive in Chicago until the following fall. Yet already, by spring of 1987, Obama had made contact with Bill Ayers's brother.

Obama's links to Bill Ayers's future colleagues don't end there. The advisory board of Obama's youth counseling network also included Anne Hallett, who would someday join with Bill Ayers to create an education foundation headed by Obama. Another school reform leader, Fred Hess, was on Obama's board. So a year before the time in 1988 when Bill Ayers emerged as the leader of Chicago's school-reform forces, Obama was bound to this network.

How did Obama manage to place what amounts to nearly the entire upper echelon of the Chicago school reform movement on the advisory board of his tiny community organization's proposed counseling network—at a time when the movement itself had only barely taken shape? The most likely answer is Ken Rolling, a key figure in Chicago's socialist politics. Rolling, a former high official of the Midwest Academy, was in charge of Obama's foundation funding. Rolling was also orchestrating the school-reform movement from behind—less out of a concern for education than in an effort to build the power and membership of Chicago's Alinskyite groups.[98] Rolling could easily have linked Obama to the leaders of Chicago's school-reform movement.

Obama's Plan Rejected

In the end, Obama's grander plans for his youth counseling network fell apart. Apparently, Harold Washington never agreed to meet with Obama and his youth counseling advisory board, or to keynote a DCP rally.[99] A letter from the DCP to Mayor Washington also contains a cryptic hand-written notation from a mayoral aide that seems to indicate Obama was "upset" to learn that his proposal had been rejected or delayed.[100] (The note is too vague to conclude this with certainty.)

If Harold Washington had decided to back the proposal, it would have been a major coup for Obama. As creator of the prototype for a city-wide program funded by millions of state dollars, Obama would have been in charge of a small fiefdom and could have built connections (and a political future) all over town. With Wright, Pfleger, and Ayers in tow, Obama would also have enjoyed periodic meetings with the mayor, just like his UNO mentors. Obama's proposal appears to have been put on hold toward the very end of June 1987. We know that Obama told Jerry Kellman of his decision to leave organizing for law school in late October of that year.[101] The failure of Harold Washington to accept Obama's youth counseling proposal may have checked Obama's immediate political ambitions, thereby pushing him out of organizing and into law school.

Education Confrontation

Before leaving for Harvard, however, Obama would join UNO for some classic Alinskyite hardball. We know that in early February of 1988, Obama planned and participated in a confrontational UNO break-in. Around this same time, Obama's DCP combined with UNO for a number of joint actions. UNO co-founder, Mary Gonzales, explained that during this period, "We were trying very hard to connect neighborhoods and he [Obama] was part of that."[102] One of these joint UNO-DCP actions took place on February 18, 1988, and involved school reform. Although Obama cannot be placed at this action with certainty, the chances of his having been there are high. After all, Obama had participated in the joint UNO-DCP landfill protest just days before. With his DCP followers going into yet another confrontational action, Obama would surely have wanted to help.

The *Chicago Tribune* of February 19, 1988, reports on a Chicago Board of Education meeting forced into hasty adjournment by a joint UNO-DCP demonstration: "Leaders of the Neighborhood Schoolhouse Coalition refused to present their reform proposal after William Farrow, chairman of the board's Education Summit Committee, would not allow all their supporters into the already packed, 120-seat board chambers."[103] Deacon Daniel Lee (presumably Will from *Dreams*) laid out the ultimatum. Although the Education Summit Committee tried to persuade the UNO-DCP protesters to present their plan, they refused to do so without the seventy-five additional supporters angrily chanting in the lobby because they couldn't fit into the hearing room.

This is a typical Alinskyite gambit, favored not only by UNO organizers, but by Obama's allies at ACORN and the Midwest Academy as well.[104] Demonstrators demand to be heard collectively at a packed public meeting, knowing full well that they will not all be able to fit. The resulting polarization when the request is denied generates anger against supposedly repressive authorities, thus intimidating political "targets" while simultaneously ginning up the energy of the group (although at the price of alienating moderate observers). Since Obama was likely present at this school-reform demonstration, along with the landfill break-in (and quite possibly additional unreported joint actions with UNO), his account of his tactics in *Dreams* begins to look like a sugary fairy tale.

Another by-product of this disruptive strategy is media attention. After the schools meeting was canceled, coalition leaders presented their plan to supporters and the press outside the chamber. The UNO-DCP proposal called for $500 million in new school funding. Powerful Illinois state senator Arthur Berman promised during the 1988 reform debate that any major new money for the schools would mean an increase in state taxes.[105] The reformers never got their money—or their tax increase.

By March of 1988, just a few weeks after the joint UNO-DCP demonstration, a wide-ranging group of school-reform activists began meeting regularly. Initially this was under the leadership of Peter Martinez, an experienced Alinskyite organizer who also worked closely with UNO.[106] This signaled that UNO had assumed a central role in what was soon to become the most powerful city-wide group pushing for school reform: the ABCs Coalition (Alliance for Better Chicago Schools). Along with UNO, of course, Obama's Developing Communities Project (DCP) was very much a part of the ABCs Coalition. We also know that Obama himself remained immersed in the school-reform crusade until he left for Harvard, since he led a busload of school-reform activists to Illinois' capital of Springfield when the movement turned to lobbying in the late spring of 1988.[107]

At some point in late 1987, Bill Ayers joined the Chicago school-reform battle. Ayers was then in his first year as a professor of education at the University of Illinois, Chicago. Of course, given his brother John's established role in this battle, Bill would have had an "in" to the school-reform coalition from the moment of his arrival in the city.

According to a 1990 article in the *Chicago Reader*, Ayers was asked to run ABCs Coalition meetings within a few weeks of the time he started to attend.[108] With the initial moderator, Martinez, closely tied to UNO, Ayers may have been perceived as a neutral figure, conveniently unattached to any existing faction.[109] With Obama deeply immersed in the ABCs coalition, and with Ayers chairing its meetings, the chances that they would have met in 1988 are high. UNO was the leading power within the school-reform coalition, and Obama's DCP was UNO's closest ally. So it's unlikely that someone leading the coalition's strategy sessions could have safely ignored Obama. During the 2008 campaign, bloggers pointed to the likelihood of an early Obama-Ayers connection via their work in the 1988 Chicago school-reform battle.[110] What we now know about Obama's ties to UNO only strengthens the point.

SECTION FOUR

SOCIALIST ORGANIZING

One last name on the advisory board of Obama's proposed youth counseling program requires attention: Dr. John L. McKnight, of the Center for Urban Affairs Policy Research at Northwestern University. The McKnight connection opens another revealing window onto Obama's ideology. Toward the end of his organizing stint, Obama approached McKnight for a recommendation to Harvard Law School. McKnight had helped to train Obama.[111] At the conclusion of his book *The Audacity of Hope*, Obama tells of asking McKnight for a recommendation (without using McKnight's name).[112]

McKnight is an expert in both health policy and community organizing. His most influential essay on organizing was published jointly with his Northwestern colleague, John ("Jody") Kretzmann (another Obama associate) in 1984, a year before Obama arrived in Chicago. It's called "Community Organizing in the Eighties: Toward a Post-Alinsky

Agenda."[113] With Obama receiving training from McKnight in the mid-eighties, he would surely have been influenced by this piece. In fact, a report in Sasha Abramsky's recent book, *Inside Obama's Brain*, confirms that Obama studied McKnight's work.[114]

In their article, McKnight and Kretzmann note that decisions affecting local economies are increasingly made in other parts of the country. That makes it harder for organizers to find local "enemies" or "targets" capable of delivering economic relief. You can't force a mayor, or even a factory manager, to re-open a steel mill if the decision to close it is made in a far-away state. The remedy, say McKnight and Kretzmann, is to organize confrontations, not over the distribution of city services (like garbage pickup or neighborhood police patrols), but over economic production itself. McKnight and Kretzmann take the Community Reinvestment Act (CRA) as their model. In the name of fairness, CRA forces banks to make high-risk "subprime" loans to low-credit customers. Many believe that CRA helped to cause the current financial crisis. Yet McKnight and Kretzmann want to impose CRA-like redistributive constraints on a whole range of industries. For example, they favor laws that would give community organizers a place on corporate boards and regulatory agencies, thereby preventing businesses from leaving a community at will. Just as ACORN inserted itself into America's banking system through CRA, McKnight and Kretzmann want organizers to press for laws that would give them influence over the entire system of production.

This movement to place constraints on capitalism "from below" was the strategy favored by the Democratic Socialists of America (DSA) in the eighties. This socialist vision, I argue, inspired Obama to become a community organizer. He learned how to go about it from his mentor John McKnight.

Forced Labor

McKnight is also an expert on health policy who has worked in close partnership with longtime Obama confidante Quentin Young. Young was a high official of the Chicago chapter of the Democratic Socialists of America.[115] Together, Young and McKnight founded the Health and Medicine Policy Research Group, which published a magazine called *Health & Medicine* in the eighties.[116] *Health & Medicine* strongly backed single-payer systems—health care run exclusively by the government. Young's influence helped turn Obama into a prominent advocate of single-payer health care, and Obama worked with Young on the health-care issue during his time in the Illinois State Senate.[117] Young was also present at the notorious kickoff event for Obama's political career at the home of Bill Ayers and Bernardine Dohrn.[118]

Health & Medicine, the magazine of the group founded by Young and McKnight, is filled with socialist themes. The Spring 1987 issue (published in the middle of Obama's Chicago organizing stint) features excerpts from the biography of "Red Emma" (leftist-anarchist Emma Goldman), along with a tribute to nurses in the Abraham Lincoln Brigade (communist-supported fighters in the Spanish Civil War).[119] A Winter 1985 issue of *Health & Medicine*, published just before Obama's arrival in Chicago, features an article supporting health care as practiced by the Marxist Sandinista Revolution in Nicaragua, and in Cuba as well.[120] McKnight himself is featured in two pieces from that Winter 1985 issue of *Health & Medicine.* In one article, he leads a discussion among community organizers looking for ways to "capture a portion" of the health-care market.[121] This is consistent with McKnight's idea that community organizations need to take control of the economy from below.

Also in the Winter 1985 issue of *Health & Medicine,* Quentin Young interviews McKnight about the latest developments in Sweden's welfare state.[122] McKnight is an expert on the Swedish system. Some of that country's most left-leaning bureaucrats actually seek out his advice. In the interview, McKnight explains to Young that at a 52 percent tax rate (not including a 15 percent national sales tax), the Swedish state has probably reached the limit of its ability to extract income from its citizens. The solution, McKnight's Swedish associates believe, is to "tax people's time." Sweden's far-left bureaucrats call this idea "care conscription." Under the plan, Swedes would be drafted to work in the state's welfare system. At the same time, the government would limit the amount of time an individual could work for his own profit. This "care conscription" would compel citizens to mop floors and provide other sorts of manual labor in Sweden's many state-run institutions.

While McKnight and Young acknowledge the radicalism of this proposal, they clearly admire the Swedish system and are at least open to the idea of compulsory citizen labor. These, then, are the values of Obama's organizing mentors and political collaborators.

Building Socialism in Our Neighborhoods

What about Obama's fellow organizers at UNO of Chicago and its successor organization, the Gamaliel Foundation. Were they socialists? We know from Rutgers political scientist Heidi Swarts, who studied the organization in recent years, that Gamaliel-trained organizers intentionally avoid open ideological talk, although they freely spout leftist jargon behind the scenes.[123] Knowing that their working-class followers will reject leftist ideology, Gamaliel organizers take care to present their ideas as "commonsense" solutions for "working families."[124] But consider Obama's account of his mentor "Marty Kaufman" in *Dreams*. Kaufman's plans for workers to take over a struggling steel mill and pressure local banks to fund it come right out of the socialist strategies of the eighties.[125]

With Greg Galluzzo's support, in 2001, Dennis Jacobsen, the director of Gamaliel's National Clergy Caucus, published *Doing Justice:*

Congregations and Community Organizing, a combination handbook and ideological guide for Gamaliel's religious organizers.[126] The book is socialist in all but name. Jacobsen decries America's corporate system, which he claims is designed to benefit the prosperous and keep the poor down.[127] The goal of Gamaliel organizers, says Jacobsen, should be to stir up public anger in order to "shake the foundations of this society."[128] Jacobsen never mentions socialism, but he does hold up communal property among the early Christians and "radical sharing" by various African groups as models for the good society.[129] Like Reverend Wright's sermon's, Jacobsen's work is shot through with anti-American themes. The underlying point is clear enough for anyone with eyes to see: America is a "sick society" whose oppressive capitalist system must be transformed out of all recognition.[130]

In January of 1988, toward the end of Obama's organizing time in Chicago, *New Ground*, the newsletter of the Chicago branch of the Democratic Socialists of America, published a report called "Community Organizing: Building Democracy and Socialism in our Neighborhoods."[131] That article identifies an "emerging consensus" among area socialists that community organizing has become an indispensable element of their political strategy. DSA members are exhorted to work within existing community organizations, to "radicalize" their efforts. That is, socialist organizers are encouraged to agitate for laws and agreements designed to constrain banks, utilities, and other elements of the capitalist system. This is Marty Kaufman's plan in *Dreams*. The 1988 *New Ground* report also cites the Citizen Action network, run by Chicago's Midwest Academy, as the leading example of a leftist approach to community organizing. These socialist community organizers were at the very center of Obama's political world.

Mike Kruglik, one of Obama's early organizing mentors, once said of his protégé: "I think Obama already had his basic beliefs and values when he got [to Chicago]."[132] So according to Kruglik, Obama's politics were well established by the time he left New York. We now know that Obama was drinking in socialist theories of community organizing during those New York years. Chicago's organizers provided Obama with new political tools, but not with a new ideology. That ideology was entrenched before Obama ever set foot in Chicago, and its name, evidence strongly suggests, was socialism.

CHAPTER 5

The Midwest Academy

ORIGINS

In the summer of 1969, the Students for a Democratic Society—SDS, the group that had carried out the most violent and radical leftist protests of the sixties—was divided and near collapse. The SDS's Weather Underground faction, including Bill Ayers and Bernardine Dohrn, was preparing to embark on its now-infamous terror spree. Although historians remember the birth of the Weather Underground from the ashes of the SDS, few have noticed that another and perhaps ultimately more influential group was quietly coming into existence at the very same time. On Labor Day 1969, a group that included past SDS national secretary Paul Booth, his activist wife, Heather Booth, onetime SDS field secretary Steve Max, and radical community organizer Harry Boyte published a pamphlet titled "Socialism and the Coming Decade."[1] Clustered several years later around an institute called the Midwest Academy, this group would go on to create a new way of blending socialism, community organizing, and electoral politics.

Obama's Secret

In many ways, the Midwest Academy is the hidden key to Barack Obama's political career. Obama's organizing mentors had ties to it; Obama's early funding was indirectly controlled by it; evidence strongly suggests that Obama himself received training there; both Barack and Michelle Obama ran a project called "Public Allies" that was effectively an extension of the Midwest Academy; Obama's first run for public office was sponsored by Academy veteran Alice Palmer; and Obama worked closely at two foundations for years with yet another veteran organizer from the Midwest Academy, Ken Rolling.

Perhaps more important, Barack Obama's approach to politics is clearly inspired by that of the Midwest Academy. Therefore, it is of no small interest that the Midwest Academy is a socialist "front group," a phenomenon supposedly consigned to the bad old days of the 1930s communist "Popular Front." The story of the Midwest Academy's transformation from a stealthy nest of radical sixties socialists into a force at the center of the Democratic Party offers unparalleled insight into Barack Obama's hidden political world.

In 2010, the Midwest Academy is as unknown as ACORN was in early 2008. Today, by contrast, any political fan can tell you something about ACORN's ideology and tactics, perhaps reeling off the names of a couple of leaders and a branch or two of ACORN's byzantine organizational empire, to boot. Yet the Midwest Academy's history, cast of characters, and organizational reach are at least as extensive as ACORN's. A bit of effort devoted to the Midwest Academy's hidden past opens the door to the heretofore secret history of contemporary American socialism—and to the heart and soul of Barack Obama's hidden political world. The accompanying charts should be of some assistance.

Midwest Academy History

1969	1971	1973	1978	1979 & After
Origins	**Alliance with Alinsky**	**Midwest Academy Founded**	**C/LEC Founded**	**Citizen Action**
Paul and Heather Booth, Harry Boyte, and Steve Max—high officials and activists of SDS—author a pamphlet, "Socialism and the Coming Decade." Their strategy envisions "conscious socialists" using community organizing to create and manage a radical mass movement capable of bringing socialism to the U.S. in the long term.	Heather Booth trains with Alinsky. Paul Booth co-leads Alinsky's new citywide organization in Chicago, CAP. **Socialist Feminism** Heather Booth works at the socialist Chicago Women's Liberation Union. CWLU partners with a day-care movement that is not overtly socialist. Strategy of 1969 essay put into practice.	Heather Booth, Steve Max, and Paul Booth train organizers and teach socialism. Harry Boyte advises from Minnesota. The Academy works closely with socialist organizations NAM and DSOC. Boyte envisions strategy for overtly populist-communitarian movement guided quietly by socialists. 1969 strategy will be attempted on a national scale.	Heather Booth co-founds and co-leads the Citizen/Labor Energy Coalition. Cooperates closely with DSOC. Co-leads with William Winpisinger, union leader and committed socialist. C/LEC is a dry run for a broader national political strategy uniting labor and community organizations in a "populist" coalition quietly guided from behind by socialists.	C/LEC transitions to a national multi-issue coalition called Citizen Action. Overtly populist and communitarian, CA is led quietly by socialists. CA's Illinois branch, IPAC, initiates successful electoral strategy with the election of Lane Evans to congress. Midwest Academy guides CA and becomes a force within the Democratic Party in the 1980s.

The Socialist Backstory

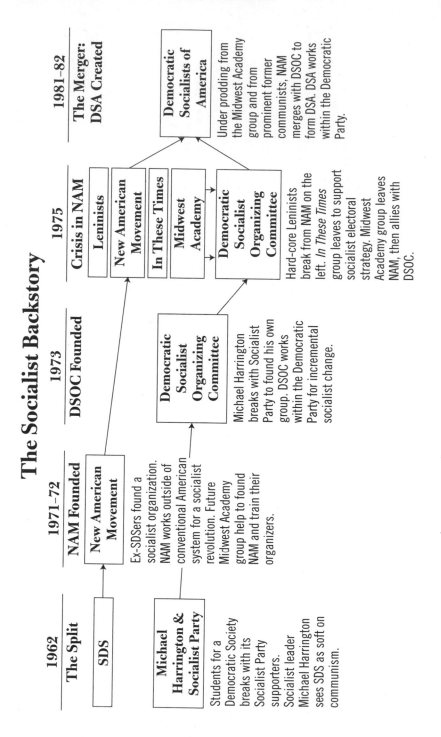

1962	1971–72	1973	1975	1981–82
The Split	**NAM Founded**	**DSOC Founded**	**Crisis in NAM**	**The Merger: DSA Created**

SDS

New American Movement

Michael Harrington & Socialist Party

Students for a Democratic Society breaks with its Socialist Party supporters. Socialist leader Michael Harrington sees SDS as soft on communism.

Ex-SDSers found a socialist organization. NAM works outside of conventional American system for a socialist revolution. Future Midwest Academy group help to found NAM and train their organizers.

Democratic Socialist Organizing Committee

Michael Harrington breaks with Socialist Party to found his own group. DSOC works within the Democratic Party for incremental socialist change.

Leninists

New American Movement

In These Times

Midwest Academy

Democratic Socialist Organizing Committee

Hard-core Leninists break from NAM on the left. *In These Times* group leaves to support socialist electoral strategy. Midwest Academy group leaves NAM, then allies with DSOC.

Democratic Socialists of America

Under prodding from the Midwest Academy group and from prominent former communists, NAM merges with DSOC to form DSA. DSA works within the Democratic Party.

The Obama Connection

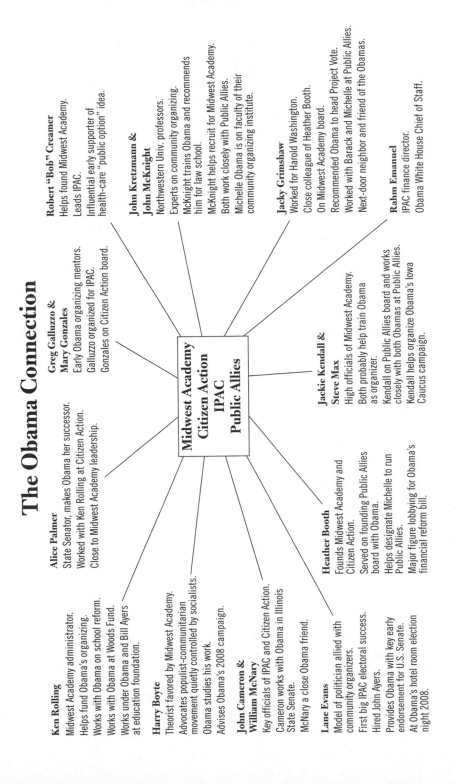

Robert "Bob" Creamer
Helps found Midwest Academy.
Leads IPAC.
Influential early supporter of health-care "public option" idea.

**John Kretzmann &
John McKnight**
Northwestern Univ. professors.
Experts on community organizing.
McKnight trains Obama and recommends him for law school.
McKnight helps recruit for Midwest Academy.
Both work closely with Public Allies.
Michelle Obama is on faculty of their community organizing institute.

Jacky Grimshaw
Worked for Harold Washington.
Close colleague of Heather Booth.
On Midwest Academy board.
Recommended Obama to head Project Vote.
Worked with Barack and Michelle at Public Allies.
Next-door neighbor and friend of the Obamas.

Rahm Emanuel
IPAC finance director.
Obama White House Chief of Staff.

**Greg Galluzzo &
Mary Gonzales**
Early Obama organizing mentors.
Galluzzo organized for IPAC.
Gonzales on Citizen Action board.

Alice Palmer
State Senator, makes Obama her successor.
Worked with Ken Rolling at Citizen Action.
Close to Midwest Academy leadership.

**Midwest Academy
Citizen Action
IPAC
Public Allies**

**Jackie Kendall &
Steve Max**
High officials of Midwest Academy.
Both probably help train Obama as organizer.
Kendall on Public Allies board and works closely with both Obamas at Public Allies.
Kendall helps organize Obama's Iowa Caucus campaign.

Ken Rolling
Midwest Academy administrator.
Helps fund Obama's organizing.
Works with Obama on school reform.
Works with Obama at Woods Fund.
Works under Obama and Bill Ayers at education foundation.

Harry Boyte
Theorist favored by Midwest Academy.
Advocates populist-communitarian movement quietly controlled by socialists.
Obama studies his work.
Advises Obama's 2008 campaign.

**John Cameron &
William McNary**
Key officials of IPAC and Citizen Action.
Cameron works with Obama in Illinois State Senate.
McNary a close Obama friend.

Lane Evans
Model of politician allied with community organizers.
First big IPAC electoral success.
Hired John Ayers.
Provides Obama with key early endorsement for U.S. Senate.
At Obama's hotel room election night 2008.

Heather Booth
Founds Midwest Academy and Citizen Action.
Served on founding Public Allies board with Obama.
Helps designate Michelle to run Public Allies.
Major figure lobbying for Obama's financial reform bill.

Trails Lead Here

An examination of the Midwest Academy gathers the threads of Obama's career around a number of themes raised earlier in this book. In the interest of clarity, let us recap them. In Chapters One and Two we encountered an incremental and pragmatic form of socialism, tied to community organizing and championed by Michael Harrington and other leaders of the Democratic Socialists of America (DSA). Working closely with Michael Harrington's DSA, the leaders of the Midwest Academy provided a real-life model for the DSA vision of a partnership between community organizing and socialism. Over the course of the 1970s, the leaders of the Midwest Academy and their supporters also played a central role in dragging the militant ex-SDSers of the New American Movement (NAM) into a more pragmatically minded alliance with Michael Harrington. We got a hint of that in Chapter Two, but the fuller story of the decade-long transformation of NAM from militance to pragmatism is well worth telling. The story of NAM and the Midwest Academy helps explain why real-life community organizers adhere to a version of socialism very different from what standard-issue treatments of Marxism might lead us to expect. In Chapter Three we also learned of a stealthy brand of socialism advocated by a theorist of community organizing named Harry Boyte. Boyte closely collaborated with the leaders of the Midwest Academy, and his vision of socialism is embodied in the work of that institution.

The Midwest Academy succeeded in synthesizing the community organizing techniques of Saul Alinsky with the sort of national electoral strategy Alinsky had long refused to countenance. Through their vision, ambition, and ideological earnestness, the leaders of the Midwest Academy turned Alinsky's localized techniques into the key to an ambitious national strategy of socialist transformation. Barack Obama, by all accounts a brilliant student of community organizing, was for years in an ideal position to drink all of this in. Michelle Obama (herself closely affiliated with the Midwest Academy) has said of her husband that he thinks of electoral politics as a kind of project in community organizing writ large: "Barack is not a politician first and foremost. He's a community activist exploring the viability of politics to make change."[2] This way of understanding electoral politics was virtually invented by the Midwest Academy. So let's have a look at the history of this extraordinary institution, and of its ties to Barack and Michelle Obama.

Pragmatic Socialism

"Socialism and the Coming Decade," the 1969 pamphlet published by the future leaders and core supporters of the Midwest Academy, took the quest for socialism in a very different direction than the Weather Underground. The Weathermen nursed wildly improbable hopes of fomenting revolution through a terrorist war waged against police, the military, and the symbolic seats of American democracy. In contrast, "Socialism and the Coming Decade" is all about long-term strategy, realistic short-term objectives, and the deep-down social change that only patient community organizing can bring. For all that, the program itself remains radical, with clear support for the Vietnamese communists and a guaranteed annual income for all Americans among its positions, for example.[3]

Even so, the SDSers behind "Socialism and the Coming Decade" counsel patience, and acknowledge that the United States of 1969 (with Richard Nixon as its new president) has entered a "nonrevolutionary period."[4] In these non-revolutionary times, we're told, "a conscious organization of socialists" needs to found and guide community organizations among the working class.[5] These neighborhood groups can mobilize workers around concrete issues like urban redevelopment and health care, thereby giving "the socialist movement relevance to the daily lives of the people."[6] Over time, patient neighborhood organizing and struggle will prepare the workers' consciousness for the socialist revolution to come.

Notice the implicit difference here between the socialist consciousness of the organizers and the less-than-fully-socialist thinking of their "mass" followers. Community organizations may be "anti-capitalist" in practice,[7] but that is not the same thing as full socialist consciousness—which according to these socialists takes time and education to develop. So beneath the surface of "Socialism and the Coming Decade" lurks the problem of precisely how honest socialist community organizers ought to be about their beliefs. Should community organizers proudly proclaim their politics and convert the masses to socialism—or quietly draw their unsuspecting followers into implicitly socialist schemes? Over time, the answer became clear. As America's "non-revolutionary period" persisted, organizers at the Midwest Academy increasingly opted for stealth.

By 1971, with the Weather Underground in the midst of its futile terror campaign, Heather and Paul Booth were following through on the more plausible program that they and their colleagues had outlined two years before in "Socialism and the Coming Decade." With the SDS a dead letter, the Booths turned toward Alinsky. This was despite, or perhaps because of, Alinsky's long-standing conviction that the SDS's organizing methods were naive and counterproductive. Heather Booth enrolled in Alinsky's fledgling Chicago organizer training institute in the summer of 1971. (Records show that Obama's original training mentor, Jerry Kellman, was a classmate of hers at the time.)[8] Meanwhile, Paul Booth was assuming the co-chairmanship of the Citizens Action Program (CAP), a pioneering city-wide community organization in Chicago that emerged out of Alinsky's new training institute. The experience and connections the Booths gained through CAP would enable them to found their own organizer training institute, the Midwest Academy, in 1973.

CAP

CAP was Saul Alinsky's attempt to organize the white middle class.[9] The rising Black Power movement of the late sixties had driven Alinsky out of organizing projects in African-American neighborhoods and left him with no choice but to shift his focus to whites. Yet Alinsky was also convinced that large-scale socialist transformation would require an alliance between the struggling middle class and the poor. The key to radical social change, Alinsky thought, was to turn the wrath of America's middle class against large corporations. After initial drives against corporate pollution and Chicago's plan to construct a crosstown expressway, CAP launched one of the first campaigns against bank "redlining," paving the way for ACORN's fateful attack on the mortgage industry decades later.

An unpublished University of Chicago doctoral dissertation in sociology by David Emmons, himself a CAP research director and organizer, offers a remarkably frank inside portrait of CAP, the Midwest Academy's immediate predecessor.[10] Emmons notes that CAP's campaign against the bank "red-lining" was pushed by "organizers who were mostly left-of-center social democrats and populists. They attributed most of the city's ills to underlying economic forces and longed for CAP to adopt an anti-corporate agenda."[11] "Social democrats and populists" is a bit of a euphemism, since the files of the Midwest Academy make it clear that CAP's organizers were largely socialist. But the interesting point here is the tension between what socialist-leaning organizers really wanted (anti-corporate campaigns) and what they sometimes had to agree to in response to their membership's interests (fighting the mayor's plan to construct an expressway). While the Weathermen were in hiding, hatching their absurdly unrealistic terror plans, the Booths and their fellow radicals were learning how to lead in the real world. In exchange for patient willingness to pursue popular projects of less-than-ultimate interest to themselves, socialist organizers could occasionally harness the power of the "masses" to actions with genuinely radical potential—like an attack on the banking system.

Having spent eighteen months in CAP, Emmons provides an informed and sobering account of the duplicitous and intentionally polarizing tactics at the center of Alinskyite organizing. For example:

CAP organizers manufactured anger: targets were baited to behave provocatively so that members would respond angrily. Frequently a cycle of rancourous protest was set off . . . CAP organizers prized angry confrontation because it created solidarity and a commitment to further action among participants. But it also created an image of militancy which repelled more conservative and frequently substantial local leaders, thus sometimes irreparably dividing neighborhoods into opposing camps.[12]

We saw exactly the same pattern in the methods Obama himself adopted under the training of Alinsky acolyte Greg Galluzzo. The CAP experience provided the Midwest Academy's organizers with a fund of these polarizing Alinskyite techniques on which to draw.

Socialist Feminism

While Paul Booth would be a board member and a power behind the scenes at the Midwest Academy, his wife, Heather Booth, would become (in 1973) the Academy's true founder and guiding force. Heather Booth was in an excellent position to observe and participate in CAP's battles of the early seventies. Yet Heather Booth's chief efforts in 1971 were devoted to organizing for socialist feminism. Booth and her early collaborator at the Midwest Academy, Day Creamer, were involved in both the Chicago Women's Liberation Union (CWLU) and the Action Committee for Decent Childcare.[13] The juxtaposition of the explicitly socialist CWLU with the less ideological daycare project—open to all women, not just committed socialists—exemplifies the strategy Booth and her collaborators had laid out in 1969's "Socialism and the Coming Decade," in which small, consciously socialist groups quietly build and guide less openly ideological mass movements. Booth's developing ideological and strategic perspective is presented in her 1971 pamphlet, written with Day Creamer and a small group of others, "Socialist Feminism: A Strategy for the Women's Movement."[14] This pamphlet was reprinted by the Midwest Academy "for historical purposes," and was sometimes used in the Academy's training sessions.

The most interesting thing about Booth's "Socialist Feminism" pamphlet is its open blending of socialism with Alinsky's intentionally non-ideological language. Alinsky was a cross between a democratic socialist and a communist fellow traveler.[15] He was smart enough to avoid Marxist language in public, however. Instead of calling for the overthrow of the bourgeoisie, Alinsky and his followers talk about "confronting power." Instead of advocating socialist revolution, they demand "radical social change." Instead of demanding attacks on capitalists, they go after "targets" or "enemies." Yet Booth and her collaborators use socialist and Alinskyite jargon interchangeably, as if their pamphlet were a sort of translation guide to the hidden socialist language of community organizing. For Booth, the Alinskyite "target" or "enemy" is openly equated with the "power of the ruling class."[16] Community organizing should "alter the relations of power," says Booth, which she elsewhere calls "weakening the power of the ruling class."[17] In Chapter Four, we saw Obama deploy a typical Alinskyite euphemism in *Dreams from My Father*. After criticizing black nationalist separatism for its inability to circumvent capitalism, Obama suggests that the only real solution for blacks is "changing the rules of power." That phrase is classic Alinskyite code for the sort of broad-scale social changes that lead to socialism. Booth's pamphlet makes the "translation" clear. So in 1971, Booth's SDS background was already combining with her Alinskyite training to produce a more self-consciously ideological brand of community organizing.

Booth's "Socialist Feminism" pamphlet also reveals the deeper reason for the Alinskyite embrace of hardball organizing tactics. Consider, for example, Booth's socialist-feminist approach to organizing around the abortion issue. Instead of simply working to expand legal protections for abortion, Booth tells feminists to figure out which corporate executives serve on the boards of churches that oppose abortion. That way, organizers can launch "direct action" campaigns against these executives, presumably, laying siege to their homes and boycotting their businesses.[18] When your ultimate goal is the overthrow of the capitalist ruling class, intimidating businessmen is not a problem. On the contrary, it moves the battle beyond conventional legal reform and toward radical consciousness—which is Booth's explicit goal. Most Americans are put off by Alinskyite tactics, implicitly feeling them to be violations of the underlying rules of fairness and civility on which society depends. Yet if in your heart you stand outside of society and hope to see the current system swept away, breaking the rules actually helps to get you where you're going. In other words, Alinsky's tactics are more than means to an end. His tactical radicalism points to an underlying socialist ideology. Thus does Booth's pamphlet reveal what Alinsky himself kept hidden.

That doesn't mean Booth herself was entirely open about her socialism. Her pamphlet does lay out an ideology—calling for free universal health care, the disarming and community control of police, collective responsibility for rearing children, and other radical goals.[19] Yet Booth is cautious and sophisticated about the relationship between "conscious socialists" and "mass organizations." The socialist Chicago Women's Liberation Union may have favored free, twenty-four-hour child care, but Booth makes it clear that it would be foolish to broach so radical a proposal to members of a "mass organization" (i.e., a group not restricted to socialists) like the Action Committee for Decent Childcare.[20] The most radical socialist-feminist goals must be revealed only gradually, and chiefly to women who seem like possible recruits to socialism. In 1971, then, two years before the founding of the Midwest Academy, Heather Booth's stealthy synthesis of socialism and Alinskyite community organizing was taking shape.

Founding NAM

As we've seen, in 1969, with the SDS in collapse, the authors of "Socialism in the Coming Decade" called for the formation of a "conscious organization of socialists." Between late 1971 and mid-1972, two authors of that document, Paul Booth and Harry Boyte, helped to found the New American Movement (NAM), a democratic socialist organization offering a home of sorts to the scattered veterans of the SDS.[21] One reason the history of NAM is virtually unknown today is that the organization was in many respects a failure. Despite grand plans to unite workers and the poor in a multi-racial revolutionary movement for socialism, NAM's membership remained minuscule. Political plans notwithstanding, NAM functioned as something of a lifestyle time-warp for aging sixties revolutionaries. Prospective new members were often driven off by the cliquish and retro feeling of it all.[22]

More important, most NAMers had a spectacularly unrealistic sense of America's readiness for a socialist revolution. There was barely any strategy at all, beyond the assumption that capitalism was teetering on the brink of failure.[23] It was taken for granted that an uncompromising and boldly articulated socialist vision would bring the "masses" flocking to NAM. Nixon's impeachment seemed to confirm NAM's hopes, and the group squandered its limited resources organizing around that crisis—only to be stunned after Nixon's resignation by the system's recuperative powers.[24] Yet the admittedly comical features of NAM mustn't blind us to its significance. We saw in Chapter Two how the eventual willingness of some in NAM to postpone their revolutionary dreams and work for socialist-friendly candidates in the here and now ultimately led to an influential alliance between Harold Washington and Chicago's socialists. The circle of organizers who would found and support the Midwest Academy were at the heart of this more realistic and effective tendency within NAM. Over the long term, the Midwest Academy group helped transform NAM into something new—creating a working relationship between modern community organizing and socialism in the process.

Early Signs of Trouble

In April of 1972, just as it was getting started, NAM sponsored an organizer training workshop conducted by Heather and Paul Booth along
with Bob and Day Creamer. The Booths had pushed the idea, partly as
a way of increasing the tactical savvy of these ex-SDSers, but really as
a way of pulling NAM in their own strategic direction. Archival documents paint a revealing picture of the splits within NAM that emerged
at this early workshop.

The NAM leaders who introduced the Booths and Creamers to the
organizing workshop took care to withhold NAM's official endorsement from the presenters. The Booths and Creamers, it was noted, had
developed their methods while working with "non-socialist organizations" and "liberal mass movements" (i.e., CAP and the daycare advocacy group), whereas many NAMers believed that revolutionary mass
organizations must be built around openly socialist ideas. At the workshop, Heather Booth defended the value of movements built around
piecemeal reforms as a way of gradually creating radical consciousness.
Booth "called on those present to fight perfectionism, correct lineism,
impossibilism, and all the other isms that have distracted the Left." [25]
In other words, Booth argued that unless NAMers lowered their revolutionary expectations and worked for gradual and only implicitly socialist change, they would never get past square one with the American
people.

The workshop included readings from Andre Gorz, whose theories,
we learned in Chapter Two, held that capitalism could be crippled and
transformed from within by a series of reforms that were far more radical in effect than they appeared to be. [26] Yet the Booths and Creamers
were pressed during the workshop to go beyond "reformism" and explain how to build mass movements with explicitly socialist consciousness. The presenters apparently avoided answering those questions
head-on. Similarly, one of the NAM leaders who corresponded with the
Booths prior to the workshop pressed them to be more specific about

the delicate question of how open community organizers ought to be about their socialism (the terms "front group" and "mass activity" in the following passage translate to "community organization"):

What is the relationship of the NAM chapter to the mass activity? Under what conditions should actions be carried out in the name of NAM? Under what conditions should it be a front group or a coalition? Who really decides, the front group or the chapter? How and when do you raise the question of socialism? How do you recruit NAM members out of a mass action? [27]

This same leader pressed the Booths to "deal with the question of illegal activity" like "violence and street tactics." "Why are these less than useful?" he wanted to know. From the beginning of NAM's existence, then, a split was developing between hardliners who saw a violent and openly socialist revolution around the corner, and a pragmatic faction content to organize and provide quiet socialist guidance to movements that were liberal in appearance, yet radical in their ultimate intention and effect.

TEACHING SOCIALISM

In the winter of 1973, a then twenty-seven-year-old Heather Booth founded the Midwest Academy as a training institute for community organizers. Steve Max was the other key trainer, while Paul Booth, Bob and Day Creamer, and a small number of other associates served on the board of directors.[28] Because many files of the Midwest Academy, along with a number of Heather Booth's personal papers, have been archived at the Chicago Historical Society, it is possible to reconstruct the internal operations of this remarkable institution through about the mid-1980s. Of course, document archives offer a very partial picture of what happens in real life. Face-to-face interactions and phone calls don't get archived. That said, the voluminous Midwest Academy records are revealing, particularly because key figures were sometimes in different cities and communicated by letter. Draft manuscripts traded among colleagues also shed light on the ideological development of the Academy's leaders. The bottom line is that the Midwest Academy archives are a window onto the inner workings of a modern-day socialist front group. With the assistance of the archives, it is possible to identify numerous links between the Midwest Academy and both Barack and Michelle Obama.

How do you train community organizers? The Midwest Academy mixed role-playing games (e.g., mock negotiations between demonstrators, steel company executives, and a mayor) with readings, lectures, discussion, and participant observation at actual demonstrations.[29] Students at the Academy's 1973 Summer Session, for example, attended a CAP bank protest and got detailed lectures from Paul Booth on CAP's history and strategy. Academy students even sang old labor songs and put their own lyrics to others. "Show the targets we can beat them!" sang the students of '73.[30]

While Academy training had a lot to say about tactics, there was plenty of opportunity to introduce students to socialist ideas as well. A session on the "political science of organizations" dissected the inner workings not only of CAP and the National Organization of Women (NOW), but of "Communist Party fronts," "Socialist Workers Party fronts," and "agitprop" (Marxist abbreviation for "agitation and propaganda").[31] There were discussions of "movement history" and "class consciousness," as well. As time went on, the Academy put more emphasis on the history of the left, exposing students to veteran activists from the thirties, of which there were many in Chicago.[32]

The most entertaining bit of evidence for the ideological training going on at the Midwest Academy is a song created by Academy staffers as a sendoff for Steve Max when he had to leave Chicago for a time. The tribute to Max, highlighting his favorite theories, was to be sung to the tune of the Internationale, the communist-socialist anthem, and included the following lyrics: "Arise a left, no more we'll mourn/We'll organize for socialism/With anti-capitalist structural reform!"[33] Not only did the Midwest Academy's leaders approve of Gorz's theory of "non-reformist reforms," they actually set it to music.

So along with contemporary socialist theory, the communist and socialist history of community organizing was actively conveyed to Midwest Academy trainees. Steve Max, the son of a prominent American communist, could draw on his Communist Party heritage to drive home these lessons.[34] Yet Heather Booth was fully involved as well. She handled much of the Academy's continuing "socialism session," which included eight weekly units covering Marx, Engels, and Lenin, moving through a century of sectarian battles, and culminating with Michael Harrington's democratic socialism and the factional struggles of the SDS.[35]

Only some students would have attended the full socialism session, but Max's references to the communist and socialist past in the regular training sessions would have been more than enough to alert Academy students to the socialist background of community organizing. If some expressed interest in learning more about socialism, they were no doubt marked out as potential NAM recruits. For example, a "Director's Report" from June of 1974 indicates that many leaders of a group in-training from Iowa State NOW "say they are socialists of sorts."[36] Most groups had to pay for Midwest Academy training, but the Academy did sessions for both NAM and Michael Harrington's Democratic Socialist Organizing Committee (DSOC) for free.[37] In the Academy's fall 1974 session, five out of twenty-two students were members of NAM.[38]

Factional tensions between the Midwest Academy and NAM continued to cause problems, however. On the one hand, the Academy's leaders wanted to get as many NAMers as possible into their program, in the hope that this would convert the group to their more stealthy, patient, and pragmatic vision of socialism. On the other hand, Steve Max's letters show that he was nervous about having to train his fellow NAMers. Max feared that when NAM's hardliners got exposed to the Academy's more prudent approach to socialism, they'd respond by "forming a caucus to fight our revisionism."[39] So Max suggested that Booth invite their close ally Harry Boyte to come to Chicago from Minnesota to attend the NAM training session. As a founder and leader of NAM, Boyte could run interference for Max in case the hardliners attacked.

SECTION TWO

SOCIALIST STRUGGLE

All of which brings us to 1974–75, a time of chaos within NAM and change for the Midwest Academy. Around this time, a crisis-ridden NAM began to break apart.[40] Three years after the New American Movement's creation, there was no sign whatever of a socialist upsurge in the United States, much less a revolution. NAM was failing. But why?

For NAM's left wing, the answer was that an undisciplined group of quarreling "democratic socialists" had failed to present America's workers with a single clear and politically "correct" ideological "line." A newly formed "Marxist-Leninist Organizing Caucus" sought a return to classic Leninist party discipline and conversion of NAM into a tightly knit group, or "cadre" organization, of professional revolutionaries.[41] At the same time, on NAM's "right" (obviously a relative term), there was frustration at the organization's refusal to consider socialist ventures in electoral politics. Most NAMers insisted that participation in America's hopelessly bourgeois electoral system would mean co-optation by capitalism and betrayal of the revolution. That stance disappointed NAMers who believed that, over time, openly socialist ideas could win electoral battles. And we already know that members loyal to the Midwest Academy were exasperated by NAM's dismissal of community organizing ventures not publicly labeled as socialist.

A Socialist Crackup

The result of these differences was confrontation and schism on the left, and quiet departures on the "right." (Again, "right" in this context means "slightly less radically socialist.") Actually, we already encountered one of the sharpest internal confrontations in Chapter Three: the rift between communist and democratic-socialist community organizers in Cambridgeport, Massachusetts, in 1974. Recall that after failing to enlist the working-class residents of Cambridgeport in their protests, a group of community organizers in that town decided to drop their Alinskyite stealth and come out openly as socialists. Honest and enthusiastic socialist exhortation, they calculated, would bring in batches of working-class recruits, where Alinskyite stealth had failed. Their new socialist honesty, however, produced only ideological in-fighting, rejection by the blue-collar residents of Cambridgeport, and organizational collapse. NAM's records make it clear that this story, told at the head of *Let the People Decide*, Robert Fisher's influential history of community organizing, was intertwined with NAM's internal crisis—something Fisher never lets on.[42] The records of the Midwest Academy's organizing ventures, combined with the backstory of the Cambridgeport fiasco, make it clear that hidden socialist maneuvering stands behind a good deal of modern American community organizing.

On NAM's "right," the leaders of the Midwest Academy, Heather Booth and Steve Max, quietly left the organization around 1975, to ally instead with Michael Harrington's politically pragmatic Democratic Socialist Organizing Committee (DSOC).[43] Harry Boyte, a close ally of Booth and Max, and their co-author on the 1969 "Socialism and the Coming Decade" paper, remained in NAM but joined Harrington's DSOC as well.[44] Around the same time, John Judis (today a writer for the liberal *New Republic*) led a pro-electoral faction out of NAM.[45] This group soon clustered around the socialist periodical *In These Times*. In Judis's words, the *In These Times* faction believed that only electoral participation could build "a majority movement for socialism that would take over the government and establish a new society."[46] We saw in Chapter Two that Harold Washington's electoral success in Chicago in 1983 generated considerable optimism at *In These Times* about the prospects for a socialist-friendly electoral movement in the United States.

NAM's breakaway "right-wing" factions were pragmatic about advancing socialism in the present, yet remained radical in their vision of the future. At best, admitted Judis in 1974, openly socialist electoral victories would be but a prelude to a broader social revolution and probable "armed struggle."[47] In a 1975 address to a conference of socialist feminists, Heather Booth criticized her comrades as "in-grown, abstract, sectarian," and "isolated from the lives of most women."[48] Socialist feminism, Booth added, has become "more like a religion than like a movement for social change." As a model to emulate, Booth proposed Ralph Nader's step-by-step anti-corporate campaigns. To build a successful movement, Booth insisted, women need concrete victories, "collective actions . . . where they see the enemy cringe in front of their eyes." Yet Booth conceded that even the best community organizing strategy in the present could only prepare the battlefield, so to speak, for the inevitable revolutionary showdown of the future. Said Booth: "Truly reaching socialism or feminism will likely take a revolution that is in fact violent, a rupture with the old ways in which the current ruling class and elites are wiped out."[49] Heather Booth's willingness to contemplate the "wiping out" of America's "ruling class," even far in the future, is disturbing, to say the least. It also casts a suspicious light on the supposed moderation of "democratic" socialists. That said, the revolutionary commitment of seventies socialists like Judis and Booth matters less for our purposes than their determination to drag modern American socialism, kicking and screaming, into the heart of America's mainstream institutions.

The Midwest Academy group may have formally left NAM in 1975, but their goal remained unification of the old and new left under a more pragmatic banner—with community organizing at the center of a reformulated socialist project. Over several years, the Midwest Academy faction largely succeeded in engineering this shift. Michael Harrington's correspondence shows that Harry Boyte made the first move, writing Harrington in January of 1974 in hopes of initiating cooperation between Harrington's DSOC and NAM.[50] Steve Max's correspondence with Heather Booth shows that he also played a key role in arranging an eventual merger of the two groups.[51]

Committee of Correspondence

With all this talk of socialism, it's important to keep in mind that the Midwest Academy remained extremely cautious, not only about mentioning socialism in its public organizing, but also about too much socialist talk in front of the organizers they trained. Not every feminist or senior citizen activist was receptive to hard-left advocacy. So in 1977, the Academy set up a discreet "Committee of Correspondence" that would allow socialist community organizers to privately exchange ideas about the relationship between their work and their ideology.[52]

The records of this group show organizers grousing about how hard it is "to get people to make the leap from seeing how big banks and other businesses are ripping them off to seeing that such practices are inherent in our economic system."[53] There were also debates about the role of violence, if any, in a socialist seizure of state power. Stealth was another topic, as in this remark by an anonymous correspondent from Washington, D.C.: "If we initially start out by talking about reallocating wealth and power, let alone about 'socialism,' we will turn too many people off to build the kind of socialist mass movement we seek."[54]

It's tough to build a socialist mass movement without mentioning socialism. Yet that is exactly what these organizers were trying to do. The most difficult problem of all—highlighted in correspondence from Steve Max and Harry Boyte—was that "every social proposal that we make must be couched in terms of how it will strengthen capitalism."[55] This is a telling admission. While Max and Boyte long for the day when political taboos melt and they can argue for the Humphrey-Hawkins Full Employment Act in openly socialist terms, they effectively admit to manufacturing shaky free market rationalizations for measures they support on socialist grounds. So the Midwest Academy's confidential Committee of Correspondence proves that at least in some cases, deceptive socialist intentions really do stand behind legislation justified in the language of free enterprise.

The Ex-Communists

Meanwhile, in the late seventies, the influx of a small but highly influential group of ex-communists into NAM was pushing the revolutionary group toward conventional American politics. In particular, two veteran communists named Dorothy Healy and Max Gordon took the lead in arguing that NAMers had to rethink their opposition to acting within the Democratic Party.[56] Ripping into NAM's simplistic, purist, and anti-electoral interpretations of Marxism, Gordon pointed to explicit calls by Engels and Lenin for participation in American electoral politics. Real Marxists, Gordon insisted, work flexibly, never isolating themselves from the working class but joining in its struggles as a way of pulling the workers ever closer to socialism. In the United States, labor votes with the Democrats, so that's where NAM must be, said Gordon. These ex-communists had painful memories of their support for Henry Wallace's third-party campaign in 1948. That third-party venture had isolated the communists from their Democratic allies and left the party vulnerable to destruction in the fifties.

The ex-communists in NAM had been profoundly shaped by the "Popular Front" of the 1930s. During that period, America's communists dropped their openly revolutionary language and presented themselves as ordinary Americans instead. The Popular Front embraced American icons like Abraham Lincoln and the Founders, but moved to redefine them in de facto communist terms. The result was by far the greatest expansion the party had ever seen. The price paid was secrecy, as communists now worked through manipulation of mass-membership organizations ("front groups") they controlled on the sly.

NAM's ex-communists defended the Popular Front against attacks from purists who preferred openly revolutionary radicalism. Never were so many Americans drawn to socialism as during the Popular Front, these ex-communists pointed out. The Popular Front may have been short on Marxist jargon, but its democratic rhetoric and stealthy coalition-building worked, swelling the Communist Party of the 1930s to unprecedented proportions.

It's tough to strike a more-radical-than-thou pose against legendary veterans of the Communist Party. Slowly but surely, then, the combined pressure of organizational failure and the ex-communists' arguments began to push the remaining NAMers into cautious electoral experimentation, and ultimately into a merger with Michael Harrington's DSOC. Ironically, it took America's veteran communists to push the remnants of the SDS into the Democratic Party.

Harry Boyte

Between NAM's crisis of the mid-seventies and the merger of NAM and DSOC in the early eighties, a steady stream of manuscripts for comment flowed from Harry Boyte, an academic in Minnesota, to the leaders of the Midwest Academy. Boyte, a longtime community organizer who in 1969 had co-authored "Socialism and the Coming Decade," along with the Booths and Steve Max, was the unofficial big-picture theorist of the Midwest Academy. Through the latter part of the seventies and the early eighties, Boyte refined the Academy's concept of a stealthy brand of incremental socialism rooted in community organizing. As a founder of NAM and, after 1975, a leader of the DSOC as well, Boyte also played a central role in arranging the merger of these two socialist groups into the Democratic Socialists of America (DSA).

Boyte's struggle with his fellow NAMers during this period ran very much in parallel with the ex-communists who had recently joined the group. In 1975, Boyte began to explicitly defend the communist Popular Front period as the model for a workable socialist strategy. With its willingness to exchange socialist jargon for American democratic language, said Boyte, the Communist Party of the thirties successfully built a coalition with "progressive sections of the ruling class—those portions of the business elite which looked toward a modernized and efficient welfare state as the 'way out' of the economic crisis."[57] Also in 1975, years before the Midwest Academy turned in earnest to electoral politics, Boyte articulated a vision of a synergy between movement-based politicians and grassroots organizing. Boyte saw this short-term political plan as part of a long-term revolutionary strategy, and freely drew on Marx, Lenin, and Mao to make his points. Yet like the ex-communists in NAM, Boyte emphasized the "strategic and realistic" side of the great communist icons, rather than their more dogmatic themes.[58]

This "Popular Front" strategy had always been implicit in community organizing. Modern community organizations themselves can best be understood as miniature front groups—little coalitions crossing ideological lines but maneuvered from behind by socialist organizers. As seen above, some NAMers even used "front group" and "community organization" as virtual synonyms. It's no coincidence, then, that NAM's new direction was engineered by an alliance of community organizers and actual veterans of the communist Popular Front.

A Popular Front strategy means stealth, and this may have been the greatest sticking point between Boyte and his fellow NAMers. In 1977, Boyte was attacked by prominent socialist strategist Frank Ackerman, in NAM's internal "Discussion Bulletin," for his refusal to openly preach socialism. Many working-class young people will respond to socialist appeals, said Ackerman, "unless, of course, we deny our existence to them, the apparent strategy of closet socialist Alinskyites."[59] Boyte's response to the "closet socialist" charge was to grant the need for sophisticated socialist strategizing behind the scenes of a broader, populist style movement.[60]

Much of Boyte's theoretical work during this period grew out of his study of America's socialist past. Early in the twentieth century, America's Socialist Party generated substantial electoral support. Yet the greatest socialist successes of that era were products of stealth. Boyte pointed to example after example of early-nineteenth-century regional parties that used populist or communitarian, rather than socialist, language to describe their radical programs. Many candidates of these regional populist parties "had a Socialist Party background but had decided that the formal language of socialism would make little headway" with Americans. In other cases, said Boyte, "middle-class socialists . . . abandoned the linguistic purity of the Socialist Party," developed a communitarian vocabulary, and worked within the Democratic Party. Some of America's most "progressive" legislation of the thirties was enacted at the state level using this stealth socialist strategy, said Boyte.[61]

In 1980, as preparations for the NAM-DSOC merger were well underway, Boyte went so far as to lobby behind the scenes for the new organization, the Democratic Socialists of America, to drop the word "socialist" from its name.[62] Boyte hadn't turned against Marx, Lenin, or Mao, of course. His desire for stealth was based on simple realism about what the American public was willing to accept. Boyte pointed out that despite the DSOC's considerable influence within the Democratic Party, it was still "frozen out of media coverage" because of the "cultural sanction" against socialism. Boyte knew that there were already plenty of "anti-capitalist" organizations that for strictly practical reasons had decided not to call themselves socialist. He believed these groups might be prepared to join a unified NAM-DSOC if the new organization was willing to drop the word "socialist" from its name. Boyte and the members of his "communitarian caucus" pushed for an end to open socialism at the DSA through the mid-eighties, yet never quite managed to bring the majority of the DSA around to the idea. Nonetheless, Boyte's emerging vision of a large-scale populist movement pushed toward radicalism by discreet socialist leaders inspired his Midwest Academy colleagues to try something new.

SECTION THREE
─────────────────────────

A NATIONAL STRATEGY

In April 1978, at a gathering of nearly seventy labor and liberal groups in Washington, D.C., the Citizen/Labor Energy Coalition (C/LEC) was launched.[63] Formed ostensibly in response to the era's energy crisis, this group was pledged to fighting for lower gas and oil prices. In fact, this brainchild of Heather Booth's Midwest Academy and Michael Harrington's DSOC was created with far broader goals in mind. C/LEC was an initial attempt to build a nationwide populist movement, quietly directed by socialists, and specifically designed to unify and revive a fragmented American left. The sixties had divided patriotic and socially conservative unionists from a generation of radicals sympathetic to socialist revolution abroad and movements for feminism and gay liberation at home. Kicking off an anti-corporate battle over energy prices was a first attempt to heal this rift, while launching a full-spectrum movement of the left under effective socialist control. The idea was to unite the working and middle classes against American corporations, thus creating a majority coalition for progressive "social change."

In time, this neglected yet influential episode in American political history gave birth to a new way of linking socialism, community organizing, and electoral politics.

C/LEC's program embodied the pragmatic and incremental political strategy shared by Harrington's DSOC and the Midwest Academy. Heather Booth co-founded a group of socialist feminists in the early seventies, yet from 1978 on, she proved willing to subordinate her commitment to feminist radicalism to the larger and more workable project of assembling a populist coalition around economic issues. For the sake of making peace with their unionist allies, Booth and the other community organizers in C/LEC also agreed to avoid the question of nuclear power. Environmental activists loathed nuclear power, while unions looked forward to jobs in nuclear plants.

Legislative Socialism

Along with a pragmatic willingness to focus on issues that would unify the left, C/LEC's leaders experimented with a new way of fighting for socialism. Instead of following the classic Marxist playbook and demanding nationalization of the energy industry, C/LEC crafted a regulatory regime that would have effectively put this sector of the economy under government control. At the same time, C/LEC called for the creation of a publically owned energy corporation to provide "competition" for private oil companies.[64] C/LEC's strategy is a little-known but important precedent for President Obama's health-care plan, with its elaborate regulatory apparatus and "public option." The president's cap-and-trade proposal is reminiscent of C/LEC's program as well.

Critics of today's cap-and-trade bill sometimes claim that its advocates tout the prospect of global warming merely as a pretext for imposing socialist-inspired government controls on the energy sector. Whether that's so or not, however, socialism surely was the hidden motive behind C/LEC's legislative plans. Heather Booth and her allies at the DSOC were clearly using popular discontent with the energy crisis as a pretext to justify their long-standing desire to socialize the economy. It was obvious to most observers in the seventies that the energy crisis had been precipitated by the newly formed OPEC oil cartel. C/LEC largely ignored OPEC and blamed the crisis instead on the structure of America's energy industry. The plan was to channel consumer anger at rising energy prices into a step-by-step de facto nationalization process. As with today's energy battle, in public C/LEC emphasized solar energy and what we now call "green jobs." Yet this seems to have been something of a cover for C/LEC's top priorities: price controls and higher energy taxes. As with cap-and-trade today, C/LEC's call for higher energy taxes was stymied by the prospect that the oil industry would pass the cost along to the consumer.

C/LEC's program was laid out in the Citizens Energy Act, submitted to Congress by Representative Toby Moffett (D-CT) and Senator

Howard Metzenbaum (D-OH) in 1980. C/LEC never expected the bill to pass in its entirety. It was far too radical for that. Yet several of the Citizens Energy Act's provisions were written into law, and the remainder of the bill inspired a variety of grassroots campaigns managed by the Midwest Academy. The goal of these campaigns was to win a place for community organizations on local regulatory boards and utility commissions—very much at the heart of socialist strategy in the late seventies and eighties. So C/LEC gave substance to the vision of a coordinated and incremental national political strategy running from grassroots organizations to the halls of Congress, and controlled by socialists behind the scenes.

Front Group

While C/LEC didn't get everything it wanted, this populist coalition won a surprising number of legislative battles. It took the conservative think tanks five or six years to figure out what this new player on the scene was up to. Beginning in 1983, a series of think-tank reports on C/LEC began to piece together the story of the socialist leadership behind the populist facade.[65] Yet conservatives in the eighties had only a very partial sense of just how deeply socialist a venture C/LEC actually was. The think-tank reports largely focused on the Democratic Socialist Organizing Committee's (DSOC) outsized involvement in the coalition. But that was only the beginning.

C/LEC was jointly headed by Heather Booth and International Association of Machinists president William Winpisinger. Conservative policy experts had only the barest inkling of how profoundly socialist each of these leaders was.[66] It was duly noted that Winpisinger had once described himself as a "seat of the pants socialist," but that apparently casual remark could be dismissed. In fact, Winpisinger was a vice chair of the DSOC. As Michael Harrington's correspondence reveals, moreover, in his capacity as head of the Machinists, Winpisinger was a major—maybe *the* major—financial supporter of the DSOC.[67]

Winpisinger's well-camouflaged views are revealed in the September 1979 issue of DSOC's newsletter, *Democratic Left*. There he talks about using the frustration of consumers caught in gas lines to undermine the capitalist system. Despite his obvious support for the grassroots socialist strategy of the day, Winpisinger was something of an unreconstructed centralizing socialist. In the pages of *Democratic Left*, he calls for "socialist central planning," "mandatory price and profit controls," "mandatory controls on all forms of income," and "a guarantee that workers' real income will be permitted to rise incrementally each year." Winpisinger freely acknowledges that his vision of "centralized economic planning and controls" cannot "possibly be executed without encroaching on . . . traditional property rights." [68]

So the think-tankers were even more right about C/LEC than they realized. Not only was DSOC helping to run the show, but Winpisinger himself was a hard-edged socialist and a high official and key financial supporter of DSOC. And this is not to mention Winpisinger's co-leader, Heather Booth. Conservative policy wonks duly noted Booth's SDS history, but had little sense of what we've already seen: how very deeply her socialist ties and convictions ran.

What does any of this have to do with Barack Obama? A great deal. As we've seen, the resemblance between C/LEC's incremental socialist strategy and the Obama administration's major legislative initiatives is striking. Also, Obama worked closely with the very people who developed and implemented C/LEC's strategy. Midwest Academy records, for example, include a letter from C/LEC's administrative director, Ken Rolling, thanking Harry Boyte for letting him know that the DSOC board had just passed a resolution "in favor of adding consumer and labor representatives to the boards of energy corporations." Rolling promises to use the resolution as a talking point. [69]

So C/LEC really was a socialist front organization, conceived as a partnership between Michael Harrington's DSOC, the Midwest Academy, and the stealthy left of the labor movement. The C/LEC idea was inspired by Harry Boyte's vision of a majority left-populist movement, guided quietly behind the scenes by committed socialists. And the conscious template for this was the communist Popular Front of the thirties. Boyte himself helped to pass the strategic ideas from the DSOC, on whose board he served, to his colleagues at the Midwest Academy. The operation, moreover, was administered by Ken Rolling, a man who funded and then worked closely with Barack Obama for years. Rolling was by no means the only source from whom Obama could have learned the Midwest Academy's stealthy and incremental blend of socialism, community organizing, and national politics. Yet with a working relationship extending over fifteen years, Rolling was surely a very important conduit of the Midwest Academy's political expertise and perspective to Obama.

Conservative charges that C/LEC was determined "to withhold from the public its underlying philosophy and goals" never got much traction in the media.[70] If Harrington's DSOC was frustrated by the press's refusal to publicize their leverage within the Democratic Party, conservatives were equally stymied by media reluctance to entertain charges of dissembling by effectively socialist citizens' groups. In general, the media treated the socialism issue as too hot to handle.

I sympathize, since I downplayed the socialism question myself during the 2008 campaign. Yet an honest encounter with Obama's organizing background virtually compels a reconsideration of this cautious policy. It turns out that stealthy and incremental socialist legislative "conspiracies" really do exist, at least in the world Obama inhabited for years.

In April of 1980, a coalition of labor and citizens' groups that substantially overlapped with C/LEC sponsored "Big Business Day." The event was intended to kick off a populist anti-corporate movement, just as "Earth Day" had launched the environmental movement a decade earlier. The keystone of the day's events was the introduction in Congress of the "Corporate Democracy Act of 1980," another regulatory wish list designed to preserve the appearance of corporate independence while nationalizing America's businesses by degrees. Big Business Day's sponsors brazenly denied that socialism had anything to do with their plans: "Ultimately, then, the issue is not regulation vs. freedom. . . . Nor is it capitalism vs. socialism. It is autocracy vs. democracy."[71] This was nonsense, of course, given the pervasive presence of socialists among the event's sponsors. Yet it nicely illustrates the Popular Front–inspired substitution of democratic language for straightforward socialist advocacy.

The VISTA Battle

So by the late seventies, the Midwest Academy had initiated a "populist" strategy combining grassroots organizing with a national legislative program. Yet community groups continued to resist electoral involvement, fearing that electoral campaigns would drain energy from local agitation and undercut the ability of organizers to control events. It took the election of Ronald Reagan to erode the traditional reluctance of Alinksyite organizers to enter the electoral arena. The Midwest Academy was at the epicenter of that tactical change.

"Bread for organizers," that's all President Johnson's War on Poverty was good for, said the revolutionary radicals of the sixties. In the seventies, President Carter placed the VISTA program (Volunteers in Service to America), a surviving remnant of the original War on Poverty, in the de facto control of die-hard radicals from the sixties, once again making the federal government a ready source of "bread" for leftist political agitation. The capture of VISTA by the left was arranged, in part, by Midwest Academy, and it was the collapse of this scheme under Ronald Reagan that finally broke the resistance of the Academy and its network to electoral politics.

Heather Booth, along with ex-SDS leader Tom Hayden and his wife, Jane Fonda, were among the key figures recommending their friend Margery Tabankin to head the federal ACTION agency under Jimmy Carter.[72] ACTION helped dispense VISTA grants, and Tabankin quickly found a way to divert VISTA money from traditional "direct service" volunteering to her community organizer colleagues. Tabankin was a friend and collaborator of many leaders within the Midwest Academy network. In fact, it was Tabankin who first drew SDS veterans Paul Booth, Heather Booth, and Bob Creamer into their alliance with Saul Alinsky in the early seventies.[73] Tabankin had worked closely with ACORN as well. Shortly after her appointment in 1977, Tabankin arranged a series of meetings in Washington, D.C., with the nation's top community organizers—many of whom also happened to be her friends. Out of those meetings came a scheme for distributing VISTA grants directly to national networks like ACORN and the Midwest Academy. This new national program made it possible to circumvent state-level grant restrictions and successfully kept the system out of the public eye for a time.[74]

Within a couple of years, however, controversy exploded. A report prepared in 1978 and published in 1979 by the investigative staff of the House Appropriations Committee detailed a series of VISTA grant abuses—especially by ACORN and the Midwest Academy. In numerous instances, said the report, ACTION had failed to observe congressional guidelines for grants, many of which were awarded noncompetitively to Tabankin's personal network of organizing colleagues.

These problems might have slowed the Midwest Academy, but it was the election of Ronald Reagan in 1980 that threatened to bring the entire edifice of American community organizing—now thoroughly dependent on federal money—crashing down. Reagan appointee Thomas Pauken replaced Tabankin at ACTION and quickly set about investigating the Midwest Academy, C/LEC, and related organizations for possible abuse of their VISTA grants. Pauken also discovered the highly politicized tracts used to train VISTA personnel—Booth's socialist feminism essay, for example.[75] Midwest Academy files show Ken Rolling, in his capacity as C/LEC administrative director, resisting Pauken's inquiries with a series of counter-demands. A hand note to Rolling from one of the VISTA grantees under investigation says: "Keep up the good job of running them around in circles."[76] But with Midwest Academy personnel increasingly distracted by investigations,[77] and with the Reagan administration determined to slash funding for what it viewed as a hopelessly politicized VISTA program, Heather Booth began to re-think the reluctance of Alinskyite organizers to enter the electoral fray.[78]

Lane Evans and IPAC

C/LEC had always been intended as merely the first volley in a far larger attempt to bring a national dimension to community organizing. Alin-sky's early writings had envisioned a grand coalition of neighborhood "people's organizations" uniting to fundamentally change American society. Alinsky created CAP (the Midwest Academy's predecessor) as an initial stab at a city-wide coalition of neighborhood groups. Heather Booth's idea was to push the coalition-building to another level, cre-ating statewide assemblies of community organizations, then knitting them together into a national coalition. Linking this collection of grass-roots groups to organized labor, Booth believed, would create a power-ful national movement of the left. So beginning in 1979 and for several years thereafter, local affiliates of the Citizen/Labor Energy Coalition began turning themselves into multi-issue grassroots groups, orga-nized into state-wide units and gathered nationally under the banner of "Citizen Action."[79]

The most established and effective of these statewide Citizen Action groups was the Illinois Public Action Council (IPAC). IPAC had actu-ally been around since 1975, and was run by Bob Creamer, a close as-sociate of Heather and Paul Booth, and of the Midwest Academy. IPAC was effectively the Midwest Academy's action arm, as well as the model for a nation-wide Citizen Action coalition. It was through IPAC that Booth and Creamer began experimenting with a blend of community organizing and national electoral politics.

In 1982, the mid-term election of Ronald Reagan's first term, IPAC and the Midwest Academy systematically targeted a downstate con-gressional district that had voted Republican in every election but one since the Civil War.[80] The famous Reagan recovery was some years into the future, and this district was struggling economically. IPAC recruited a young, activist legal aid attorney, Lane Evans, to make the run as a Democrat.[81] IPAC then trained both Evans and his campaign staff and launched a district-wide informational canvass designed to help Evans. The Evans campaign's script could have been written by Harry Boyte. (Who knows? Maybe it actually was.) Evans ran as a populist, yet highlighted conservative and communitarian themes like family, faith, hard work, and patriotism. The difference was that Evans reinterpreted these values, always linking them to anti-corporate themes.[82] Once elected in this historically conservative district, Evans compiled one of the most anti-Reagan voting records in the House. On entering office, Evans also helped co-found the Congressional Populist Caucus, the hoped-for vehicle of a new national movement of the left.[83]

Was Evans's affinity for "populism" a cover for socialism? Evans certainly would not have called himself a socialist. Yet like Harold Washington, Evans worked closely with socialists, and was touted by both *In These Times* and the Chicago chapter of the Democratic Socialists of America (DSA).[84] Evans was one of seven congressmen affiliated with DSA's national "New Directions" coalition, and was singled out by Chicago DSA for special endorsement as "someone with whom we can work with on an ongoing basis."[85] Chicago DSA had two members working full-time on the Evans campaign, and Chicago's DSA newsletter called Evans "extremely progressive"—a description these socialists would not have used lightly.[86]

Behind the scenes, IPAC itself was dominated by socialists. According to a 1981 article in DSA's national newsletter, IPAC was in the process of shifting "from the usual reform targets of citizens groups (shut offs, street lights, metro fares) to naming, and questioning, the basic economic structure of the society."[87] A number of socialists served on IPAC's governing board. The founding national convention of Citizen Action (of which IPAC was the most powerful component) featured a well-received and openly socialist address by Michael Harrington.[88]

IPAC's program was filled with concrete legislative proposals, centering on various schemes for public ownership and wider distribution of "the fruits of production." A September 1983 *New York Times Magazine* piece on the Citizen Action phenomenon focused on IPAC. Said the *Times*: "At the heart of the movement is an element of class struggle."[89] The *Times* framed that struggle as "populist," but once you've read through the files of the Midwest Academy, the "populism" of IPAC and the Citizen Action network is revealed as an appealing public face for socialism.

A number of significant figures in Barack Obama's world had close ties to IPAC and the Midwest Academy. Obama's early mentor, Greg Galluzzo, organized for IPAC just before he and his wife Mary Gonzales founded UNO of Chicago.[90] Gonzales is listed in Midwest Academy files as a member of Citizen Action's national board in 1981, where she served alongside Heather Booth, Bob Creamer, and other Midwest Academy luminaries.[91] This was at the very time Gonzales and Galluzzo were founding UNO, and almost certainly means that UNO of Chicago was a member of the IPAC coalition. If so, the same would very likely have applied to Obama's own Developing Communities Project. IPAC's finance director, by the way, was a young fellow named Rahm Emanuel.[92] Whatever Emanuel's politics at the time, he would surely have understood that many IPAC members saw themselves as socialists guiding an overtly "populist" movement from behind.

On election night 2008, former Congressman Lane Evans, then battling Parkinson's Disease, was honored to be a guest in Barack Obama's hotel suite.[93] Obama has repeatedly expressed admiration for Evans, and even credited his 2004 Senate victory to Evans's early support. Yet the history of IPAC casts Obama's admiration of Evans in a new light. Evans was very much a creature of IPAC and the Midwest Academy. If Evans offered Obama a swift and critically important downstate endorsement in 2004, that was likely at the urging of Obama's former colleagues at IPAC and the Midwest Academy. In any case, Obama's longtime admiration for Evans may have less to do with that U.S. Senate endorsement, significant though it may have been at the time, than with what Lane Evans represents to Chicago's community organizers. Evans is the very model of successful synergy between grassroots organizing and national politics. Evans's "populist" stance enabled him to hold a historically conservative congressional district for twelve terms, all the while compiling one of the most liberal records in Congress. To Chicago's socialists, moreover, Evans was, at minimum, a fellow traveler, if not perhaps, more quietly, one of them.

John Ayers and Jan Schakowsky

From 1983 to 1986, Bill Ayers's brother, John Ayers, served on Lane Evans's congressional staff. It is possible that Evans and Ayers first connected through IPAC and the Midwest Academy. Recall that IPAC trained both Evans and his campaign staff, so IPAC was clearly in a position to suggest staffers to Evans as well. Heather Booth's personal correspondence contains a letter on House stationery from John Ayers, along with a card identifying him as Congressman Evans's "Special Projects Coordinator." Ayers had clearly met with Booth on several occasions, since he refers to their recent ninety-minute meeting by saying: "I always learn so much when I talk with you." [94]

Ayers writes Booth to arrange an Evans address to the Midwest Academy's annual summer retreat, but also to solicit Booth's input and cooperation in the just-forming Congressional Populist Caucus. In a hand-written memo accompanying his letter, Ayers explains who Heather Booth is to members and staffers of the Populist Caucus, and lets them know that she would like to address the group. Ayers explains to his colleagues that Booth hopes to involve the Congressional Populist Caucus in formulating an economic program designed to draw community organizations into local and national political campaigns. [95] In 1987, just after finishing his service with Congressman Evans in Washington, Ayers moved back to Chicago and connected with Obama. Lane Evans, John Ayers, the Midwest Academy, and Barack Obama all seem to have been part of the same political circle.

Although the extent of her direct ties to Barack Obama are unclear, it's worth noting that Congresswoman Jan Schakowsky, who represents Chicago's immediate northern suburbs, exemplifies the close ties between IPAC, the Midwest Academy, and the Chicago chapter of the Democratic Socialists of America. Schakowsky was program director of IPAC from 1976 to 1985, and directed its Utility and Energy campaigns during the C/LEC years.[96] On an application for a Midwest Academy administrative training session, she lists Heather Booth as a reference, jokingly calling Booth her mother.[97] Midwest Academy files include numerous letters from Booth thanking Schakowsky for helping to train students, during the seventies.[98] Documents from the mid-eighties list Schakowsky as one of the Academy's "associate trainers."[99] Schakowsky eventually married IPAC head Bob Creamer, and had worked closely years before on consumer campaigns with Jackie Kendall, a colleague and successor of Heather Booth as Midwest Academy director.[100] In short, Jan Schakowsky had close ties to the Midwest Academy's core leadership.

Files from the Chicago chapter of the Democratic Socialists of America show Schakowsky as an active member. For example, in the February/March issue of *Chicago Socialist,* Schakowsky reports on IPAC's annual conference, its role in the Evans campaign, its political program, and the continuing role of DSA members on IPAC's board.[101] A 1986 copy of *DSA News* reports on some of Schakowsky's initial electoral forays in a section titled "DSAers on the Move."[102] In Congress, Schakowsky has been a leading crusader for health-care reform and, as we saw in Chapter One, was featured in a famous video clip revealing the radical long-term ambitions of health-care-reform supporters.

The Secret Revealed

In 1982, just after the Democratic Socialists of America (DSA) was formed out of a merger of Michael Harrington's DSOC and NAM, DSA began publishing a "discussion bulletin" called *Socialist Forum.* This was to be a strictly internal periodical where DSAers could freely air ideas, disagreements, and sensitive information. The first issue of *Socialist Forum* featured "A Socialist's Guide to Citizen Action," by John Cameron.[103] Cameron, a staffer at IPAC and its national umbrella organization, Citizen Action, wanted to clue his new colleagues in to the socialist backstory of this growing political force. Essentially, Cameron was inviting his fellow socialists to join Citizen Action, while also subtly warning them away from attempts to turn the organization into an openly socialist entity. In other words, without quite using the term, Cameron was letting his colleagues know that Citizen Action was a socialist front group.

Cameron duly notes Citizen Action's overtly "neo-populist" ideology, but explains as well that "most of its key leaders probably consider themselves socialists." According to Cameron, many DSAers, especially in the Northeast and Midwest, "are part of Citizen Action—as staff or in other activist roles." The state-wide affiliates tend to be headed by ex–New Lefters, he adds. Cameron then explains Citizen Action's pragmatic avoidance of hot-button cultural and foreign policy issues, and notes its recent expansion into the electoral arena. Interestingly, Cameron describes Citizen Action's economic proposals as a "transitional program," socialist jargon for a program of gradual transition from capitalism to socialism. In short, Cameron used DSA's new discussion bulletin to reveal the socialist secret of Citizen Action.

About a year later, in 1983, DSA field director Leo Casey followed up with a still franker report on Citizen Action in *Socialist Forum*.[104] Casey argued that Citizen Action's electoral turn was pulling it toward an ever more open and across-the-board leftist position, little different from that of the DSA itself. Yet Casey also acknowledges Citizen Action's political reticence:

> In my estimation, the bulk of Citizen Action leadership would privately profess a socialist politics well within the DSA spectrum. A few have joined DSA and publicly identified themselves as members; Steve Max [the Midwest Academy's curriculum

director] is the most prominent example of this group. But for the most part, socialist sentiments are not expressed in public.[105]

Casey goes on to defend this policy of secrecy, noting that Citizen Action personnel have already been attacked for their SDS background, and could hardly afford to have their socialist views made public as well. In a fascinating passage, Casey goes on to explain how carefully Citizen Action's leadership monitors and controls its degree of public socialism:

> As Citizen Action has grown in size and influence, its leadership has grown more confident in assuming more progressive positions and less cautious about the presence of open socialists in its ranks. There were a number of indications at this year's Midwest Academy retreat—both in the form of public symbols and gestures (which are carefully thought through and chosen by the leadership) and in private conversations with key Citizen Action figures—that the general tenor of the leadership is to seek more cooperation and common work with DSA, and to welcome our participation in their organizations.[106]

Casey goes on to acknowledge problems with Citizen Action, including "staff domination" and "opaque political processes known only to an inner circle."[107] Nonetheless, Casey admits that DSA's openly socialist approach to coalition building isn't working very well, and gently hints that joining Citizen Action as its openly socialist wing may be a solution. In any case, it is abundantly clear from Cameron's and Casey's pieces that, although Citizen Action, its IPAC affiliate, and the Midwest Academy had made elaborate efforts to avoid being labeled as socialist front groups, that is exactly what they were.

John Cameron's piece ends by suggesting that Citizen Action's stealth and DSA's openly socialist approach represent two competing strategies for promoting "progressive social change in America."[108]

The verdict on which strategy will work, says Cameron, will take time to emerge. If DSA's openly socialist strategy had succeeded we would know about it, of course. Yet what if Citizen Action's stealthy strategy for socialist-inspired change had succeeded instead? How would we know it? There would be a popular alliance between grassroots groups and left-leaning labor unions, on the one hand, and successful "progressive" politicians affiliated with that movement, on the other. In this strategy, socialism per se would be active only behind the scenes of an overtly populist-communitarian progressive coalition.

This latter strategy was authored, above all, by Harry Boyte. Obama first encountered it in New York, where he likely read Boyte's books and watched Boyte debate his stealthy organizing strategy at the 1985 Socialist Scholars Conference. Although Boyte and his Midwest Academy allies, Heather Booth and Steve Max, succeeded in breaking NAM's revolutionary impatience—and in merging NAM with Harrington's more pragmatic DSOC—Boyte and his "communitarian caucus" ultimately failed to persuade the newly formed Democratic Socialists of America to abandon socialist language and adopt a full-on stealth strategy. Outside of DSA, however, Boyte and the Midwest Academy faction succeeded. Their stealthy plan to launch a populist-communitarian movement quietly directed from the background by socialists became the keystone of modern community organizing. Boyte, Booth, and Max had settled on this plan as far back as their original SDS manifesto in 1969.

Boyte, Booth, and Max surveyed their new movement in a co-authored 1986 book, *Citizen Action and the New American Populism*.[109] The book is filled with socialist ideas framed in populist-communitarian language:

> Populism revives the central view of economics articulated by our nation's founders . . . that all forms of economic enterprise and private property . . . are charges over which we are stewards for the broader community.[110]

They follow up these principles with proposals for worker representatives holding half the seats on corporate boards, legal restrictions on the movement of businesses, and the rest of the socialist program of the era.[111] Although co-authors Boyte, Booth, and Max were key figures in the development of modern American socialism, the subject of socialism never openly comes up in their book. As it was published by some of Chicago's most prominent community organizers in the midst of Obama's own Chicago organizing stint—during a time when Obama reportedly was "obsessively" reading material about his new profession—it's reasonable to assume that the future president read this book.[112] Given the extent of his contact with the Midwest Academy, it's also reasonable to assume that Obama understood perfectly well that behind the "new populism" lay socialism.

SECTION FOUR

THE OBAMA CONNECTION

In 2008, Harry Boyte was an advisor to the Obama presidential campaign.[113] In the summer of that year, Boyte completed a policy paper on "civil engagement" with co-author Carmen Sirianni, of Brandeis University. In other words, Boyte was helping to coordinate Obama's efforts to link his political success to grassroots movement building—very much a continuation of the Midwest Academy's political strategy. The text of the 2008 Boyte-Sirianni policy paper was personally approved by Barack Obama.[114] Sirianni, by the way, spoke at New York's Socialist Scholars Conferences from 1983 through 1985, when Obama was in New York. At the Cooper Union Conference, for example, Sirianni addressed the panel "After the Revolution: Marxism and Utopianism," and was listed in the program as the author of *Workers Councils and Socialist Democracy*. Who knows whether Obama may have run into Sirianni at those early conferences, but she was clearly a part of

Harry Boyte's socialist world. At any rate, Barack Obama's connection to Harry Boyte apparently runs from the days of the Socialist Scholars Conferences right up through the 2008 presidential campaign.

Chicago DSAer John Cameron, author of "A Socialist's Guide to Citizen Action," was also at the center of the alliance between Chicago's socialists and Mayor Harold Washington. In Chapter Two, I recounted the early relationship between Harold Washington and NAM, followed by the alliance between Washington and DSA during the mayoral campaign of 1983. Much of the material I drew on for that account was authored by John Cameron in various socialist publications. So it's of interest that in Sasha Abramsky's 2009 book, *Inside Obama's Brain*, Cameron is identified as both a "longtime staffer for Citizen Action" and an Obama colleague and fan.

According to Abramsky, Cameron first encountered Obama at a meeting in Obama's Illinois State Senate office.[115] It would appear, then, that during his Illinois State Senate years, Obama was working closely with Citizen Action by way of this prominent Chicago socialist. This is particularly important because we have no office records from Obama's State Senate years. During the 2008 campaign, the group Judicial Watch claimed that Obama had handled his State Senate records in such a way as to avoid leaving a "paper trail."[116] If Obama was hiding something, it was probably his close and continuing relationship with the radical community organizations he'd worked with for years prior to his political career. In any case, Obama's ties to Cameron and Citizen Action indicate ongoing links to the Midwest Academy network. From his position on the board of the Woods Fund, between 1993 and 2002, Obama also channeled money to the Midwest Academy for years. In cannot be said, therefore, that Obama's radical organizing background and socialist network were irrelevant to his later political career.

Sources ranging from Obama-friendly author Sasha Abramsky, to the indefatigable libertarian blogger Trevor Loudon, to *In These Times* journalist David Moberg confirm the close friendship and political alliance between longtime IPAC/Citizen Action legislative director

William McNary and Obama.[117] Loudon has also unearthed ties between McNary and Chicago's Democratic Socialists of America. Taken in isolation, Obama's links to radical activists like Cameron and McNary may seem insignificant. This perhaps is part of the reason why the investigations of Loudon and other bloggers into Obama's radical network have failed to gain wide notice. (It's also fair to say that some of these blogger-identified radical connections are either unconvincing or insignificant.) Situated in the broadest ideological, political, personal, and historical context, however, the dense network of ties between Obama and Chicago's radical left becomes more disturbing, not less.

Chicago in New York

Although Obama's many links to the Midwest Academy's network certainly grew exponentially when he moved to Chicago, the Academy's reach likely extended to Obama's New York years as well. We've seen evidence that Obama was studying Harry Boyte's writings during his NYPIRG organizing days. NYPIRG itself was part of the Midwest Academy network. Steve Max's letters to Heather Booth from New York include references to contacts with NYPIRG,[118] and NYPIRG leader Don Ross was an invited observer at the founding conference of Citizen Action.[119]

The "Social Movements" panel at the 1983 Cooper Union Socialist Scholars Conference may well have introduced Obama to his new profession of community organizing. That panel was organized by Peter Dreier, whose conference talk, I argued in Chapter Two, was probably worked up in an article Dreier published in the July 23, 1983, issue of *The Nation.* That article centers on Citizen Action's strategy of harnessing grassroots movements to the campaigns of politicians plucked from the ranks of community organizers. Dreier himself helped to train Midwest Academy students at a session in late 1978 or early 1979 and corresponded with Heather Booth at the time about ways to link community organizing and politics.[120] It's also of no small interest that Peter

Dreier was an advisor to Obama's 2008 presidential campaign.[121] John Atlas, Dreier's co-author on the *Nation* article, attended the Midwest Academy's summer 1983 retreat and caucused afterward with John Cameron, Leo Casey, and a large group of other DSAers present at the event.[122] These DSAers argued out the implications of the growing Citizen Action network for socialist strategy. So Obama's conversion to community organizing at the April 1983 Cooper Union Socialist Scholars Conference was inspired, in a sense, by the Midwest Academy's increasingly successful "neo-populist" (and covertly socialist) strategy. In the mid-eighties, the alliance between socialism and community organizing was the talk of the socialist world, and the Midwest Academy's new strategy was at the center of the excitement. This was the apparently intoxicating world that Obama entered at the Cooper Union in 1983.

Ken Rolling and Alice Palmer

As the Citizen Action network increasingly moved into electoral organizing, the leaders of the Midwest Academy realized that their strict focus on economic issues would be difficult to maintain. Supporting congressional candidates would inevitably raise issues of foreign and defense policy. So Citizen Action decided to experiment with organizing on these issues as well. The move into international issues was fraught with danger, not only of splitting the coalition, but also of publicly exposing Citizen Action's underlying socialism. Perhaps for these reasons, Citizen Action's foreign policy efforts never gained significant traction. Nonetheless, for at least a couple of years, from about 1984 through 1985, Citizen Action had an active foreign policy wing.

Citizen Action's International Affairs Committee was headed by two people who would go on to play important roles in Barack Obama's career: Ken Rolling and Alice Palmer. Rolling would someday supply funding for Obama's organizing ventures, would work with him on

Chicago school reform, would serve with him at the Woods Fund, and in the latter nineties would run the Chicago Annenberg Challenge under the leadership of Obama and Bill Ayers. Alice Palmer would go on from her work with Citizen Action to become an Illinois state senator representing Hyde Park and other sections of South Chicago. Eventually Palmer would select Obama as her political successor. Obama may well have had a direct connection to Palmer through the Midwest Academy. In any case, before choosing Obama as her political successor, Palmer would surely have received extended reports on his abilities and political leanings from her one-time partner Ken Rolling, and from her other Midwest Academy colleagues as well.

In 1984 and 1985, Rolling headed up the Citizen Action International Affairs Committee's efforts on Central America, while Palmer concentrated on South Africa. Rolling's Central America work for Citizen Action provides plenty of evidence for his socialist sympathies. Rolling, for example, represented Citizen Action and the Midwest Academy at a Chicago celebration of the sixth anniversary of the Nicaraguan Revolution. He also visited Nicaragua in August of 1984 with other Citizen Action leaders and staffers.[123] On that trip, Rolling and his group met with CDS, the Sandinista Defense Committee, "the largest community based organization in Nicaragua."[124] Rolling and the other Citizen Action delegates clearly saw these local Sandinista regime defense committees as the counterparts of their own community organizations in the United States. Literature in the Citizen Action International Affairs Committee files idealizes "neighborhood democracy" under the Sandinistas and acknowledges the Marxist character of the regime.[125] On meeting with Nicaragua's own neighborhood organizers, Rolling's delegation immediately moved to set up an exchange. Rolling then personally hosted Milagros Leyton, director of the Secretariat for International Relations for the Sandinista Defense Committee, during Leyton's visit to the summer 1985 Midwest Academy retreat. Leyton slept at Rolling's home, and along with participating in the retreat, visited IPAC's offices to meet and brief the staff.[126]

The Academy Retreats

There is an excellent chance that Obama himself attended this 1985 Midwest Academy retreat. The Academy's summer retreats were the Chicago counterpart of the New York Socialist Scholars Conferences, and there is substantial overlap between the panelists at both conclaves. In fact, too many characters mentioned elsewhere in this book spoke at the 1985 Midwest Academy retreat to list. Suffice it to say that attendance at this or future Midwest Academy retreats would have quickly introduced Obama to the full cast of characters of Chicago's socialist organizing world. Obama arrived in Chicago in June of 1985, just a month or two before the August 2–4 Academy retreat, which he surely would have wanted to attend.

Several panelists at the Midwest Academy's 1985 retreat deserve mention. Alice Palmer moderated a South Africa panel, a topic of long-standing interest to Obama, and could have struck up an immediate relationship with her future successor here. Also, Obama's key organizing mentors, Greg Galluzzo and his wife Mary Gonzales, headlined a panel on "Organizing Through Existing Institutions." With two of his new mentors lecturing on the topic of his own work, attendance at this session was probably obligatory for Obama. Harry Boyte spoke at this conference on "What It Means to be a Democratic Populist." Lane Evans addressed this and subsequent Academy retreats as well. The 1986 retreat featured a presentation by Jan Schakowsky and a joint Boyte-Booth-Max press conference on their just-published book, *Citizen Action and the New Populism*. Again, this only scratches the surface of the links between the networks outlined in this book and the list of presenters at the Midwest Academy's annual summer retreats.[127]

By the mid-eighties, Midwest Academy retreats and related conferences began to have an impact on the Democratic Party. National news accounts started portraying the Midwest Academy/Citizen Action network as the "progressive" rival of the centrist Democratic Leadership Council.[128] Harry Boyte's populist-communitarian ideas got some play in the press, and by the 1987 Midwest Academy retreat, all six official or prospective Democratic presidential candidates addressed the gathering.[129] The Midwest Academy was accumulating real political power. Their stealthy socialist strategy had succeeded where Michael Harrington's relative openness had failed.

The Campaign for Human Development

Indirectly, the Midwest Academy was responsible for funding Obama's Chicago organizing, which began in June of 1985. Key support for Obama's early work came in part from the Campaign for Human Development (CHD), probably the largest funding source for community organizing in the United States. Other early funding for Obama's organizing flowed from Chicago's Woods Charitable Fund, the left-leaning foundation on whose board Obama and Bill Ayers later served. In both cases, the Midwest Academy's Ken Rolling likely had a major role in dispensing this money.

Before taking on a leading administrative role at the Midwest Academy and its related ventures, Rolling earned a master's degree in theology from a pastoral seminary, and maintained close ties to the Catholic left.[130] In the late sixties, the Campaign for Human Development (nowadays renamed the Catholic Campaign for Human Development), grew out of Saul Alinsky's alliance with radical elements in the Catholic Church. Rolling served on CHD's National Committee, which advised on grant allocations, and Rolling would likely have had particular sway over grants to Chicago applicants. Rolling appears to have left CHD's National Committee sometime after 1985, probably to avoid any conflicts with his new administrative role at Chicago's Woods Fund. Rolling did consulting for Woods in 1985, helping to expand the foundation's support for community organizing to roughly double its earlier levels. By 1986, Rolling had joined Woods as program director and went on to a long career at that foundation—and a long partnership with Barack Obama. So by moving from CHD's National Committee to Woods in 1985–86, Rolling likely had a role in authorizing both of Obama's major early sources of funding.

While Rolling served on CHD's National Committee, he was also a top administrator for the Midwest Academy. And although Rolling formally left the Midwest Academy when he moved from part-time consulting for Woods to full-time employment, he likely remained a de facto force for the Midwest Academy's interests while working at Woods. Heather Booth certainly saw Rolling's move to the Woods Fund in this light, Academy files show.[131] Rolling is a good example of how the Midwest Academy has long supplied the infrastructure, so to speak, for much of American community organizing. When radical Catholics or left-leaning foundation leaders want to know which community organizers to support, they turn to the Midwest Academy for advice. As we saw, the Carter administration did the same thing when it wanted to know who to put in charge of the VISTA program. The Academy was the hidden hand guiding a great deal of financial support for community organizing in the seventies, eighties, and nineties, and Ken Rolling was point man for the Midwest Academy's efforts in this regard. Rolling was a big supporter of ex–Jesuit priest Greg Galluzzo, Obama's mentor and co-founder of both Chicago UNO and the Gamaliel Foundation. Initially, Rolling probably supported Obama as a Galluzzo protégé, although Rolling and Obama soon developed an independent relationship.

The Campaign for Human Development has long drawn intense criticism from traditional Catholics and conservatives.[132] CHD receives its many millions of funding dollars from a special church collection, usually held on the Sunday before Thanksgiving. Critics argue that parishioners have no idea that money they believe is going to traditional charitable activities is in fact supporting the radical politics and controversial tactics of groups like ACORN. On top of that, CHD-funded groups have sometimes supported practices that contradict Catholic teaching, like abortion or condom distribution. Critics also cite CHD for its scarcely disguised attacks on the free market and de facto involvement in partisan politics. Some say that CHD is socialist in all but name. Because the Midwest Academy worked hand in glove with CHD, its files contain an abundance of material validating these concerns. I'll restrict myself to a quick look at CHD's ideology, since Obama's CHD ties yield yet more evidence of covert socialism in his organizing network.

SOCIALIST HAND SIGNALS

Reading CHD documents of the mid-eighties is like playing charades. The secret word is "socialism," and CHD seems to be trying everything from stomping the ground, jumping up and down, and turning itself into a pretzel to convey what it sees as the answer to our nation's troubles, without actually saying "socialism." The basic assumption behind CHD, we are told, is that there are "serious structural flaws in the [capitalist] system," which suggest the need for "structural reform." [133] The answer is a new system of "social rights" in which "the freedom of the dominated takes priority over the liberty of the powerful." [134] Poverty cannot be transcended through middle-class success, because poverty itself is created by America's "economic system and political structures." The answer is to "go beyond the traditionally accepted claims of the free enterprise system." So what exactly is wrong with America's economic system? It "lacks fundamental planning for the good of all." [135] Or consider this tidbit from a speech to supporters by eighties CHD head (and former ACORN member) Reverend Marvin Mottet: "While some tout the merits of our system under the banner, 'democratic capitalism,' a more appropriate description might be 'democracy for capitalists.' " [136]

As we've seen, the files of the Midwest Academy overflow with undisguised socialism—meant for organizer eyes only. CHD's variation on this strategy was to come as close as possible to openly touting socialism, without ever actually uttering the forbidden word. This was partly to forestall criticism, but also because classic Catholic teaching supports the right to own private property. So explicit endorsement of socialism was not permitted. The CHD documents acknowledge this, yet also admit to actively promoting the long-term "socialization of property ownership."[137] In effect, then, CHD adopts the incremental strategy of modern democratic socialists: Work slowly from within the system, laying long-term foundations for the transition from capitalism to socialism. Subtleties and prevarications notwithstanding, once you dip into Midwest Academy files, the ideology that pervaded the upper echelons of the community organizing world—and that governed the funding of Obama's early work—is easy enough to identify. It's called socialism.

Obama's Academy Training

Evidence strongly suggests that Obama himself trained at the Midwest Academy. While Heather Booth retained ultimate control of the Academy for many years, she ceded command of day-to-day operations in 1977.[138] Jackie Kendall served as Midwest Academy director during Obama's early organizing years, and first met Obama shortly after his arrival in Chicago. Deeply impressed, Kendall remembers telling her husband:

> I just met somebody we're going to say we knew him when. He just had some quality about him, something special. I can count the number of times I've said that on one hand. It was just a presence and self-assurance about him at such a young age.[139]

Where did Kendall meet Obama and interact with him long enough to make such an assessment? It could have been at the 1985 Midwest Academy retreat, just after Obama's arrival in Chicago, but Kendall might also have encountered Obama at a Midwest Academy training session, which she and Steve Max jointly ran in those days.[140]

According to Sasha Abramsky's book *Inside Obama's Brain*, in the mid-1980s, Obama "went through a series of 'organizing schools' in Chicago," at the Gamaliel Foundation and other locales.[141] Other than Gamaliel, there were only two organizing schools in Chicago at the time, and the Midwest Academy was one of them. A "Midwest Academy Report to the Board" of July 1987 includes the following note: "In addition we worked with a new training institute in Chicago (Gamaliel Foundation) to help develop a training program for Church based organizations."[142]

In 1987, there was little to the Gamaliel Foundation beyond UNO of Chicago, Obama's Developing Communities Project, and the groups run by Obama's mentors Jerry Kellman and Mike Kruglik. As the head of one of Gamaliel's four groups, it seems very likely that Obama would have worked directly with the Midwest Academy to design the Gamaliel Foundation's new training program. This is all the more likely since, in late 1987 or early 1988, after Obama handed daily control of the Developing Communities Project to a successor, he spent time training Gamaliel organizers.[143] In other words, Obama himself was probably helping to run the organizer training program designed for Gamaliel by the Midwest Academy, and so would likely have worked closely with the Academy to draw that program up. Moreover, in an informal yet important sense, both Barack and Michelle Obama ultimately became officials, of sorts, for the Midwest Academy. To understand how that happened, let's return for a moment to one of Obama's early organizing mentors—and the man who recommended Obama for law school—John McKnight.

Public Allies

Midwest Academy files contain a couple of letters exchanged between McKnight and Heather Booth in 1978–79.[144] McKnight, a professor of urban affairs at Northwestern University, had invited Heather Booth to address one of his classes, and it's clear from their exchange that Booth and McKnight saw this classroom appearance as a venture in organizer recruitment. McKnight thanks Booth, calls her presentation "superb bait for the cause," and quotes a student praising Booth's "evangelical" tone. "It's clear that we'll recruit a few organizers from the quarter," says McKnight. Booth writes back asking McKnight to refer students to one of her workshops and explains that she has student intern positions available as well. The socialist flavor of the classroom exchange is clear, since Booth appends to her letter a reply to a student request for a definition of the word "cadre." ("Cadre" is socialist jargon for the inner leaders of a revolutionary movement.) Beyond revealing links between the Midwest Academy and one of Obama's mentors, this exchange helps explain the role Barack and Michelle Obama would eventually play in recruiting students to the Midwest Academy's training ventures.

In 1992, shortly after Barack Obama returned to Chicago from Harvard Law School, he joined the founding advisory board of a group called Public Allies. The archived files of the Midwest Academy do not extend to this date, unfortunately, but material on Public Allies is available from other sources. Documents outlining the early structure and purpose of Public Allies can be found in the archives of ACORN, housed at the Wisconsin Historical Society. Also, a limited number of early newsletters from the Chicago branch of Public Allies are preserved at the Chicago Historical Society. These and other records indicate that the Chicago chapter of Public Allies was an extension, of sorts, of the Midwest Academy. The core purpose of the Chicago Public Allies was to draw young people into community organizing, and clearly the Midwest Academy would have been able to use this organization as a recruiting mechanism.

Public Allies was founded by Vanessa Kirsch, a Democratic Party activist and leader of a network of "young progressive women."[145] Kirsch designed Public Allies to connect young people to left-leaning community organizations, non-profits, and government agencies. A stress on "diversity and multiculturalism" was common to the organization, but the three local pilot programs would each have a unique focus. The Washington branch would concentrate on placements in government, for example, while the Chicago program would focus on drawing young people into community organizing.[146] Heather Booth, then in Washington, D.C., was on the founding board of Public Allies. The only two board members then resident in Chicago were Midwest Academy director Jackie Kendall and Barack Obama, identified in 1992 as a "writer" (presumably because he was working on *Dreams from My Father*).[147]

In short, The Chicago branch of Public Allies was a sort of extension of the Midwest Academy. In fact, an early notice in a periodical for Chicago organizers instructs interested parties to write Public Allies care of the Midwest Academy.[148]

While we lack detailed Midwest Academy records from this period, a Chicago community organizer named Mark S. Allen provides some information of interest. After working with Obama during the future president's initial Chicago organizing stint, Allen says:

> I went away to college and got my first paid community organizer job with a group called CITIZEN ACTION and Midwest Academy and worked directly under the leadership of women named Heather Booth and Jackie Kendall. It was through the Midwest Academy that I would later get more insight into the leadership of Michelle Obama in that the Academy would be a partner in working with Michelle Obama and the group PUBLIC ALLIES in training young people for public service.[149]

How exactly did Public Allies and the Midwest Academy work together?

Public Allies Chicago had two core programs, each of which appear to have been linked to the Midwest Academy. Every year, Public Allies would recruit thirty or so young people between the ages of eighteen and thirty and place them in ten-month apprenticeships at various community organizations.[150] Some of these groups might appear relatively apolitical (eg., the Girl Scouts), while others fit the model of Alinskyite community organizations.[151] The apprentices, called "Allies," would receive "training in a variety of workshops relating to social change and community development." They would also attend lectures and meet an extensive network of community leaders working for "social change." [152] These apprentices were also broken up into teams and assigned to work and train with various members of the Public Allies Advisory Board.[153] In a second program, Public Allies would recruit up to one hundred additional young adults to be honored as one of "Tomorrow's Leaders Today." [154] As part of the selection process for this award, prospective honorees participated in "training workshops on social issues" and were connected to a "network of resources." [155]

In short, Public Allies functioned as a training and recruitment funnel into the Midwest Academy network. Young activists would cycle through the programs, receive Midwest Academy training, and no doubt would be privately assessed by Academy leaders in the process. A few of the most promising recruits would surely have been approached after initial training to involve themselves more deeply in the Midwest Academy's ventures.

Barack Obama was a member of the original Public Allies national board of directors.[156] After persuading the board (really, Heather Booth and Jackie Kendall of the Midwest Academy) to hire Michelle to head the Chicago office, Obama stepped aside to avoid a conflict of interest.[157] Yet Barack did eventually become a member of the Public Allies Chicago Advisory Board, along with current presidential aide Valerie Jarrett and several other figures of interest. Midwest Academy director Jackie Kendall was on the Chicago Public Allies Advisory Board, along with John "Jody" Kretzmann and Jacky Grimshaw.[158]

Kendall, Kretzmann, Grimshaw

Jackie Kendall, we've seen, likely helped to train Obama when he first moved to Chicago. Beginning in 1982, Kendall took charge of the Midwest Academy's day-to-day operations.[159] In recognition of her work at the Midwest Academy, in 1999 Kendall received the Debs-Thomas-Harrington award, the annual honor conferred by the Chicago chapter of the Democratic Socialists of America.[160] Kendall not only worked closely with Barack and Michelle during their time at Public Allies, but was part of the team that developed the 2007 training program at "Camp Obama" for volunteers going into Iowa.[161] Obama's win in the 2008 Iowa Caucuses, of course, was the critical turning point in his fledgling presidential campaign.

In the early nineties, John Kretzmann was project director of the Center for Urban Affairs and Policy Research at Northwestern University. There Kretzmann was a close colleague of, and frequent co-author with, John McKnight, another key Obama mentor and the man who recommended Obama for law school. Obama closely studied the jointly authored work of Kretzmann and McKnight. The vision of community organizing sketched out by these two authors was effectively a guidebook to the socialist organizing strategy of the day. McKnight, an admirer of some of the Swedish welfare state's most radical plans, also worked closely with prominent socialist Quentin Young on health-care policy. Kretzmann and McKnight formed a special institute for community organizing at Northwestern, which was closely linked to Public Allies. In fact, Michelle Obama was an original faculty member of Kretzmann-McKnight's community organizing institute.[162] Obviously, then, McKnight and Booth found a way to regularize the recruiting relationship they tentatively began back in 1978, when Heather Booth enthusiastically addressed McKnight's class—introducing them to the socialist term "cadre" in the process.

Yet another player of note here is Jacky (sometimes Jackie) Grimshaw. Grimshaw, a longtime top political aide to Mayor Harold Washington, was also on the Public Allies Advisory Board, and sits today on the Midwest Academy board of directors as well.[163] Grimshaw is a longtime colleague of Heather Booth. Grimshaw is also the Obamas' next-door neighbor in Chicago, and it's obvious from Sasha Abramsky's book *Inside Obama's Brain* that the Grimshaw and Obama families are close.[164] Along with Michelle, Barack was very active in Public Allies, lecturing recruits and helping to train them in community organizing.[165] In a sense, through Public Allies, Barack Obama himself became a Midwest Academy trainer. Since the Public Allies Advisory Board was heavily involved in the actual training, both Obamas would have worked closely with Grimshaw, as well as Kendall and Kretzmann, in the early nineties.

In 1987, Grimshaw and Heather Booth were jointly honored with the Debs-Thomas award by the Chicago Democratic Socialists of America. The Midwest Academy files contain Heather Booth's speech from that award ceremony, from which it is clear that Booth worked directly under Grimshaw on Harold Washington's 1987 re-election campaign—another example of the electoral alliance between Chicago's socialists and the Harold Washington administration.[166] Grimshaw and Heather Booth also participated in public speaking events under the sponsorship of Chicago DSA.[167] Given the fact that Grimshaw currently sits with Heather and Paul Booth and Jackie Kendall on the Midwest Academy board of directors, Grimshaw's ties to Booth and the Academy have clearly only deepened with time. We also now know that it was Grimshaw, along with other Chicago community organizers (probably including Booth), whose recommendation secured Barack Obama's post at the head of Illinois Project Vote in 1992.[168] In sum, both Barack and Michelle Obama have close and longstanding ties to a thoroughly socialist network of community organizers, politicians, and political activists centered on the Midwest Academy.

Robert Creamer

The most interesting connection of all between the Midwest Academy and the Obama administration may run through Robert Creamer, a member of the Academy's founding board and one-time head of the Illinois Public Action Council (IPAC), the oldest and most important group in the Academy's Citizen Action network. As we've seen, IPAC was also the very model of a socialist-controlled community organizing front group. To this point, I've used the name "Bob" Creamer, taking my lead from the many familiar references in the Midwest Academy Records. Now, however, Robert Creamer offers a running commentary on the Obama administration at a popular liberal blogsite, the Huffington Post. Creamer is also a powerful political consultant, with a list of clients that includes ACORN, the SEIU, and the Democratic Congressional Campaign Committee.[169] He has, as well, served a prison term after pleading guilty to tax evasion and bank fraud.[170]

The Creamer-Obama link has already been highlighted by some of the Obama administration's most vociferous critics.[171] It's been noted that this Democratic strategist with a criminal record was an organizing instructor at Camp Obama during the 2008 presidential campaign. The book Creamer wrote while in prison, *Listen to Your Mother: Stand Up Straight! How Progressives Can Win,* is often credited with shaping the administration's strategy on health-care reform. Creamer was an important early advocate of what we now call the healthcare "public option," clearly an idea along the lines of C/LEC's public energy corporation. As an influential health-care reform strategist in Congress, Creamer's wife, Representative Jan Schakowsky, has certainly had plenty of opportunities to carry his ideas to the highest political levels. It's also of interest that Creamer's book carries endorsements from Obama mentor and UNO of Chicago co-founder Greg Galluzzo, and from SEIU head and frequent White House visitor Andrew Stern.[172]

Most intriguing of all, Creamer seems to have ties to top Obama advisor David Axelrod. Axelrod contributed a blurb to Creamer's 2007 book, endorsing it as a "blueprint for future victories."[173] Axelrod was also one of many left-leaning politicos who submitted friendly letters to the court when Creamer came up for sentencing in 2006.[174] At his Huffington Post blog, Creamer has expressed strong confidence in Axelrod's commitment to "fundamental progressive change."[175] It would at least appear that one of the most powerful leaders of the Midwest

Academy and its associated network has considerable connections to, and influence on, the course of the Obama administration.

While Creamer's critics have pointed to his criminal record, his Alinskyite radicalism, and his apparent influence on some of the key figures formulating the administration's health-care reform strategy, the earlier history linking both Creamer and Obama to the Midwest Academy and its stealthily socialist organizing empire is not well understood.

Everybody Knew

Is it conceivable that Obama could have been ignorant of the socialist politics shared by his many colleagues from the Midwest Academy network? No, it is not. Obama had to know that his mentors and colleagues were socialists. We know from an Occidental College acquaintance that Obama was a hard-core Marxist-Leninist in 1980. By 1983 he had entered the world of democratic socialism and, through it, the profession of community organizing. Given Obama's experience at New York's Socialist Scholars Conferences, and his voracious reading on "revolutionary" topics in the mid-eighties, he would have recognized the signs of socialism all around him.

At the 1987 Midwest Academy retreat, which Obama could easily have attended, Jackie Kendall introduced Heather Booth to the crowd by mentioning the Debs-Thomas award Booth had just received.[176] (The award was named after the American Socialist Party leaders, Eugene V. Debs and Norman Thomas.) Obama would certainly have understood the socialist reference. This is simply one example of what would have been many such references over the years. Barack Obama almost surely had Midwest Academy training, which we know touched frequently on socialist topics. In fact, in conjunction with Public Allies, Obama himself effectively became a Midwest Academy trainer.

Could the Midwest Academy and its circle have accepted and promoted Barack Obama to so high a level if they had not been confident of his socialist leanings? That seems next to impossible. We've seen how sensitive the Academy was about public exposure of its socialism. Recall that even a prominent socialist observer like Leo Casey referred to the Academy's "opaque political processes known only to an inner circle." Barack and Michelle Obama were part of that inner circle. They had to be trusted to get inside. Midwest Academy staffers entertain each other by making up songs about Marxist theory. Obviously, anyone admitted to this charmed circle would have to be reliable. Choosing Obama for the original Public Allies board of directors was an act of trust. So was accepting Barack's recommendation of Michelle to direct the Chicago chapter of Public Allies. Sitting together on a small board and working closely together in the Public Allies organizer training program would have required political compatibility.

The socialist sympathies of State Senator Alice Palmer are similarly not in doubt.[177] Why did she choose Obama as her political successor in 1995? Palmer was a Midwest Academy veteran and could easily have tapped her ex-colleagues Ken Rolling, Heather Booth, and Jackie Kendall for an assessment of Obama's politics, based on years of joint work. Would Palmer and her network have accepted Obama as her successor if they had not been confident of his socialist leanings? Palmer and her Midwest Academy circle were savvy and tactically ruthless socialist ideologues. It's tough to imagine them surrendering Hyde Park's State Senate seat to someone who was not "one of them." We know that Obama had to win Palmer's approval in a series of meetings in the late spring of 1995, where he would have presented to her his progressive bona fides.[178] Surely Obama himself would have pointed Palmer to her old colleague Ken Rolling and the rest of the Midwest Academy network to vouch for him.

We know that Palmer introduced Obama as her successor at a get-together at the home of Bill Ayers and Bernardine Dohrn. Ayers was a self-confessed "small c communist" who was even then managing an education foundation in partnership with Obama. Dohrn was a life-long socialist. Palmer was a socialist veteran of the Midwest Academy, and may well have known Obama for years through the Academy retreats and her colleagues there. At a minimum, Palmer's socialist colleagues would have provided a full history of Obama. Prominent DSA leader Quentin Young was also present that day.[179] Young would have had access to his close colleague John McKnight's assessment of Obama, based on years of cooperation.

In sum, Obama was anointed Alice Palmer's political successor by a roomful of socialists, each of whom had access to an enormous amount of information about his deepest political convictions. The obvious implication of all this is that Obama was chosen to succeed Alice Palmer in the Illinois State Senate because, like Palmer and her close political circle, Obama was a socialist.

The story of the Midwest Academy reveals the hidden truth about Barack Obama's politics—and more. In a sense, the Academy's history is a tale of the quiet radicalization of the Democratic Party. Heather Booth went on from the Academy to serve the Democratic Party in various capacities.[180] In 1993, after decades of playing defense, the election of Bill Clinton made it possible for Booth to assertively fight for her top priority. Booth joined the Democratic National Committee as the national outreach coordinator of the battle for the Clinton health-care plan.[181] Considerable overlap exists between the socialist program of "change" for America and the most sweeping proposals of the Democratic Party. In the eighties and nineties, socialists found a comfortable—and quiet—way to fight for their preferred policy outcomes within the Democratic Party. Barack Obama, evidence strongly suggests, was one of them.

CHAPTER 6

ACORN

SECTION ONE

ACORN'S SOCIALISM

Prior to its recent troubles, ACORN (The Association of Community Organizations for Reform Now) was the largest and most influential community organization in the United States.[1]

Among other activities, ACORN was notorious for fraudulent voter registrations, in-your-face protest tactics, alleged abuse of government funds, and helping to precipitate the banking crisis of 2008. ACORN presents itself as a pragmatic "action organization," democratic in structure and devoted to producing concrete results for poor people.[2] In fact, however, as this chapter will show, ACORN is a classic social-ist front group. ACORN is a variation on the "new populist" model: a broadly leftist "mass organization" guided quietly from behind by socialists.

Secrecy and Crisis

Barack Obama understands this. As far back as his introduction to
community organizing at the Cooper Union Socialist Scholars Conference of 1983, Obama grasped the socialist backstory of his chosen profession. Obama's ties to ACORN are broad, deep, longstanding, and
intimate. Behind the scenes, ACORN worked cooperatively with leaders of the Midwest Academy and other figures from the socialist networks laid out in this book. ACORN was part and parcel of Obama's
socialist world.

For that reason, Obama's attempts to minimize and deny his
ACORN connection during the 2008 campaign were both deceptive and in bad faith. Although enough information has been publicly
available since 2008 to show this, new material from the archived files
of ACORN at the Wisconsin Historical Society decisively proves the
point. This new documentary evidence sheds considerable additional
light on Obama's relationship to ACORN. The truth about ACORN—
and about Obama's extensive ties to this group—provides yet more evidence that the president of the United States may indeed be a socialist.

The extraordinary repository of internal ACORN documents at
the Wisconsin Historical Society allows us to reconstruct the history
of this controversial group. Arguably, Barack Obama is president today because of the financial crisis that erupted during the 2008 presidential campaign. How remarkable it would be if ACORN did in fact
have a significant role in precipitating that crisis—and if Obama misled
the country during the campaign about the nature of his ties to that
group. Evidence strongly suggests that both of these things are true. In
the eighties and nineties, ACORN helped drag America's banking system into the business of subprime lending. During these same decades,
Obama did everything in his power to support ACORN's work.

Subprime

The problem of ACORN's role in the financial meltdown raises the complex issue of the place of economic crises in American socialist strategy. The question is not merely whether ACORN's banking campaign precipitated the financial crisis, but whether the group's socialist sponsors may actually have intended to do so—by a variation on the strategy of "orchestrated crisis" laid out by longtime ACORN advisors Richard Cloward and Frances Fox Piven in the sixties.[3] It is very unlikely, I think, that ACORN could have anticipated the path by which its banking campaign helped to destabilize America's financial system. In a more general sense, however, there is a relationship between the phenomenon of financial crisis and the actions—and intentions—of ACORN and its socialist advisors.

It would be a mistake to treat the question of ACORN's socialism as if it were somehow separate from this group's troubling tactics, or its assault on America's banking system. On the contrary, ACORN is important because, more than any other community organization, it succeeded in putting the model of de facto socialization of the economy "from below" into practice. By combining locally based campaigns against banks with a sophisticated national lobbying operation, ACORN managed to gain significant influence over a core sector of the American economy. While I don't expect to resolve the question of the precise degree of ACORN's responsibility for the financial crisis that began in September 2008 here, new evidence from the Wisconsin archives suggests that the group's effect was substantial. More than we've known, ACORN served as a catalyst for the spread of risky subprime mortgage lending throughout the financial system. As we trace the history of Barack Obama's ties to ACORN, the inside story of ACORN's role in the rise of subprime lending will unfold side by side. Obama's support for ACORN deepened as ACORN's involvement in the banking system grew. (The accompanying charts should help to clarify the history and organizational ties in question.)

Project Vote 1992

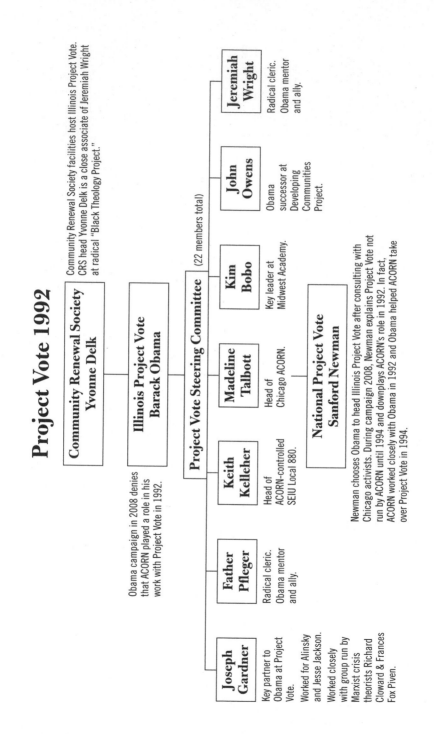

Community Renewal Society
Yvonne Delk

Community Renewal Society facilities host Illinois Project Vote. CRS head Yvonne Delk is a close associate of Jeremiah Wright at radical "Black Theology Project."

Illinois Project Vote
Barack Obama

Obama campaign in 2008 denies that ACORN played a role in his work with Project Vote in 1992.

Project Vote Steering Committee   (22 members total)

Joseph Gardner

Key partner to Obama at Project Vote.

Worked for Alinsky and Jesse Jackson.

Worked closely with group run by Marxist crisis theorists Richard Cloward & Frances Fox Piven.

Father Pfleger

Radical cleric. Obama mentor and ally.

Keith Kelleher

Head of ACORN-controlled SEIU Local 880.

Madeline Talbott

Head of Chicago ACORN.

Kim Bobo

Key leader at Midwest Academy.

John Owens

Obama successor at Developing Communities Project.

Jeremiah Wright

Radical cleric. Obama mentor and ally.

National Project Vote
Sanford Newman

Newman chooses Obama to head Illinois Project Vote after consulting with Chicago activists. During campaign 2008, Newman explains Project Vote not run by ACORN until 1994 and downplays ACORN's role in 1992. In fact, ACORN worked closely with Obama in 1992 and Obama helped ACORN take over Project Vote in 1994.

ACORN's History and Banking Campaign

National Welfare Rights Organization

1966–1969

ACORN's predecessor group, guided by Marxist "crisis strategists" Richard Cloward and Frances Fox Piven. Cloward and Piven remain closely tied to ACORN.

ACORN Founded

1970

Wade Rathke founds ACORN in Arkansas. Sees ACORN as successor to socialist Arkansas group from 1930s.

People's Platform

1978–1979

ACORN issues de facto socialist platform as part of entry into national politics. Works with socialists at Democratic Party.

ACORN Theorizes

1979

ACORN leadership, apparently inspired by Marxist theorist André Gorz, pledges to take advantage of crisis to transform society.

Squatting

1983–1985

ACORN enters Chicago in 1983. Begins to seize abandoned homes to give to members. ACORN leader says this shows ACORN's lack of belief in private property.

Banking Campaign Early Stages

Mid-1980s

ACORN learns to block bank mergers with housing discrimination complaints. Pressures banks to cooperate with its loan counseling program.

S&L Bailout Leads to ACORN-Friendly Legislation

1989

ACORN eager to take advantage of banking crisis to get legislative backing for its loan counseling program. ACORN lobbyists tip close votes and win major victories.

GSE Act Citibank Campaign Clinton Contacts

1992

Democrats let ACORN write key legislation pulling Fannie Mae and Freddie Mac into subprime-loan business. ACORN launches aggressive campaign against Citibank. Chicago ACORN pressures Fannie Mae to support its housing program. Socialist crisis theorist Peter Dreier works with ACORN, Midwest Academy, and incoming Clinton team.

Clinton Administration

1993

ACORN works to get subprime lending spread throughout entire financial system. Gains wide access to top Clinton officials. HUD Secretary Cisneros helps ACORN and offers it government money. ACORN devises schemes to hide the money trail.

ACORN Meets with Clinton

1994

ACORN meets with President Clinton, who promises to use executive, rather than legislative, means to spread subprime lending far beyond parts of banking system covered by the Community Reinvestment Act. Evidence that fear of ACORN-sponsored legislation pressured "non-banks" into "voluntary" subprime lending. Clinton promises to amplify the pressure.

Obama and ACORN 1992–96

Motor-Voter Lawsuit
Barack Obama

Obama serves as lead attorney for ACORN in suit to force Illinois to implement the federal "Motor-Voter" law. This is the only ACORN tie Obama would acknowledge during campaign of 2008. Evidence suggests he also consults with HumanSERVE group created by Marxist theorists Richard Cloward and Frances Fox Piven.

Small Schools
Madeline Talbott
Bill Ayers

Chicago ACORN head Madeline Talbott works with Bill Ayers to create ACORN-controlled mini-schools. Obama works with Ayers to fund this program.

Banking Campaign
Madeline Talbott

Chicago ACORN launches bitter attack on Citibank in 1992. Obama sues Citibank for housing discrimination in 1994. Obama works to increase funding for ACORN at Woods Fund of Chicago, with a report that reveals knowledge of organizer attacks on local businesses.

Illinois Project Vote
Keith Kelleher
Carol Harwell?

Obama puts Madeline Talbott and Keith Kelleher on Project Vote steering committee in 1992. ACORN takes over Project Vote in 1994. Registration drives likely meant to help New Party candidates. Obama briefs new national Project Vote head Leslie Watson-Davis on the transition and offers to help raise money for the ACORN-controlled group. Obama also pressures Keith Kelleher to put his future campaign manager, Carol Harwell, on Project Vote executive committee.

Progressive Chicago
Keith Kelleher

Progressive Chicago is a "front group" for the New Party. It allows progressives to indirectly help the New Party without alienating Democrats. Keith Kelleher tries to draw Obama into the New Party via Progressive Chicago. Obama is receptive. Top Obama aide Carol Harwell works closely with Progressive Chicago, perhaps to lay groundwork for New Party endorsement of Obama.

New Party
Madeline Talbott

New Party in Chicago controlled by ACORN and SEIU Local 880. A substantial number of Democratic Socialists of America also in party. New Party program is de facto socialist. Obama seeks and gets New Party endorsement in first run for office. Endorsement requires candidates to join the New Party. Evidence strongly suggests Obama offered to do free legal work for New Party.

Chicago ACORN

ACORN Proper	SEIU Local 880
Madeline Talbott	Keith Kelleher

Obama helps obtain funding for ACORN from Woods Fund of Chicago and, in cooperation with Bill Ayers, from the Chicago Annenberg Challenge. Obama helps train ACORN leaders in yearly seminars. ACORN members work in Obama's election campaigns.

Front Group

The idea that ACORN is a socialist front group is hardly unprecedented, including among socialists. An influential theorist of community organizing has made largely the same claim. In his 1980 essay "Socialist Incubators" Peter Dreier argued that a variety of community organizations—ACORN prominent among them—were pushing a series of concrete reforms that added up to a step-by-step socialist program for the United States, even if that fact hadn't yet dawned on the full membership of these groups.[4] A leading figure in the Democratic Socialists of America, Dreier went on to develop an influential behind-the-scenes relationship with ACORN, helping to guide the group's assault on the banking system.

The pattern here reaches back to ACORN's predecessor group from the sixties, the National Welfare Rights Organization (NWRO). Marxist theorists Richard Cloward and Frances Fox Piven helped to found that group and guided it with a strategy derived from communist organizing techniques of the 1930s. NWRO sought a socialist transformation of the United States. The idea was to flood state and local welfare systems with more applicants than they could possibly afford to carry. Cloward and Piven believed that this "break the bank" strategy would force President Johnson and a liberal Democratic Congress to bail out overburdened state welfare systems with a federally guaranteed annual income.[5]

Yet Cloward and Piven weren't particularly interested in open socialist proselytism. True, they believed that as welfare recipients shed traditional American notions of self-sufficiency and learned to demand government support as their right, a kind of de facto anti-capitalist mentality would take hold. For Cloward and Piven, however, socialist transformation depended less on conscious ideological conversion of the poor than on stoking their sense of entitlement and rage. This picture—of sophisticated Marxist strategists guiding activist organizers (some socialist and some not) and a larger body of ideologically unselfconscious members—is the very image of a socialist front group.

Going Semi-Public

ACORN carried this pattern forward to the seventies and beyond, although the new organization was vastly more cautious about advertising its socialist subtext than NWRO had been. Cloward and Piven published their famous "break the bank" strategy openly in *The Nation* magazine in 1966, and explained their Communist-inspired machinations in detail in their 1977 book, *Poor People's Movements: Why They Succeed, How They Fail*.[6] These two socialist strategists continued to advise ACORN behind the scenes, along with socialist colleagues like Dreier.[7] In the eighties and nineties, however, you'd need to attend a Socialist Scholars Conference or read an obscure journal like *Social Policy* to grasp the Marxist character of community organizing. Stealth was the order of the day.

With a bit of digging, however, it's possible to see clearly the underlying ideology of ACORN's leadership. A series of memos and articles from 1979 suggests that ACORN's leadership was drawing on the work of Marxist theorist Andre Gorz to develop their long-term strategy. Gorz's writings have a special appeal for socialist community organizers, and we saw in the last chapter that the leaders of the Midwest Academy frequently assigned writings by Gorz. A 1979 internal memo from Danny Cantor, then ACORN's head organizer in St. Louis, explicitly draws on Gorz's notion of "non-reformist reforms" as a model for ACORN's work. Cantor went on to co-found the ACORN-sponsored New Party, with which Obama ran during his first political campaign in 1996. Today, Cantor heads New York State's controversial Working Families Party, founded in close association with ACORN.[8]

Cantor's memo was dated February 1979, so it's of interest that Peter Dreier's influential paper on Gorz, "The Case for Transitional Reform," came out in the January–February issue of *Social Policy* in 1979. (We learned in Chapter Two that Dreier convened a panel on community organizing at the Cooper Union Socialist Scholars Conference where Obama was converted to the profession.) Drawing on Gorz, Dreier's overall strategy was to first establish quasi-socialist institutions at the heart of capitalist society—ACORN's role in the banking system very much fitting the bill. In the short run, these de facto socialist groups would push society toward gradual "democratic" change. In the long run, perhaps, they'd serve as the vanguard of a revolution. The second part of Dreier's strategy was to inject "unmanageable strains into the capitalist system, strains that precipitate an economic and/or political crisis," by which Dreier meant a "revolution of rising entitlements" that "cannot be abandoned without undermining the legitimacy of the capitalist class." In the short run, Dreier said, "the process leads to expansion of state activity and budgets, and . . . to fiscal crisis in the public sector. In the longer run, it may give socialist norms an opportunity for extension or at least visibility."

Given the dates of Dreier's article and Cantor's memo, it would seem that Cantor invoked Gorz under the influence of Dreier's essay. Cantor apparently misspelled Gorz as "Gortz," another indication that he was drawing on Dreier's *Social Policy* piece, and not on his own reading of Gorz.[9]

It's also of interest that the September–October 1979 issue of *Social Policy* features an article called "ACORN: Taking Advantage of the Fiscal Crisis." The piece was jointly written by ACORN's chief organizer, Wade Rathke, ACORN's director of research, Seth Borgos, and ACORN's campaign coordinator, Gary Delgado. Published only months after the Dreier piece, this essay by ACORN's top leadership reads like a response to Dreier that shouts "Me, too!" Neither Dreier nor socialism are explicitly mentioned, yet the message ACORN's leadership brings across in this piece is that the seemingly specific and immediate reforms they organize around are ultimately intended to challenge "the structural foundation of society from which unequal distribution of goods and services derives." Referring to the economic woes of the late Carter administration, ACORN's leaders say: "We view the fiscal crisis . . . as an opportunity to seize power for low- and moderate-income people," and an opportunity to "project a vision of a new society to our constituency."

In short, in late 1979, ACORN's top leadership announced in *Social Policy*, the key forum for the socialist intelligentsia of American community organizing, that they were on board with the sort of program articulated by Dreier months before. The content and timing of the Cantor memo suggests that ACORN's leadership was directly inspired by Dreier's piece. It's probably no coincidence, then, that Peter Dreier had an important advisory role in ACORN's subsequent banking campaign, and arguably served as ACORN's most vocal public defender during the organization's post-2008 period of crisis.[10]

In sum, between the subterranean socialism of the leadership's writings and Dreier's behind-the-scenes work with the organization, ACORN fits the pattern of a socialist front group.

A Socialist Platform

In their piece for *Social Policy,* ACORN's leadership points to what they call a "People's Platform" as one of the tools they use to "project a vision of a new society" to their constituency. ACORN adopted this People's Platform, the most systematic public expression we have of ACORN's political ideology, at its 1979 convention in St. Louis.[11] The creation of that platform was part of a four-year plan, initiated in 1976, to inject ACORN into national politics. In that 1976 memo, ACORN toyed with the idea of running its own presidential candidate in 1980.[12] That never happened, of course (not in 1980, anyway), but in the late seventies and early eighties, ACORN did begin to operate an inside/outside strategy on the Democratic Party. ACORN ran delegates to Democratic conventions and pushed platform planks, while pressuring the party from outside with its trademark aggressive protests. ACORN may have taken longer than the Midwest Academy to worm its way into the heart of the Democratic Party, yet it started earlier and finished stronger.

The adoption of the People's Platform in 1979, along with ACORN's increasing focus on national politics, was noticed by America's socialists. In the pages of the DSOC newsletter, *Democratic Left*, many planks from ACORN's People's Platform were itemized, including the creation of a public energy corporation to compete with private companies, a national health-care system controlled by neighborhood committees, strong laws mandating low-income lending, reserved seats for low-income people on the boards of banks, and others planks along the same lines. While acknowledging ACORN's self-portrayal as "pragmatic" and "non-ideological," *Democratic Left* made it clear that ACORN's platform was socialist in all but name:

Democratic socialists must participate in and support [ACORN's] efforts, not as ideological outsiders with a separate agenda, but as committed allies in the same struggle.[13]

The internal "discussion bulletin" of NAM, the other major democratic socialist organization of the late seventies (shortly to merge with DSOC), came to the same conclusion:

ACORN is not simply a neo-Rooseveltian tendency in the Democratic Party. ACORN is an integral part of the evolving forces of socialism, *even if not consciously so* [emphasis original] . . . it is an organization of people's power in the communities, and is thus central to the institutional framework of a future democratic socialism . . . NAM chapters should work in and with ACORN as much as possible in cities where community organizing is a major focus of our work.[14]

The author seems to have underestimated the extent to which the top leadership of ACORN, if not the majority of foot soldiers, was

aware of the group's underlying socialist message. Despite its democratic pose, ACORN's socialist-friendly leaders pulled the organization's strings—another reason it makes sense to see ACORN as a front
group.

After the adoption of its People's Platform in 1979, ACORN geared
up to run delegates to the 1980 Democratic National Convention. The
goal was to inject elements of their newly formed program into the national Democratic platform. After years of effort, Michael Harrington's
Democratic Socialist Organizing Committee (DSOC) had successfully
captured about a quarter of the seats on the 1980 Democratic platform
committee. So ACORN and DSOC formed an alliance to shape the
program of the national Democratic Party.[15]

Another indicator of ACORN's ideology is the leadership's strong
sense of continuity with American socialist history. The first ACORN
handbook for new organizers, published in 1976–77, features ACORN
leader Wade Rathke's tribute to H. L. Mitchell, leader of the Southern Tenant Farmer's Union (STFU).[16] STFU was an Arkansas socialist group from the 1930s that Rathke saw as a predecessor of sorts to
ACORN (which also started in Arkansas). Rathke's handbook piece
highlights STFU's Socialist Party origins, and includes a picture of
Mitchell with early Socialist Party leader Norman Thomas. ACORN
has carefully avoided the socialist label in public, yet its internal training material gets the ideological message across, not least to novice organizers with eyes to see.

SECTION TWO

CHICAGO ACORN

In February of 2010, the House Committee on Oversight and Government Reform issued a staff report under the leadership of Ranking
Member Darrell Issa (R-CA). The report was called "Follow the Money:

ACORN, SEIU and their Political Allies."[17] The report "found there was no real separation between ACORN and its affiliates. ACORN is a single corrupt corporate enterprise composed of a series of holding companies and subsidiaries that are financially and operationally dependent upon the main corporation."[18] Chicago-based SEIU (Service Employees International Union) Local 880 is specifically cited by the report as an example of the substantial intertwining of ACORN and its SEIU affiliates, which involves not only financial but political "codependence."[19] Obama had dealings with both Chicago ACORN and SEIU Local 880, so it's important to keep in mind that separate identities notwithstanding, SEIU 880 is in reality a part of ACORN.

The Issa staff report's first finding was: "ACORN and SEIU's illegal agreements, and the crimes committed in furtherance of these agreements, constitutes a criminal conspiracy."[20] In this connection, the report noted the existence of "hundreds of ACORN bank accounts, shell organizations incorporated under different sections of the internal revenue code, and even an ACORN controlled accounting firm (Citizen's Consulting Inc.) that helps ACORN obscure the true use of charitable donations and taxpayer funds."[21] ACORN's records will allow us to see from the inside the organization's extraordinary capacity for spinning off groups meant to disguise its own controlling role.

It's critical to keep this pattern in mind when trying to make sense of Obama's own ties to ACORN. ACORN's facility for manufacturing and quietly orchestrating the work of multiple organizations extends beyond financial matters, into the political realm. I take no position here on the alleged crimes outlined in the Issa report. But I do want to show that Obama's ties to SEIU Local 880, the New Party, a group called "Progressive Chicago," and Project Vote all ultimately lead back to ACORN. In a sense, ACORN's apparent capacity for creating financial "shell organizations" is an extension of and variation on its predilection for spinning off political front groups. Up to now, these layers within layers of affiliated groups have obscured the extent of Obama's involvement with ACORN.

Militant Actions

The records of Chicago-based Illinois ACORN at the Wisconsin Historical Society, which extend from Illinois ACORN's founding in 1983 to about 1994, are filled with indications of the group's trademark hardball tactics. For the most part, the Illinois records (unlike ACORN's more extensive national records) are confined to yearly reports, meeting minutes, and newspaper clippings, with only the occasional lengthy memo. Undoubtedly, Chicago ACORN leaders communicated mostly in person or over the phone, whereas ACORN's scattered national leaders more often had to resort to memos. Even so, the Illinois records provide fascinating glimpses of Chicago ACORN's modus operandi.

Chicago ACORN board minutes from 1984 describe an action against Illinois governor James Thompson: "We caught him by surprise, and demanded that he support the Affordable Budget Plan. He agreed to investigate and meet with us again. (At first he had said he would not meet at all, but after 200 people surrounded him at a ceremony, he changed his mind.)"[22] A 1984 Great Lakes Regional Report says of ACORN's Chicago branch: "the work-in at the Options Exchange and the take-over of a utility hearing were good, militant actions that finally got us into one of the dailies, for the first time in our nine months."[23] A month later, Chicago ACORN leader Madeline Talbott was self-critical: "We failed to produce enough troops to mess up opening day of the Options Exchange in our jobs campaign, and failed to produce enough political pressure to stop them from cutting the opening [d]ay ribbon."[24]

ACORN Chicago's January 1985 year end report includes tidbits like, "We took over the [utility rate] hearing and had a fine time."[25] A 1988 annual report lists as a failing "too many hit and run actions without enough follow-up."[26] Illinois ACORN's files are dotted with the occasional arrest record and notations about court appearances resulting from its "direct action" campaigns.[27] Chicago ACORN leader Madeline Talbott's personal spiral notebooks, while mostly filled with appointments and addresses, include occasional reflections of interest: "Anger is a tactic/100 go wild/can take the heat, want the impact/small room: don't lose control of anger/*they will too*/always try to take away strongest tools in negotiating."[28]

In his 2008 history of Chicago-based SEIU Local 880 (very much a part of ACORN), 880's head organizer, Keith Kelleher, stresses the special role of Alinskyite direct-action tactics in his local's campaigns. According to Kelleher, SEIU Local 880 used "guerilla tactics that included sending busloads of members to the home of owners and managers."[29] With pride, Kelleher adds that these tactics "inflicted a degree of reputational damage on primary and secondary targets of a wholly different nature than typical labour-management fights at that point in America's history."[30]

We've seen that national ACORN began moving into politics in the late seventies. By the early eighties, when ACORN arrived in Chicago, the traditional aversion of Alinskyite organizers to electoral politics was well on the way out. SEIU 880, for example, focused on organizing home health-care workers, many of whom were employed by the Illinois Department of Rehabilitation Services (DORS). So SEIU ran plenty of "actions" against state officials. Busing protesters to the state capital of Springfield in 1985, for example, 880 "seized the front doors" of DORS and "marched, singing and chanting, into the offices of the department secretary."[31] SEIU 880 used these protests to persuade Illinois to eliminate competitive bidding on home health-care contracts, thus raising wages with pre-set rates.[32]

All of which provides some context for our upcoming examination of Barack Obama's work with Illinois ACORN and SEIU 880 when he ran Illinois Project Vote in 1992. Kelleher emphasizes that 880's work with Obama's Project Vote in 1992 allowed the union to "build and cement" an important relationship with the future state senator.[33] The implication is that Obama's later work in the Illinois State Senate was of use to SEIU 880 on the myriad issues tying it to the state. So a great deal more than voter registration was at stake in Obama's work with ACORN and SEIU in 1992. That was simply one moment in a long-term political alliance in which ACORN/SEIU provided political troops to Obama, while receiving foundation funding and legislative help from the future president.

Squatting

When Obama first arrived in Chicago in 1985, ACORN's push for subprime lending was in its infancy. The focus of Chicago ACORN's housing campaign in the mid-eighties was squatting. Protesters would break into abandoned homes, seize them for designated ACORN members, and begin to make repairs. A picture in the April 8, 1989, *Chicago Tribune*, for example, shows a group of ACORN protesters with bullhorn and crowbar prominently displayed.[34] That protest appears to have melted away when police arrived, but other squatting efforts had more success. Sometimes neighbors were happy to see an abandoned property taken over and fixed, and sometimes banks under pressure agreed to hand foreclosed properties over to ACORN. Pointing to an obscure and unenforced statute, ACORN claimed exemption from arrest for criminal trespass on the grounds that they were beautifying abandoned property.[35] Yet the group also pushed for new legislation that would explicitly legalize their "homesteading."[36] In a 1986 article, Chicago ACORN leader Madeline Talbott concedes the illegal character of the squatting campaign and emphasizes her care in trying "not to let people squat in really high risk situations."[37]

Why, exactly, was ACORN squatting? If the group wanted homesteading legislation, why not fight for it through conventional political channels and stop the illegal seizures? This apparently reasonable question totally misses the Alinskyite point. In part, ACORN wanted those houses because the hope of being selected as an "owner" brought new recruits into the organization. ACORN works by appropriating goods from businesses or the state, then doling them out as a way of luring in new members. This is another "polarizing" Alinskyite win/win, of the type favored by Obama's organizing mentors. If ACORN seizes a house and gets to keep it, the organization wins. But if politicians or businesses step in and prevent a seizure, anger spreads among the squatters (stirred up by ACORN's organizers, of course), who are bound that much more closely to the group by their rage. So going the respectable route, and calling for homesteading legislation won't do. ACORN feeds off high-risk actions that push the limits of the law.

There's something else involved as well. In his history of ACORN's early years, Gary Delgado assigns squatting an ideological meaning. Recall that Delgado was an author, along with Wade Rathke, of "ACORN: Taking Advantage of the Fiscal Crisis," the 1979 article that communicated ACORN's de facto socialist sympathies and bragged about the group's ability to "project a vision of a new society to our constituency." Delgado helped organize and author ACORN's "People's Platform," and in his history of ACORN he is clearly miffed that the platform couldn't be even more explicitly radical than it was. So Delgado points to ACORN's squatting campaign as proof of the group's genuinely skeptical attitude toward the idea of private property.[38] In other words, ACORN's squatting campaign was socialist *in practice*. Property was literally confiscated "from below" and dispersed to the poor. With its organized squatting, ACORN really was projecting a vision of a new society to its constituents. And that vision was decidedly not capitalist.

Obama Meets ACORN

We know that Obama first made contact with Chicago ACORN through its leader Madeline Talbott. Talbott was a powerful figure within the organization, serving as director of ACORN's Great Lakes/ Prairie Region branch and playing a major role in ACORN's national campaigns.[39] A 2008 *Newsday* article by Letta Taylor and Keith Herbert on Obama's early organizing—especially his role in the asbestos campaign—says that Talbott "initially considered Obama a competitor.

But she became so impressed with his work that she invited him to help train her staff."[40]

What exactly does this mean? While Obama doesn't show up in the Illinois ACORN/SEIU 800 archives until 1992, it's possible to put together at least a plausible picture of what Obama's initial contacts with ACORN might have involved. The key is to follow archived accounts of the Altgeld Tenants United (ATU), the local ACORN group active at the Altgeld Gardens public housing project where Obama did his initial organizing.

Altgeld Tenants United was closely allied with UNO of Chicago's Mary Ellen Montes, who led a coalition of activists opposed to the expansion of area dumps run by Waste Management.[41] Like ACORN, Montes and UNO favored hardball tactics, and ACORN's files indicate participation in blockades at dumping sites around 1985, as well as arrests and court appearances related to those actions.[42] Obama's own Developing Communities Project was effectively an extension of UNO of Chicago, and Obama himself worked closely with Montes planning and carrying out an aggressive action against Waste Management in 1988.[43] So ACORN was a core part of Obama's organizing network from the start.

ATU appears to have been put together by ACORN organizer Steuart Pittman.[44] ACORN's national records show Pittman playing a leading role in ACORN's banking campaigns of the nineties. Yet Pittman disappears from the ACORN Illinois records after early 1985. Perhaps he was transferred to another city. In any case, sometime shortly after Pittman's departure, ATU fell on hard times. By 1986–87, the peak of Obama's own activities at Altgeld, ATU, once one of ACORN's strongest outposts, was listed as "a weak group." The report added: "We have not found a way to move enough dues here to support an organizer."[45]

Why the trouble? In the late eighties, Chicago ACORN was willing to live without a full staff of organizers for the sake of establishing an ACORN Housing Corporation and gearing up for a major housing-banking campaign.[46] ACORN was beginning to wake up to the immense financial, political, and organizational opportunity represented by its mortgage campaigns. ACORN was willing to sacrifice other projects to get that housing effort into gear. By the 1988 year end report, however, ATU had snapped out of its dormancy and come to life. The report calls ATU "a recently reactivated group with a hot issue: asbestos."[47]

So ACORN, which arrived in Chicago in 1983, was flourishing at Altgeld by 1984 and working closely with Obama's future allies and mentors at UNO of Chicago by 1985, the year Obama himself arrived in Chicago. The departure of ATU's original organizer, Steuart Pittman, appears to have weakened the group. Meanwhile Chicago ACORN's increasing interest in housing and banking left it with a thinned-out and inexperienced field-organizing staff for several years. Altgeld Tenants United went dormant from 1986 to 1987, the very time Obama arrived at Altgeld and took his Developing Communities Project through its most celebrated actions.

It's easy to see, then, why Chicago ACORN head Madeline Talbott "initially considered Obama a competitor" but later "became so impressed with his work that she invited him to help train her staff." At a minimum, it would seem, Obama briefed ACORN staffers on his asbestos campaign so that they could revitalize ATU and carry on the battle after his departure in 1988.

In any case, we know that Obama and Talbott hit it off during his initial organizing stint, and that this bond became the basis of a deepening relationship with ACORN after Obama's return to Chicago from law school and his work with Project Vote in 1992. Obama's apparently generous cooperation with ACORN in the eighties makes perfect sense, given ACORN's alliance with UNO of Chicago and Obama's own ambitions. Obama wasn't interested in freezing an organizing competitor out of Altgeld Gardens. On the contrary, he wanted to forge his own alliance with a group that could help him with future political campaigns. That turned out to be a very wise move.

SECTION THREE

HITTING THE BANKS

"You've got only a couple thousand bucks in the bank. Your job pays you dog-food wages. Your credit history has been bent, stapled, and mutilated. You declared bankruptcy in 1989. Don't despair: You can still buy a house."[48] So began an April 1995 article in the *Chicago Sun-Times* that went on to direct prospective home buyers fitting this profile to ACORN's loan counseling program. Considered in the wake of the subprime mortgage crisis of 2008, encouraging customers like this to buy homes seems little short of madness. At the time, however, those who supported ACORN's lending program saw it as both an embodiment of economic justice and a force for civil rights.

By 1995, when that Chicago newspaper article made its appearance, Barack Obama's political fortunes were deeply entangled with ACORN. Gearing up for his first run for office in 1996, Obama was pouring money into ACORN's coffers from his position on the board of two liberal Chicago foundations. By 1995, Obama had also been personally training ACORN leaders for some time. That same year, Obama represented ACORN in a lawsuit designed to force the state of Illinois to enforce the federal "Motor-Voter" bill. And while running formally on the Democratic Party ticket, Obama received the endorsement of—and almost certainly joined—the "New Party," jointly controlled by Chicago ACORN and the Chicago Democratic Socialists of America (DSA). With ACORN members serving as foot soldiers in Obama's first and subsequent political campaigns, the partnership was complete.

The year 1995 was also a culmination of sorts for ACORN's intrusion into the financial system. By 1995, ACORN had solidly established its profitable loan counseling program, had helped to pull Fannie Mae and Freddie Mac into the subprime mortgage business, had established itself as a powerful partner of the Clinton administration on housing policy, and had helped to push subprime mortgage lending through the financial system as a whole.

The degree of ACORN's involvement in the subprime mortgage crisis of 2008 is subject to debate. Skeptics argue that the Community Reinvestment Act (CRA), which ACORN used to force banks into making high-risk loans to low-credit customers, could have influenced at most only about a quarter of the loans at the base of the financial meltdown.[49] It's true that the crisis of 2008 was a confluence of many factors, and that CRA loans were only a piece of the puzzle. What the skeptics miss, however, is the degree to which ACORN served as a critical catalyst, using a combination of local protest actions and national lobbying to spread subprime lending far beyond the confines of CRA-controlled banks. ACORN may not have been the only cause of the subprime mortgage crisis, but a good deal of evidence points to its substantial role in laying the foundations of the debacle. While some of that evidence is already public, the archives of ACORN at the Wisconsin Historical Society shed considerable new light on this issue.

Obama clearly understood and supported the hardball tactics ACORN used in its campaign against Chicago's banks. During the years 1992 through 1995, when Obama's relationship to Chicago ACORN deepened, housing was the overwhelming focus of its work. During his initial organizing stint in Chicago, Obama likely helped ACORN cover for the weakness of its field operations as it geared up for its run at the banks. On his return to Chicago in 1992, ACORN's housing and banking operations were in full force, and Obama was pleased to offer ACORN training, funding, legal representation, advice, and political alliance. So let's trace the story of ACORN from Obama's departure for law school in 1988 through 1995, when Obama's Chicago-based political alliance with ACORN reached maturity, and when ACORN's extraordinary efforts to transform America's banking system came to fruition.

Never Waste a Crisis

The Community Reinvestment Act (CRA) of 1977 called on banks to fulfill their charters by meeting "the convenience and needs" of the communities they served.[50] That vague admonition had little effect on the level of subprime lending until the huge increase of mergers in the mid-eighties gave ACORN and other community groups a lever against the banks. ACORN learned that filing a CRA challenge during the critical period after a large acquisition or merger had been assigned a completion date was the key to success. These agreements turned on time-sensitive issues, like the market value of stock, and could be undermined by delay or bad publicity. So even though no CRA challenge during this period actually won on the merits, holding mergers hostage to delay enabled ACORN to force lending concessions from the banks.[51]

Supposedly, ACORN's challenges objected to discrimination against minority loan applicants, and targeted banks were ostentatiously accused of outright racism. Yet internal documents make it clear that ACORN's real enemy was not the discriminatory application of lending standards, but the standards themselves.[52] ACORN understood very well that most minority applicants were rejected for lack of a down payment, poor credit histories, or other income-related issues. ACORN's real goal was the lowering of lending standards, and this is what posed so great a danger to the financial system.

Nonetheless, the basis for CRA challenges remained weak until 1989, when a crisis in the Savings and Loan system and the call for a federal bailout provided ACORN with an ideal opportunity to change the rules. We saw ACORN's leaders publishing a 1979 article: "ACORN: Taking Advantage of the Fiscal Crisis." Ten years later, the same theme of using a financial crisis as an opportunity for redistributive reform appears again throughout ACORN's publications and internal documents.

With an intense national lobbying effort, ACORN managed to mobilize support from allies like the Conference of Mayors, the United Auto Workers, the Leadership Conference on Civil Rights and others to insert three key provisions into the S&L bailout of 1989.[53] Federal Home Loan District Banks were required to contribute a portion of their profits to a housing fund that groups like ACORN could tap into. Low-income loan counseling operations (of which ACORN's was the most prominent) would also get priority access—at below-market prices and below-market financing—to a large share of the homes the government took over from insolvent S&Ls. Finally, changes to the Home Mortgage Disclosure Act required the extensive collection of data by race, creating a raft of opportunities for claims of discrimination under the Community Reinvestment Act.

Unfortunately, these new racial statistics would be used to create the misleading impression of discrimination in instances when not race but credit histories and other financial factors were actually at work. In a last-minute effort to torpedo these legislative changes, Republican senator Phil Gramm of Texas circulated a letter condemning the provisions as a kind of "piracy". "The special interest housing organizations that would profit from these provisions loudly promote them, but the people who will pay have been told next to nothing."[54] According to Gramm, the ACORN-backed provisions would cost the taxpayer more than $13 billion in property sales that otherwise would have been used to offset the cost of the bailout. President George H. W. Bush came close to vetoing the bailout over the ACORN-backed provisions, yet relented at the last minute when offered concessions on other issues. The original ACORN-supported provisions passed only narrowly in the House—in one case by a margin of only two votes—with special help from Democrats like Joseph Kennedy (D-MA), Barney Frank (D-MA), and Nancy Pelosi (D-CA).[55] The House provisions were accepted only reluctantly in conference by the Senate. There is no reason to doubt ACORN's internal conclusion that without its intense lobbying efforts, these provisions would likely have failed.

Land Grab

Those 1989 legislative changes were a huge boon to ACORN. Housing and banking issues now moved to the very center of its efforts nationally. The new openings for housing agitation also brought help from figures we've encountered elsewhere in this book. Peter Dreier and John Atlas, frequent collaborators and leading socialist strategists, now joined hands with both ACORN and the Midwest Academy's coalition, Citizen Action, to plan a national housing campaign. ACORN's files from this period include banking strategy memos from Peter Dreier to leaders of ACORN and the Midwest Academy, and memos from Jackie Kendall and Steve Max of the Midwest Academy in reply.[56] Behind the scenes, the national campaign to expand subprime lending was being planned and coordinated by leading socialist organizers. Dreier, who helped to popularize the idea of taking advantage of a crisis, drove home the point again in a 1991 memo on continuing housing scandals: "These scandals constitute both a crisis and an opportunity."[57]

The provisions ACORN successfully inserted into the 1989 Savings and Loan bailout certainly had a galvanizing effect on its Chicago office.[58] Short-staffed with inexperienced organizers when Obama left for law school in 1988, Chicago ACORN had turned the problem around by 1991, when it ended the year with eight well-schooled field organizers.[59] The next year, 1992, was a breakthrough, as the new organizers and their expanded campaigns against banks resulted in a major expansion of Chicago ACORN's loan counseling program. By the end of 1993, ACORN's Chicago office had added two organizers entirely dedicated to housing protests and two full-time loan counselors.[60]

Chicago ACORN head Madeline Talbott, who had allied with Obama during his early organizing stint, was the sparkplug of this expansion. Talbott was a specialist in ACORN's "direct action" protests, and was also a key planner of ACORN's national banking campaign.[61] In February of 1990, only months after the congressional breakthroughs of 1989, Illinois regulators held what was believed to be the first-ever state hearing to consider blocking a thrift merger for lack of compliance with the Community Reinvestment Act. The challenge was filed by Talbott against Bell Federal Savings and Loan Association. Bell complained that ACORN pressure was undermining its ability to make financially responsible loans. Increasingly, Bell maintained, it was being boxed into an "affirmative-action lending policy."[62] The following years saw Talbott featured in dozens of stories about pressuring banks into higher-risk minority loans.

In April 1992, Talbott filed another precedent-setting complaint using the "community support requirements" of the S&L bailout of 1989.[63] Within a month, ACORN organized its first "bank fair" at Malcolm X College and found sixteen Chicago-area financial institutions that preferred negotiation with ACORN to disruptive protests.[64] Two months later, Talbott announced plans to conduct demonstrations in the lobbies of area banks that refused to attend an ACORN-sponsored national bank "summit" in New York.[65] She insisted that banks show a commitment to minority lending by lowering their standards on down payments and underwriting—for example, by overlooking bad credit histories. By September 1992, the *Chicago Tribune* was describing Talbott's program as "affirmative-action lending" and ACORN was issuing fact sheets bragging about relaxations of credit standards it had won on behalf of minorities.[66]

ACORN's national archives include a 1991 memo from Talbott to all ACORN offices recommending a plan that "makes some cash for us and keeps the lead on this campaign in [ACORN's] hands."[67] Talbott then explains her bank-fair strategy and lists the many ways participating banks can be induced to financially support ACORN. Chicago's Talbott was blazing the trail of ACORN's national grassroots campaign against the banks.

Was ACORN's housing activism really motivated by socialist-inspired compassion for the poor, or was the huge financial success of ACORN's banking campaign becoming a motive in and of itself? We don't necessarily have to choose between these explanations.

ACORN's leaders were ideologically committed to the goals of their group, and no doubt viewed anything that profited ACORN itself as in the best interests of the poor—and of "the cause." Prospective ACORN "homesteaders" were required to participate in at least five ACORN-sponsored "community events" (read "demonstrations"). "It's not just about a house" explained one ACORN leader, adding: "What the ACORN Housing Corporation does is indoctrinate you about what being a neighbor is, what being a community is." [68] Although loan applicants counseled by ACORN received titles to their rehabbed homes, ownership of the land beneath their houses remained with ACORN. ACORN leases also limited the ability of homeowners to move out of their properties, or to sell their homes to anyone but ACORN Housing Corporation. As one ACORN leader explained, this policy "helps maintain ACORN's connection to the product of its labors." [69] Some might see all this as greedy double-dealing on the part of an organization supposedly working for the good of the poor. In the end, however, the proud indoctrination and constraints on private ownership built into ACORN's housing program were entirely consistent with the group's underlying socialist ideology.

Fighting Fannie

ACORN's burgeoning efforts to undermine credit standards in the aftermath of the 1989 changes to the Community Reinvestment and Home Mortgage Disclosure acts taught it a valuable lesson. However much pressure ACORN put on banks to lower credit standards, tough requirements in the "secondary market," run by quasi-federal housing agencies Fannie Mae and Freddie Mac, served as a barrier to change. Fannie Mae and Freddie Mac buy up mortgages en masse, bundle them, and sell them to investors on the world market. Back then, Fannie and Freddie refused to buy loans that failed to meet high credit standards. If, for example, a local bank buckled to ACORN pressure and agreed to offer poor or minority applicants a 5 percent down-payment rate, instead of the normal 10 to 20 percent, Fannie and Freddie would refuse to buy up those mortgages. That would leave all the risk of these shaky loans with the local bank. So time and again, local banks would tell ACORN that, because of standards imposed by Fannie and Freddie, they could lower credit standards by only a little.[70]

This substantial barrier to its plans reinforced ACORN's determination to combine its high-pressure Alinskyite "outside" strategy with a growing "inside" reliance on Washington lobbyists. Somehow ACORN would have to undercut credit standards at Fannie Mae and Freddie Mac. Only then would local banks consider making loans available to customers with bad credit histories, low wages, virtually nothing in the bank, and even bankruptcies on record. It's evident that ACORN's initial encounter with Fannie Mae went poorly. A July 12, 1991, internal ACORN "Alert" castigates Fannie Mae for being "totally unwilling to accommodate us."[71] In response, ACORN had its friends in Congress introduce bills compelling Fannie Mae and Freddie Mac to support subprime lending and called on its local groups to begin intense lobbying efforts with their own congressional representatives. ACORN's "Alert" warned that Fannie and Freddie were "on the warpath" against this legislation and called the two agencies "even more formidable opponents than the banking industry."

ACORN won this showdown, playing a major role in the passage of the "GSE Act" of 1992. House Banking chairman Henry Gonzales "informally deputized" ACORN and other community groups to draft that law's affordable housing mandates.[72] The result was the imposition of low-income loan quotas on Fannie Mae and Freddie Mac and a loosening of agency underwriting standards to accept down payments of 5 percent or less, and to ignore poor credit histories more than a year old. This is how the *Chicago Sun-Times* could send readers with bankruptcies and other credit impairments to ACORN for loans.

ACORN had succeeded in dragging Fannie Mae and Freddie Mac—kicking and screaming—into the subprime mortgage business. And ACORN wasn't done yet. In obedience to its new legislative mandates,

Fannie Mae held a bank fair in Chicago in the fall of 1992. Although ACORN wasn't invited, the group decided to make Fannie an offer it couldn't refuse. According to Chicago ACORN's Year-End/Year-Begin Report for 1992–93:

> Fannie Mae rolled into town in the fall announcing their bank fair. We went into their planning meeting and reminded them they couldn't hold a bank fair without us. We got them to give us $25,000 to do turnout. We promised them over 500 and the thought of our people marching into their bankfair helped to bring them around in national negotiations.[73]

So ACORN's intimidation tactics not only made the group a tidy twenty-five thousand dollars for turnout efforts that likely cost it little, a message was sent that Fannie Mae's subprime lending mandates would have to be fulfilled through direct cooperation with ACORN. This move would pay off handsomely for ACORN down the road.

SECTION FOUR

ACORN IN CAMPAIGN '08

Our narrative has now reached 1992, when Barack Obama's dealings with Chicago ACORN enter more fully into the light of day. Before exploring new evidence illuminating the ACORN-Obama relationship, it will be useful to review the controversy over the president's early work with ACORN.

My One and Only

Obama's ties to ACORN were a hotly debated topic during the 2008 presidential campaign. In early October, Republican presidential nominee John McCain's campaign ran an Internet ad attacking ACORN for voter registration fraud, intimidation tactics, and pressuring banks to make the same kind of risky loans that caused the financial crisis. McCain's ad stressed what it called Obama's "long and deep" ties to the group, including the reported mid-eighties request by Chicago ACORN head Madeline Talbott that Obama train her staff, and a published report that Obama had run training classes for ACORN in the nineties as well.[74] Then, in an October 10, 2008, memo, the McCain campaign charged that in 1992, when Obama directed Chicago's Project Vote, he was effectively running "an arm of ACORN."[75] It should be noted that in May of 2008, at National Review Online, I authored what was quite possibly the first in-depth article spelling out Obama's ties to ACORN, followed by several other pieces on the topic.[76] Directly or indirectly, the McCain Internet ad was likely influenced by that work.

For its part, the Obama campaign energetically denied his ACORN connection, acknowledging only that Obama "represented ACORN in a successful lawsuit" (requiring Illinois to enforce the federal "Motor Voter" law). Obama's "Fight the Smears" website listed three pertinent "facts":

Fact: Barack was never an ACORN community organizer.

Fact: Barack was never an ACORN trainer and never worked for ACORN in any other capacity.

Fact: ACORN was not part of Project Vote, the successful voter registration drive Barack ran in 1992.[77]

When Obama himself was asked by an ABC News reporter on October 14, 2008, to comment on Senator McCain's charges, he replied:

Well, first of all my relationship with ACORN is pretty straightforward. It's probably 13 years ago when I was still practicing law, I represented ACORN, and my partner in that investigation was the U.S. Justice Department, in having Illinois implement what was called the Motor Voter law, to make sure people could go to the DMVs and driver's license facilities to get registered. It wasn't being implemented. **That was my relationship and is my relationship to ACORN.** There is an ACORN organization in Chicago. They've been active. As an elected official, I've had interactions with them. But they're not advising my campaign. We've got the best voter registration in politics right now and we don't need ACORN's help. [Emphasis added.][78]

Obama reiterated this point on October 15, in the third presidential debate with John McCain, this time making an even more explicit claim that his legal representation of ACORN was his only involvement with that organization:

The **only** involvement I've had with ACORN was I represented them alongside the U.S. Justice Department in making Illinois implement a Motor Voter law that helped people get registered at DMVs. [Emphasis added.][79]

Around the same time, two professedly non-partisan fact-check groups took up the issue. Politifact rated McCain's claim that Project Vote was "an arm of ACORN" when Obama ran it "false." Politifact then went further and said that it had found no evidence that ACORN and Project Vote "had a relationship" during the 1992 voter registration drive.[80] On October 18, 2008, about a week after Politifact's foray into the issue, Factcheck.org consulted with Sanford Newman, who headed Project Vote nationally in 1992, and who chose Obama to run the group's operation in Illinois. Newman emphasized that Project Vote didn't start working exclusively with ACORN until after 1992. Yet Newman conceded that "ACORN may have been one of dozens of organizations that participated in registration drives that year with Project Vote personnel like Obama."[81]

Finally, an October 11 *New York Times* article by Stephanie Strom noted yet more evidence of Obama's work with ACORN when he ran Project Vote in 1992.[82] According to a post by Sam Graham-Felsen, a blogger at Obama's own website, Obama himself had linked his 1992 work with Project Vote to ACORN. In a meeting at which he sought the presidential endorsement of ACORN's leaders, Obama reportedly said: "Even before I was an elected official, when I ran Project Vote voter registration drives in Illinois, ACORN was smack dab in the middle of it, and we appreciate your work."[83] (In May of 2009, a controversy erupted over a report that the editors of the *New York Times* had acted, shortly after the publication of this article, to cut off Strom's continuing investigations into Obama's ACORN ties.)[84]

Evasion and Falsehood

The next development came well over a year later, in February of 2010, when what appears to be the original video of Obama's endorsement appeal to ACORN's leadership finally surfaced. The original video clip has since been withdrawn from the Internet, but its inclusion in a television broadcast yields a transcript of Obama's private campaign remarks to ACORN:

> I definitely welcome ACORN's input. You don't have to ask me about that. I'm going to call you even if you didn't ask me. When I ran Project Vote, the voter registration drive in Illinois, ACORN was smack dab in the middle of it. Once I was elected there wasn't a campaign that ACORN worked on down in Springfield that I wasn't right there with you. Since I have been in the United States Senate, I've been always a partner with ACORN as well. I've been fighting with ACORN, along side ACORN, on the issues you care about my entire career.[85]

The contrast between Obama's proud but private affirmation of his longtime relationship with ACORN and his denial of that relationship during the campaign is striking. When we combine already public information with the archival record, Obama's campaign posture on the ACORN question emerges as a combination of lawyerly evasion and outright falsehood. While it's true that the McCain campaign went too far in calling Chicago Project Vote an "arm of ACORN" when Obama ran it, nearly everything else the McCain campaign alleged can be confirmed. The fact-checkers, on the other hand, were, at best, less than thorough, since they ignored a good deal of readily available evidence that would have called Obama's claims into question. At worst, these purportedly neutral fact-checkers may have had a bias that prevented them from finding easily available information bearing directly on the Obama-ACORN controversy. The fact-checkers also relied uncritically on former Obama colleagues, who had every reason to cover for the candidate.

We've already seen that Stephanie Strom's *New York Times* article, published a week before Factcheck.org's piece, included an Obama-friendly blogger's report that Obama himself had bragged to ACORN about his work with them in 1992. Yet Factcheck ignored that report and concluded instead that "Project Vote and ACORN may or may not have worked together in Chicago that year [1992]."[86] Yet a March 2007 article in the *Washington Post,* long pre-dating both fact-checks, provides clear evidence that Obama worked directly with Chicago ACORN leader Madeline Talbott during the 1992 Project Vote campaign:

Fellow community organizer Madeline Talbott said Obama mastered the [Alinsky] approach. She remembers a successful 1992 voter-registration drive that he ran for Project Vote. "He says things like, 'Do you think we should do this? What role would you like to play?'" said Talbott, chief organizer for Illinois ACORN. "Everybody else just puts out an e-mail and says, 'Y'all come.' Barack doesn't do that."[87]

Yet, according to PolitiFact: "We also didn't find any evidence to indicate the two organizations [Project Vote and ACORN] had a relationship during the 1992 Illinois drive."[88] Apparently, testimony by the leader of Chicago ACORN quoted in the *Washington Post*, not to mention testimony by Obama himself unearthed by the *New York Times* a week later (and by me months before) was too difficult to find.[89]

Keith Kelleher, the head of Chicago's ACORN-controlled SEIU Local 880, published a history of 880 in the spring of 2008. This was readily available on the Internet and is referred to in the 2010 congressional report on ACORN sponsored by Congressman Darrell Issa (R-CA). In that article, Kelleher explains SEIU 880's ACORN tie and goes on to say:

> Local 880 and Illinois ACORN joined forces with a newly-invigorated voter registration group, Project Vote, run by former community organizer (and current Democratic presidential candidate and U.S. Senator) Barack Obama, to bring other community groups under the Project Vote umbrella and move a large-scale voter registration program for U.S. Senator Carol Moseley Braun.[90]

Kelleher's testimony is important for several reasons. Not only was this available evidence of Obama's direct work with ACORN when the ACORN controversy erupted in the 2008 campaign, it also suggests that the ACORN-SEIU role in Obama's Project Vote's coalition was special. According to Kelleher, ACORN and SEIU 880 worked with Obama to bring other community groups into the coalition. In other words, ACORN was at the core of Obama's coalition, while other groups were on the periphery. Kelleher's suggestion of a special role for ACORN-SEIU in Obama's Project Vote coalition is confirmed by archival evidence. Kelleher's account also contrasts sharply with national Project Vote head Sanford Newman's 2008 claim that, at best, ACORN may simply have been "one of dozens of organizations" working with

Chicago's Project Vote that year. Notice also that Kelleher lets it slip that ACORN's work with Project Vote in 1992 was intended to "move a large-scale voter registration program for U.S. Senator Carol Moseley Braun." As a rule, given legal requirements for tax-exempt voter registration work, Project Vote coalition members are careful to maintain a facade of non-partisanship. So much for evidence bearing on the Project Vote issue that was already public at the time of campaign 2008's ACORN controversy. Now let's have a look at what the original documents reveal.

SECTION FIVE

PROJECT VOTE REVEALED

Records of Barack Obama's work with Illinois Project Vote in 1992 can be found in the files of SEIU Local 880, archived at the Wisconsin Historical Society. Recall that the congressional staff report sponsored by Darrell Issa found that "there was no real separation between ACORN and its affiliates. ACORN is a single corrupt corporate enterprise composed of a series of holding companies and subsidiaries that are financially and operationally dependent upon the main corporation." The report cited Chicago-based SEIU Local 880 as an example of the substantial intertwining of ACORN and its SEIU affiliates, entailing both financial and political "codependence."

The records of both Illinois ACORN and SEIU Local 880 confirm this assessment. The two groups shared the same office, and staffers were instructed to answer the phone as either "ACORN" or "Union," depending on which lines were called.[91] More important, both groups reported to ACORN's chief organizer, Wade Rathke. It's apparent, moreover, that in the office division of labor, SEIU 880 head Keith Kelleher handled much of the voter registration paperwork for both Chicago ACORN and Local 880.[92] So what do the records show?

Fight the Power

On June 1, 1992, Illinois Project Vote issued a press release for its public kickoff.[93] The release quotes Obama explaining the need for Project Vote by pointing to the recent rioting in Los Angeles—six days of disturbances that drew the National Guard, the U.S. Army, and finally the United States Marines into the largely African-American neighborhood of South Central Los Angeles. Fifty-three people died, about two thousand were injured, and thirty-six hundred fires were set during these riots, which were sparked by the acquittal of police officers who had beaten an African-American suspect, Rodney King, after he allegedly resisted arrest following a high-speed chase. The riots played out between April 29 and May 4, just four weeks prior to Obama's press release.[94] In that release, Obama concentrated on linking the riots to electoral politics, saying: "The Los Angeles riots reflect a deep distrust and disaffection with the existing power pattern in our society." To change that power pattern, Obama argued, "people on the bottom of the economic ladder" need to register and vote.

While that June press conference was the public kickoff of Illinois Project Vote's 1992 campaign, work had gotten under way two months before, when a select group was invited to join the Project Vote steering committee. An April 28 letter invited SEIU Local 880 head Keith Kelleher to be a member of that committee.[95] The invitation was on letterhead from the Community Renewal Society, and was signed by Yvonne V. Delk, executive director of that group, by Obama, as Illinois state director of Project Vote, and by Obama's partner at Project Vote, Joseph Gardner, commissioner of Greater Chicago's Water Reclamation District. This letter presented registration of poor and minority voters as a way to shift the strategies of both political parties: "Both the Republicans and the Democrats have focused their attention on 'courting the so called middle class,' because low income and minority persons are not expected to register and vote. We feel that it is time that political leadership recognized the needs and interest of all citizens."

Obama's co-signatories on that letter, Yvonne Delk and Joe Gard-
ner, were part and parcel of the hard-left network we've been exploring
throughout this book. In Chapter Three I told the story of the Black
Theology Project (BTP), followers of black liberation theologian James
Cone, a group of whom traveled to Cuba to enthusiastically support
Castro's revolution. Jeremiah Wright sat on the board of that group and
twice went to Cuba with BTP. Yvonne Delk sat on the BTP board with
Wright and helped to organize BTP's Chicago chapter, which met at
Wright's church beginning in late 1986, not long before Obama himself first met Wright.[96] Obama may have used his Wright connection to
get Delk's Community Renewal Society to provide facilities for Project
Vote. Obama may even have met Delk at Black Theology Project meetings in the mid-eighties. Obama's work with Delk at Project Vote shows
a significant link to Wright's radical network.

Joe Gardner served as director of field operations for Harold Washington's historic 1983 campaign for mayor of Chicago, and in the wake
of Washington's death, Gardner emerged as a rising political star in
Chicago.[97] A longtime official of Reverend Jesse Jackson's Operation
PUSH, Gardner had been Jackson's chief negotiator in the development of economic "covenants" with American corporations.[98] If many
viewed this as a valuable service to minorities, others saw Jackson's
high-pressure campaigns against allegedly biased corporations as an
only slightly less egregious form of de facto extortion than that practiced by ACORN. A Chicago community organizer named Mark S.
Allen reports that, on Gardner's recommendation, he (Allen) worked
with Obama in the mid-eighties. According to Allen, Obama regularly
attended Saturday morning Operation PUSH registration forums run
by Gardner in 1986.[99]

Gardner had also been a community organizer for Saul Alinsky's
Chicago group, the Woodlawn Organization, in the 1970s.[100] Gardner
may have met Heather Booth back then, when she was training with
Alinsky and working with his Chicago-wide alliance, CAP. In any case,
Gardner was a close ally of Booth, who helped lead Gardner's metro-

politan sanitary district commissioner election drive in Chicago's Lakefront district.[101] Finally, Gardner was on the board of Human SERVE, the voter registration group run by Richard Cloward and Frances Fox Piven.[102] Marxist theorists Cloward and Piven had a longstanding relationship with ACORN and its predecessor group, the National Welfare Rights Organization. In their later work, Cloward and Piven hit on the idea of provoking polarizing battles around voter registration as the key to a socialist transformation of the United States. Their ultimate goal was to drive the Democratic Party to the left, thus dividing the country along class lines. These ideas were discussed at the Cooper Union Socialist Scholars Conference where Obama discovered his vocation as a community organizer.

Clearly, a peek into almost any element of Obama's political network tends to uncover connections to almost every other piece of the puzzle. The socialist thinkers, community organizers, and radical theologians Obama relied on were all politically allied. The cross-connections are multiple and variable. The broadly socialist political orientation remains constant.

OBAMA'S NETWORK

A list of the twenty-two-member steering committee of Project Vote's "Chicago Coalition" provides yet another glimpse of Obama's political network.[103] Both Chicago ACORN's Madeline Talbott and SEIU Local 880's Keith Kelleher were on Obama's Project Vote steering committee. This, of course, is consistent with the accounts we've already seen from both Talbott and Kelleher of their work with Obama in 1992. It also shows that ACORN and SEIU 880 stood at the center of Obama's Project Vote coalition, bringing other groups into the fold, yet enjoying a special standing.

Kim Bobo, a leader in the nineties of the powerful socialist front group the Midwest Academy, was also on Obama's steering commit-

tee, along with Reverend Jeremiah Wright, Father Michael Pfleger, and
Obama's successor at the Developing Communities Project, John Owens. Sokoni Karanja, an influential member of Wright's congregation
and a close Obama associate, was on the steering committee as well.
An August 1992 *Chicago Sun-Times* piece about Project Vote highlights training sessions taking place in the basement of Wright's Trinity
United Church of Christ.[104] Clearly, then, Obama's interest in Reverend Wright extended beyond strictly spiritual matters.

Despite Project Vote's officially non-partisan status, it was very
much a part of the successful effort to elect Carol Moseley Braun to the
U.S. Senate in 1992. In a sense, Obama was allied with Heather Booth
in this effort, since Booth—arguably the queen of socialist politics in
Chicago—served as field director for Moseley Braun's campaign.[105]
Technically, Booth was no longer director of the Midwest Academy, yet
she surely continued to enjoy tremendous de facto power there. Kelleher's papers include records of his contacts with Heather Booth.[106]
Kelleher wanted Booth to arrange for Moseley Braun to appear at a
"multi-purpose" ACORN event at which voters would be registered,
but where the focus would be on ACORN's banking campaign and
Moseley Braun's political pitch. If there was any separation at all
between Project Vote's supposedly non-partisan efforts, the Moseley
Braun campaign, and ACORN's banking activism, it is impossible
to discern it from Kelleher's writings. In 1992, Obama, ACORN,
the Moseley Braun campaign, Reverend Wright, Father Pfleger, and
the Midwest Academy were all part of a single tightly interconnected
political alliance. This is entirely consistent with ACORN's own conception of its voter registration work. Internal ACORN documents
stress that its voter registration activities should never be conducted
in isolation, but always be tightly bound to ACORN's recruiting efforts
and issue campaigns.[107] That is one reason why Obama's voter registration work with ACORN matters. Obama's decision to place Chicago ACORN and SEIU Local 880 on Project Vote's original steering
committee advanced ACORN as an organization. ACORN's leaders

were very clearly part of a select group of Obama's closest political associates.

Shaking with Anger

ACORN's banking campaign was running full speed throughout the Moseley Braun campaign. In September of 1992, ACORN's banking activism and Chicago ACORN's work for Carol Moseley Braun would dramatically intersect. The tale begins with ACORN's campaign against Citibank, one of the few major national financial institutions that refused to join ACORN's loan program. Citibank left a July 1992 ACORN-sponsored bank "summit" without agreeing to cooperate. Within days, five hundred singing and chanting ACORN members "stormed" Citicorp's New York headquarters, in what one ACORN official called "an old-fashioned takeover."[108] At that point, Citibank agreed to talk, but without committing to cooperation beyond that.

The storming of Citicorp kicked off a carefully coordinated national effort to crush remaining resistance from America's banks to "voluntary" cooperation with ACORN's subprime mortgage programs. A July 18, 1992, strategy memo from ACORN head Wade Rathke begins, "Clearly we are riding a bronco here."[109] Rathke assigned Steuart Pittman to coordinate the national banking effort. (This is apparently the same ACORN operative who organized tenants at Chicago's Altgeld Gardens housing project in 1984, just before Obama's arrival.) Chicago ACORN's Madeline Talbott was to serve as the campaign's national "field director," whipping up "mass actions" against carefully targeted banks across the country.[110] One thing ACORN and the banks agreed on was the resemblance between ACORN's banking campaign and an extortion racket. Rathke ends his July 18 memo with a reference to "all of our joking about extortion of the banks." A follow-up memo from one of ACORN's legislative lobbyist notes that many of the banks at ACORN's summit "clearly viewed us as an extortion ring."[111]

The foundation had now been laid for a dramatic confrontation between Chicago ACORN and Citibank. This clash left ACORN's banking campaign coordinators buzzing for weeks. Chicago Citibank staffers had been summoned to an August 29 ACORN rally and were seated on a stage looking out on four hundred ACORN and Local 880 members as ACORN banking expert Ernestine Whiting berated them unmercifully before the crowd—presumably for racism and greed. Whiting was about to temper her attacks with at least a bit of praise when U.S. Senate candidate Carol Moseley Braun showed up to address the crowd. This left the Citibank people "shaking with anger" and "embarrassed and stewing on stage." Said one memo, "By the end of the rally the negotiations were irretrievable. The Citibank representatives took everything personal. They felt they had been set up for a 'good old fashioned blind-sided sucker punch.'" The "meeting ended with a 10 minute shouting match," after which the female Citibank CRA officer was literally pulled out of the room by a male colleague as she was getting ready to physically attack one of ACORN's female leaders.[112] Apparently, the Carol Moseley Braun appearance that Keith Kelleher had arranged with Heather Booth, in conjunction with Project Vote, set off one of ACORN's more notorious banking clashes. The records do not show how much Obama knew about this, but it was the talk of his ACORN colleagues for weeks. In any case, as a civil rights attorney filing housing discrimination suits in Chicago, Obama surely knew about ACORN's high-pressure attack on area banks. Obama was co-counsel in a 1994 suit against Citibank for alleged racial discrimination in its mortgage policies.[113] Obama might have coordinated that suit with ACORN. In any case, it's clear that, despite his denials in 2008, Obama's 1992 Project Vote alliance was deeply entangled in ACORN's broader organizing work.

It took a while for ACORN to bring Citicorp to heel, but the bankers were afraid to walk away from the table, so ACORN ultimately got its way. Meanwhile, in late 1992, two ominous events transpired behind the scenes. On October 20, 1992, prominent socialist strategists and ACORN allies Peter Dreier and John Atlas sat down with a high

ACORN official and Marc Weiss, presidential candidate Bill Clinton's senior policy advisor on housing.[114] Weiss emphasized his desire to reverse President Reagan's elimination of politicized VISTA grants. Weiss argued, however, that reversing Reagan's "de-funding of the left" would better be done by "hiding" financial support for ACORN inside nondescript government programs than by an open battle to revive a controversial program like VISTA. ACORN agreed with this tactic of stealth. ACORN also endorsed a big-picture Atlas-Dreier housing strategy paper for the new administration. In a second ominous development, Congresswoman Maxine Waters (D-CA) invited a top ACORN lobbyist to write a piece of legislation designed to grant ACORN everything it wanted from federal housing policy.[115]

SECTION SIX

THE CLINTON ADMINISTRATION

In November of 1992, Carol Moseley Braun won her Senate seat and Bill Clinton won the presidency. Obama moved on from Project Vote to a civil rights law practice in Chicago. Meanwhile, Chicago ACORN's banking campaign pressed on. Thanks in great part to ACORN's lobbying, Congress imposed low-income lending quotas on Fannie Mae and Freddie Mac in 1992, while Chicago ACORN's threat to invade Fannie Mae's bank fair helped force the agency to cooperate with ACORN's loan-counseling corporation nationally. The result was a 1993 Fannie Mae pilot program led by Chicago ACORN's Madeline Talbott. According to the *Chicago Sun-Times,* this partnership of ACORN and Fannie Mae was designed to make mortgages available to borrowers "with troubled credit histories."[116] In time, this initiative would provoke a brand-new form of financial trouble for the nation.

Meanwhile, in the nation's capital, ACORN was ushered through the doors of power. National ACORN's files from 1993 are filled with records of visits to high officials of the Clinton administration, including White House chief of staff Mack McLarty, Clinton confidant and associate attorney general Webster Hubbell, and officials of the president's Domestic Policy Council and National Economic Council.[117] The Senate Banking Committee even asked for advice on "ACORN-type pork" (the committee's phrase, not ACORN's) to include in a banking bill.[118] ACORN's agenda at this point reached far beyond the Community Reinvestment Act, although ACORN did want to see CRA "strengthened." ACORN's real goal going into the Clinton administration was to spread the lending provisions of the Community Reinvestment Act throughout the financial system as a whole. This had already begun with the imposition of low-income lending quotas on Fannie Mae and Freddie Mac, and ACORN was determined to push the process further.

Elated

The most ACORN-friendly Clinton administration official of all was Secretary of Housing and Urban Development Henry Cisneros. A delegation of top ACORN leaders and lobbyists left their first meeting with Cisneros "elated."[119] Famous as one of the first Hispanic mayors of an American city, Cisneros had established a working relationship in his home of San Antonio with a largely Hispanic community group called COPS (Communities Organized for Public Service). COPS's ground-breaking political pressure techniques were developed by Ernesto Cortez, an organizer for the IAF (Industrial Areas Foundation), the organizing institute founded by Saul Alinsky himself.[120] COPS was the model Obama mentors Greg Galluzzo and Mary Gonzales had in mind when they founded their own largely Hispanic community group, UNO of Chicago, in 1980.[121]

So when ACORN met with Housing Secretary Cisneros, it found a friend. The first of many meetings between ACORN and Cisneros lasted for two uninterrupted hours, instead of the one hour originally scheduled. Already, at that first meeting, Cisneros promised ACORN help with what were soon to become the Clinton administration's signature changes in low-income lending policy—at Fannie and Freddie and elsewhere. Cisneros then asked ACORN's leaders for detailed information on their organizing techniques, which he wanted to compare to tactics used by COPS. He asked if ACORN was "adversarial," forcing politicians into yes-or-no answers like COPS (and like UNO of Chicago—and Obama himself). Cisneros made his approval of these tough tactics clear. Without being asked, Cisneros also requested ideas on ways HUD could channel money to ACORN and other community organizations. This last topic is what added an hour onto the meeting.

Their first encounter with Cisneros set ACORN's top leadership buzzing. Although they were elated, ACORN's officials worried that government money would turn them into a political target.[122] Memories of the old VISTA scandals and similar controversies lingered. Just days after that first meeting with Cisneros, ACORN head Wade Rathke issued a long memo (with copies to Madeline, Zach, and Steuart, among others, presumably Madeline Talbott, Zach Polett, and Steuart Pittman). The memo was a masterpiece in the art of hiding money trails—penned by the master himself. Rathke wraps up his tour of possible schemes for camouflaging federal dollars by saying:

> I think pragmatically the politics are such that we would be wise to resist grants and/or contracts directly to ACORN, Inc. but try and either set up separate corporations . . . or use existing corporations . . . that are less overtly moving the money directly into ACORN, Inc., though in truth it would be going there in other ways. Certainly having CORAP [an older and controversial ACORN stand-in entity] did not completely insulate us from problems, but I can not believe it is smart for him [Cisneros] or for us to leave our ass hanging in the wind waiting to be kicked.[123]

Specific legal accusations aside, this certainly seems consistent with the general picture of ACORN's financial shell games sketched out by Congressman Issa and other ACORN critics.

Discrimination

ACORN didn't quite have carte blanche within the Clinton administration, which had its pro-business elements as well. Occasionally ACORN had to battle administration opponents, at which times ACORN seemed particularly good at getting its hands on memos it was not supposed to see (no doubt through leaks from allies in the bureaucracy).[124] On one occasion, ACORN led a successful behind-the-scenes charge to torpedo the nomination of a banking regulator who was hostile to their approach.[125] ACORN had clout.

ACORN also seems to have played a significant behind-the-scenes role in Assistant Secretary for Fair Housing Roberta Achtenberg's efforts to push subprime lending through the broader financial system. By the mid-nineties, the Community Reinvestment Act applied only to about a quarter of the banking system. Yet Achtenberg made key regulatory changes that had the effect of pressuring the other three-quarters of America's mortgage industry into greater subprime lending.[126] In particular, Achtenberg ruled that, regardless of any intention to discriminate, policies that ended up granting proportionally more loans to some groups than others would be considered discriminatory. So if blacks in some cities happened to have shakier credit histories than whites (a common phenomenon), banks would be punished even for applying exactly the same lending standards to both blacks and whites. Achtenberg's new definition of discrimination helped push even institutions not covered by CRA into the business of shaky subprime lending. ACORN pressed Achtenberg hard on this and other issues, at times with help from Housing Secretary Cisneros.[127] So when ACORN denies responsibility for the financial meltdown by pointing to the limited jurisdiction of the Community Reinvestment Act, it is being disingenuous. ACORN used its considerable influence within the Clinton administration to spread the practice of subprime lending well beyond those sections of the banking system controlled by CRA.

Bill Ayers

On April 20, 1993, having heard a presentation from ex-Weatherman Bill Ayers, then an education expert at the University of Illinois, three hundred ACORN members began shouting and chanting "Small Schools Now! Small Schools Now!" pressing local officials to sign on to Ayer's project.[128] Ayers had become a consultant to Chicago ACORN on his signature issue: creating miniature "schools-within-schools" built around themes, such as peace and Afro-centrism. The catch phrase "small schools" was really a euphemism for what would more accurately have been called, "leftist political schools."

Working with Ayers, ACORN's plan was to set up a series of ACORN-controlled mini-schools in Chicago. Although banking was ACORN's top priority in the early to mid-nineties, education was a major ACORN initiative during these years. After linking up with Bill Ayers to run a foundation called the Chicago Annenberg Challenge, Obama himself would soon be deeply involved in ACORN's education efforts. I'll leave further discussion of ACORN's education program to the chapter on Obama's relationship to Bill Ayers. It's important to keep in mind, however, that alongside Chicago ACORN's preoccupation with its mortgage campaign, the group's educational partnership with Bill Ayers was getting off the ground in 1993.

THE NEW PARTY

Along with ACORN's move to gain a foothold within the public school system by creating its own mini-schools, the group's other major priority in 1993—after housing—was the creation of a third political party under de facto ACORN control. Along with a considerable number of prominent American socialists, ACORN was a key force behind the formation of the "New Party." Obama first ran for office with New Party endorsement, and while Obama and his supporters vehemently deny it, substantial evidence indicates that Obama himself was a member of the New Party. The New Party was far to the left of the mainstream Democratic Party, although its "fusion" strategy allowed it to endorse candidates running on the Democratic line. Like the Citizen/ Labor Energy Coalition, the New Party is best understood as an attempt to build a mass-based political front for a largely socialist party leadership.

Obama Denies It

Obama's tie to this far-left, ACORN-controlled third party explains a lot about why he denied his ACORN connection during the 2008 campaign. Although Obama's selection of ACORN and SEIU Local 880 to be on Project Vote's steering committee in 1992 was a real boon to those groups, it's hard to see why Obama didn't just confess his 1992 alliance with Chicago ACORN. That connection could likely have been acknowledged and minimized without serious political damage. The deeper problem for Obama was that his ACORN connection went well beyond Project Vote and included membership in an ACORN-controlled third political party, far to the left of the American mainstream. Public awareness of that third-party connection could have done serious harm to the Obama campaign in 2008. So it was apparently worth deceiving the public to keep the full picture of Obama's involvement with ACORN out of sight.

To this day, few Americans know anything about the controversy over Obama's ties to the New Party. Along with other critics, I wrote about Obama's New Party connection during the 2008 campaign, yet the mainstream press avoided the issue.[129] This is another reason why popular perceptions of Obama's politics continue to differ so greatly. American conservatives who read online sources tend to know things about Obama's radical political past that the broader public has never heard.

After I wrote about Obama's New Party ties, late in the 2008 campaign, Obama's "Fight the Smears" website came out swinging—calling my claim that Obama had been a New Party member a "crackpot smear."[130] As Obama's critics buzzed about the New Party issue, *Politico*'s Ben Smith—a prominent media gatekeeper—poured cold water on the idea that there was anything particularly radical about the New Party, or that Obama himself had been a member. Smith's source for these denials was New Party co-founder Joel Rogers. Smith and I then had several sharp exchanges about Obama's New Party ties.[131]

Through the medium of Ben Smith, New Party co-founder Joel Rogers first moved to quash concerns about Obama's New Party connection by denying that the New Party ever had members at all.[132] If nobody was a New Party member, of course, Obama could hardly have been one. Rogers also stressed to Smith that the New Party's contemporary successor, New York State's Working Families Party, had endorsed Hillary Clinton—and even some Republican State Senate candidates. Rogers then described the New Party platform for Smith as favoring "national health insurance and wage insurance, quality education, and environmentalism," all ideologically "well within the left half of the Democratic Party," Smith concluded. As for the charge that the New Party was socialist, Rogers said that socialism meant placing the "means of production under public ownership." "The New Party was never about that," Rogers maintained.

Rogers's claims about the New Party were thoroughly misleading. The New Party certainly did have members. In fact, the New Party's own publications called Obama a member. It's tough to see how taking contemporaneous New Party documents at their word constitutes a "crackpot smear." It's true that the New Party's successor, the Working Families Party, endorsed Hillary Clinton and the occasional Republican, but its fusion strategy is designed to use co-endorsements to pull the rest of the political spectrum to the left. One of the reasons liberal New York Republican state senator Deirdre (Dede) Scozzafava raised a national furor among Republicans when she ran for Congress in 2009 is that she had repeatedly been endorsed by the Working Families Party. Republicans across the country were outraged that Scozzafava had run with support from this far-left, ACORN-controlled group.[133] Moreover, Joel Rogers understood perfectly well that in the eighties and nineties America's socialists had shifted their strategy away from (immediate) nationalization of the means of production. After all, Rogers himself was one of the most important advocates of taking control of the economy indirectly, "from below," by gaining a place for groups like ACORN in the boardrooms and financial centers of capitalism.[134]

The New Party's platform was also far more radical than platitudes like "quality education" and "environmentalism" indicate. So Rogers's self-interested denials of New Party radicalism—and of Obama's own New Party membership—were deeply misleading. This was already clear from information in the public domain, but I have new evidence from the ACORN archives at the Wisconsin Historical Society that allows us to follow Obama's path to membership in the New Party in greater detail.

A Radical Party

Before examining the archival material pertaining to Obama's own New Party ties, let's review the evidence for the New Party's radicalism— and its links to ACORN. The files of Illinois ACORN/SEIU 880 at the

Wisconsin Historical Society reveal internal debate about how ideologically open the New Party ought to be. In an early strategy memo, New
Party co-founders Daniel Cantor and Joel Rogers called on the party to
publicly advocate "social democracy." Cantor and Rogers wanted the
New Party to be "an explicitly social democratic organization, with an
ideology roughly like that of Northern European (e.g., Swedish) labor
movements."[135] A party standing on the left side of Sweden's political
spectrum would clearly be radical by American standards—and a far
cry from Rogers's portrayal of the New Party's stance to Ben Smith.
That's exactly why one New Party figure took issue with Cantor/Rogers
and called instead for the New Party to use "less ideologically charged"
public language—even as that critic confessed personal agreement with
Cantor's and Rogers's far-left political preferences.[136]

Other internal ACORN/New Party documents articulate the modi-
fied socialist strategy of the day, calling for a "pragmatic" leftism that
rejects ideological purity and instead favors "organizing the private
economy to serve public ends."[137] In other words, instead of nationalization, the New Party hoped to use a combination of government
regulation and devolution of power to community groups like ACORN
to create "popular and democratic control over the economy."[138] The
agenda here was simply socialism by other means. A sympathetic article on the New Party in the newsletter of the Democratic Socialists of
America got the message—treating the New Party's political goals as a
kind of stand-in for socialism.[139]

The New Party's nineties platform was actually an updated version
of the superficially "populist"—but de facto socialist—program favored
by Obama's future mentors and colleagues at the Midwest Academy
in the late seventies and early eighties.[140] Echoing Midwest Academy
strategy, the New Party downplayed controversial social issues like
abortion, gay rights, and affirmative action, instead using economic
campaigns to build a national majority coalition along class lines.[141]
There is certainly overlap between the New Party platform and the
liberal agenda of today's Democratic Party—including "card check"

unionization laws and early advocacy for what we now call "cap-and-trade" pollution taxes.

Yet the New Party also envisioned a program of constraints on America's businesses that was far to the left of the Democratic Party. Announcing that "our major economic problem is not the government, as conservatives claim, but American enterprise itself," the New Party called for a "demanding Federal code of social responsibility" that would subject all private companies to "standards of social usefulness." Businesses abiding by this code would be "eligible for 'most favored company' status, with attendant benefits." The New Party also called for a "Corporate Democracy Act" much like the one backed by the Midwest Academy and its anti-business coalition partners back in 1980.[142] So the New Party was a reincarnation in the nineties of the stealth-socialist electoral and legislative politics practiced by the Midwest Academy more than a decade before. This time, however, Obama was right in the middle of it.

A Socialist Party

Joel Rogers's denials to Ben Smith notwithstanding, then, the New Party's program was an effectively socialist grab for public control over the economy. The strategy was to leave the private economy formally intact, while turning it into a hollow shell in practice. Leftist observers said as much, acknowledging, with a wink, the New Party's reluctance to be labeled socialist, while pointing out that its actual policies would be considered "radical" even by European standards.[143] Joel Rogers himself touted the New Party in the Marxist journal *New Left Review*, in terms that made his party's underlying socialism clear.[144]

The New Party was chock full of prominent American socialists. The papers of Frances Fox Piven contain letters from New Party co-founder Danny Cantor inviting the large delegation of New Party members speaking at the 1993 Socialist Scholars Conference to a socialist workshop on the New Party, with a large group photo afterward.[145] Many of these individuals—Frances Fox Piven, Manning Marable, Barbara Ehrenreich, Cornel West—had been prominent at the Socialist Scholars Conferences Obama attended in the mid-eighties (see Chapter Two). Recall that New Party co-founder Danny Cantor himself had been enamored of Marxist theorist Andre Gorz back when he worked for ACORN in 1979.

During the 2008 presidential campaign, I bracketed the question of the New Party's alleged socialism.[146] The issue struck me as fraught with definitional complications, and ultimately unnecessary to settle, given the fact that the New Party was far to the left of the Democratic Party. Having been forced by my study of Obama's past to confront the socialism question, I am now convinced that it is fair, revealing, and important to label the New Party an effectively socialist group. In 2008, I made note of the fact that about a quarter of New Party members in Chicago came from the Democratic Socialists of America (DSA). Yet I also emphasized that the vast majority of Chicago New Party members were associated with Chicago ACORN or SEIU Local 880, rather than the DSA.[147] It's now clear, however, that ACORN itself is a socialist front group. So the New Party was a coalition of open socialists from the DSA and a larger, "mass-based" socialist front group called ACORN. These sorts of partially stealthy hard-left coalitions are what enabled sophisticated American socialists in the post-sixties era to exercise large-scale political power.

Fronting for ACORN

The New Party was also very much a front for ACORN—and this was particularly so in Chicago. According to the most informative published history of the New Party: "Wade Rathke, ACORN's lead national organizer, was in on the founding discussions that led to the New Party, and the group's political director, Zach Polett, also came to play a big role in guiding New Party field organizing for the party [in Chicago and Little Rock]."[148] Illinois ACORN/SEIU Local 880 documents confirm this.

Madeline Talbott and Keith Kelleher were clearly running the New Party on the ground in Chicago, while coordinating their moves with Zach Polett at ACORN central in Little Rock.[149] The national newsletter of the Democratic Socialists of America also treats the New Party as essentially the "electoral arm" of ACORN and its allied SEIU locals.[150]

A fascinating July 1993 exchange between Zach and Wade (presumably ACORN political director Zach Polett and ACORN head Wade Rathke) specifies ACORN's ultimate interest in the New Party.[151] In these memos from the ACORN archive, Polett notes resistance by many potential recruits to joining a third political party. Polett asks Rathke if it might be a better idea to drop the formal party plan and instead explore a technically non-party vehicle like that being used by the Ross Perot movement at the time. Rathke replies that while he hopes for the national success of the New Party, his real long-term goal for ACORN is the creation of a true third party with its own ballot line in cities where ACORN is strong. In short, the New Party in Chicago was essentially an electoral front for ACORN. Of course, the New Party had not yet achieved its own separate ballot line in Chicago in 1996. So when Obama first stood for public office he ran on the Democratic line. Yet by enthusiastically accepting the endorsement of the New Party—and the party membership that acceptance entailed—Obama was cementing his relationship with ACORN, and, in effect, sending out a message that he would be ACORN's man in the Illinois State Senate.

Illinois New Party documents are filled with references to individuals we know are part of Obama's political network, and some other interesting characters as well. It's not always clear whether Obama's close political associates had actually joined the New Party, but many of them were on lists of recruiting prospects. Jeremiah Wright was apparently suggested as a possible New Party recruit by Joe Gardner, Obama's partner at Project Vote.[152] Gardner himself cooperated extensively with both the New Party and the party's front group, "Progressive Chicago."[153] John ("Jody") Kretzmann, a longtime associate of both Barack and Michelle Obama, was on the New Party mailing list, along with Obama's successor at the Developing Communities Project, John Owens.[154] There was also a New Party contingent from the Committee of Correspondence—an even more hard-line Marxist organization than the Democratic Socialists of America.[155] This included prominent former SDSer Carl Davidson, who was singled out for a special invitation from Talbott and Kelleher to join the New Party's leadership.[156] Longtime Obama colleague and prominent Chicago socialist Quentin Young also hosted an early New Party fundraiser.[157]

Pursuing Obama

As leaders of both the New Party and Chicago ACORN, Madeline Talbott and Keith Kelleher had several reasons to pursue Obama in 1993. Talbott was copied on a March 1993 memo from Zach Polett reporting on a meeting with Marxist theorists, longtime ACORN supporters, and voter registration activists Richard Cloward and Frances Fox Piven. Cloward and Piven foresaw the need to build up a stable of civil rights lawyers around the country to bring suits to force compliance with the Motor Voter Act.[158] No doubt Talbott quickly realized that Obama was a candidate for the job in Illinois, which in fact he got two years later, in 1995. In 1993, the Illinois New Party also badly needed a competent lawyer to provide it with pro bono (free) legal assistance.[159] On top of that, as a well-connected Chicago leftist who had worked closely with ACORN in 1992 and was famous as the first black editor of the *Harvard Law Review*, Obama surely stood out as a possible future New Party electoral candidate. What plays out in New Party/ACORN/SEIU 880 files in 1993, then, is a systematic campaign to woo Obama into a deeper relationship with Chicago ACORN and its electoral arm, the New Party.

In 1993, Keith Kelleher initiated a series of meetings with prominent Chicago leftists he viewed as potential future members of the New Party. To facilitate the recruitment process, the New Party/ACORN/SEIU 880 created a front group called "Progressive Chicago." Supposedly the purpose of Progressive Chicago was to reunite the coalition that had elected Harold Washington mayor.[160] In fact, Progressive Chicago was designed as a buffer that would allow individuals and groups that might be uncomfortable working directly with a third party to provide the New Party with indirect support.[161] In other words, work with Progressive Chicago would allow politically connected leftists to help the New Party, without angering their Democratic Party allies. Ultimately, of course, Progressive Chicago was designed to serve as a recruitment funnel into the New Party. Kelleher's private meetings with prominent Chicago leftists throughout 1993 were intended to scout out potential New Party recruits, whom he would at first simply try to draw into a public association with Progressive Chicago.

In May of 1993, Kelleher met with former top Harold Washington political aide Jacky Grimshaw.[162] We learned in Chapter Five that Grimshaw was a close colleague of Heather Booth and a strong supporter of Booth's socialist front group, the Midwest Academy. Grimshaw was also a close colleague of Barack and Michelle Obama at Public Allies and is currently the next-door neighbor of the Obamas in Chicago. Grimshaw's recommendation to Sanford Newman at Project Vote, along with support from other Chicago organizers, helped Obama secure his position at the head of Illinois Project Vote in 1992.[163] Kelleher's hand notes from his meeting with Grimshaw show her recommending Obama as a possible New Party recruit, along with Midwest Academy leader Jackie Kendall and Obama's early organizing mentor at UNO of Chicago, Mary Gonzales. Meanwhile, New Party files in June of 1993 contain indications that obtaining free legal advice for the New Party was becoming an increasingly urgent priority. This gave Kelleher yet another reason to court Obama.

On July 27, 1993, Keith Kelleher personally met with Obama about a possible association with Progressive Chicago—and ultimately the New Party.[164] Kelleher's hand notes from that meeting show that, like so many other potential New Party recruits, Obama was interested, yet also cautious about anything that might jeopardize his relations with the Democratic Party. Supposedly, the New Party's "fusion" strategy was designed to solve this problem, by allowing New Party candidates to cooperate with other parties as well. Yet fusion or not, prospective New Party members were understandably cautious about offending the Democrats by joining a third party.

According to Kelleher's hand notes, Obama told him that he was "more than happy to be involved" in New Party/Progressive Chicago affairs. On the other hand, Obama said he would be cautious about anything that might offend regular Democrats, and emphasized that he had no desire to "force people" into the New Party. Obama was clearly cagey and cautious, apparently telling Kelleher that he could attend a meeting (presumably of Progressive Chicago, but perhaps also of the New Party itself), yet couldn't "put too much time into it." Among others, Obama listed Alice Palmer (three years before he succeeded her in the Illinois State Senate) and Danny Davis (who eventually ran for Congress with the New Party) as potential New Party candidate recruits.

About two weeks later, New Party co-founder Daniel Cantor sent Obama a letter copied to Kelleher, to the other New Party co-founder, Joel Rogers, and to Rogers's wife, Sarah Siskind. Siskind was a lawyer in the Madison, Wisconsin, office of Obama's law firm and herself did important legal work defending the New Party's ability to run "fusion" candidates on state ballots. Siskind sometimes reported on her legal progress to ACORN head Wade Rathke.[165] In his letter to Obama, Cantor says that, based on what Sarah Siskind has already said to him about Obama, he (Cantor) expects that Obama ought to be quite interested in the New Party. Cantor encloses a batch of New Party literature and invites Obama to have a "serious discussion" with party theorist Joel Rogers about the New Party's purpose and strategy, on one of Rogers's frequent trips to Chicago.[166]

Need a Lawyer

A couple of months later, in a September 30, 1993, report on New Party activities to Danny Cantor, Keith Kelleher returns to the difficult issue of finding an affordable lawyer for the party. Kelleher notes that Sarah Siskind was planning to speak with "Barack" about doing legal work for the New Party, "but I have had no response from either of them" for a month. Kelleher then calls the task of finding a New Party lawyer a "major problem," noting that other potential candidates had been scared off for fear of offending the Democrats.[167]

A month later, on November 2, 1993, a memo from Keith Kelleher to Madeline Talbott appears to indicate that Kelleher has finally heard back from Obama. Kelleher has located a couple of attorneys willing to do legal work for the Illinois New Party. The problem is that none of these lawyers will work for free. Kelleher appears to think that Obama might help to lighten the cost of choosing one of these prospective attorneys, Steve Saltsman:

> He [Saltsman] said that we would control what his price will be by the stuff we ask him to do. He also said he could meet within the next week with us and/or the candidate. I did not ask Saltsman if he could work with Barack or have Barack do a lot of the work but Saltsman was open to teaching our members and staff to do a lot of the legal legwork, so he may not have a problem working with Barack.[168]

While Keith's (presumably Keith Kelleher's) meaning here cannot be known with certainty, the most reasonable interpretation, I think, is that Obama has let Kelleher know that he is—or may be—willing to do pro bono legal work for the New Party, so long as it does not involve openly taking on the role of the New Party's attorney in Illinois. Kelleher clearly seems to think that the New Party would be able to save money on legal fees if Saltsman were to farm out some of his work to

Obama. So it seems likely that Obama finally did get back to Kelleher and express a willingness to do at least some pro bono work for the party on a quiet basis.

If it's true that Obama gave at least a qualified indication of willingness to do legal work for the New Party, it also seems likely that Obama would have taken advantage of the opportunity to meet with Joel Rogers about the party's broader aspirations. Keep in mind that Obama did enthusiastically accept the New Party's endorsement in his first run for office in 1995–96. Given that, Obama's active consultation and cooperation with the party's leaders in 1993 seems all the more likely. Documents indicate that Steve Saltsman did eventually do legal work for the New Party.[169] It's unclear how long Saltsman's work continued, or whether Obama was ever involved. At a minimum, however, Obama seems to have given Kelleher reason to expect cooperation on a pro bono, or at least low-cost basis.

On the last day of 1993, a formal letter on Progressive Chicago letterhead inviting Obama to attend a meeting of the group went out under the signatures of Joe Gardner, Obama's partner at Project Vote the year before, and Ron Sable.[170] Sable was a prominent Chicago activist, a member of the socialist New American Movement (NAM), and a leading member of the Chicago chapter of the Democratic Socialists of America. Sable was also a board member of the Illinois Public Action Council (IPAC), the socialist-controlled community group most closely associated with Chicago's Midwest Academy.

Raising Money

The bulk of records from Chicago ACORN and SEIU Local 880 at the Wisconsin Historical Society extend through 1993. These records, however, do include a small archive box with just a few files from 1994. Inside that box is a remarkable packet of material—four attached memos from June of 1994—that cast substantial new light on Barack Obama's dealings with ACORN.[171] We saw that in the third presidential debate of 2008, Obama claimed that the only involvement he'd had with ACORN was his role as the group's attorney in a case involving enforcement of the federal Motor Voter law. When the McCain campaign alleged that, as head of Illinois Project Vote in 1992, Obama had effectively run an arm of ACORN, the Obama campaign denied that ACORN had played any part in Project Vote's work in 1992. Sanford Newman, the national head of Project Vote in 1992, also widely let it be known that it was not until 1994 that Project Vote was formally placed under the ACORN umbrella.

We already know that these campaign disclaimers were deeply misleading, since documentary evidence confirms that Obama worked closely with Chicago ACORN and the ACORN-controlled SEIU Local 880 on the steering committee of Project Vote in 1992. And of course we've just seen evidence of continuing cooperation in 1993 between Obama and the ACORN-controlled New Party, as well as the New Party's front group, Progressive Chicago. The documentary evidence from 1994 shows that Obama was also working closely with Project Vote, even as it came under direct ACORN control. In fact, Obama was apparently scheming in 1994 to ensure that his close ally and future campaign manager, Carol Harwell, would enjoy a prominent position within an ACORN-managed Project Vote. So while much was made in 2008 of the fact that Obama ran Project Vote in Illinois well before ACORN assumed formal control, Obama in fact remained deeply involved with Project Vote, even as it was incorporated into ACORN.

In 1994, ACORN assumed formal control of Project Vote, now to be led by Leslie Watson-Davis. The packet of memos in the files of SEIU Local 880 comes from the period when ACORN was consolidating full control of Project Vote, June of 1994. During that time, Local 880 head Keith Kelleher was negotiating with Obama's close associate Carol Harwell, who was pressing Kelleher to place her on the Project Vote executive committee—on terms that would cut her political competitors out of Project Vote or reduce their power within the group, or both. At the same time, Leslie Watson-Davis traveled to Chicago to explore potential funding sources for Project Vote in Illinois. The memos show Obama helping Watson-Davis, even as he was pressuring Kelleher to grant favorable terms to his ally, Harwell, within the new, ACORN-controlled Project Vote.

In a memo reporting to Zach Polett at ACORN headquarters on her Illinois trip, Watson-Davis recounts her meeting with Obama.[172] The two spent an hour together, during which time Obama thoroughly explained Project Vote's 1992 funding sources. Watson-Davis adds that Obama "is willing to work with me as host of a small, major dollar, reception for individuals who write personal checks of $1,000 plus." So Obama was not only cooperating with the ACORN-run Project Vote in 1994, he was offering to help them raise money. Watson-Davis appears to have received extensive advice from both outgoing Project Vote head Sanford Newman and Heather Booth on whom to meet in Chicago. This suggests that Booth was an important Newman contact and implies that Booth herself may have played a role, along with her close political ally Jacky Grimshaw, in convincing Newman to select Obama to head up Illinois Project Vote in 1992.[173]

Barack Is Very Influential

Even as Obama was offering financial help to Leslie Watson-Davis, he appears to have been withholding critical information from Keith Kelleher, in order to give his close associate and soon-to-be campaign manager Carol Harwell leverage in her negotiations with Project Vote. Kelleher apparently thought of Harwell as a hard-bitten, foul-mouthed, and not particularly appealing partner. In a memo to the leadership of ACORN and Project Vote, Kelleher toyed with the idea of ditching Harwell altogether, even at the possible cost of alienating Obama and losing fund-raising connections that only Obama and Harwell could provide. This is a long, fascinating, and detailed memo. Some excerpts, however, will convey the flavor:

I caution you that she [Harwell] is heavily organizing me around
these issues [the nature of her possible role with Project Vote]
and I believe Barach [*sic*] has told her of the national relationship
between me, ACORN and Project VOTE . . . She clearly wants
to work with Project VOTE but is not against doing it on her
own. I assume from what she says, with Barack and company. . . .
I asked her to get a copy of that list to me. She said she would
talk to Barack, who I have already called and received nothing
from. . . . Throughout the conversation, she kept referring to
Barack and how she would have to check with Barack about that
and this, and that Barack thinks this and that . . . But it is clear
to me that Barack is very influential in this and probably orchestrating a lot of it. . . . Although on several items concerning over-
head and Barack's advice on budget, etc. she said "Fuck Barack,
I don't think we need all that bullshit this time . . ." . . . . Anyway,
Barack seems to be the key to this plan. . . . I mean, what can I
say about Carol except, "Fuck her, let's hire Bob Hurd . . ." Seriously, though, I think we have a relationship, if one can have a
relationship with Carol. She has attended almost all of the Progressive Chicago meetings, perhaps with an eye to pulling this off
all the time.[174]

An interesting detail here is Harwell's regular attendance at meetings of Progressive Chicago. One of the memos in this packet is from
KK to WR (almost certainly Keith Kelleher to Wade Rathke) in which
Kelleher asks Rathke's advice about the future structure of Progressive
Chicago.[175] Kelleher makes it clear that most of the regular attendees
at meetings of Progressive Chicago were staffers of left-leaning politicians (who presumably might someday want to run with New Party/
Progressive Chicago support). While Kelleher interprets Harwell's regular attendance at Progressive Chicago meetings as her maneuvering
for a choice role within an ACORN-controlled Project Vote, it seems
quite likely that Harwell was also protecting and cultivating Obama's

prospects of running with New Party/Progressive Chicago support. We know that just a year after these memos were written, Obama would launch his first political campaign, with Harwell as his manager. At the time he wrote the memo, of course, Kelleher did not know this.

What makes this extraordinary is that, during the 2008 presidential campaign, Harwell herself was quoted on the Fight the Smears website saying: "Barack did not solicit or seek the New Party endorsement for state senator in 1995."[176] Enough evidence is already public to show that this is false, as we'll see. In any case, it is at least arguable that, in direct contradiction to her own claims, Carol Harwell herself was actually soliciting a New Party endorsement on Obama's behalf—by virtue of her close cooperation with the New Party's front group, Progressive Chicago.

An October 10, 1994, memo to all ACORN offices from Political Director Zach Polett took up the subject of ACORN's national Motor Voter strategy. That memo includes the following notice: "We have retained Barack Obama with the Davis, Miner law firm on a contingency basis to represent ACORN as local counsel in a suit against the state [of Illinois]."[177] Whether Carol Harwell ended up getting a position on the executive committee of Illinois Project Vote, and if so, on what terms, is unclear. At any rate, Obama's pressure on behalf of Harwell's bid for influence within Project Vote certainly doesn't seem to have damaged his standing with ACORN. On the contrary, four months after the Harwell negotiations, Obama was representing ACORN in a major lawsuit.

During the 2008 campaign, Obama was often described by news reports as being one of a team of lawyers representing ACORN in the Motor Voter battle.[178] Obama did call in other attorneys from his firm for help. Yet this ACORN memo, along with numerous references to Obama in the files of Richard Cloward and Frances Fox Piven's HumanSERVE group, refer to Obama—and Obama alone—as ACORN's attorney.[179] Clearly, it was the Obama connection that drew ACORN to the law firm of Davis, Miner. And although we have little beyond legal papers and a few fax coversheets, it's likely that Obama was consulting on the Motor Voter case with Cloward and Piven's group as well (probably by phone), just as Human SERVE itself was closely consulting with ACORN.[180]

More than ten years before, at the Cooper Union Socialist Scholars Conference at which he decided to become a community organizer, Obama heard Frances Fox Piven open the proceedings, and quite possibly also heard Peter Dreier outline the path from community organizing to politics, through groups like ACORN and Citizen Action. A decade later, Obama was well and truly ensconced in this socialist organizing network. During the 2008 presidential campaign, the only relationship with ACORN Obama would admit to was acting as the group's attorney in the Motor Voter suit. It's clear, however, that Obama's work for ACORN on that suit was simply one event in what was in fact a continuing and ever-deepening political partnership.

SECTION EIGHT

CRISIS AND DECEPTION

ACORN Meets Clinton

In late July of 1994, a delegation from ACORN met with President Clinton at the White House. It was a landmark moment in ACORN's continuing efforts to pull the Clinton administration into its various subprime lending schemes. ACORN's goal was clear: "Our #1 agenda item for the meeting is extension of CRA to non-banks."[181] In other words, ACORN wanted to extend the reach of the Community Reinvestment Act to the three-quarters of the financial system not yet covered by its most important legal weapon. That would hand ACORN a lever with which to force subprime lending onto mortgage companies, mutual funds, and insurance companies—bringing vastly more money into ACORN's loan counseling program in the process. ACORN also sought to bolster Clinton's support for the extensive help it was already receiving from HUD Secretary Cisneros and Assistant Secretary Achtenberg.[182]

In 1994, ACORN's direct-action campaign was also focused on drawing ever more sectors of the financial system into its lending schemes. ACORN's presentation to Clinton at the White House highlighted the organization's just-negotiated $10 million agreement with Allstate to buy mortgage backed securities issued by Fannie Mae, for loans originated under an ACORN program run through Nations-Bank.[183] ACORN had captured the banks, and even Fannie Mae. Now it was aiming to rope insurance companies into its loan counseling program. ACORN's highest priority was convincing Clinton to support these efforts.

President Clinton had to squeeze his meeting with ACORN into a day on which he was hosting a summit between Jordan's King Hussein and Israeli prime minister Yitzhak Rabin. Even so, Clinton managed to give the group half an hour, chiefly to discuss extension of CRA to non-banks. As the meeting began, ACORN president Maude Hurd presented Clinton with an ACORN T-shirt, which the president modeled and promised to wear jogging the next day. ACORN then explained the need to extend CRA to non-banks, presenting the Allstate deal as a model. According to ACORN political director Zach Polett, "Clinton jumped on this like white on rice." While Clinton explained that he probably couldn't get a bill to ACORN's liking through Congress, he promised to use "the executive power of the president" to achieve the same ends.[184]

A National Economic Council staffer in attendance added that the mutual fund industry had already approached the administration to see how it might promote subprime lending. It seems that Wall Street was using the promise of cooperation to forestall legislation intended to extend CRA to non-banks—like the bill written for Maxine Waters by ACORN. Warming to the idea of drawing mutual funds into the subprime lending business, Clinton told his aides to "take this up in earnest." At this point in his memo recounting the meeting, ACORN's political director exalts: "This could open up a whole new front for the CRA campaigns, negotiations, and victories."[185]

Create a Crisis?

So while much debate has centered on the impact of the Community Reinvestment Act on the financial meltdown, the real story of ACORN's influence goes far beyond CRA. With substantial help from the Clinton administration and its congressional allies, ACORN was coordinating a campaign of regulation and political pressure designed to spread the practice of subprime lending far beyond the limited sector of the financial system covered by CRA. Analysts like American Enterprise Institute scholar Peter J. Wallison have long argued that, although the CRA itself did not produce enough weak loans to create the financial crisis, CRA initiated a degradation in the quality of mortgages that eventually spread across the broader financial system. Wallison cites Fannie Mae and Freddie Mac, along with Clinton administration policy—especially as set by HUD (i.e., Secretary Cisneros)—as key channels through which the dangers of CRA were generalized.[186] What emerges from the archival evidence is the extent to which ACORN was acting behind the scenes to orchestrate this entire process.

Was ACORN's banking campaign part of an intentional effort to provoke a financial meltdown—a sort of variation on the strategy of orchestrated crisis popularized by ACORN advisors Richard Cloward and Frances Fox Piven in the sixties? I think the answer to this question is both "no" and "yes." It's dubious that either ACORN or its socialist advisors had a specific plan to use the group's banking campaign to provoke a national mortgage crisis. Cloward and Piven's plan to flood local and state welfare systems with recipients until President Johnson and the Democratic Congress created a guaranteed annual income was very specific. Moreover, it would have been difficult in the 1990s to even envision the complex chain of events by which

ACORN's efforts ultimately contributed to the financial meltdown of 2008.

On the other hand, it does seem possible—even likely—that in a more general sense, ACORN's mortgage activism was part of an overall strategy that did seek to contribute to, and certainly to take advantage of, periodic crises in capitalism. We know this because Peter Dreier, an influential advisor to ACORN's banking campaign, authored such a strategy. Dreier's idea (almost certainly influenced by Cloward and Piven, with whose work he was quite familiar) was to provoke an entitlement crisis that would undermine America's fiscal health, thus opening the way to socialism as a solution. A federally sponsored subprime lending policy would fit nicely into this scheme. In a sense, ACORN's plan was a socialist "twofer," putting the federal government indirectly on the hook for lending at Fannie Mae and Freddie Mac, while also handing the country's most radical community group significant influence over the core of American capitalism. Its tough to see why Dreier would have devoted so much effort to ACORN's banking campaign if it didn't advance his plans for encouraging a transition from capitalism to socialism.

In a sense, Dreier's work helped to "regularize" the orchestrated crisis strategy of Cloward and Piven. No longer would it be necessary to specify a particular path by which a crisis would be provoked. A "transitional strategy" for socialism could simply be pegged to a general expansion of government guarantees beyond the system's breaking point. Although it would be impossible to know where and when the next crisis would break out, the point was to keep pushing for unsustainable government largesse, while standing ready to take full advantage of the resulting crises to transform the system, bit by bit. This "reformist" stance replaced the premature revolutionary activism of the sixties and early seventies and allowed community organizers to connect their local and piecemeal efforts to a long-term socialist strategy. Barack Obama cut his teeth in a world in which this was the default political stance.

A Pattern of Deception

Although evidence from the Illinois ACORN/SEIU Local 880 archives runs out in mid-1994, we know how the story ends. In 1995–
96, Obama ran for the Illinois State Senate, with New Party support.
As a condition of that endorsement, Obama surely became an active
member of this far-left, ACORN-controlled party. In 1995, Obama
also represented ACORN in its suit to compel enforcement the federal
Motor Voter bill. That same year, in partnership with Bill Ayers, Obama
took control of an education foundation called the Chicago Annenberg
Challenge, from which he and Ayers channeled money into ACORN's
education projects. During this same period, Obama continued to
teach seminars on "power" for ACORN leaders, as he had for some
time.[187] To top it off, in 1995, Obama helped engineer a major increase
in funding for community organizing at the Woods Charitable Fund,
supervising a report on the issue in close consultation with Chicago
ACORN's Madeline Talbott.[188] That report made it clear that Obama
was perfectly aware of ACORN's use of high-pressure tactics against
area businesses. After all, Obama's friend, Chicago ACORN head
Madeline Talbott, was the national field director of ACORN's "direct-
action" assault on America's banks. Finally, ACORN members served
as foot soldiers in Obama's first and subsequent political campaigns, in
gratitude for his longstanding ties to this group.[189] (A number of these
issues will be taken up in the following chapter.) It's tough to see how
Obama's ties to ACORN could have been much closer.

During the 2008 presidential campaign, New Party co-founder Joel
Rogers attempted to keep a lid on this can of worms with the claim that
the New Party never had members to begin with. When pressed, Rogers clarified his meaning: The New Party in Illinois never had its own
line on the ballot, so that voters could formally register only as Republicans or Democrats.[190] Yet precisely because it had not yet achieved a
separate line on the ballot, Chicago's New Party devised other ways to
incorporate members. Members joined the New Party in 1995–96 by

signing up and paying dues. Moreover, candidates endorsed by Chicago's New Party were required to sign a contract mandating "a visible and active relationship" with the party.[191] There is no good reason why Obama would have been exempted from this requirement.

The evidence that Obama did in fact join the New Party and sign this contract is very strong. Above all, the Spring 1996 issue of the New Party's official organ, *New Party News*, explicitly calls Obama a New Party member.[192] That issue of *New Party News* even features a picture of Obama posing with other victorious New Party–endorsed candidates. Although Obama's salty-tongued 1996 campaign manager, Carol Harwell, claimed at the Fight the Smears website in 2008 that "Barack did not solicit or seek the New Party endorsement for state senator in 1995," persuasive contemporaneous evidence to the contrary exists.[193] An article on the New Party in the September–October 1995 issue of *New Ground,* the newsletter of the Chicago Democratic Socialists of America, describes Obama as one of a group of local politicians publicly appealing for New Party endorsement at a July 1995 party meeting.[194] Another leftist publication from the period, the *Progressive Populist,* also identifies Obama as a New Party member.[195]

Is there any evidence that Obama maintained the "visible and active relationship" with the New Party required by the endorsement contract he almost certainly signed? There is. A report on the New Party in the July–August 1996 issue of *New Ground* reports on Obama's participation in a New Party meeting where he expressed his gratitude for party support and invited members to join his task forces on voter education and voter registration.[196] In a January 2009 article in *The Progressive*, longtime Madison, Wisconsin, activist and writer John Nichols recalls appearances with Obama at New Party gatherings in the mid-nineties: "When we spoke together at New Party events in those days, he [Obama] was blunt about his desire to move the Democratic Party off the cautious center where Bill Clinton had wedged it."[197] So the claim that Obama was a New Party member in 1995–96 is supported by powerful evidence from the period in question. Denials in the present by supporters with every reason to protect Obama, like New Party co-founder Joel Rogers, are far less reliable than contemporaneous evidence. Just compare Carol Harwell's denials with the evidence of what she and Obama were actually doing at the time.

During the 2008 controversy over Obama's ACORN ties, the Fight the Smears website was forced to backtrack on its denial that Obama had ever been an ACORN trainer.[198] My own initial National Review Online piece on Obama's ACORN ties dug up a 2003–4 *Social Policy* article by Chicago ACORN leader Toni Foulkes that recounted Obama doing leadership training for the group on a yearly basis.[199] When the McCain campaign cited this article, the Obama camp was forced to confess the training and modify its denial at the Fight the Smears website. (By the way, when the ACORN controversy broke during the 2008 campaign, *Social Policy* pulled the Foulkes article from the Web. By then, however, the cat was out of the bag.)[200] Given the fact that a famous profile of Obama's first political campaign in the *Chicago Reader* also refers to his leadership training for ACORN, it's extraordinary that Obama ever denied this fact in the first place.[201]

The article by Foulkes and the profile in the *Chicago Reader* both characterize Obama's relationship to ACORN as long-standing and close. In December of 1995, for example, the *Reader* quotes Chicago ACORN leader Madeline Talbott saying:

> I can't repeat what most ACORN members think and say about politicians. But Barack has proven himself among our members. He is committed to organizing, to building a democracy. Above all else, he is a good listener, and we accept and respect him as a kindred spirit, a fellow organizer.[202]

Given all this, it seems fair to say that Barack Obama knowingly lied about his ties to ACORN during the 2008 campaign. But while a "lie" is certainly included in the problem, I think something much larger than a single infraction against the truth is at stake here. Obama's suppression of his ties to ACORN is part of a systematic and deeply-lying pattern of deception about his radical political past. Obama's campaign stance was so completely at odds with existing information on his ACORN ties—not to mention the archival evidence—that it is a matter for wonder that the candidate kept to his story, and did so with a straight face. Obama could have confessed more, I think, if full exposure of his ACORN ties hadn't threatened to unravel his entire radical network. As we've seen, rightly understood, Obama's ACORN connection encompasses everything from Reverend Wright, to Bill Ayers, to the Midwest Academy, to socialist crisis theorists like Richard Cloward, Frances Fox Piven, and Peter Dreier, to the socialist thinkers behind the New Party. The role of ACORN in the financial crisis was raised by McCain, and this turned the ACORN issue into political dynamite as well. ACORN is at the center of Barack Obama's political world, and the very immensity of that fact required nothing less than a brazen attempt at deception when the issue emerged in 2008. Yet the story of ACORN is Obama's story, too.

CHAPTER 7

Ayers and the Foundations

Barack Obama and Bill Ayers—that famously unrepentant revolutionary terrorist of the sixties—were longstanding political partners. For eight years, Ayers and Obama worked together at two leftist Chicago foundations. Obama praised Ayers's writings and funneled major financial support to the projects of Ayers and his radical allies. Ayers helped launch Obama's political career and joined with the future president in the battle over an Illinois juvenile crime bill. Ayers played an important role in elevating Obama to the position of board chairman at the Chicago Annenberg Challenge, an education foundation Ayers himself helped create. Evidence suggests that Obama was responsible for bringing Ayers onto the board of the Woods Fund of Chicago, where the two worked together to increase funding for radical community organizations, including ACORN and the Midwest Academy. Evidence also suggests that despite official denials the Obama-Ayers connection long predates 1995, when the Obama camp claims it began.

SECTION ONE

WHY AYERS MATTERS

Why is all this important? The Obama-Ayers relationship was a topic of intense controversy during the presidential election of 2008. I ought to know, since the attempt to block my research into the Obama-Ayers partnership—and then to prevent me from talking about my findings on the radio—helped inject the Ayers issue into the campaign.[1] Unfortunately, the controversy in 2008 got sidetracked on the question of whether Obama knew about Ayers's notorious activities as a member of the terrorist Weather Underground group in the late sixties and early seventies. True, Obama's willingness to fund and work with an unrepentant ex-terrorist is a legitimate and important issue. But the deeper significance of the Obama-Ayers alliance is what it tells us about Obama's politics in the present.

It turns out that Ayers was only the most visible component of Obama's radical network. In fact, making sense of the Ayers-Obama relationship requires a quick tour of virtually the entire socialist organizing community described in this book. Ayers worked closely with ACORN, supported the same sort of anti-capitalist and anti-American education programs favored by Jeremiah Wright, and maintained alliances with a number of prominent sixties radicals who largely retained their Marxist views. Like so many other partners in Obama's political world, Bill Ayers hoped to see the United States transformed into a socialist state. Ayers was actually just one of a series of former leaders of the radical SDS (Students for a Democratic Society) who worked with Obama throughout the future president's years in Chicago. These sixties veterans may have postponed their short-term revolutionary plans, but they never abandoned their core socialist beliefs.

During the 2008 presidential campaign, Chicago mayor Richard Daley floated the classic defense of the Ayers-Obama relationship. Let's not "keep re-fighting 40 year old battles," said the mayor. Yes, Daley conceded, "people do make mistakes in the past." But invoking Ayers's more recent work on public education, he added: "You move on. This is a new century, a new time. He [Ayers] reflects back and he's been making a strong contribution to our community."[2] Although Ayers escaped prosecution for terrorism on a technicality, the image Mayor Daley conjured was that of a repentant ex-con who goes straight after years in the slammer, devoting himself to community service to make up for his youthful crimes. In no way does that image describe what Bill Ayers has been up to.

Small c

Ayers is not sorry for the Weather Underground's terrorism, so it's hard to see how he can be forgiven. More important for our purposes, Ayers is a self-described communist, with a small c, who still yearns to see America's capitalist system overthrown by a violent revolution.[3] That is why Ayers is "unrepentant," why he keeps republishing old Weatherman texts, and why he writes memoir after memoir about his terrorist past. Ayers wants to leave a record that will be of use to radical activists in the present—and potential revolutionaries of the future. You can learn all about Ayers's revolutionary hopes in publications that few but his sympathizers have the patience to read.[4]

In his present-day battles, however, Ayers has put aside openly revolutionary rhetoric. It took Ayers a decade on the run from the law to recognize what his ex-SDS colleagues at the Midwest Academy had accepted years before: that America is in a "non-revolutionary period," during which patient community organizing and influencing the education system are the best ways to produce a socialist wave of the future. Although Ayers appears less committed to secrecy than his colleagues at the Midwest Academy, he is an excellent modern-day example of the shift from an openly revolutionary socialist stance to a stealthy "Popular Front" strategy. A careful student of his Communist Party forbears, Ayers understands his strategic and tactical shift in just these terms.[5]

So in channeling foundation money to the projects of Ayers and his radical allies, Obama was offering crucial support to Chicago's thriving contingent of socialist organizers and educators. That would be a story even if Ayers had never planted a single bomb forty years ago. This isn't a question of guilt by association, in other words, but of guilt by participation.

It's perfectly fair to judge a politician by the projects he funds and the allies he advances. Obama's foundation work was a major component of his pre-presidential career, and Ayers was arguably Obama's most important partner in the foundation world. Ken Rolling, one of the few who could challenge Ayers for that honor, was a long-time official of the crypto-socialist Midwest Academy. So Obama's foundation service was part and parcel of his longstanding allegiance to Chicago's socialist world.

While Obama's help with Ayers's projects would be news even if Ayers had never lifted a terrorist finger in the sixties, it's impossible to understand Ayers's socialist present without examining his Weatherman past. The projects in education, community organizing, and juvenile justice that Ayers and Obama jointly funded for eight years were all understood by Ayers as a way of advancing, in a non-revolutionary era, the basic political strategy outlined by the Weather Underground decades before. So let's return to the world of the Weathermen, focusing less on bombings than on the role of community organizing, education, and juvenile justice in their revolutionary plans. With that as background, we can trace the development of the foundation-based partnership of Ayers and Obama, and understand its purpose in the way that Ayers himself would have seen it.

SECTION TWO

COMMUNITY ORGANIZING, WEATHERMAN-STYLE

Bill Ayers may be best known as "a revolutionary anarcho-communist, small c, intent on overthrowing the government," but he was very much a community organizer as well.[6] In fact, the two identities overlap. Ayers first met his future wife, Bernardine Dohrn, as the two of them were emerging from community organizing stints with the SDS, Dohrn in Chicago and Ayers in Cleveland. "Activism and organizing," they had decided, "would become our way of life."[7] The SDS's community organizing schemes all flopped, however. Young SDSers were paralyzed by a vision of "participatory democracy" in which all decisions would be unanimously agreed upon and organizers would facilitate the plans of "the people," who inconveniently wanted no part of their would-be benefactors' socialist goals.

SDS's community organizing outpost in the middle of Cleveland's black ghetto, where Ayers worked, was known for being particularly ingrown and ineffective. The organizer commune once held a twenty-four-hour meeting to decide whether to take a day off and go to the beach.[8] Yet in Ayers's view, to become a community organizer was to enroll as "a volunteer in the army that would take on the American monster, end the American nightmare. . . ."[9] In other words, Ayers believed that community organizing among inner-city blacks would ignite a revolution. In Ayers's eyes, America's ghettos were "internal colonies," domestic counterparts of Third World nations oppressed by American imperialism. Just as Cuba and Vietnam had rebelled against America and embraced socialism, so, too, would America's internal colony of blacks lead a socialist uprising here at home. Here's how Ayers and Dohrn made the connection between inner-city community organizing and revolution in the Weather Underground's definitive 1974 tract, *Prairie Fire*:

The Black struggle for self-determination is the strategic leading force of the US revolution. . . . By fighting for control over their communities, schools, jobs and their future as a people, Black people also push forward the overthrow of the existing power relations in the entire society. . . . Organized struggles in local areas and the ongoing day-to-day battles of Black people are often not as visible as the actions and rebellions of a high-tide period. But they are urgent and necessary in the development of a people's movement.[10]

Hot Town

When rioting swept through black sections of Cleveland in the summer of 1966, Ayers took it as a sign of the revolution to come. Yet the riots and the accompanying rise of the Black Power movement spelled the end of the SDS's organizing ventures among blacks. Now militant black leaders like Stokely Carmichael insisted that white radicals leave the ghettos and instead convince whites to support the Black Power movement.[11] This enforced shift to political work with the white working class led Ayers and the emerging Weatherman faction to develop what may well be the most bizarre community organizing technique in history.

In the spring of 1969, Ayers was part of a group called the Jesse James Gang or the Action Faction. Although the James Gang was Marxist, it downplayed theory in favor of an "aggressive confrontation politics" that would provide a living model of the revolution for all to follow.[12] In April of 1969, the James Gang, led by Ayers and a coauthor, Jim Mellen, submitted a proposal to the SDS National Council for a summer community organizing project in Detroit that would ultimately lead to a wild new way of pushing the masses toward revolution. Named after a hit song by the Lovin' Spoonful, the proposal was called "Hot town: summer in the city."[13]

Ayers and his Action Faction meant to lead by example, stressing "the propaganda effect of the very existence of whites who are on the side of blacks against the system." The James Gang was looking for spectacular ways to demonstrate its commitment to a black-led and Third World–inspired revolution. The assumption was that the shock of seeing whites defending radical Black Panthers and Viet Cong warriors would wake up America's working-class youth to their own oppression by "the system," thus stampeding them into the camp of liberation. Insisting that militant blacks were the vanguard of social-ist revolution was a slap at the SDS's more traditional Marxist faction, which emphasized class and rejected race-based politics. Yet the hot-town strategy also effectively acknowledged that the American system could not be overthrown without help from the white working class— whether blacks led the revolution or not.

Ayers's revolutionary vision was uncompromising. In the hot-town proposal, he demanded a "total, fundamental economic and social transformation in which the working class overthrows and liquidates the ruling class." It's worth keeping these genocidal plans in mind when considering Ayers's claims to have bombed only property, not people, during the Weatherman's terrorist days.

Ayers's hot-town organizing strategy was a conscious break from the passivity and self-preoccupation of the SDS's earlier organizing strate-gies. "In our past organizing we incorrectly thought that SDS people should totally follow the direction of the people with whom they were working," said Ayers. In contrast to this passivity, an Alinskyite orga-nizer would have subtly seized upon neighborhood complaints to push the people toward effectively socialist policies, without ever admitting that this was his goal. Yet, intending to spark a revolution by radical ex-ample, Ayers now had something much bolder than Alinskyite stealth in mind.

Spontaneous Anti-Pig Consciousness

Before we find out what sort of actions Ayers's hot-town community-organizing strategy led to, we need to consider the formal birth of the Weatherman faction at the disastrous June 1969 SDS national convention. Here, just two months after Ayers's hot-town strategy was floated, the SDS was torn apart (and soon destroyed) in a three-way struggle between the traditionally Marxist faction, Progressive Labor, and two revisionist Marxist factions, Revolutionary Youth Movements I and II.[14] The three groups were spread out along an ideological spectrum. On one end, the more traditionally Marxist Progressive Labor rejected race-based politics and insisted that radicalizing America's working class was the key to revolution. In the middle was Revolutionary Youth Movement II, which argued that the black nationalist struggle was a sparkplug of the revolution, yet also accepted the centrality of the white working class to any revolutionary struggle. RYM II was led by Mike Klonsky, Carl Davidson, and Marilyn Katz, among others. (As we'll see, all three of these SDSers remained active in Chicago politics for years, eventually entering Obama's political orbit.) At the other end of the spectrum came RYM I, also known as the Weathermen, led by Ayers, Dohrn, and a handful of others. While the Weatherman faction did not reject the revolutionary importance of the white working class, they stressed the "vanguard" character of Third World revolutionaries and America's black "internal colony." For the Weathermen, white supremacy was the lynchpin of America's oppressive society. That meant backing the resistance of nationalist groups like the Black Panthers was the best way to destroy the American system.

The essentials of the Weatherman terror strategy—which featured bombings of police and military installations—were already visible in the group's founding statement for the June 1969 SDS convention. Their idea was to put dramatic acts of resistance to "the pigs" (i.e., the police and the army) at the center of the revolutionary struggle. Violent conflicts with the pigs would serve as the catalyst of revolution, bringing the true nature of American oppression home to the public. In the Weatherman view, the highest form of community organizing would use attacks on pigs to spark off a violent, neighborhood-based conflagration:

> Thus the pigs are ultimately the glue—the necessity—that holds the neighborhood-based and city-wide movement together; all of our concrete needs lead to pushing the pigs to the fore as a political focus . . . till either winning or getting pigged [i.e., being jailed or killed by the police or army] . . . developing spontaneous anti-pig consciousness in our neighborhoods [is necessary] to an understanding of imperialism, class struggle, and the state.[15]

For Ayers and the Weathermen, then, revolution and community organizing were two sides of the same coin. Community organizing would galvanize white working-class youth to follow America's own rebellious internal colony of inner-city blacks into the revolutionary fray. The inspiration for it all would be the continuing revolt of that de facto external colony, Vietnam, against the American monster. Abandoning SDS's passive community organizing techniques, the Weathermen would galvanize revolutionary consciousness by boldly setting an example of aggressive resistance to the American system—and the pigs who defend it. Radicalized elements of the white working class would willingly follow. The end result: socialist revolution.

The combination of low comedy and high treason that emerged from Ayers's theory of community organizing may seem today like something akin to madness. Yet, less than a year before the hot-town proposal was drafted, massive SDS-led demonstrations at the 1968 Democratic National Convention in Chicago provoked a violent, nationally televised confrontation with the police. That conflagration sparked a huge upsurge in SDS membership. Ayers believed that a wave of neighborhood-based confrontations would have the same effect.

Throwing Punches

Just a month after the descent of the SDS into chaos at its June 1969 convention, the Weatherman gathered in Detroit to put the hot-town community-organizing strategy into practice. The prototype action took place in July, at greater Detroit's white working-class Metro Beach.[16] A squadron of Weathermen marched onto the beach passing out literature and carrying a Viet Cong flag. The white working-class men on the beach, some of whom were Vietnam vets, did not take kindly to this. Fistfights broke out, in which the Weathermen held their own, after which they marched off the beach in good order, still carrying their Viet Cong flag. The flyer likely handed out on the beach that day was a call to arms:

> Cats are being fucked over *everywhere*. Like, what is there to do? You can go to school, but we know their schools are just jails. They've even got pigs there to make sure we don't make any "trouble" for the jail wardens . . . It doesn't make any difference where you work, cause it's all jive shit . . . SDS is recruiting an army right now, man, a people's army, under black leadership, that's gonna fight against the pigs and *win*!!![17]

But how do you build an army by attacking your recruits? Somehow the Weathermen had gone from compliantly following the wishes of the people they were trying to organize to punching them in the mouth. Ayers explains the theory in his memoir, *Fugitive Days*: "Working class youth can never be won to a movement that is soft and overly cerebral . . . when they see us raising the question of power and contending for control, they will join us in droves."[18] Accurate insofar as it goes, this snippet is also a vintage bit of Ayers obfuscation. No one who reads Ayers's beautifully crafted memoirs would realize what Weatherman community organizing actually amounted to—challenging working-class kids to a fight by waving Viet Cong flags in their faces.

Although the Metro Beach action apparently recruited no one to the cause, it was held up by the Weathermen as an organizing model for the nation. What followed was still more extraordinary.

Now it was the Weatherwomen's turn to smash both imperialism and sexist stereotypes at a blow—literally. At Michigan's McComb Community College, nine female Weatherpeople marched into a class of some fifty students taking a sociology final. The Weather-invaders blocked the exits and began lecturing the students on American imperialism, the black colony, and the "dual position" of white students as both oppressor and oppressed. When the teacher and several men tried to leave the room, the nine Weatherwomen stopped them with karate skills. At a follow-up action in Pittsburgh's predominantly white working-class South Hills High School, seventy-five Weatherwomen marched through the halls carrying Viet Cong flags, war whooping, and shouting "jailbreak." Again, the idea was that once these students saw Americans who sided with the Viet Cong, whites who sided with blacks, and women who didn't act like traditional women, they'd drop their reactionary ways and flock to the revolution.[19]

It was all a disastrous failure, of course. This sort of community organizing involved no prior groundwork and ultimately amounted to nothing but a series of unprovoked attacks by outsiders on the very people they were supposed to organize. If anything, these fruitless organizing schemes helped push the desperate Weathermen into their bombing campaign—on the theory that pumping up their revolutionary exhibitionism would somehow bring in more recruits.

Schools and Prisons

To understand Ayers's work with Obama in the nineties, we'll also need to take a brief look at the Weatherman view of education and juvenile justice. Weather-logic on both topics follows from what we've already learned. The SDS community organizing collective in Cleveland intended its group decision-making and abandonment of private property to stand as a model for the socialist society of the future. The same could be said for Ayers's education projects. The schools Ayers ran in Ann Arbor and Cleveland were designed to serve as "oppositional institutions"—tiles in a revolutionary mosaic.[20] Ayers's theory of education rejected conventional rules—and certainly anything resembling patriotism—encouraging kids to challenge the American system instead. As might be expected from its race-based theory of revolution, Weather-ideology heartily embraced ethnic and racial consciousness in education, along with the need for blacks to challenge existing power arrangements by seizing control of their local schools.[21]

The Weathermen viewed America's juvenile justice system in light of their revolutionary hopes. By "imprisoning large sectors of the young militant [black] population," wrote Ayers, America was committing a sort of counter-revolutionary genocide.[22] So Ayers's plan was that legions of imprisoned black youth would form the vanguard of a revolution. The Weathermen were particularly fond of an observation by Black Panther George Jackson:

> You will find no class or category more aware, more embittered, desperate or dedicated to the ultimate remedy—revolution. The most dedicated, the best of our kind—you'll find them in the Folsoms, San Quentins and Soledads.[23]

For Ayers and his Weather-compatriots, then, black prisoners were the crucial catalysts of the coming rebellion. Instances in which black resistance inspired white prisoners to follow suit were of special interest. Here was the revolutionary plan in nucleus, especially since, for the Weathermen, the ultimate prison was America itself.

Bombs

The Weathermen pored over manuals teaching blasters how to collapse buildings with a few well-placed explosives. Ayers's girlfriend, Diana

Oughton, and her co-conspirators died in an accidental explosion as they were creating a nail-bomb designed to tear through the flesh of "pigs"—soldiers and their dates at a dance.[24] Here is how an unrepentant terrorist writes about his past: "Everything was absolutely ideal on the day I bombed the Pentagon. The sky was blue. Birds were singing. And the bastards were finally going to get what was coming to them."[25] Adds Ayers: "I can't quite imagine putting a bomb in a building today—all of that seems so distinctly a part of then. But I can't imagine entirely dismissing the possibility, either."[26] These words were published in 2001, when Obama and Ayers were serving together on the Woods Fund Board.

In a number of writings published during and after the period when he was working directly with Obama, Ayers has explained why he defiantly refuses to apologize for his terrorist past. To apologize, says Ayers, would be to "convert," to surrender his opposition to capitalism and America's white supremacist society.[27] Surrender would only discourage revolutionaries of the future, the very people Ayers hopes to inspire. Ayers and Dohrn have republished their Weatherman writings and explicitly endorsed their original critique of American society. They regret their "bombastic" rhetoric and the ideological in-fighting with fellow socialists, but in substance Ayers and Dohrn stand by their Weatherman credo today.[28] Ayers assures us that he is still a "small c" communist, and adds: "I don't believe for one minute that the system, the way it's drawn up now, is democratic."[29]

But while you can find all this in Ayers's writings about his Weatherman past, in his day-to-day work on community organizing, education, and juvenile justice, Ayers was careful to disguise the extent of his radicalism. Essentially, Ayers adopted a version of the Popular Front stealth he'd rejected years before. In a classic Popular Front move, for example, Ayers stopped calling America a "marauding monster," and instead started touting famous American rebels as models. Praising John Brown's 1859 armed insurrection against slavery, for example, was a way of keeping revolutionary hope alive without openly condemning America.[30] Once Ayers's students learned to see America's prison system as a new form of slavery, they'd realize that armed insurrection might be needed again. Yet Ayers stopped openly preaching revolution and left it to his students to make the connections.

So as Ayers emerged from his fugitive days, he embarked on a career advocating politicized education, the dismantling of America's prison system, and community organizing strategies designed to advance these goals. Ayers moderated his rhetoric and refrained from punching the people he hoped to organize. Yet his goals remained unchanged—the creation of a minority-led mass movement for socialist change in America. To fund his efforts, Ayers turned to Chicago's leftist foundation world, and this eventually brought him into a close alliance with Barack Obama.

Obama Meets Ayers?

To understand the Obama-Ayers partnership, we'll need to trace the history of the foundations where they did their joint work. Yet the record of Obama's ties to Ayers is hotly contested. While all parties now agree that Ayers and Obama worked together in 1995 at an education foundation called the Chicago Annenberg Challenge, there is good reason to believe that their relationship extends further back in time than either man will admit. We saw why in Chapter Four, where we learned that in 1988, Ayers led a coalition for Chicago school reform in which Obama and his organization, the Developing Communities Project, played an important role. It's tough to see how Ayers and Obama could have avoided working together at that time.

We also learned that Bill Ayers's brother John was not only a key player in the Chicago school-reform movement, but a part of Obama's political network as early as 1987. Obama made contact with John Ayers even before John's brother Bill arrived in Chicago. On top of that, Obama was working with just about every leader in the movement for Chicago school reform months before Bill Ayers arrived on the scene. Ayers has said that his very best friends in Chicago are the people he worked with during the school-reform battles of the eighties.[31] Obama was a member in good standing of that circle from the start. How, then, could Obama have avoided meeting Ayers in the eighties? Indeed, knowing Ayers's closest friends and colleagues—not to mention working directly with Ayers at two foundations for years—how could Obama have failed to be aware of either Ayers's terrorist past or his socialist commitments in the present?

SECTION THREE

SOCIALISM AND THE FOUNDATIONS

With the shift from the violent world of the Weathermen to the courteous calm of foundation board meetings, the shouting goes out of our tale. There is drama in this new phase of the struggle, however. Our story now traces the slow-motion takeover of Chicago's Woods Charitable Fund by Barack Obama's socialist allies, the ascent of Obama himself at both the Woods Fund and the Chicago Annenberg Challenge (a foundation Ayers created), and Obama's elevation of Ayers to the board of the Woods Fund.

Now it becomes a game of "follow the money." The question is no longer "Who's punching whom?" but "Who's funding whom?" Following the crisscrossing connections in Obama's socialist organizing network can be daunting, and a chart is provided to clarify the connections.

The difficulty of following this ballgame without a program has served to protect Obama for years. It takes patient detective work to uncover the significance of a simple list of foundation grantees. Fortunately, we already know something about the major players in this story: ACORN, the Midwest Academy, Obama's leftist organizing mentor John McKnight, Bill Ayers, and Bernardine Dohrn. Keep in

Obama, Ayers, and the Foundations

Wieboldt Foundation

Anne Hallett
Executive Director, 1986–93
Funds Obama, 1987–88.
On Obama's advisory board, 1987.
Major funder of school reform.
Works with John Ayers.
Co-founds CAC with Bill Ayers.

Stanley Hallett
Longtime Wieboldt board member.
Wieboldt Exec VP through 1985.
Wife Anne runs Wieboldt, 1986.
Helps pioneer Community Reinvestment Act.
Funds Northwestern U. Urban Studies Center.
Hired by Cuba to help develop Havana.

**John McKnight &
John Kretzmann**
Work with Stanley Hallett at Northwestern.
Kretzmann on Wieboldt board.
McKnight advises Wieboldt board.
McKnight's group favors Cuban medical system.
Obama studies their organizing theories.
Both work closely with Barack and Michelle.

Woods Fund

Ken Rolling
Key Woods Administrator for Community Organizing, 1985–95.
Former Official of Midwest Academy.
Funds Obama's early organizing.
Funds school reform.
Works with Obama on 1995 report.
Leaves Woods to direct CAC under Obama and Ayers.

Barack Obama
Board member, 1994–2002.
Funds projects of Ayers, Dohrn, and Khalidi.
Works closely with ACORN.
Greatly expands ACORN funding.
Funds Midwest Academy.
Brings Ayers onto Woods board.
Funds McKnight and Kretzmann.

Bill Ayers
Joins Woods board in 1999, just after Obama's 1998 stint as Woods board chairman.
Helps Obama increase funding to favored groups such as ACORN and Midwest Academy.
Expands funding for leftist juvenile justice groups.

Chicago Annenberg Challenge (CAC)

**Bill Ayers &
Anne Hallett**
Co-found CAC in 1995.
Help select Obama as board chairman.
Ayers heads policy group, "The Collaborative."
Ayers and Hallett "joined at the hip."

Barack Obama
Board chairman, 1995–99.
Board member till 2001.
Keeps funding flowing to Ayers and his allies, even after they lose formal control of purse strings.
Obama and Ayers lure Ken Rolling from Woods to direct CAC.
Obama keeps money flowing to controversial parent organizing plan.

Ken Rolling
Helps keep money flowing to community organizers.
Internal CAC evaluations criticize administrators for lack of educational expertise.
CAC's projects fail to improve test scores.

mind that when we narrate the history of Chicago's leftist foundations, we are actually tracing the financial outlines of modern American socialism.

After introducing a few more key players—in particular, the Wieboldt Foundation's Anne and Stanley Hallett—the story of the joint rise of Bill Ayers and Barack Obama within Chicago's foundation world can commence in earnest. To aid in our investigation of Obama's foundation world, I will draw on nearly complete collections of the hard-to-find Woods Fund and Wieboldt Foundation annual reports for the period in question.

The three foundations we'll be looking at—Woods, the Chicago Annenberg Challenge (CAC), and Wieboldt—share a common commitment to supporting community organizing. Because of community organizing's radicalism—and especially because of its confrontational tactics—very few foundations, even liberal ones, have been willing to devote significant resources to the profession.[32] Woods, CAC, and Wieboldt were the great exceptions. In planning and personnel, Woods, CAC, and Wieboldt overlapped, and Obama was at the very center of their alliance.

Anne and Stanley Hallett

Let's begin with the Wieboldt Foundation. To the best of my knowledge, it has never been reported that Obama's early community organizing work was supported, not only by the Woods Fund and the Campaign for Human Development, but also by the Wieboldt Foundation. Obama's Developing Communities Project received grants from Wieboldt in 1987 and 1988, and Wieboldt also supported the Gamaliel Foundation, where Obama served as a trainer.[33] That financial support tied Obama more deeply to a radical network that Ayers would soon join.

The key figure here is Anne Hallett, who was Wieboldt's executive director in 1987, when it began supporting Obama. Along with

Obama colleague, Midwest Academy official, and Woods Fund program director Ken Rolling, Hallett was the largest funder of community organizing in Chicago. Hallet and Ayers went on to co-found the Chicago Annenberg Challenge, which Obama headed, and where Ken Rolling served as executive director. In other words, Obama, Ayers, Rolling, and Hallett formed a closely allied group, working together in a variety of positions at a series of foundations. Hallett, for example, once described her relationship to Ayers as "joined at the hip."[34] Most important, Obama, Ayers, Rolling, and Hallett were deeply a part of Chicago's socialist world.

Anne Hallett's husband, Stanley Hallett, was a powerful figure at Wieboldt, and likely played a role in elevating her to the position of executive director. Stanley Hallett was a longtime Wieboldt board member and simultaneously served as Wieboldt's executive vice president.[35] Although he remained a lifetime "member" of the foundation, Stanley Hallett resigned from the board of directors in 1985, perhaps to avoid a conflict of interest when, in 1986, his wife, Anne, a community organizer with a special interest in education, was appointed Wieboldt's executive director and secretary.[36]

Stanley Hallett, who died in 1998, was a fascinating, influential, and somewhat mysterious character on Chicago's political scene. A 1998 profile of Hallett in the *Chicago Reader* highlights his insistence on staying out of the limelight.[37] Hallett helped found the Chicago bank that served as a model for the Community Reinvestment Act, the law that compels banks to write risky subprime mortgages. Hallett also served on the board of the Woodstock Institute, the Chicago think tank behind much of the agitation for government-enforced subprime lending.[38] Obama, by the way, worked closely with the Woodstock Institute during his time in the Illinois State Senate.[39]

Stanley Hallett was a longtime supporter of Alinskyite community organizing. He helped found the Center for Urban Affairs at Northwestern University and worked closely there with his younger colleagues, John McKnight and John Kretzmann, longtime associates of

Barack and Michelle Obama, and closely tied to the Midwest Academy as well. Obama studied the writings of Kretzmann and McKnight, which embodied the socialist organizing strategy of the era.[40] Essentially, Kretzmann and McKnight saw the Community Reinvestment Act as a prototype for a far broader program of constraints imposed on businesses by a partnership of government and grassroots community groups. So, again, we're looking at a densely packed network of leftists tied to the Wieboldt Foundation, with multiple connections to Obama.

Why was Stanley Hallett so intent on avoiding publicity? Perhaps it had something to do with his political convictions. The January 1988 issue of *New Ground,* the newsletter of Chicago's Democratic Socialists of America, contains the following notice under the heading, "Organizer's Report":

> Our February meeting will be addressed by Dr. Stan Hallett of the Center for Urban and Policy Studies, Northwestern University. Dr. Hallett, who has just recently returned from Cuba where he had been hired by the Cuban government to work on urban renewal plans for Havana, will speak on the possibilities of neighborhood-based economic development within the constraints of a Communist regime.[41]

We've already seen that Hallett's colleague at Northwestern, John McKnight, served as a consultant for the most left-leaning social planners in Sweden, and helped publish a magazine that touted the healthcare systems of communist countries like Cuba and Nicaragua as models for the United States. McKnight recommended Obama for law school and worked closely with Barack and Michelle during Michelle's time at Public Allies. It would appear that the cluster of leftist academics the Obamas were so closely tied to were running a consultancy service for international socialism.

A Socialist Network

Following Wieboldt's lead, the Woods Charitable Fund turned itself into the second great source of foundation money for community organizing in Chicago—and one of only a handful of foundations friendly to Alinskyite organizing in the country. It's common for family-run foundations to be pulled leftward after their creator's demise, and the story of the Woods Fund is a classic example of a traditionally liberal family-run foundation being "captured" by leftist radicals. Obama was a major player in Woods's radical faction, and appears to have brought Ayers onto the foundation's board to strengthen his camp.

The Woods Charitable Fund was established in 1941 by Frank H. Woods, who made his money in coal. The foundation was largely run by the Woods family until 1980, when Frank H. Woods, Jr., one of the most involved family members, died. Up to then, the Woods Fund had focused on supporting the arts, and charities like the United Way, with a few civil rights groups thrown in. After Woods Jr.'s death, outside staffers and board members were recruited, including former Midwest Academy administrator Ken Rolling. Rolling and his colleagues promptly began to pull the foundation leftward.[42]

Throughout the eighties, the Woods Fund provided extensive financial support to nearly every radical group that mattered to Obama. The socialist-tinged connections and interconnections are dizzying. (No need to master every detail. Just get the feel of it.) We learned in Chapter Five, for example, that Ken Rolling personally hosted a top neighborhood organizer for Nicaragua's Marxist Sandinista regime during a visit to the Midwest Academy Retreat of 1985. During the same period, Rolling was funding ACORN's "homesteading" program—a campaign of illegal housing seizures, seen by ACORN's leaders as a way of undermining the very concept of private property.[43] UNO of Chicago—the radical Hispanic counterpart to ACORN—also received extensive financial support from Woods under Rolling.[44] Obama mentors and UNO of Chicago founders Greg Galluzzo and Mary Gonzales (closely

tied to the crypto-socialist Midwest Academy) were highly favored by
Academy alumnus Rolling. Not only was their work at UNO of Chicago
supported, Woods also funded the couple's more ambitious regional
organizing consultancy, the Gamaliel Foundation (to which Obama remained close right through his time in the U.S. Senate).[45]

Rolling also funded the Midwest Academy directly.[46] There was
Woods money for the Health and Medicine Policy Research Group as
well.[47] This was the organization, co-founded by radical Obama mentors Quentin Young and John McKnight, that held up the health-care
systems of Cuba and Nicaragua as models for America. As we've seen,
McKnight and his colleague John Kretzmann were closely tied to the
Midwest Academy and to both Barack and Michelle Obama, and to the
Gamaliel Foundation as well. Kretzmann and McKnight crafted their
socialist-friendly community organizing theories at Northwestern University's Center for Urban Affairs & Policy Research, which we saw
above was founded by Stanley Hallett, who worked for the Cuban government helping to plan the development of Havana. Hallett's center
for urban affairs received regular support from Rolling at Woods.

Increasingly, then, the Woods Fund had been commandeered as a
funding source by Chicago's—and Obama's—tightly interconnected
socialist network. As a "small c" communist who worked closely with
many of these players during the Chicago school-reform battle (another
campaign heavily supported by Rolling), Bill Ayers would someday be
a perfect fit for the Woods Fund board.

In 1993, the battle between the conventionally liberal family faction
and the radical organizers reached a climax. After "intensive debate,"
the foundation broke in two.[48] The Lincoln branch would continue to
be called the Woods Charitable Fund and would keep on supporting
the arts and conventional charities. The Chicago branch would now
incorporate separately as the Woods Fund of Chicago, focused on support for community organizing. The foundation's endowment was
divided, with Chicago taking 70 percent.[49] For the pro-community-
organizing faction in Chicago, there was still work to be done. It

would take years before virtually all the Chicago money was funneled to Obama's organizer allies. Nonetheless, with the formal creation of two separate foundations, Ken Rolling and his fellow radicals had effectively won. For all practical purposes, the Woods family's money had been captured.

Obama Takes Charge

Here's where Obama came in. Directly and indirectly, he had been supported by Woods for years. In 1992, for example, Rolling had directed a grant to Michelle Obama's Midwest Academy–affiliated group, Public Allies.[50] Now, in 1994, as the Woods Fund split in two, Obama was selected by Rolling's faction to sit on the new Chicago entity's board.[51] As one of only five foundation directors, Obama wielded considerable influence from the start. In fact, Obama was quickly put in charge of a comprehensive review of, and report on, the Woods Fund's support for community organizing.[52] This report laid the groundwork for a major increase of financial support for Obama's allies.

Obama and Ken Rolling worked together on the review process, aided by an advisory panel chaired by Obama. The advisory panel consisted of UNO of Chicago co-founder Mary Gonzales, Midwest Academy board member Jacky Grimshaw, former UNO of Chicago organizer Josh Hoyt, organizing theorist John Kretzmann, Jeremiah Wright's close supporter Sokoni Karanja, and Chicago ACORN head Madeline Talbott.[53]

The report that emerged from Obama's review of the Woods Fund's community organizing program reveals him as the leading player in a good cop/bad cop game. Obama's foundation job was to keep the money flowing to his controversial organizing cohorts by putting a respectable public face on a radical profession. Woods Fund support for Obama's allies had an importance that went far beyond the money itself. The staged confrontations, intimidation tactics, and "civil disobedience" practiced by Alinskyite organizers tend to scare even liberal foundations away. As the Obama-supervised report puts it: "Some funders . . . are averse to confrontational tactics, and are loathe [*sic*] to support organizing for that reason. They essentially equate organizing with the embarrassment of their business and government associates."[54] As one of the few foundations to support community organizing for its own sake, Woods Fund money acted as a Good Housekeeping Seal of Approval, offering political cover to other foundations interested in funding the hard-left. Obama sought to capitalize on this effect, not only by increasing Woods support for organizers, but by distributing the Woods report to a national network of potential funders.[55]

Formally, the Woods Fund claimed to be "non-ideological." According to the report: "This stance has enabled the Trustees to make grants to organizations that use confrontational tactics against the business and government 'establishments,' without undue risk of being criticized for partisanship."[56] Yet, under Obama's guiding hand, and in close coordination with Chicago ACORN head Madeline Talbott, Woods now more than doubled ACORN's funding (just as ACORN's campaign against Chicago's banks was at its height).[57] Since we know that ACORN volunteers served as the shock troops of Obama's early political campaigns, that would seem to raise the specter of partisanship.[58] It is at least possible, in other words, that Obama used his position at a supposedly non-partisan foundation to direct money to an allegedly non-partisan group, in pursuit of what were in fact nakedly partisan ends.

SECTION FOUR

THE CHICAGO ANNENBERG CHALLENGE

The release of the Obama-supervised Woods Fund report on community organizing in April of 1995 brings us up to the edge of the Ayers controversy. While there's good reason to believe that Ayers and

Obama had known each other at least since 1988, no one now disputes that the two had numerous contacts beginning in 1995. In that critical year, Bill Ayers and Anne Hallett teamed up to create an education foundation called the Chicago Annenberg Challenge (CAC), whose board of directors Obama chaired. Later that year, Obama was introduced as the designated successor of State Senator Alice Palmer at a small gathering of Palmer's supporters at the home of Bill Ayers and Bernardine Dohrn. Throughout campaign 2008, and since, the Obama camp has labored to deny or downplay the obvious implication of these two episodes: that Barack Obama and Bill Ayers were close political allies. Yet a good deal of evidence suggests that the Ayers-Obama partnership was strong and long-standing, and that Obama has been trying to hide this fact for years.

In a sense, we've already learned the most important lesson of the Ayers controversy. Ayers himself was the tip of the iceberg—merely the most notorious figure in a much larger socialist network supported by Obama through his work at Chicago's leftist foundations. Precisely because Ayers himself was so deeply enmeshed in that network, the Obama camp's persistent denials in 2008 that Ayers had anything to do with Obama's selection as CAC board chairman rang false.

Obama in Ayers's Network

We learned in Chapter Six that Ayers was working closely with ACORN in 1993. Chicago ACORN's Madeline Talbott headed ACORN's national education campaign. A 1993 memo from Talbott to the head organizers at all ACORN offices makes it clear that the real purpose of the schools campaign was to recruit parents to ACORN, with educational concerns playing a distant secondary role. Talbott worked closely with Ayers, whose ethnically themed "schools within schools" program offered ACORN a model for carving a mini-empire out of the Chicago public school system. Talbott's plan was to attack the prestigious citywide system of "magnet" schools set up for students with higher test scores. By creating a furor of protest surrounding those schools, Talbott hoped to force the city to allow ACORN to set up a counter-system of Afro-centric "small schools" under its own control.[59]

Ayers's Weatherman ideology, which he has never abandoned, views the seizure of schools by radical black community groups as the long-term key to building a movement for socialism in the United States. Obviously, Ayers and Talbott were made for each other. In 1994, Ayers brought Talbott into the working-group planning to create a Chicago education foundation with grant money from the wealthy conservative donor Walter Annenberg (another case of foundation money being captured by radicals).[60] That same year, Talbott was working closely with Obama on the Woods Fund community-organizing advisory board, while Obama was busy channeling a massive increase in funding to ACORN. So a year before he became CAC board chairman, Obama was already effectively funding Ayers's education work with ACORN.

That same year at Woods, Obama was also funding former Wieboldt director Anne Hallett's Cross City Campaign for Urban School Reform, the fiscal agent for which was Leadership for Quality Education, a group headed by Bill's brother, John Ayers.[61] We've seen that Hallett helped support Obama's organizing work and served on the advisory board of Obama's youth counseling program along with John Ayers in 1987. Sokoni Karanja, former Woods board member and prominent member of Jeremiah Wright's congregation, was both close to Obama and a key member of Ayers's education team.[62] The cross-connections go on almost endlessly. In short, the year before Obama was chosen to head CAC, he was already well known to Ayers's inner circle.

Ayers Launches Obama

The Chicago Annenberg Challenge was Bill Ayers's brainchild, with Anne Hallett as his close ("joined at the hip") partner. The foundation's internal evaluations characterize its first year in particular as the period when CAC was "founder-led."[63] It is simply inconceivable that Obama could have been elevated to the chairmanship of a foundation created by Bill Ayers—at his moment of maximum power—without Ayers's enthusiastic consent. Since CAC was funding Ayers's pet projects and those of his closest allies, Ayers could hardly have been neutral about the man chosen to head the board, which was in charge of dispensing the money.

We now know that Ayers did in fact put Obama into the chairmanship of CAC's board. Apparently drawing on an interview with Ayers himself, David Remnick's recent biography of Obama states that "Ayers helped bring Obama onto the Annenberg board."[64] This extraordinary admission, made in passing and without comment by Remnick, flies in the face of the Obama campaign's repeated denials in 2008 that Ayers had any role whatever in elevating Obama to the CAC chairmanship.

It's important to emphasize that, at this point, President Obama's credibility on the matter of his radical political past is virtually nil. We saw in Chapter Six that candidate Obama's denial of any tie to ACORN beyond his role as the group's lawyer in a single case was spectacularly false. Now we've learned that Obama worked closely with Chicago ACORN head Madeline Talbott at the Woods Fund and was the key figure on the Woods board advocating massive increases in money for community organizers—a huge portion of which went to ACORN. Since even Obama's sympathetic biographer has now revealed (without comment or explanation) that the Obama campaign's central contention about Ayers in 2008 was false, how can we now believe the president's denials about his radical past?

We certainly can't trust David Remnick's account of the Ayers-Obama relationship. Remnick's biography of Obama relies uncritically on his interview with Ayers, a man who's confessed that his own memoirs bear, shall we say, a complicated and circuitous relationship to the truth.[65] According to Remnick, Ayers claims to have hosted Obama's political coming-out party strictly as a favor to State Senator Alice Palmer.[66] Yet Palmer told CNN's Drew Griffin in 2008 that she "in no way" organized the event.[67] Ayers's claim to Remnick that he wasn't really "into" Obama because of the future president's "moderation" is completely unconvincing.[68] After all, it was at Ayers's behest that Obama was put in charge of dispensing money to Chicago's most radical activists. Obama's conduct at CAC reveals him to have been a reliable supporter of Ayers's most troubling projects and actions. It's extraordinary, moreover, that Remnick's biography has virtually nothing to say about Obama's foundation work. Maybe that's because it is impossible to tell the story of Obama's foundation experience without facing up to the reality of the future president's extensive partnership with Bill Ayers.

Pledge Allegiance

By ordinary standards, the Chicago Annenberg Challenge was an expensive failure. Together Obama, as head of CAC's money-dispensing board, and Ayers, as head of its policy-making "collaborative," spent well over $100 million, with no discernible improvement in the test scores of low-performing schools. Tellingly, this judgment that CAC failed to improve educational performance in Chicago's public schools was made by the foundation's own evaluators.[69]

Can we attribute CAC's failure to the sheer impossibility of improving inner-city schools? Not at all. During the same years CAC flourished, Chicago schools established clear standards, began high-stakes testing, ended social promotion, forced thousands of students to attend summer school to advance a grade, and put failing schools on probation. That pushed up test scores city-wide, "with no statistically significant differences in student achievement between Annenberg schools and demographically similar non-Annenberg schools."[70]

Even so, by the standards of Ayers and Obama, CAC was a success. That's because, in the eyes of Obama and his radical circle, CAC's real purpose was to channel money to the enterprise of community organizing. In this it succeeded admirably. Instead of funding schools directly, CAC required schools to affiliate with "external partners," which actually got the money. Proposals from prospective external partners committed to teaching traditional math and science skills were rejected. Community organizers like ACORN and Obama's own Developing Communities Project got the money instead.[71] Programs established by these groups focused more on political consciousness, Afro-centricity, and bilingualism than traditional education.[72]

Ayers's "small schools" projects were perfect examples of the type. One of Ayers's creations was a "peace school," where students celebrated United Nations–themed events instead of traditional American holidays. As part of his rhetorical makeover, Ayers has soft-pedaled his overt anti-Americanism.[73] The infamous 2001 picture of him standing on the American flag, published just as his Weatherman memoir was being released, was an imprudent, if revealing, exception.[74] In his education work, Ayers inculcates loyalty to "the world" as a substitute for overt anti-Americanism. In his edited 1998 collection, *Teaching for Social Justice*, Ayers includes the story of a teacher who, instead of leading her students in the pledge of allegiance to the American flag, leads them in an alternative "pledge allegiance to the world."[75]

Another of Ayers's projects, Telpochcalli, was an Aztec-themed school that catered primarily to Mexican immigrants. Telpochcalli insisted on "full bilingualism" and its intense focus on Mexico's language and culture made it controversial. Not only native English speakers but even some Spanish-speaking parents pulled their kids out for fear that children were learning English too slowly.[76] Telpochcalli and some of Ayers's other "schools within schools" were housed in a district where the local school council was controlled by UNO of Chicago—another connection to Obama's radical network.[77] As CAC's board chairman, Obama was funding all of these projects.

Ayers's partner in the small schools movement was Mike Klonsky, the ex-SDSer who led the faction of the Revolutionary Youth Movement from which Ayers and the Weathermen split off in 1969. Their old differences over the precise extent to which minorities would play leading roles in the revolution had been patched up—but not forgotten. Now, Ayers's and Klonsky's joint work promoting radical politics through ethnically themed schooling was a fulfillment of their sixties-vintage socialist theories.

Ayers's education theories explicitly downplay achievement tests in favor of political activism.[78] It's hardly a surprise, then, that CAC failed to raise test scores. In Ayers's eyes, schools should be "sites of resistance" to an oppressive system. The point, he says, is to "teach against oppression," against America's history of evil and racism, thereby forcing social transformation.[79] If Obama was really too moderate for Ayers's taste, why would the ex-Weatherman have trusted his young colleague to decide whether to fund projects guided by so controversial a theory of education?

Why Annenberg Failed

Again and again, Obama came through for Ayers. CAC was restructured after its first year, due to ethical concerns. Under the initial arrangement, community activists at the Ayers-run collaborative were effectively recommending that the CAC board fund their own projects. So after the first year, all decisions on grants were made by the Obama-headed board alone. Ayers and Hallett were stripped of their ex-officio status as board members. Yet, while the apparent threat of self-dealing was removed, Obama kept the money flowing to Ayers and his inner circle for years. It was as if the restructuring had never happened.[80]

Internal evaluations attributed CAC's failure to the board's reluctance to de-fund community groups that had very little in the way of actual educational expertise (think ACORN).[81] Yet we've seen that education was always secondary for these organizers, who were much more interested in recruiting parents to their groups than in raising kids' test scores. Obama's own "youth counseling program," formulated back in 1987 with the help of the same people who went on to create CAC, focused on parental recruitment as well. When CAC's one relatively conservative board member objected to the focus on organizing parents at the expense of education, Obama intervened to keep the money flowing.[82]

CAC's internal post-mortem also fingered the hiring of an executive director with no real educational experience as a major source of the foundation's failure.[83] This was no mere oversight. Obama and Ayers hired Midwest Academy veteran Ken Rolling away from the Woods Fund to run CAC. Rolling had been a hidden force behind the Chicago school-reform movement. Rolling's motivation had little to do with education. Instead he hoped to hand power and recruits to the city's community organizers.[84]

CAC's failure, therefore, had nothing to do with either bad luck or the inherent difficulty of the task, and everything to do with the shared desire of Obama and Ayers to funnel a very large pot of money to the city's most radical community organizers. This was leftist political patronage, pure and simple. Ayers chose Obama for the job because he knew Obama could be trusted to support Chicago's socialist network. After all, Obama was already doing the very same thing at the Woods Fund. As we'll see, Obama eventually returned the favor and brought his trusted ally Ayers onto the Woods Fund Board.

Ayers's old SDS associates from the SDS's Revolutionary Youth Movement faction (before it split with the Weathermen) were very much a part of Obama's world. As we've seen, Ayers worked closely on his small-schools projects with former RYM leader Mike Klonsky.[85] Obama funded those projects for years. The former leadership of RYM, Klonsky, Carl Davidson, and Marilyn Katz, retained their socialist views and now belonged to the Committees of Correspondence—a Marxist group to the left of even the Democratic Socialists of America.[86] Davidson worked closely with the New Party, which Obama joined for his 1995–96 state senate run.[87] Davidson, Klonsky, and Marilyn Katz helped organize the October 2002 demonstration where Obama first went public with his opposition to the Iraq war.[88]

SECTION FIVE

OBAMA AND AYERS AT WOODS

Although Ayers would not join the Woods Fund board until 1999, long before that, under Obama's sway, Woods began to direct money toward Ayers's projects, and the projects of his wife and former Weather Underground leader Bernardine Dohrn. In 1995, when Obama was already helping to fund Ayers's education projects as CAC board chair, Woods directed major support to Ayers's small schools workshop, and to Anne Hallett's Cross City Campaign for Urban School Reform.[89] That was a major show of support from Obama, and a way of opening up a second stream of money for Ayers and Hallett should their CAC funding be shut off on grounds of self-dealing. Woods continued to support Ayers's and Hallett's education projects for years.[90]

OBAMA FUNDS DOHRN

In 1996, with Obama now vice chair of the Woods board, funding began to flow as well to Bernardine Dohrn's Children and Family Justice Center at Northwestern University School of Law.[91] So in the same year Obama won his first run for political office—with a campaign kicked off at Ayers's and Dohrn's home—Woods began funding the couple's projects. For someone we're now supposed to believe wasn't really "into" a "moderate" like Obama, Ayers was making out pretty well.

There is nothing remotely moderate about Bernardine Dohrn's understanding of the American legal system. In her 2009 memoir-polemic with Ayers, *Race Course Against White Supremacy*, Dohrn lays out a critique of American society straight out of the Weatherman worldview. For Dohrn, America's justice system is simply a modern version of the "slave ship," and our prison system a veritable political "gulag."[92] From Dohrn's perspective, violence is less the fault of criminals than of America's "structurally racist" society. Welfare reform laws and low-wage work—themselves forms of "state violence"—are the real crimes, says Dohrn. The implications of Dohrn's writings are clear. Since Americans suffer from pervasive and structural "state violence," mass violence against the state would be entirely justified. While Ayers and Dohrn had abandoned their terror tactics, you can see why they've refused to either apologize or rule out future terrorism. They still believe revolution is justified. It's obvious as well that Ayers and Dohrn continue to see a minority-led rebellion against America's prison system as the best long-term hope of sparking off a socialist revolution.

This is the ideology that lay behind Dohrn's juvenile justice projects, which Obama began funding in 1996. Dohrn's picture was featured in a special profile at the head of the Woods Fund's 1996 Annual Report.[93] This was no fluke. A year after he began to fund Dohrn's juvenile justice projects, Obama allied with Ayers in the fight against a new Illinois juvenile crime bill. This was clearly a new phase in what was to become an extended working relationship between Obama, Ayers, and Dohrn.

Obama Appoints Ayers

Once you piece together all the available information, it's apparent that it was Obama who placed Ayers on the Woods Fund Board in 1999.[94] After all, in 1999, Obama had served for five years as board chair of the Chicago Annenberg Challenge, a foundation created by Bill Ayers. Not only had Ayers and Dohrn launched Obama's political career at their home, but Obama had worked closely with Ayers during the 1997–98 battle over the Illinois juvenile crime bill. Along with Obama at the state capital, Bernardine Dohrn's Juvenile Justice Center at Northwestern University was probably the strongest public voice against that bill.[95] Since Woods was channeling significant support to Dohrn's center during the battle, it's evident that Ayers, Dohrn, and Obama were strong political allies.[96]

Obama's only year of service as Woods Fund board chair, moreover, was 1998.[97] Presumably this is when Ayers was actually recruited to the board and when the groundwork for his 1999 appointment was laid. So Obama used his moment of maximum formal power at Woods to recruit Ayers to the board.

In the unlikely event that placing Ayers on the Woods Fund Board was actually someone else's idea, it's inconceivable that the board would have followed through without Obama's enthusiastic agreement. After all, no one at Woods could have known Ayers better or worked with him longer than Obama. Whoever first suggested that Ayers join Woods, Obama's approval would have been critical. But why beat around the bush? In the immortal words of Bob Dylan, you don't need a weatherman to know which way the wind blows. Ayers's elevation to the Woods Fund Board was obviously Obama's doing.

Not a Moderate

With Ayers on the Woods Fund board, Obama now had the ideal ally to push the foundation toward yet another increase in support for his community organizing allies. We've seen that, drawing on his Weatherman ideology, Ayers regards agitation around education, community organizing, and juvenile justice as the best way to build a movement for socialism in a non-revolutionary period. Now Ayers and Obama together helped usher in a new set of Woods policies, formally announced in the 2001 Woods Fund Annual Report.[98] The new "strategic objectives" not only increased support for community organizing, but favored fewer—and larger—grants for a select set of favored groups. Among the main beneficiaries of this new largesse were ACORN, the Midwest Academy, and a variety of leftist advocates on juvenile justice issues.[99]

The new strategic objectives also emphasized coordinated efforts by leftist think tanks and radical community groups to influence legislation in Springfield. With Ayers's help, in other words, Obama was now

able to fund an expertly guided grassroots movement to help him with
his legislative campaigns.

The 2001 Woods Fund annual report contains a long case study of
an Obama-funded coalition at work. The report was co-authored by
Joshua Hoyt, one of Obama's old colleagues from UNO of Chicago.[100]
Hoyt proudly tells the story of how a foundation-funded grassroots
coalition called United Power for Action and Justice was able to win
a major expansion of health insurance in Illinois "in the midst of the
worst state budget crisis in two generations." Of course, the Illinois
budget crisis has only worsened since then, advanced by exactly this
sort of entitlement expansion.

One of the most interesting things about Hoyt's report is its core tactical message: "A good cop/bad cop dichotomy can be useful." United
Power's policy experts consciously worked to remain on friendly terms
with legislators on all points of the political spectrum, yet worked behind the scenes to encourage the hardball Alinskyite confrontation tactics of their grassroots allies. Hoyt's account teaches us an important
lesson about Obama. The president is not a moderate. He is instead
a classic Alinskyite "good cop." Obama's role is to provide a veneer of
moderation to what is in fact a radical enterprise, all the while encouraging his tactically ruthless Alinskyite supporters. It took Bill Ayers
more than thirty years to discover an organizing strategy that worked.
With Obama's help, he finally found one.

A Campaign Controversy

The truth about the extended political partnership between Ayers and
Obama stands in sharp contrast to the president's famous April 2008
campaign claim that Ayers was "just a guy who lives in my neighborhood." By the summer of 2008, a number of bloggers had noticed the
contradiction between Obama's portrayal of his relationship with Ayers and publicly available information on the Chicago Annenberg Challenge, which Obama and Ayers jointly headed. When my attempts in

August of 2008 to examine the CAC records housed at the University of Illinois Chicago Library were blocked, the controversy exploded onto the public stage.

Although I had been repeatedly assured by UIC Library officials that I would be allowed to examine CAC records, just before I boarded my flight for Chicago, top library officials mysteriously intervened to bar access. They justified their decision by a series of evolving and inconsistent explanations. I then launched a public campaign at National Review Online to persuade UIC officials to allow access to the records.[101] The university was deluged with emails and protests.

Based on reporting by the *Chicago Tribune* and Freedom of Information Act requests by myself and others, I was later able to provisionally reconstruct what had happened.[102] Former CAC executive director Ken Rolling apparently intervened to deny me access to the records after being tipped off by an unidentified library official on the same day I contacted UIC, August 11, 2008. Rolling later claimed that he had called the library on his own that day, but it's impossible to believe he would have spontaneously phoned to block access to the CAC records on the same day I asked to see them. Rolling appears to have offered a highly questionable series of legal claims as a way of building a case to completely withdraw the records from university control. The burgeoning public campaign to release the records soon doomed that move to failure.

By the time UIC relented and allowed me to see the CAC records, I entered the UIC Special Collections Reading Room with local and national media, as well as a phalanx of aides from both the Obama and McCain campaigns. But while Chicago media reported on the controversy, the national media remained virtually silent. A day after I began to look through the records, most of the reporters stopped searching the archives. Although the online conservative community had been in an uproar from the moment I was refused access to the records, the mainstream press was able to keep the CAC story largely out of the public eye.

Having turned up records of CAC board meetings attended jointly by Obama and Ayers, I was invited to appear on the radio with Chicago's widely respected talk-show host Milt Rosenberg to present my findings and discuss the Obama-Ayers relationship. The Obama campaign turned down an offer to send a representative to debate me and instead launched an all-out campaign to bar me from the radio. Thousands of callers inundated the radio station demanding that my appearance be canceled, while an Obama campaign spokesman phoned the station to insist that I be barred.[103] The radio station was housed in Chicago's famous Tribune Tower, whose soaring lobby, the "Hall of Inscriptions," is carved with stirring defenses of freedom of speech and the press: " 'Give me liberty to know, to utter and to argue freely according to my conscience, above all other liberties'—Milton." I studied the inscriptions as I waited in the lobby.

The radio show was dominated by callers demanding that I be barred from speaking. All they knew about me was what they'd been told by the Obama campaign—that I was a "right-wing hatchet man," a "smear merchant," and a "slimy character assassin," perpetrating one of the "most cynical and offensive smears ever launched against Barack."[104] Of course, this "smear"—that Bill Ayers worked directly with Barack Obama at the Chicago Annenberg Challenge and had a role in appointing Obama to the board—has now been confirmed by myriad documents, and even by Obama's sympathetic biographer, David Remnick.

A month later I reported the findings of my research in a *Wall Street Journal* op-ed piece.[105] After informing the Obama campaign of the gist of my argument and requesting a response, I published their statement in full, along with my rebuttal, at National Review Online.[106] Ten days later, the *New York Times* took notice of the controversy, publishing a piece that acknowledged a working relationship between Obama and Ayers, but did everything possible to minimize its extent and significance.[107] The article relied on the Obama campaign and Obama's supporters in Chicago as sources, without quoting the views of critics like myself or the intrepid liberal blogger Steve Diamond, who did yeoman's work detailing the Ayers-Obama relationship during the campaign.[108] As a result, while many were up in arms about the Ayers affair, the broader public never heard both sides of the story. At least as important, the national press refused to report on the Obama campaign's efforts to suppress the story itself.

In any case, as I've emphasized repeatedly, Bill Ayers was never anything more than an important clue to a much larger mystery. Ayers's notoriety turned him into a particularly noticeable tear in the carefully woven fabric of Obama's moderate image. A few more tugs and the cloak itself would unravel, revealing the socialist secret beneath. That is why the Ayers story had to be suppressed.

CHAPTER 8

Jeremiah Wright

The political truth about Barack Obama was revealed during the 2008 presidential campaign, when video clips of sermons by Reverend Jeremiah Wright made it impossible to deny the radicalism of the candidate's spiritual advisor and mentor. It's not that Obama shared Reverend Wright's belief that, say, the United States government had created the AIDS virus as an instrument of genocide against black people. It's rather that Obama put up with nonsense like that because he shared Wright's socialist worldview.

Obama saw Wright as an important element of his long-term political strategy. As a politician-organizer, Obama hoped to inspire and mobilize a movement of the religious left. That movement was to be led by an activist black church under the guidance of preachers like Wright. That is why Obama featured Wright's "audacity of hope" theme in his career-making keynote address at the 2004 Democratic National Convention, and made the phrase the title of his second book. Wright—and the radical black-church movement he represented—was to be an important element of Obama's populist-bred, socialist-led coalition.

Reverend Wright's basic political stance is very much along the lines of the Socialist Scholars Conferences, UNO of Chicago, the Gamaliel Foundation, ACORN, the Midwest Academy, and Bill Ayers.

The difference between these other radicals and Wright is the latter's indiscretion. Wright got caught boldly shouting the sort of things the other inhabitants of Obama's political network believed, but typically buried under sugary rhetoric, or just keep quiet about—or restricted to obscure publications none but the converted ever bothered to read. Wright's famous "God damn America" remark followed an oration blaming black poverty and imprisonment on the government—and implicitly on America's entire political and economic system. Bill Ayers made these sorts of points constantly in his latter-day writings, but with a good deal more rhetorical subtlety.[1] We've seen that Ayers eventually dropped his more extreme Weatherman rhetoric, even as he charted his new life course by the original Weatherman forecast. For Wright, on the other hand, even on the matter of rhetoric, it might as well still have been 1969.

So the point is not merely that Obama has always known about Wright's beliefs and deceived the public when he claimed not to have known. The deeper point is that Obama chose Wright as his political and spiritual advisor because he largely shared his former minister's politics.

CONTEXT

"Sound bites" and "snippets"—that's how Reverend Wright and his supporters dismissed the explosive excerpts from his sermons, played frequently on television at the height of the Wright affair in the spring of 2008. If only we understood the broader context within which Wright had damned America and blamed the United States for the terrorist attacks of 9/11, apologists insisted then, the storm would pass.[2] As early as March of 2007, when challenged by conservative FOX News host

Sean Hannity about some of his more controversial beliefs, Wright had insisted that his faith be placed within the broader context of the "black liberation theology" created in the late sixties by James H. Cone, the Charles A. Briggs Distinguished Professor of Systematic Theology at Union Theological Seminary.[3] For those unfamiliar with the scholarly left, Cone's academic pedigree seems proof of reasonableness and respectability. Once you actually read Cone's theology, however, it's evident that the only thing worse than quoting Jeremiah Wright out of context is quoting him in context. More important, a bit of digging reveals that Obama was well acquainted with the radical theology that inspired his favorite preacher.

James Cone published *Black Theology and Black Power*, the founding text of black liberation theology, in 1969.[4] That pivotal year saw the birth of the Weathermen from the ashes of the SDS, and the programmatic beginnings of what would someday become the Midwest Academy. Black liberation theology was another radical survivor of that era. While Obama and his supporters have tried to portray his church's theology as well within the mainstream, Trinity United Church of Christ was in fact an outlier. The writings of Cone's followers are filled with attempts to come to grips with the overwhelming rejection of their radical political theology by mainstream black churches.[5] But while Cone's theology is little more than a leftist relic of the sixties for most black churches, in select university-based divinity schools and a few congregations, it lives on. Cone himself cites Wright's Trinity as the church that embodies his theology more fully than any other.[6] So Obama arguably belonged to the most radical black church in the country.

On Cone's own account, *Black Theology and Black Power* is written in the voice of an angry black man.[7] Cone, in fact, demands and commends anger in black liberationist preachers. In the book, Cone sometimes addresses or refers to whites as simply "the oppressor" or "whitey."[8] The black intellectual's goal, says Cone, is to "aid in the destruction of America as he knows it."[9] Such destruction requires both black anger and white guilt. To stir that guilt, the Black Power theologian must tell the story of American oppression so powerfully and precisely that white men will "tremble, curse, and go mad, because they will be drenched with the filth of their evil."[10]

So what exactly is "Black Power"? Here, Cone follows Malcolm X, defining it as "complete emancipation of black people from white oppression by whatever means black people deem necessary."[11] Like the radical anti-colonial theorist Franz Fanon, on whom he sometimes draws, Cone sees violent rebellion as a transformative expression of the humanity of the oppressed. For example, Cone defends those who looted during the urban riots of the late 1960s as affirming their "being," rather than simply grasping and destroying.[12]

Cone also makes a point of leveling strident attacks against white liberals. According to Cone, "When white do-gooders are confronted with the style of Black Power, realizing that black people really place them in the same category with the George Wallaces, they react defensively, saying, 'It's not my fault' or 'I am not responsible.' "[13] But Cone insists that white, liberal do-gooders are every bit as responsible for black suffering as the most dyed-in-the-wool segregationists. Well before it became a cliche, Cone boldly outlined the case for institutional racism—the notion that "racism is so embedded in the heart of American society that few, if any, whites can free themselves from it."[14]

For Cone, the deeply racist structure of American society leaves blacks with no alternative but radical transformation or withdrawal. So-called Christianity, as commonly practiced in the United States, is actually the racist Antichrist. Cone believes that, theologically, "Malcolm X was not far wrong when he called the white man 'the devil.' "[15] The false Christianity of the white-devil oppressor must be replaced by an authentic Christianity fully identified with the poor and oppressed. This, in turn, requires "the replacement of middle-class consciousness with 'black consciousness,' " with "a theology which confronts white society as the racist Antichrist, communicating to the oppressor that nothing will be spared in the fight for freedom."[16]

Cone's radicalism is evident in his rejection of anything short of total social revolution—a revolution justified because, in Cone's view, black life in America is essentially a slow-motion version of the Jewish Holocaust.

OBAMA AND CONE

So Jeremiah Wright's angry rhetoric, grounded in his conviction that America is racist to the core—even genocidally so—is indeed fully backed by black liberation theology. Trinity's famous rejection of "middle-classness" has a similar theological basis. Wright's most infamous statements were not momentary outbursts, as his defenders in the campaign implied, but deliberate products of a developed theological tradition instead.

As for Obama, he understood his pastor's theology perfectly well. During the 2008 campaign, the Obama camp acknowledged that Cone's writings were regularly included in packets of material handed out to new members of Wright's Trinity United Church of Christ.[17] Obama, however, refused to answer oral or written inquiries in 2008 about his knowledge of Cone's work.[18] In the few cases where interviewers obliquely raised the issue of black liberation theology, Obama sidestepped the question and steered the conversation toward the "social gospel."[19] An obscure footnote in Sasha Abramsky's 2009 book, *Inside Obama's Brain*, however, quotes Obama mentor John Kretzmann confirming that Obama did indeed read Cone during his days as a community organizer in Chicago—the very time he met Wright.[20] Indeed, Obama surely learned of black liberation theology even earlier, at the Socialist Scholars Conferences in New York.

Given this record, not to mention Obama's well-known affinity for Malcolm X and Franz Fanon, on whom Cone freely drew, we have every reason to believe that Obama settled on Trinity United Church of Christ in full knowledge of Wright's radical theological views. In fact, a large body of evidence fairly screams that Obama joined Wright's church precisely *because* of those radical views.

CHURCH HISTORY

In the early sixties, Trinity United Church of Christ was one of the few predominantly black congregations in the liberal United Church of Christ denomination. In those days, the goal of the civil rights movement was integration, and Trinity's decidedly middle-class congregation embraced that goal with enthusiasm. With the rise of the Black Power movement in the late sixties, however, Trinity's integrationist congregants found themselves out of step with the times. Attendance fell sharply until 1972, when Wright came on board, charged with developing a more black-identified style of worship.[21]

But Trinity wasn't prepared for the extremes of Wright's liberationist theology—or the extent of his Afro-centrism. After Wright revamped Trinity's worship, attendance shot way up. Yet within three years, all the members who had originally invited Wright had left the church. By 1983, yet another group of prominent church members uncomfortable with Wright's approach went elsewhere. In 1978, a national official of the United Church of Christ attempted to distance UCC from Wright's church, calling it a "cult" (only months after the Jonestown suicides) and accusing Wright of having an "ego problem." This official was eventually forced to apologize to Trinity.

Wright's nominal Afro-centrism was supercharged in the eighties when he visited Africa for the first time. Never entirely comfortable with Cone's claim that whites had succeeded in stripping blacks of their culture, Wright started emphasizing continuities between Africa and what he would soon begin to call "Africans in America" (rather than "American blacks").[22] Around this time, Wright ramped up his Africa-related activism—one of the first things that caught Obama's eye about Wright's church.[23]

But Wright never abandoned Cone. On the contrary, what was distinctive about both Wright and Cone was their blending of black-identified politics with a scarcely concealed Marxism. Prompted by his contacts with Latin American liberation theologians and his growing cooperation with Michael Harrington's Democratic Socialists of America, Cone made it clear in the eighties that he wanted to see American capitalism replaced by some form of democratic socialism. "I do not think that racism can be eliminated as long as capitalism remains intact," wrote Cone in 1982.[24] Not long afterward, Cone appeared at the 1984 Socialist Scholars Conference, following which he visited Cuba along with a group of followers that included Jeremiah Wright. "Perhaps what we need today," wrote Cone, "is to return to that 'good old-time religion' of our grandparents and combine it with a Marxist critique of society. Together black religion and Marxist philosophy may show us the way to build a completely new society."[25]

Cone's coy formulations frame his approach to socialism as that of an outsider in search of ways to cooperate with socialists. This allows Cone and his followers to avoid the socialist label, while embracing socialism in substance. We know that Wright splashed a glowing account of his trip to Cuba across the pages of his *Trinity Trumpet* church newsletter. It was obvious from that account that Wright and his fellow black liberation theologians supported Cuba's communist revolution and viewed it as a model for the United States. Any politically sensitive observer—and Obama was surely that—would quickly have picked up on the socialist tenor of Wright's theology.

THE AUDACITY OF COMMUNISM

The 1988 "Audacity of Hope" sermon that had so storied an effect on Obama invoked the privation and oppression of "black and brown" citizens in Africa and the rest of the world. To a superficial ear, the sermon may seem simply to call for aid to the world's hungry. For

those attuned to Wright's theology, however, it contains a barely disguised attack on Western capitalism, which Wright believes is the true
cause of the suffering and privation of the "black and brown" world.[26]
"White folks' greed runs a world in need," as Obama quotes Wright
in *Dreams*.[27] This view, by the way, echoes the Marxist "dependency
theory" we saw Obama drawing on during his time in New York.

Obama biographer David Remnick describes one of Wright's favorite sermons, an oration that stresses Martin Luther King's radical side.
According to Remnick, Wright's sermon maintains that King "was not
the plaster saint of popular memory but, rather, a rebellious minister
who opposed 'the maniacal ménage à trois' of militarism, capitalism,
and racism."[28]

We saw in Chapter Three that Obama likely attended a panel featuring James Cone at the 1984 Socialist Scholars Conference, where it was
argued that Martin Luther King, Jr., had experienced a late-life conversion to democratic socialism. Wright pushes the same line. Recall that
Wright's 1984 trip to Cuba with Cone shortly after that year's Socialist
Scholars Conference was billed as a seminar in honor of Martin Luther
King. It was on this trip that Jesse Jackson courted controversy by publicly chanting, "Long live President Castro! Long live Martin Luther
King! Long live Che Guevara!"

King's supposed late-life rejection of capitalism was a favorite
Wright theme. You can find it discussed not only in his sermons but in
Wright's column in *Trumpet Newsmagazine*. In 2005, Wright converted
his *Trinity Trumpet* church newsletter into a glossy national "lifestyle
magazine for the socially conscious." *Trumpet* is filled with radical politics, from Wright's regular column to the writers he featured—many of
them on staff at Trinity Church. In a January 2007 column, Wright tries
to spin Martin Luther King's late-life opposition to the Vietnam War as
a challenge to America's economic system:

> When one goes against the war, one tampers with the financial
> institutions and the financial system that was put in place by the
> Founding Fathers of this country to keep the rich, rich!

Dr. Martin Luther King's sermon at Riverside put him at odds with a government that is only interested in protecting business interests. He was attacking the financial institutions of our country when he came out against the war.[29]

Obviously, Wright is not a fan of the financial system put in place by America's Founding Fathers. The same issue of *Trumpet* contains a piece by freelance writer Obasi A. Kitambi that conveys the flavor of the magazine's take on capitalism:

> The Western world's insistence on pimping people, places and economies in support of capitalist imperialistic wet dreams of excessive booty and international penetration is the . . . crutch [of colonialism and imperialism].
> The consistent pasty face of this level of domination makes it difficult for non-westerners to believe that race is not one of the defining criteria for membership in this economic boys club.[30]

Harshly spoken anti-capitalist tirades are so pervasive in Wright's sermons and publications that Obama had to have seen them.

CHOOSING A CHURCH

An abundance of evidence indicates that, when Obama chose Wright as his pastor, he knew exactly what he was getting into. Alvin Love, one of the ministers Obama consulted with before joining Trinity, quotes Obama saying: "I don't want to join a church for convenience' sake. I want to be serious and be comfortable wherever I join."[31] So Obama did not approach his choice of a religious home lightly. Obama biographer David Remnick explains that another pastor advising Obama, L. K. Curry, recommended Wright after hearing of Obama's strong interest in "social justice."[32] Remnick goes on to explain that if Obama had merely been in search of a large and influential church, he could have chosen a popular Pentecostal church on the South Side whose minister, Reverend Arthur Brazier, had worked with Saul Alinsky years before. Brazier told Remnick that Obama preferred Wright because "Reverend Wright is more into black liberation."[33] Wright himself told Remnick that Obama actually hesitated to join Trinity for fear that it might be "too upwardly mobile."[34] Clearly, Obama took Trinity's pledge to struggle against "middle-classness" very seriously. In short, Remnick makes the case that Obama chose Wright out of a specific preference for Wright's politically oriented theology.

Yet, while he provides a good deal of what appears to be damning information, Remnick rescues the president by relying on assurances from Obama's original organizing mentor Jerry Kellman that back when Obama chose Trinity, the "political pronouncements by Wright that, two decades later, plagued Obama's Presidential run were not yet in evidence."[35]

This is utter nonsense. It also fits a pattern in Remnick's relatively uncritical book. Drawing on his interviews with Obama's former colleagues, Remnick repeatedly conveys damaging information withheld by the president's friends during the 2008 election, only to neutralize the effects of those revelations with false assurances from his sources. Obama's college friends tell Remnick that they were socialists at Occidental and that Obama shared their views, while insisting that the young socialist Obama was never particularly doctrinaire. Bill Ayers apparently reveals that he did in fact help select Obama as chairman of the Chicago Annenberg Challenge, yet assures Remnick that he was never really that "into" a "moderate" like Obama. We've seen that these assurances are false. Kellman's claim that Wright only recently developed the habit of courting of political controversy is false as well.

As early as 1984, Wright had been cited on the *Wall Street Journal*'s op-ed page as the American contact used by communist intelligence agencies to arrange a visit to Cuba by Cone's religious circle.[36] The op-ed piece gave Cone's group the benefit of the doubt, generously claiming that they had merely been manipulated by the Cuban government. In reality, Wright touted his Cuba trip on the pages of his *Trinity Trumpet* newsletter, with a story making it clear that he and his fellow black liberation theologians saw Cuba's communist system as a model and inspiration for American blacks. Wright couldn't have felt manipulated by the revelation that Cuba's government had used his visit for propaganda purposes, since he personally led yet another delegation of black liberation theologians on a return visit to Cuba in 1996, only a year before he first met Obama. Obviously, Wright was practiced at in-your-face political antics well before 2008.

In *Dreams from My Father*, Obama explains that when he first met his future pastor, Wright warned him that some preachers thought him too radical. Wright also warned Obama that some clergy considered him not radical enough.[37] That is hardly proof of moderation. Wright's Black Muslim and Afro-centric colleagues saw him as too moderate simply for remaining Christian. Trinity's motto, "Unashamedly Black and Unapologetically Christian," expresses the duality of its stance—to the liberationist left of most Christian churches and to the right of Black Muslim or "Kemetic" (Afro-centric) sects (to the "right," simply in the sense of remaining Christian). We've seen from our quick tour of Cone's theology that there was nothing moderate about this black liberationist stance.

CEREBRAL

Drawing on interviews conducted before the 2008 Wright controversy broke out, Obama biographer David Mendell has shown that part of the bond between Obama and Wright was intellectual. Wright's University of Chicago experience allowed him to relate to Obama on a more "cerebral" level than other ministers Obama might have chosen, says Mendell. "We talked about race and politics," Wright told Mendell, adding, "I was not threatened by those questions."[38]

So let's add up what we know about Obama's initial encounter with Wright. Obama was looking for a serious religious home, not simply a respectable place to park. Wright had been recommended to Obama as the local minister most devoted to "social justice." And around the time he met Wright, Obama was also reading James Cone's work. Obama even hesitated to join Wright's church for fear that it might be considered too middle class. Wright offered Obama genuine intellectual companionship, and they discussed race and politics in depth.

Given all this, it's obvious that Obama had to have understood Wright's radical politics from the start. Moreover, Wright and Obama must have discovered their mutual links through Cone's Black Theology Project and the Socialist Scholars Conferences early on. It took Wright less than five minutes to justify himself to Sean Hannity in 2007 by highlighting his status as a James Cone disciple. Once the topic of Wright's radicalism came up with Obama—which we know it did right away—the pastor would have quickly explained to Obama that he was one of Cone's foremost disciples. Surely Obama would then have told Wright about his encounters with leading black liberation theologians at the Socialist Scholars Conferences in New York. Then there are the repeat anti-American trips to Cuba. Remember, Wright proudly touted the whole Cuban experience to his parishioners in *Trinity Trumpet,* so why would he have hesitated to tell Obama? How better for Wright to prove his leftist credentials to a young radical worried that Trinity might be too middle class than by recounting his Cuban escapades?

The Cuban adventure aside, if Obama had only familiarized himself with James Cone's writings—and we already know that he did—that by itself would be enough to prove Kellman's assurances wrong. Just about every radical statement Wright has ever made echoes an equally over-the-top pronouncement by Cone. So from the moment Obama joined Trinity United Church of Christ, he fully understood that Wright was a prominent follower of the strident and socialist-friendly

James Cone. The conclusion is unavoidable: That is precisely why Obama chose Wright's church.

SOKONI KARANJA

One of Obama's ways of distancing himself from Wright after the 2008 campaign controversy broke was to say that he had not so much joined Trinity because of its pastor as to be part of the larger congregation.[39] Given Obama's writings in praise of Wright, as well as testimony from several sources that the two enjoyed a close friendship, this claim was an obvious evasion.[40] Yet Obama's distancing strategy contained a kernel of truth. He did in fact form ties to other Trinity congregants, especially Sokoni and Ayana Karanja. Yet through Obama's little-known alliance with the Karanjas, we find still more evidence that Obama had to have known about his church's disturbing radicalism.

Obama had a close and longstanding working relationship with fellow Trinity United Church of Christ congregants, Sokoni and Ayana Karanja. In 1971, Sokoni Karanja founded the Centers for New Horizons (generally called "Centers"), to operate a series of daycare centers constructed by the Chicago Housing Authority. The curriculum at Centers is Afro-centric, featuring birthday celebrations for figures like Malcolm X, for example. In 1982, three years before Obama's arrival, Centers began operating an early learning center at Altgeld Gardens, the Chicago public housing development where Obama did his organizing.[41] Around the same time, Sokoni Karanja became one of the first Woods Charitable Fund board members not from the Woods family.[42] The Woods foundation funded Obama's early organizing work, and Obama eventually joined the Woods Fund board.

Sokoni Karanja was a member of the Illinois Project Vote advisory board when Obama ran that organization in 1992.[43] In 1994, Obama and Sokoni Karanja co-founded the Lugenia Burns Hope Center, a community-organizer training institute on Chicago's South Side.[44] Obama himself taught classes there. Sokoni's wife, Ayana, a professor of anthropology and Africana literature, helped run the Lugenia Burns Hope Center.[45] As a Woods Fund board member, Obama kept foundation money flowing to the Centers for New Horizons and the Lugenia Burns Hope Center for years after Karanja's departure from Woods.[46] So Obama did have important alliances with Trinity members other than Reverend Wright. But what exactly would Obama's ties to Sokoni and Ayana Karanja have taught him?

Sometime around 1982, Ayana Karanja headed a group of Trinity congregants who wrote and and assembled a collection of essays to be used during the yearly "Church-Wide Study Course Week." This volume, *Perspectives, a view from within, a compendium for churchwide study,* contains essays by Sokoni Karanja and other influential Trinity congregants.[47] For example, Wright's longtime theological collaborator, Iva Carruthers, has an essay in *Perspectives.* Wright contributes an essay as well, along with an introduction to the collection.

Sokoni Karanja's essay in *Perspectives* is pervaded by the same anti-capitalist anger that motivates Reverend Wright. Karanja focuses on the three great evils confronted by American blacks: racism, sexism, and capitalism. According to Karanja, capitalism "exploits through control of police powers, all earthly resources and protects property and profits above human concerns."[48]

The interesting twist in Karanja's essay is the way he uses capitalism to explain the dysfunctional aspects of black "intimacy":

> The cash connection grows out of the commodity character of society. It is informed by several capitalistic assumptions. . . . Here we observe older and younger Black men pursuing young Black girls with money and material accouterments as the only points of attraction, and p——y the only objective. [The letter "p" followed by four blank letter-spaces appears in the original.][49]

At this point, Karanja launches into classic Marxist language, describing the "species alienation" created by capitalism and again connecting this to problems between black men and women:

> Community development goals are thwarted by the incessant drive for more and more p——y. . . . P——y is our point of focus and conflict precisely because of the powerlessness imposed on all us by a capitalist, racist, and sexist system.[50]

The cure for all this, in Karanja's eyes, is "African-centered socialization, inspiration, education, and respect guided by the *Nguzo Saba* (unity, collective work and responsibility, cooperative economics, faith, creativity, purpose and self determination)."[51] In other words, a more collectivist economic framework inspired by Afro-centric values is the cure for the exploitative social and sexual practices imposed on the black community by capitalism. This certainly embodies the blending of Afro-centrism and socialism championed by Reverend Wright. Karanja also makes it clear that these same principles inform the curriculum at the Centers for New Horizons.

NOT ENOUGH MELANIN

The *Perspectives* compendium, assigned annually for week-long study by all members of Trinity United Church of Christ, contains a good deal of disturbing material. Iva Carruthers, one of Wright's theological colleagues, devotes her essay to advocating the development of "melanic deficiency theories." This refers to the Afro-centrist belief that the lack of the chemical melanin in white skin accounts for the superiority of black culture. If you object that such theories are pseudo-scientific, Carruthers replies that Western science itself is a method of oppressive control.[52] Another essay in the compendium suggests that the large number of black volunteers in America's army amounts to a form of racial genocide—a product of America's unjust economic system.[53]

Contrary to assurances from Obama's Alinskyite organizing mentor Jerry Kellman, then, it's clear that back in the 1980s, when Obama first encountered Wright, Trinity Church's members were exposed to statements every bit as disturbing and radical as the ones that got Wright into trouble in 2008. Attacks on capitalism, pseudo-biological theories of race and culture, and accusations of American genocide against blacks were commonplace at Trinity for decades. Kellman's testimony is a transparently bogus attempt to cover for Obama. Yet for years, the mainstream American press has relied on Jerry Kellman— a very interested party, to say the least—for accurate information on Obama's past.

We've already learned that, from the beginning of his tenure at Trinity, Wright ran into trouble with many in the congregation. We'll see that these troubles continued for years. Not everyone at Trinity was happy with Wright's wilder pronouncements, and many left his church. Yet the congregants whose work was compiled in *Perspectives* were Wright's strongest supporters. Some of them were also Obama's close associates. With the entire congregation studying these essays and others like them on a yearly basis, Obama had to have known what Wright and Trinity were all about. Obama's close partnership with Sokoni and Ayana Karanja would have made this clear as well. It's even possible that Obama would have consulted with Karanja before finally choosing Trinity, since Karanja at that time was a board member at the Woods Fund, which was supporting Obama's work.

WRIGHT'S POLITICAL HISTORY

If Jeremiah Wright's socialist sympathies drew Obama to Trinity United Church of Christ, there were other factors as well. Wright was a political player on the Chicago scene. The extent of Wright's political influence has not been properly appreciated. And Wright's way of exercising his power shows that Obama had to have worked closely with his pastor on substantive political issues.

It's tough to exaggerate the extent to which Jeremiah Wright believes that religion and politics are intertwined. In his own words:

> There was no separation biblically and historically and there is no separation contemporaneously between "religion and politics". . . . The Word of God has everything to do with racism, sexism, militarism, social justice and the world in which we live daily.[54]

In his contribution to the *Perspectives* anthology, Wright proudly touts his interest in political education:

> Educating constituents as to all the nuances and subtleties of the racist political system operative in Chicago, and suggesting ways to address that system as free children of the Most High King, is a very definite part of our ministry at Trinity.[55]

Over and above the political education he offered his congregation, Wright was active in Chicago politics. When Harold Washington was still a congressman, Wright served on his education task force.[56] Documents in the Harold Washington Archives and Collections indicate that Washington's education task force encouraged then mayor Jane Byrne to appoint Jeremiah Wright to the Chicago school board. We even have a copy of Wright's resume and his application for the post, which includes his answers to a series of questions about his views on Chicago's school system.

From his columns in *Trumpet Newsmagazine,* we already know something about Wright's views on education. His main concern is to teach children about "white supremacy." Here is how Wright put it in the days following Hurricane Katrina:

We need to educate our children to the reality of white supremacy. . . . We need to educate our children about the white
supremacist's foundation of the educational system. . . . When
the levees in Louisiana broke, alligators, crocodiles and piranha
swam freely through what used to be the streets of New Orleans.
That is an analogy that we need to drum into the heads of our
African American children (and indeed all children!). . . . In the
flood waters of white supremacy . . . there are also crocodiles,
alligators and piranha! . . . The policies with which we live now
and against which our children will have to struggle in order to
bring about "the beloved community," are policies shaped by
predators.[57]

That was Wright in 2006 speaking freely in his own publication. It's
perhaps more remarkable that on his application to Mayor Byrne for
a school-board appointment in 1982, Wright promised to advocate
for programs designed to educate Chicago school children about "the
racism which is rampant from the Board room to the classroom."[58]
As someone who believes that the entire American system is racist to
the core, Wright-endorsed programs in racism education might have
raised, shall we say, a bit of controversy for Chicago's school board.
On his application for Mayor Byrne's appointment to the school board,
Wright even promised to work for the abolition of the system of mayoral appointments to the school board. Clearly, Wright has been habitually reckless in speech—another reason why Obama surely knew
his pastor's outlandish political views from the start.

Wright's board-of-education flame-out in 1982 didn't stop him from
playing an important role in Harold Washington's mayoral campaign in
1983. Wright helped lead the coalition of black clergy that propelled
Washington's candidacy to success. Wright actually drafted the advertisement, signed by a group of clergymen, that helped launch the Harold Washington crusade in Chicago's black community in 1983. The
large group of congregants who left Trinity that same year did so in the

belief that Wright had become too political. Wright tells this story himself, in a little-known article where he adds: "My work with the political process says something about my conception of ministry." Wright tells us that he was actively involved in the Harold Washington campaign "at every level" during both the 1983 and 1987 elections. Once in office, Washington appointed Wright to the City College Board.[59]

All this is directly relevant to Obama's relationship to Wright. Wright was on the advisory committee of Obama's proposed youth counseling network. Obama had hoped to meet periodically with Mayor Washington, with his advisory committee in tow. By including Wright on that panel, Obama was showing Harold Washington that he had the approval and partnership of one of the mayor's most prominent supporters. In other words, Obama's connection to Wright had a strongly political character from the start. Obama wanted access to Harold Washington's administration, and Wright was a way in.

A SENATOR BEFORE OBAMA

The most striking—and hitherto unreported—fact about Wright's political past is the fact that, even before Barack Obama, Wright had yet another Illinois state senator in his congregation. His name was Howard B. Brookins, Jr.[60] After serving two terms in the Illinois State House, Brookins was elected to the Illinois Senate in 1986, and re-elected to a four-year term in 1988. So when Obama first encountered Wright, in 1987, Trinity United Church of Christ already had its very own state senator—further proof of Wright's kingmaker status.

Obama appears to have taken pains to avoid leaving a paper trail during his years in the Illinois State Senate. In contrast, Howard Brookins did preserve some of his legislative papers at the Abraham Lincoln Presidential Library in Springfield, Illinois. Sufficient material exists to offer us an intimate glimpse of the way Jeremiah Wright relates to a state senator from his own congregation.

Wright had no compunction about offering Brookins detailed advice on legislation, including instructions on how to contact other members of Wright's political network. Consider the following excerpt from a 1985 "Dear Howard" letter from Wright:

> [P]lease be in contact with our senator, Senator Dawson, and our good friend, Senator Richard Newhouse, to urge them to please support SB721 (The Economic Development Emergency Employment Development Act), and to support the Amendment to the DCCA appropriation, which will make it possible to begin this program on July 1st—this coming fiscal year!
>
> Please also be in dialogue with Senator Howard Carroll. Ask Senators Dawson and Newhouse to emplore [*sic*] Senator Carroll to push this important jobs program bill.[61]

Wright goes on to describe precedents for the proposed law in other states and to offer additional strategic advice. He sends copies of his letter to Brookins to Senators Newhouse and Dawson, but not to Senator Carroll. To say that Wright was a politically involved pastor is obviously an understatement.

Wright was not above using Trinity's congregation to put pressure on Brookins on very specific legislative issues. A 1990 letter to Brookins from Wright begins:

> Please be aware that I have asked the members of the church to talk with you to ask you to take back to the black legislators and any other colleagues and cohorts that you have down in Springfield, to ask them to be sure to override this line item please![62]

It's evident from these letters that Wright was less concerned to influence Brookins's votes—no doubt Brookins and Wright agreed on most things—than to push his senator-congregant into assembling legislative coalitions.

Brookins fought hard on behalf of the interests of Wright's inner circle. In 1983, Sokoni Karanja's Centers for New Horizons got into serious trouble with the Illinois Department of Children and Family Services (DCFS). Centers owed DCFS seventy-seven thousand dollars, yet had no funds to pay the debt. At first, DCFS canceled the state's contract with Centers as punishment. Later the state relented and agreed to renew Karanja's contract on condition that the debt would be paid. Brookins intervened aggressively on behalf of Karanja, calling on DCFS to forgive the debt. When the state refused, Brookins threatened to draft legislation forgiving the debts of all such programs. How the matter was finally resolved is unclear.[63]

Reverend Wright may have been directly involved in this fracas, since the application he submitted for the school-board appointment in 1982 indicates that he had served for the past three years as treasurer of Karanja's Centers for New Horizons. Had Wright himself mismanaged the money Karanja's Centers owed DCFS? In any case, as an Illinois state senator who co-founded a community organizer training institute affiliated with Sokoni Karanja's Centers for New Horizons, Obama fit right into Wright's political network.

In 1983, when Brookins made a concerted effort to secure the appointment of blacks to the Illinois State Board of Education, he turned to Reverend Wright for help. Brookins solicited Wright's recommendations on potential candidates, and duly wrote to each of them proposing that they send in resumes. Brookins told all of the potential candidates for the State Board of Education that he'd gotten their names from Wright. One of the names Wright submitted to Brookins was that of Iva Carruthers, Wright's theological partner at Trinity—whose *Perspectives* essay promoted the melanin-deficiency theory of culture.[64]

This, then, is the sort of access and influence Wright had come to expect from an Illinois state senator in his congregation: detailed advice on votes and coalition-building, aggressive intervention in his allies' dealings with the state, and major influence over nominations for government posts. Since Brookins was in office at the very moment Obama began his own close association with Wright, Obama would likely have seen something of the Brookins-Wright partnership in action. How likely is it that Obama could have maintained Wright's support without offering his pastor at least some significant influence on his own political world?

David Mendell, who had access to both Wright and Obama, and whose very friendly biography of Obama was published well before the 2008 Wright affair, called Wright Obama's "counselor and mentor." [65] In fact Mendell offers a fairly detailed account of the future president's political consultations with Wright as Obama was deciding whether to throw his hat into the ring for the U.S. Senate. [66]

When the Wright controversy broke in the spring of 2008, Obama denied having sought political—as opposed to religious—advice from his pastor. [67] Yet Obama's claim is plainly contradicted even by a friendly biographer. When we combine Mendell's account with the Brookins papers, it's obvious that Wright served as a political mentor to Obama. That is the relationship Wright would have expected, and anything less than that could have endangered Obama's standing with this important power on Chicago's political scene. From Reverend Wright's point of view, in fact, the very separation between politics and religion that Obama invoked to distance himself from his pastor in 2008 was an imaginary distinction.

SHOCK IN THE PEWS

Once you've read through several years of Jeremiah Wright's columns in *Trumpet Newsmagazine*, it's next to impossible to believe that Obama could have remained ignorant of his pastor's political views. Wright oozes politics from every pore, and his in-your-face style is a constant. Wright repeatedly drives home the same set of points. If you missed it in last Sunday's sermon—or column—you'll surely hear or read it again, in slightly different words, within a few weeks.

Although Wright's available *Trumpet* columns only go back to late 2004, we know his wild rhetoric was nothing new. In January of 1994, for example, Wright went on a tirade against the United States during his keynote address for a ministerial installation ceremony at a Philadelphia church. There he called America "the number one killer (in other countries)" and railed against "pop-up pastors—part punk and part pimp" who "say what the administration wants to hear and keeps the Negroes in line." According to the *Philadelphia Tribune*, when Wright added, "God has got to be sick of this shit," a number of those in the pews were shocked at the use of an obscenity in church. Given the fact that Philadelphia mayor Ed Rendell and various other local politicians were in attendance, we certainly can't call Wright shy.[68] David Remnick reports that Wright gave largely the same sermon—including the obscenity—a year earlier at another installation ceremony in Washington, D.C.[69] Clearly, then, Wright was controversial from an early date, and spoke his most shocking lines repeatedly.

WHAT OBAMA KNEW

One example of Wright's thematic repetitions stands out, because it arguably points to Obama's knowledge of the very views that set off the Wright affair in 2008. By 2004, Wright was tangled up in a protracted war with a faction in his own congregation over his remarks about 9/11. We also know that around April of 2004, Obama was attending Wright's services on a near-weekly basis. During the same period, a *Chicago Sun-Times* reporter who interviewed Obama at length about his churchgoing habits described Wright as Obama's "close confidant." In other words, we know that the very same controversial claims that got Wright in trouble in 2008 were being made at Trinity during a period when Obama himself was likely listening.

One of the most controversial Wright sermon "snippets" endlessly looped on video during campaign 2008 featured his response to the

9/11 attacks. Wright's remarks were delivered on September 16, 2001, the first Sunday after the destruction of the World Trade Center. At the climax of that sermon, Wright angrily shouts: "We have supported state terrorism against the Palestinians and black South Africans and now we are indignant because the stuff we have done overseas is now brought right back into our own front yards. America's chickens! Are coming home! To roost!"[70] So what got Wright into trouble during the presidential campaign was his holding America's support for Israel ("state terrorism against the Palestinians") responsible for 9/11.

In fact, this was no passing "snippet." Wright had apparently made same political point in his sermons long after 9/11. In the January 2005 issue of *Trumpet*, Wright not only repeats his 9/11 charges, but angrily attacks the efforts of those in his own congregation who want him to stop such talk. Here is Wright:

> It is a war [in Iraq] that does not take into account what it is the Saudis have been saying to us since 9-11-01. That part of the Arab world told us clearly that the attacks on the World Trade Center and the Pentagon had to do with our government's shameful and shameless support of Zionism . . . we ignore the real enemy in this "war against terrorism!" We don't want to tell the truth about Israel as a country. We don't want to be honest as to what caused the attacks on 9-11-01.[71]

Here Wright was making the very same point that sparked a national scandal when it was shown on television in 2008. Not everyone at Trinity was happy with Wright's endless political tirades, however. This is how Wright took them on:

> What I find most interesting, however, is that when I mention these things [the connection between Israel and 9/11] from the pulpit of Trinity United Church of Christ, I get attacked (by our own members!) as being "too political," or I get attacked as a

person who is turning our worship services into a political rally when people do not come to church to hear about politics. They want to hear about "Jesus!" . . . Trying to talk to this level of ignorance is like trying to talk to elementary school students about DNA. In the meantime, however, these so-called "members" continue to write me "hate mail." They continue to denigrate my 33 years of service.[72]

It appears as though the Iraq War gave Wright repeated occasions to make the same point about American responsibility for 9/11 that he'd made after the terror attack itself. In fact, the conflict over Wright's incessantly politicized sermons had kicked off a virtual civil war within Trinity, to the point where Wright was openly attacking his own congregants in the pages of his nationally distributed magazine.

To repeat, we know that in late March or early April of 2004, Obama assured a *Chicago Sun-Times* reporter that he was attending Trinity on a virtually weekly basis.[73] That reporter also called Wright Obama's "close confidant." How likely is it, then, that Obama could have been unaware of Wright's view of 9/11, or of the bitter internal conflict roiling his church in 2004? Yet so far from picking up and leaving the congregation (as Oprah Winfrey had years before, out of concern with Wright's inflammatory talk), Obama went on to write a book with a title borrowed from one of Wright's sermons.[74]

OBAMA'S PLANS FOR WRIGHT

The truly troubling thing about Obama's relationship with Wright is not the future president's mere awareness and tolerance of his pastor's extremism, but Obama's broader political plans for Wright. Even if Obama did reject AIDS conspiracy theories and melanin-based interpretations of culture, the extent of his political agreement with Wright nonetheless remains disturbing. Obama's goal was not to repudiate

Wright's religious radicalism, but to channel its fervor into an effective and permanent activist organization.

How do we know this? We know it because Obama himself has told us.

Consider Hank De Zutter's "What Makes Obama Run," a 1995 political profile of Obama published by the *Chicago Reader* just as Obama was embarking on his first run for office.[75] De Zutter writes that Obama rejects "the unrealistic politics of integrationist assimilation—which helps a few upwardly mobile blacks 'move up, get rich, and move out.' " This statement might surprise those who think of Obama as the epitome of integrationism. Yet Obama's repudiation of integrationist upward mobility is fully consistent with his career as a community organizer, his general sympathy for leftist critics of the American system, and his membership at Wright's Trinity Church. Obama, De Zutter tells us, "quickly learned that integration was a one-way street, with blacks expected to assimilate into a white world that never gave ground." These statements match closely to Wright's characterization of assimilated blacks as "sell-outs," and to Wright's justifications for Afro-centric education as well.[76]

But Obama's real interest in Wright and the other radical preachers he worked with was the role the clergy might play in building a radical political movement. In that 1995 profile, Obama criticizes "the politics of black rage and black nationalism"—although less on substance than on tactics. Obama upbraids the politics of Black Power for lacking a practical strategy. Instead of diffusing black rage by diverting it to the traditional American path of assimilation and middle-class achievement, Obama wants to capture the intensity of black anger and use it to power an effective political organization. Obama says "he's tired of seeing the moral fervor of black folks whipped up—at the speaker's rostrum and from the pulpit—and then allowed to dissipate because there's no agenda, no concrete program for change." The problem is not fiery rhetoric from the pulpit, then, but merely the waste of the anger it stirs.

De Zutter insists that "the lack of collective action among black churches" is a "favorite topic" of Obama's. Obama, we're told, is sharply critical of churches that try to help their communities merely through food pantries and community service programs." Obama rejects the strictly community-service approach of apolitical churches as part of America's unfortunate "bias" toward "individual action." Obama believes that what he derogates as "John Wayne" thinking and the old "right wing . . . individualistic bootstrap myth" needs to be replaced: "We must unite in collective action, build collective institutions and organizations." So as Obama first ran for office in 1995, he was using exactly this sort of communitarian language recommended by the Midwest Academy as a surrogate for socialism.

Back then, Obama's plans for more collectively oriented forms of social and political action depended on leadership from the black church: "Obama . . . spoke of the need to mobilize and organize the economic power and moral fervor of black churches. He also argued that as a state senator he might help bring this about faster than as a community organizer or civil rights lawyer." Says Obama, "We have some wonderful preachers in town—preachers who continue to inspire me—preachers who are magnificent at articulating a vision of the world as it should be." Obama continues, "But as soon as church lets out, the energy dissipates. We must find a way to channel all this energy into community building." Obama seems to be holding up Jeremiah Wright as a positive model for the wider black church. In 1995, then, Obama didn't want Trinity's political show to stop. His plan was to spread it to other black churches, then harness Trinity-style activism to a political movement of the left.

Obama presents these same ideas in his 1988 essay, "Why Organize: Problems and Promise in the Inner City." This piece was written shortly after Obama first cemented his alliance with Reverend Wright. The following excerpts show very clearly what Obama hoped to get out of the relationship:

Nowhere is the promise of organizing more apparent than in the traditional black churches. Possessing tremendous financial resources, membership and—most importantly—values and biblical traditions that call for empowerment and liberation, the black church is clearly a slumbering giant in the political and economic landscape of cities like Chicago.[77]

After acknowledging his frustration with apolitical black churches focused only on traditional community service work, Obama lays out his vision: "Should a mere 50 prominent black churches, out of thousands that exist in cities like Chicago, decided to collaborate with a trained and organized staff, enormous political changes could be wrought."[78] Give me fifty Jeremiah Wrights, Obama is saying, tie them to a network of grassroots activists like ACORN or the Gamaliel Foundation, and we can revolutionize urban politics.

So the goal of a politically awakened and organized black church was no side issue for Obama, much less a merely personal spiritual matter. It was the signature theme of the future president's grand political strategy during the era of his alliance with Wright. Obama didn't simply understand and tolerate his mentor's radical political views, which are extreme by any measure. Rather, he wanted them spread far and wide.

Together with Bill Ayers, Obama also funded highly politicized programs in Afro-centric education from his position as board chair of the Chicago Annenberg Challenge. Just as Jeremiah Wright and Sokoni Karanja advocated a kind of blending of Afro-centrism with socialism, the Afro-centric programs Obama and Ayers funded through Annenberg had a strong anti-capitalist component. The "rites of passage" movement that inspired the educators Obama funded was designed to replace the (supposed) American values of "capitalism, competitiveness, racism, sexism, and oppression" with a more collectivist culture modeled on African society.[79] Although Obama may not have bought every historical claim of these Afro-centrist educators, he obviously found the anti-individualist and anti-capitalist themes that inspired them congenial.

CAMPAIGN CRISIS

When the Jeremiah Wright controversy broke in the spring of 2008, Obama emerged with a series of excuses, explanations, and justifications. Supposedly, he'd never heard Wright condemn America, blame our foreign policy for the terror attacks of 9/11, or make other comparably outrageous statements. The controversial remarks continuously looped on video were but tiny and atypical fragments of Wright's distinguished thirty-year career, we were assured. Mostly, Obama said, Wright talks about Jesus, God, faith, values, caring for the poor and family. Nor, Obama maintained, had he sought Wright's political counsel. When he joined Trinity, Obama said, he was committing to a church, not to Wright. Obama also reminded us that Wright had performed many charitable works in Chicago.[80]

Each of these responses was deeply dishonest. Obama surely had heard wildly radical statements by Wright, since they were not only constant, but a topic of great controversy at Trinity Church during a period when Obama was in frequent attendance. The broader context of Wright's black liberation theology—with which Obama was quite familiar—is at least as disturbing as Wright's most notorious statements, if not more so. Wright openly denies the distinction between religion and politics, disdaining preachers who refuse to connect Jesus to liberationist militancy. Obama has indeed taken political counsel from Wright, and Wright's history strongly suggests that this was a common occurrence. Obama greatest hope, in fact, was to build a political movement around Wright and preachers like him. Wright's inner circle of followers at Trinity were every bit as radical as their pastor, and this was Obama's circle as well. Obama spent a career advocating politicized religion and derogating conventional charity, only to hide behind Wright's charitable work when the campaign controversy broke. Finally, Obama and Bill Ayers jointly funneled foundation money to radical education programs that echoed Wright's anti-capitalist Afrocentrism.

So it was only through a collection of egregious falsehoods that Obama managed to stave off political disaster.

In his 2009 memoir, Obama campaign manager David Plouffe blames himself for the Obama camp's failure to properly research the Jeremiah Wright issue, or to game out responses in case some inflammatory statement by Wright should become a campaign issue. "We were in denial," Plouffe concludes.[81] Plouffe manfully shoulders responsibility for the Wright fiasco, but I suspect that someone else was actually at fault.

In February of 2007, a front-page investigative article in the *Los Angeles Times* suggested that Obama may have taken too much credit for the anti-asbestos crusade he recounts in *Dreams from My Father*.[82] This was one of the first negative Obama stories of the campaign. Determined not to be caught flat-footed by attacks, as John Kerry had been in 2004, the Obama camp sprang into action. Campaign research director Devorah Adler was charged with digging up the real identities of characters from *Dreams*, so she could write a rebuttal.

The odd detail here is that Adler had to determine the true identities of the characters in Obama's memoir on her own, when, as *Chicago Sun-Times* columnist Lynn Sweet remarked, "It would have seemed simpler for her to ask Obama."[83] It would appear, then, that Obama was reluctant to let even his own campaign research director question him directly about his past. Could this also explain why the Obama camp was "in denial" about Reverend Wright? Obama is apparently reluctant to speak freely about his past, even to those responsible for defending him.

Obama's socialist past is his secret. Reverend Wright is one of several gateways to the truth about that past. No wonder Obama did everything in his power in 2008 to suppress the truth about his relationship to Jeremiah Wright.

CHAPTER 9

State Senate Years

Barack Obama's years in Chicago between his graduation from law school in 1991 and his election to the U.S. Senate in 2004 contain many mysteries. Deepening ties to ACORN and the Midwest Academy during this period, as well as the story of his foundation work with Chicago's left, are part of what Obama's been hiding. Obama's twelve years as a lecturer at the University of Chicago Law School, from 1992 until his election to the U.S. Senate in 2004, and his eight years in the Illinois state senate, from 1997 through 2004, are poorly understood as well. Obama appears to have worked to eliminate any paper trail from his State Senate days. During campaign 2008, Obama also declined to be interviewed for a *New York Times* story on his law school career.[1] The main point of that story was that Obama had hidden his legal and political views from his University of Chicago colleagues. Keeping his convictions out of sight is something Obama does well.

An attempt to penetrate the mystery of Obama's years in the Illinois state legislature reveals further connections with Chicago's socialist world. Obama's career as a state senator, moreover, shows him utilizing the patient incrementalism of an Alinskyite organizer on behalf of his long-term radical goals.

Yet, if the full extent of Obama's radicalism has been kept under wraps, it should nonetheless have been obvious in 2008 that Obama was far from the post-racial, post-ideological, post-partisan politician presented to the country by the mainstream press and the Obama campaign alike. Obama's public record in the Illinois state legislature reveals him to be profoundly race-conscious, exceedingly liberal, free-spending even in the face of looming state budget deficits, and partisan. Seen in the light of his state legislative career, moreover, the president's associations with radical figures like Bill Ayers, Bernardine Dohrn, Jeremiah Wright, Father Michael Pfleger, and Reverend James Meeks clearly emerge as intentional political partnerships, rather than peculiar instances of personal misjudgment. The socialism question aside, the press averted its eyes in 2008 from even the most obvious contradictions in Obama's carefully tended personal myth.

UNIVERSITY OF CHICAGO LAW SCHOOL

Let's begin with Obama's twelve years as a lecturer at the University of Chicago Law School. That *New York Times* story on Obama's law faculty days portrays him as an "enigmatic" figure. According to the *Times*, the future president often left his fellow faculty members "guessing about his precise views."[2] The University of Chicago has a strong tradition of intellectual give and take, centered on a system of workshops attended by faculty and interested students. Having spent much of my own time at the University of Chicago organizing and participating in these workshops, I can confirm that the byplay is intense. Had Obama showed up at a workshop, he would have been pressed to justify his views in detail—in a way that would have required him to bring his most fundamental beliefs to the surface. It's of interest, then, that Obama largely avoided the law school's workshops, leaving all but his immediate friends on the faculty mystified about his views.

Obama frequently taught the work of Lani Guinier, whose controversial writings on ways to reconfigure the electoral system to increase the number of minority officeholders forced President Clinton to withdraw her nomination as assistant attorney general for civil rights in 1993. Obama's conservative-libertarian law school colleague, Richard Epstein, believes that Obama learned from Guinier's example "not to put his name to anything that could haunt him politically."[3] In fact, despite twelve years of teaching at Chicago's law school, Obama published not a single academic article. David Franklin, a former Obama student who teaches law school today, believes that Obama agreed with Guinier's proposals.[4] Yet Obama carefully avoided saying so at the time. It seems likely that something beyond mere professorial reserve explains this silence.

Biographer David Remnick describes a moment when the normally cautious Obama "let his guard down" in class and told his students what he actually thought about the issue of reparations for slavery:

> He agreed entirely with the *theory* of reparations. But in practice he didn't think it was really workable. You could tell that he thought he had let the cat out of the bag and felt uncomfortable. To agree with reparations in theory means we go past apology and say we can actually change the dynamics of the country.[5]

Remnick tells this story to make the point that Obama is a moderate pragmatist, like his law school colleague and friend Cass Sunstein, who is also reluctant to get "too far ahead of the electorate."[6] But is it fair to describe someone who favors slave reparations, in principle—and likely agrees with the radical ideas that forced the withdrawal of Lani Guinier's nomination—as a moderate? The fact that Obama is politically astute enough not to push these ideas prematurely is cold comfort for someone concerned about the president's inner convictions and long-term intentions. After all, the implication of this "pragmatism" is that the moment Obama thinks one of his radical ideas is politically feasible, he'll put it forward, in one form or another.

President Obama has scrupulously avoided justifying his health-care reform plans on the grounds of racial injustice. Yet in his second book, *The Audacity of Hope,* Obama writes that "a plan for universal health-care coverage would do more to eliminate health disparities between whites and minorities than any-race specific programs we might design."[7] Obama then adds: "An emphasis on universal, as opposed to race-specific, programs isn't just good policy, it's also good politics."[8] It's not that Obama opposes preferential treatment by race. On the contrary, he heartily approves of such preferences. Yet Obama recognizes that, as president, he'll get far better political results with race-neutral programs than with preferential treatment. So putting together Obama's writings with what we've learned about his views on reparations, it seems likely that the president thinks of universal health-care reform as, in part, a race-neutral and roundabout way of making up for a history of racial injustice.

I'm not arguing that President Obama's health-care crusade is nothing but a roundabout form of reparations. On the contrary, I think what attracts the president to socialism is the way it combines demands for racial redress with a universal program of wealth redistribution. When push comes to shove, I'd say it's actually the universal character of socialist ideology that most appeals to Obama. Nonetheless, the radicalism exemplified by Obama's "merely" theoretical approval of slave reparations tells us something about the ideology behind his support for universal health care. Knowing that, but for purely practical barriers, Obama would willingly redistribute massive amounts of wealth to make up for slavery, we see that the president favors not only redistribution but class-based guilt, in principle. That puts him well down the road to socialism.

STUDENT SOCIALISTS

Although Obama did everything in his power to hide his radical views from his conservative-libertarian colleagues at Chicago's law school, he was on close and friendly terms with a few liberal professors like Cass Sunstein and Elena Kagan—both of whom have received major appointments from the president.[9] Reports agree as well that Obama was on very good terms with his students. Left-leaning law students in particular flocked to Obama's classes.[10] That is why the largely student-initiated endorsement of Obama by the Chicago branch of the Democratic Socialists of America (DSA) in his first run for legislative office is so revealing.

Because back issues of Chicago DSA's newsletter, *New Ground*, are available online, it has long been known that Obama was endorsed by this socialist group during his first campaign for office in 1995–96.[11] The full significance of this endorsement has not been appreciated, however. Naturally, it would be unfair to take every endorsement of a liberal-leaning candidate by some socialist group as evidence of that candidate's socialism. As I've argued throughout this book, socialists groups often ally with and support liberal factions within the Democratic Party. That does not automatically make these liberal groups socialist.

On the other hand, Obama's endorsement by the Chicago DSA in 1996 is of a different order. Out of the many Chicago-area Democrats running for office in the primary or general elections in 1996, Chicago's DSA endorsed only four: Danny Davis (for the U.S. House of Representatives), William "Willie" Delgado (for the Illinois House of Representatives), Patricia Martin (for judge of the Cook County Judicial Circuit), and Barack Obama (for Illinois Senate).[12] Obviously, this tiny list was part of a selective effort to back a few Democratic candidates considered friendly to socialist ideas. It's also highly significant that in 1996, the New Party, controlled by ACORN and the SEIU, but also supported by a significant contingent from DSA, endorsed these same four candidates—and only one additional candidate not on the DSA list.[13] In short, during his first run for legislative office, Obama was one of a small and select group of candidates endorsed by Chicago's openly socialist DSA, and by the de facto socialist New Party as well.

The New Party knew Obama chiefly through his years of cooperation with ACORN. Chicago DSA knew Obama through organizer circles, but especially through the very large and active Young Democratic Socialist chapter at the University of Chicago. The minutes of the January 20, 1996, meeting of the Chicago DSA Executive Committee indicate that Katie Romich, representing the University of Chicago DSA, was present and took the initiative to recommend Obama for endorsement. Romich also announced that Obama would speak at an upcoming forum sponsored by the University of Chicago DSA.[14] So while Obama may have been a mystery to the law school's conservative-libertarian professors, his students—to whom everyone agrees he was quite close—felt sufficiently confident of Obama's political convictions to recommend him for endorsement by Chicago's premiere socialist group.

A SOCIALIST FORUM

Obama's appearance at the student-sponsored DSA "Economic Security Forum" at the University of Chicago on February 25, 1996, was revealing in a couple of respects. Obama made his usual rhetorical bow to conservatives as well as liberals, presenting himself as someone who would combine the best of both worlds. Yet by American standards, Obama's actual proposals were decidedly radical, and immediately recognized by his socialist supporters as an attempt to import a European-style welfare state to America.[15] Four years later, in 2000, when Obama tried unsuccessfully to win Bobby Rush's seat in Congress, Chicago's DSA remained technically neutral. DSA's description of the two candidates in its newsletter, however, clearly tilts toward Obama. According to *New Ground*, Bobby Rush "hasn't always been the ideal Congressman from a left perspective . . . When Obama participated in a 1996 [University of Chicago Young DSA] Townhall Meeting on Economic Insecurity, much of what he had to say was well within the mainstream of European social democracy." [16]

Why did Obama take the risk of appearing at this socialist-sponsored forum in 1996, given his caution about exposing his radical political views? The answer may be that he was forced into the open by a bitter electoral battle. Only three days before the DSA Executive Committee meeting at which he was recommended for endorsement by his student supporters, Obama's main challenger, Alice Palmer, withdrew from contention. [17] Palmer herself held the seat Obama was running for, and had personally anointed him as her successor. After her loss in a special election for Congress, however, Palmer decided to fight Obama for the seat she had earlier promised to vacate. Obama challenged the validity of the signatures on Palmer's nominating petitions and was able to knock her off the ballot. [18] Yet he probably agreed to appear at the Young Democratic Socialist forum before he knew for sure that Palmer would withdraw.

Palmer's entry into the race with Obama had split Hyde Park's left. Palmer herself was a hard Marxist. Not only had she co-chaired the Midwest Academy's International Affairs Committee with longtime Obama colleague Ken Rolling, but for several years, Palmer edited an opinion magazine called *New Deliberations* that was obviously socialist in character (sample article title: "Socialism Is the Only Way Forward"). [19] Obama critic David Freddoso has already reported Palmer's attendance in 1986 at the Twenty-seventh Congress of the Communist Party of the Soviet Union, followed by her praise of the USSR and criticism of the United States in the communist *People's Daily World*. [20] Palmer's papers are filled with similar material—an engraved invitation to the first anniversary celebration of the Marxist revolution in Grenada, for example. [21] It is, of course, both disturbing and revealing that Palmer had originally hand-picked Obama as her successor after lengthy consultations with the future president.[22]

In this Hyde Park/South Side district, support from the hard-left would be critical to an electoral victory. Chicago's socialists were already extremely well-disposed to Alice Palmer, so once she decided to challenge Obama, he knew he would have to fight for DSA's endorsement. Bringing his radical views more out into the open than usual to please his student supporters and garner the DSA nod would have been worth it for Obama at this critical juncture. Obama was fortunate that the University of Chicago Young Democratic Socialists were at a high point of size and influence in 1996, with a large and growing number of "cadre" (politically reliable members willing to commit significant time and effort to the group).[23] The DSA Executive Committee, on the other hand, was short on cadre at the time, and in a poor position to contradict its youth branch, had it been so inclined.[24] The importance of a DSA endorsement, and Obama's likelihood of taking it away from Palmer through his student supporters, probably explains this rare bit of socialist openness on the part of a usually hyper-cautious Obama.

POST-RACIAL?

Coverage of Obama's State Senate career in two local papers provides an essential resource for reconstructing this important phase of the president's life. Obama's neighborhood newspaper, the *Hyde Park Herald,* has long opened its pages to local and state elected officials. As a state senator, Obama wrote more than forty columns for the *Herald* under the title "Springfield Report," between 1996 and 2004. Even more revealing are hundreds of articles chronicling Obama's activities in the pages not only of the *Hyde Park Herald*, but also of another South Side fixture, the *Chicago Defender*. For more than one hundred years, the *Defender* has been an influential voice of Chicago's black community. I'll draw extensively in this chapter on material from both of these papers, in combination with Obama's own columns in the *Herald.*

To a remarkable degree, Obama shared Jeremiah Wright's anti-as-similationist views on the topic of race. That is surprising to Americans first introduced to Obama through his powerful keynote address at the 2004 Democratic National Convention. There he famously said: "There is not a Black America and a White America and Latino America and Asian America—there's the United States of America."[25] That sounds like an expression of faith in a color-blind consciousness of the kind expressed in Martin Luther King Jr.'s dream that his children would one day be judged, not by the color of their skin, but by the content of their character.

In fact, while Obama clearly recognizes the political benefits of race-neutral programs, he is by no means opposed to race-based politics. On the contrary, during his years in the Illinois State Senate, race-based policies were an Obama specialty. Political necessity may have forced Obama to downplay that approach during his presidency. Yet it's worth noting that during his years as a state senator, Obama strongly supported race preferences, set-asides, and other race-based measures.[26]

Obama once tangled with another state senator, Mary E. Flowers, when she broke with her black colleagues to support the placement of a riverboat casino in a non-minority neighborhood. Responding to Obama's criticisms, Flowers said: "The Black Caucus is from different tribes, different walks of life. I don't expect all of the whites to vote alike. . . . Why is it that all of us should walk alike, talk alike, and vote alike? . . . I was chosen by my constituents to represent them, and that is what I try to do."[27] Given Obama's supposedly post-racial politics, it's notable that he should have been the one demanding enforcement of a black political agenda against an independent legislator like Flowers. This little history lesson serves as a reminder that we cannot depend on Obama's soaring rhetoric to convey the truth of his inner convictions.

POST-IDEOLOGICAL?

Well into the Obama administration, when a major question for debate has been whether the president is a socialist, it may be tough to remember how successfully candidate Obama was able to shed the liberal label in 2008.[28] I've argued throughout this book that Alinskyite organizers consciously disguise their socialist views by presenting themselves as pragmatic problem solvers. That is exactly what Obama did in 2008. Certainly, the mainstream press and a substantial segment of the electorate bought this characterization, although it plainly contradicted Senator Obama's voting record—the most liberal in the U.S. Senate at the time.

Local press coverage of Obama's Illinois State Senate days provides abundant additional evidence of the future president's longstanding liberalism. Although Obama rejected the liberal label in 2008, when he unsuccessfully ran for Congress in 2000 he freely characterized himself and his opponents as "all on the liberal wing of the Democratic party."[29] Obama lost that race to incumbent congressman Bobby Rush, a former Black Panther who received a 90 percent rating in 2000 and a 100 percent rating in 1999 from the liberal Americans for Democratic Action. Both years the American Conservative Union rated Rush at zero percent.[30] The *Hyde Park Herald* noted that there was "little to distinguish" Obama from Rush ideologically.[31] We've seen that the Chicago branch of the Democratic Socialists of America remained neutral in that 2000 race, while describing Rush as a disappointment to the left and informally tilting to Obama. Given Rush's 100 percent liberal voting record in 1999, Chicago's DSA obviously had high standards for leftism. Obama met those standards.

To see just how leftist both Bobby Rush and Obama were in 2000, consider a moment from one of their debates. When Rush bragged that, since entering Congress, he hadn't voted to approve a single defense budget, Obama pounced, accusing Rush of having voted for the Star Wars missile defense system the previous year.[32] In 2002 and 2004, the *Chicago Defender* praised Obama, sometimes calling him "progressive," sometimes a genuine "liberal."[33] Combine all this with Obama's U.S. Senate voting record and its clear that his refusal of the liberal label during campaign 2008 was patent nonsense.

One of the most interesting characterizations of his views comes from Obama himself, who laid out his U.S. Senate campaign strategy for the *Defender* in 2003: "As you combine a strong African-American base with progressive white and Latino voters, I think it is a recipe for success in the primary and in the general election."[34] Obama consciously constructed his electoral strategy on a foundation of leftist ideology and racial block voting.

While the great majority of Obama's columns in the *Hyde Park Herald* deal with state and local issues, it's interesting that one of his few nationally focused columns is a plea for readers to support Al Gore, rather than Ralph Nader, in the 2000 presidential election.[35] Obama opens his column by noting how many people he's heard complaining that both George Bush and Al Gore are beholden to the same "big money interests." While Obama makes a point of agreeing with some of Nader's criticism of the major parties, he rests his case for Gore on differences between Republicans and Democrats on issues like Supreme Court appointments, abortion, affirmative action, the environment, and school vouchers. Far from criticizing Nader's agenda, Obama implicitly presents himself as someone who could gladly support Nader, were it not for the danger of wasting a vote. It's interesting that so many of the policy differences Obama points to as reasons for favoring Democrats are classic sixties-style issues—just the kind of polarizing culture-war conflicts Obama claimed to have transcended during the 2008 campaign. In the end, Hyde Park voted 91 percent for Gore, 6 percent for Bush, and 3 percent for Nader.[36] In an election that divided the country down the middle, this provides some sense of just how left-leaning Obama's home district was.

ALLIANCE WITH AYERS

Obama's leftist views are nowhere more evident than on the subject of crime, a central concern of his during his years in the Illinois legislature. While crime has declined as an issue on the national scene, Obama's treatment of the topic provides a clear sense of his political leanings. The crime issue also brought Obama into an active alliance with Bill Ayers, Bernardine Dohrn, and other elements of his radical network. So Obama's approach to crime is well worth exploring in depth.

Knowing that Illinois was headed for a major reform of its juvenile crime laws, Bill Ayers dropped his usual focus on education and, in 1997, published *A Kind and Just Parent,* a blistering critique of the Illinois juvenile justice system.[37] Ayers was following the lead of his wife and former Weatherman leader, Bernardine Dohrn, who had founded and directed the Children and Family Justice Center at Northwestern University.[38] In 1996 and perhaps earlier, Dohrn was gearing up for a major public battle on juvenile sentencing reform. Ayers, Dohrn, and Obama were very arguably the three most powerful voices in Illinois opposed to the modest strengthening of the state's juvenile justice laws debated and finally passed in 1997–98. All signs point to the fact that Obama was actively working with Ayers and Dohrn during this period. It also seems likely that Obama understood perfectly well that the views of this famously radical couple on both crime and American society were virtually unchanged from their Weatherman days.

Steven A. Drizin, an associate of Dohrn's Northwestern center (who is also thanked in Ayers's book), was a member of the study commission that produced the proposed reform of the Illinois juvenile justice system in 1997.[39] (Despite being on the commission that produced the reform proposal, Drizin was an energetic critic of just about every prosecutor-favored provision in the bill.) So Ayers, Dohrn, and Obama knew the juvenile justice bill was in the offing a year or more ahead of time.

Certainly, it's conceivable that Ayers and Dohrn discussed the juvenile justice issue with Obama when they helped launch his career in 1995 at a campaign event in their home. In fact, the focus of Ayers and Dohrn on the upcoming juvenile justice debate may go a long way toward explaining their special interest in Hyde Park's State Senate seat. Recall that Obama was also serving as board chair of the Ayers-founded Chicago Annenberg Challenge from 1995 through 1999, and working directly with Ayers there. On top of that, just as Obama became vice chair of the Woods Fund board in 1996, that foundation began supporting Dohrn and the work of her juvenile justice center at Northwestern. Dohrn was even featured in the Woods Fund annual report of 1996 as a model grantee. So in 1996, Dohrn's colleague, Steve Drizin, was fighting the emerging juvenile justice reform within the state study commission, Ayers was finishing his book on the topic, and Obama was funneling foundation money to Dohrn's center in preparation for a legislative battle in which he, Ayers, and Dohrn would be the key voices against the new juvenile crime bill.

Shortly after its appearance in 1997, Obama gave Ayers's juvenile crime book what the *New York Times* called a "rare review" (not actually a full review but a warm endorsement) in the *Chicago Tribune*, calling it "a searing and timely account."[40] While Ayers's views have remained constant since the sixties, his rhetoric now varies greatly, depending on context. Eager to influence the public debate on juvenile crime, Ayers kept his language in *A Kind and Just Parent* relatively tame—even if the substance of his views was as radical as ever. The title itself, as Ayers explains in the book, is meant to "bristle with irony" as a comment on an American "society out of control."[41] In other words, Ayers's views in *A Kind and Just Parent* are identical to his notorious comments to a *New York Times* interviewer in 2001 that the notion of the United States as a "just and fair and decent place . . . makes me want to puke."[42] Yet in his 1997 book, Ayers expressed his hatred of the United States only indirectly, through irony. Of course, a sensitive reader like Obama would have easily picked up on Ayers's radicalism, rhetorical subtleties notwithstanding.

A Kind and Just Parent is a thoughtful and beautifully written book, which provides revealing and sometimes disturbing glimpses of life at a Chicago juvenile detention facility. The book also virtually defines the phrases "liberal guilt" and "soft on crime." While recounting horrific crimes—and even his own mugging—Ayers focuses on the terrified insecurity of the perpetrators, rather than harm to the victims.[43] Testifying at the trial of a young felon he'd been tutoring, Ayers calls him "nervous, a little shy . . . eager to please." The prosecutor responds: "Would you call shooting someone eight times at close range 'eager to please'?"[44] Actually, Ayers effectively does do this, opening his book with the claim that a young murderer had "slavishly followed the orders" of his gang leader, rather than acting of his own free will.[45]

Ayers opposes trying even the most vicious juvenile murderers as adults. More than that, he'd like to see the effective abolition of the prison system itself. Drawing on the radical French philosopher Michel Foucault, Ayers argues that prisons impose conformity and obedience on society, falsely causing us to distinguish between "normal" and "deviant" behavior. Ayers wants prisons replaced by a form of home detention.[46] He also pointedly compares America's juvenile justice system to the mass detention of a generation of young blacks under South African apartheid.[47]

It's obvious that *A Kind and Just Parent* uses high-toned academic theories to convey the very same points Ayers himself made more bluntly in his Weatherman days—for example, that America's prison system is a racist plot to clear the streets of the kids most likely to make a socialist revolution. We saw in Chapter Seven that Dohrn has made such points fairly openly as recently as 2009. Obama could hardly have missed the radical substance of the book he praised so highly in 1997, even if Ayers's rhetoric was toned down a bit for purposes of public debate.

Obama was certainly sympathetic to Ayers's radical take on America's prison system. Obama once bragged that he had consistently fought against the "industrial-prison complex," a favorite phrase of people like Jeremiah Wright, who see America's criminal justice system as secretly driven by capitalist greed.[48]

JUVENILE JUSTICE

Although the bill Obama, Ayers, and Dohrn fought so hard to sink in 1997–98 was written by prosecutors and sponsored by a Republican ex-prosecutor, it was neither simplistic nor partisan. Aware of evidence that sending juveniles to adult prison can backfire and raise recidivism rates, the bill's supporters met rehabilitation-minded critics halfway. The bill was an early example of "blended sentencing," in which juveniles who have committed serious crimes are given both adult and juvenile sentences. As long as the offender doesn't violate parole and takes part in rehabilitation programs, he never serves the adult sentence. But should the offender violate the conditions of his juvenile sentence, the adult punishment kicks in. That gives young offenders a powerful incentive to do right, putting toughness in the service of offering kids a second chance.

Most people think of blended sentencing as an innovative compromise.[49] To those on the far left, however, blended sentencing is nothing but mean-spirited punishment in a friendly guise.[50] So when the Illinois blended-sentencing bill was introduced in 1997, both Obama and Bernardine Dohrn were cited by the *Chicago Sun-Times* as the key public voices against the bill.[51] (Recall that Obama was funding Dohrn's work through the Woods Fund at the time.)

Meanwhile, Obama worked with the Illinois black legislative caucus to slow the bill's progress, specifically challenging the blended-sentencing provisions.[52] While one report has Obama negotiating with the bill's proponents for a compromise, Obama's actual aim seems to have been to scuttle the entire bill.[53] We have this on the authority of someone who may be Michelle Obama herself. Michelle Obama organized a University of Chicago panel about Bill Ayers's crime book in November 1997, just as the battle over the juvenile justice bill was heating up. That panel featured Barack himself, who was identified in the press release as "working to block proposed legislation that would throw more juvenile offenders into the adult system."[54] So this event was very much a joint Obama-Ayers effort to sink the juvenile justice bill. Obama's plug of Ayers's book in the *Chicago Tribune* the following month was part of the same effort. Obviously, Obama, Ayers, and Dohrn were active political partners.

In January 1998, a front-page headline in the *Defender* broadcast Obama's claim that the juvenile justice bill might be on the verge of failure.[55] Obama hoped that opposition to the bill's sentencing provisions by the black caucus would combine with Republican worries that the bill could force expensive jail construction (on the theory that the deterrent effect of blended sentencing would fail, thereby forcing more juveniles into adult prisons). Obama's hopes were wildly off-base. The juvenile justice bill passed overwhelmingly. Given his ambitions for higher office, Obama was no doubt reluctant to vote against the final bill. A last-minute and largely cosmetic adjustment to the blended-sentencing provisions by the governor appears to have provided sufficient political cover for the bill's harshest critics, including Obama, to come around and support it.[56]

Also in 1998, according to *The Hill,* a Washington newspaper, Obama was one of only three Illinois state senators to vote against a proposal making it a criminal offense for convicts on probation or bail to have contact with a street gang. A year later, on a vote mandating adult prosecution for aggravated discharge of a firearm in or near a school, Obama voted "present," and reiterated his opposition to adult trials for even serious juvenile offenders.[57] In short, when it comes to the issue of crime, Obama is on the far left of the political spectrum, and very much in synch with his political allies Ayers and Dohrn.

In his 2001 memoir *Fugitive Days,* published while he was still serving on the Woods Fund board with Obama, Ayers tells the story of a glittering party thrown by a Chicago foundation in honor of his book on juvenile crime.[58] With so many wealthy and powerful civic leaders in attendance, Ayers joked about the event privately with friends, calling it the Ruling Class Party. When one of the juvenile ex-offenders Ayers points to as a model heard Ayers talking this way, the young man asked what "ruling class" meant. Ayers then offered his young follower an impromptu lecture on Marxism, explaining that a revolution would someday sweep away ruling-class types like the ones who were throwing this party for Ayers himself. The young man, worried that he might be betraying Marxism, asked Ayers if he should keep building up his small business—the key to his turn away from crime. "Absolutely," answered Ayers. Just make sure to be on the side of the revolution when it comes.

This little anecdote nicely illustrates some things we should already know. At the very time he was working with Obama, Ayers was still an enthusiastically revolutionary "small c communist," who had not at all abandoned his revolutionary hopes. Ayers had merely reduced the intensity of his rhetoric, accepting the support of Chicago's elite, while reverting to his old radical talk privately with friends. Was Obama one of these friends? Probably. Obama worked directly with Ayers at the Chicago Annenberg Challenge and on the juvenile crime bill. David Remnick, who blithely accepts Ayers's bogus assurances that he was actually cool to Obama, reports that Michelle Obama was a dinner guest at the Ayers's home in the mid-nineties.[59] At the Annenberg project, Obama worked not only with Ayers, but with the ex-Weatherman's inner circle of supporters for years. How could Obama have failed to know who Ayers was and what he still believed?

The other interesting thing about this anecdote is that it shows how even Bill Ayers—the hardest of hard-core socialists—was willing to accept and even encourage private enterprise under certain conditions. Ayers still looked forward to a violent revolution, yet even for this onetime revolutionary, the road to socialism now required gradual subversion of the capitalist system from within.

AYERS AND KHALIDI

Obama's ties to University of Chicago professor Rashid Khalidi are part of a broader web of connections between Obama, Ayers, and Chicago's leftist foundations. Although Khalidi denies having been a spokesman for the Palestine Liberation Organization in the 1970s, the evidence that he was is very strong.[60] To make sense of the ties between this prominent Palestinian activist and Obama's radical world, keep in mind that Obama was a frequent dinner guest in the Khalidi home.[61] At the same time, Bill Ayers was a friend to both Rashid Khalidi and his wife, Mona.[62]

Laying out the connections between this trio chronologically is revealing. In 1995, Ayers helped select Obama as board chair of the Chicago Annenberg Challenge, then launched Obama's political career at his home, with his close friend Khalidi present.[63] From 1996 to 1998, Obama funded Ayers's wife and fellow radical Bernardine Dohrn through the Woods Fund and worked with both Ayers and Dohrn in the fight against the juvenile crime bill. In 1999, Obama brought Ayers onto the board of the Woods Fund. In 2000, the Khalidis hosted a fundraiser for Obama's congressional run against Bobby Rush.[64] Soon after, Obama and Ayers began channeling Woods Fund money to the Arab American Action Network, a group founded by Rashid and Mona Khalidi (and viewed by some as harshly anti-Israeli).[65] So Obama's move to bring Ayers onto the Woods Fund board created two likely votes on this tiny seven-member board in support of Khalidi's projects, thereby helping to consolidate Obama's political support, via Khalidi. Once again, Ayers had served as a lynchpin of Obama's political fortunes.

RACIAL PROFILING?

Obama's signature crime legislation was his effort to combat alleged racial discrimination by the Chicago police. In 2003, the *Defender* said Obama had "made a career" out of his annual battle for a bill against "racial profiling."[66] For years, Illinois Republicans had bottled up Obama's profiling bills.[67] When State Senate control passed to the Democrats in 2003, the bill finally passed—just in time to boost Obama's U.S. Senate campaign. Obama touted his anti-profiling bill as a "model for the nation."[68] Unfortunately, there's a defect in the model.

Obama is often commended for carefully consulting with the police during the negotiations that led to the final racial-profiling bill. With the Democrats in control, however, the police had little choice but to work with Obama. As Obama himself noted at the time, the police never abandoned their opposition to the bill.[69] Police doubts were entirely justified. Obama's bill is a deeply flawed exercise in precisely the sort of grievance-driven, race-based politics that fuels legislation on racial preferences and minority set-asides. All of these so-called remedies falsely leap from statistical evidence of racial disparities to claims of discrimination. In the case of racial profiling, disproportionate police stops of black or Hispanic motorists in no way prove discrimination.

Manhattan Institute scholar Heather Mac Donald's powerful work on supposed racial profiling by police has shown that drug-interdiction traffic stops track closely to the ethnic identity of those in charge of the drug trade in a given area.[70] Sometimes that involves black or Hispanic minorities, and sometimes it doesn't. The point is that police stops are based on good crime intelligence, not racism. Mac Donald rightly points out that without baseline information on the ethnic identities of those actually committing crimes, statistical disparities in traffic stops in no way prove police racism.

Unfortunately, Obama's *Hyde Park Herald* column defending his work on racial profiling is an almost textbook example of the sort of bad statistical arguments Mac Donald debunks.[71] Not only does Obama use baseline-free statistics, he makes still bolder and more questionable accusations against the police. According to Obama: "Racial profiling may explain why incarceration rates are so high among young African-Americans—law enforcement officials may be targeting blacks and other minorities as potential criminals and are using the Vehicle Code as a tool to stop and search them." Obama's claim that high black incarceration rates are due to racist traffic stops is utterly fanciful (Mac Donald's research is clear on this issue as well).[72] Obama's column takes a leaf right out of Jeremiah Wright's playbook (not to mention Ayers and Dohrn), stoking the worst sort of race-based conspiracy theories.

Indeed, Obama's racial-profiling crusade shows his political alliance with Wright, Pfleger, and Meeks in action. Obama's long-term political goal was to organize "liberationist" black churches. So it's no surprise to see the *Hyde Park Herald* praising Obama in 2001 for organizing a "grassroots lobbying effort" on racial profiling featuring not only the ACLU and the Mexican American Legal Defense and Education Fund, but also appearances by Meeks and Pfleger.[73] Jeremiah Wright's church was represented in the effort by an associate pastor. So Obama's drive for racial-profiling legislation brought to fruition his longstanding goal of organizing Chicago's most liberationist black churches for political purposes. Wright, Meeks, and Pfleger are known for their demagogic denunciations of white racism.[74] Obama's racial-profiling bill fit squarely in that tradition. Obama played the legislative "good cop," while the preachers no doubt spoke more abrasively. When you see Obama's writings on racial profiling, however, it's evident that there's little real difference between his position and the more harshly expressed views of his liberationist allies.

SPEND, SPEND, SPEND

Important though it was to State Senator Obama, the crime issue ran a distant second to his real passion: social welfare legislation. Obama was very much a redistributionist during his years in the Illinois legislature, where his fondest hope was to help lead America into another massive war on poverty. Obama openly calls for a massive renewal of expensive anti-poverty programs in his book *The Audacity of Hope*.[75] So it makes sense that, with the exception of his secondary interest in race and crime, Obama's state legislative career essentially boils down to a series of spending measures.

Obama was a master of incrementalism. His method was to find the smallest, most appealing spending proposal possible, pass it, then build toward still more spending on the same issue. It would have been tough, for example, to vote against an Obama bill exempting juvenile prisoners from paying for medical services.[76] Obama's long-term plan, of course, was to keep expanding health-care entitlements in incremental steps, until no one but the government was in charge.

In a 2007 speech to Al Sharpton's National Action Network (NAN), Obama challenged the group to find a candidate with a better record of supporting the issues they cared about. Intrigued by Obama's challenge, Randolph Burnside, a professor of political science, and Kami Whitehurst, a doctoral candidate, both at Southern Illinois University—Carbondale, decided to put Obama's Illinois record to the test. The scholars studied bills sponsored and cosponsored by Obama during his eight years in the Illinois State Senate.

The revealing results of this study were published in the *Journal of Black Studies* in 2007.[77] Burnside and Whitehurst created two bar graphs, one charting bills for which Obama was the main sponsor, arranged by subject, and a second chart displaying bills Obama joined as a cosponsor.[78] In the graph of bills of which Obama was the main sponsor, the bar for "social welfare" legislation towers over every other category. In the graph of Obama's co-sponsored bills, social welfare legislation again far exceeds every other category, although crime bills are now visibly present in second place, with tax and regulation bills close behind. According to Burnside and Whitehurst, other than social welfare and a sprinkling of government regulation, "Obama devoted very little time to most policy areas."[79]

Given this record on spending, it's no surprise that the president's fingerprints are all over Illinois's ever-growing fiscal crisis. The Illinois state budget had been in a widening crisis since 2001. By 2007, an influential committee of top Chicago business leaders warned that Illinois was swiftly "headed toward fiscal implosion." [80] Things have only gotten worse since then.

A watershed moment in Illinois's fiscal decline came in 2002, when crashing receipts and Democratic reluctance to enact spending cuts forced Republican governor George Ryan to call a special legislative session. While Ryan railed at legislators for refusing to rein in an out-of-control budget, the *Chicago Tribune* spoke ominously of an "all-consuming state budget crisis." [81] Unwilling to cut back on social welfare spending, Obama's partner and political mentor, Senate Democratic leader Emil Jones, proposed borrowing against a windfall tobacco settlement due to the state. [82]

That idea sent the editorial pages of the *St. Louis Post-Dispatch* and the *Chicago Tribune* into a tizzy. [83] The papers hammered cut-averse legislators for "chickening out," for making use of "tricked up numbers," for a "cowardly abdication of responsibility," and for sacrificing the state's bond rating to "short-term political gains." Critics repeatedly pointed out that borrowing against a one-time tobacco settlement—instead of balancing the budget with regular revenues—would be a recipe for long-term fiscal disaster. [84]

What was Obama's position while all this was going on? In his *Hyde Park Herald* column, Obama actually promoted the tobacco securitization plan and railed against Governor Ryan for "balancing the budget on the back of the poor." [85] Obama also voted to override the governor's cuts in programs like bilingual education. Yet far from "balancing the budget on the back of the poor," Governor Ryan had actually trimmed evenly across all of Illinois's most expensive programs. [86] While the governor did manage to force a number of cuts, the relentless opposition of Obama and his Democratic colleagues had its effect. When Democrats added control of the governorship and State Senate to their existing control of the House a year later, it emerged that the state's deficit was $5 billion, far larger than anyone had realized.[87] Since Obama's Democratic allies took full control of the state, it's been a swift downhill tumble toward fiscal implosion for Illinois.

On the national level, we're experiencing a grand-scale version of what happened to Illinois as Democrats took control of that state. Obama's small and carefully targeted spending bills of the nineties were expressly designed to win passage by a Republican-led State Senate. With a Democratic Congress at his back, on the other hand, President Obama can now go to town on spending. What looked like Obama's legislative moderation in Illinois was really never anything other than an incremental strategy for achieving his far more ambitious long-term spending plans.

INCREMENTAL RADICALISM

A good term for Obama's legislative strategy in Illinois might be "incremental radicalism." On health care, at least, Obama's long-term plans for Illinois were no secret. Working with his socialist colleague, activist Quentin Young, Obama repeatedly proposed a state constitutional amendment mandating universal health care.[88] Obama openly favored a "single-payer" system at the time.[89] Before the 2002 budget crisis hit, Obama planned to use the windfall tobacco settlement to finance his statewide health-care plan. That would have effectively hidden the enormous cost of the new health-care system from the taxpayer until it was too late to scale the changes back. The same sort of fiscal trickery has been essential to the president's national health-care-reform plan.

While he openly touted single-payer as the long-term answer in Illinois, Obama simultaneously proposed an ever-expanding range of baby steps as a way of gradually reaching his ultimate goal.[90] As president, Obama has moved in giant leaps on health care, while simultaneously denying that single-payer is his true goal. It's tough to take this denial seriously, given the president's open support of single-payer in Illinois.

Obama's incremental radicalism no doubt shapes his approach to a broad range of other issues. The president moves gradually toward what are in fact radical goals, usually denying what those long-term plans really are. This strategy is a direct application of Alinskyite gradualism and stealth to the legislative realm.

BIPARTISAN?

Obama's vaunted reputation for bipartisanship, based on his Illinois State Senate record, was always less than meets the eye. There has always been a group of centrist Republicans, less fiscally conservative than their colleagues, in the Illinois legislature. Many are from districts where the parties are closely balanced. It was easy enough for Obama to get a few of these Republicans to sign on to modest spending bills, carefully targeted toward the most sympathetic recipients. The problem with Obama's bipartisanship is that it was largely a one-way street. Overcoming initial opposition from Catholic groups, for example, Obama sponsored a typically incremental abortion bill requiring hospitals to inform rape victims of available morning-after pills.[91] Yet Obama rejected compromise on the same issue when he voted against a bill that would have curbed partial-birth abortions.[92] So Obama is bipartisan only when that means asking Republicans to take tiny steps toward his own long-term goals. When it comes to moving a bit in the other direction, Obama shows Republicans the door. Obama voted against a bill that would have allowed people with a court order protecting them from the approach of a specific individual to carry a concealed weapon for self-defense.[93] Bipartisanship for thee, but not for me. That's how Obama ended up with the most liberal voting record in the U.S. Senate.

What looked to some in 2008 like bipartisanship was really just Obama's "good cop" routine. The sort of grassroots coalitions Obama favored consciously made use of a good cop/bad cop strategy. Policy experts worked courteously and cooperatively with all sides, while quietly encouraging the Alinskyite intimidation tactics of their community-organizer allies. Community-organizer good cops are not pragmatic centrists. They're ideological radicals in moderate guise. Obama's incremental radicalism depends on this good-cop veneer. Yet his post-partisan pragmatism was never sincere. The signs were there in 2008 for anyone who cared to look. Unfortunately, few did.

CHAPTER 10

The Obama Administration

G iven all that we've learned of Obama's history, I believe the best way to understand the president's policies is to see them as a series of steps designed to slowly but surely move the country closer to a socialist ideal. Yet precisely because Obama moves gradually, without an announced ideological plan, the ultimate meaning of his policies will always be subject to dispute. The danger, in fact, is that we will be irreversibly down the path toward socialist transformation before we recognize as a nation what's at stake. The strategy of achieving socialism through a series of "non-reformist reforms," so popular among America's community organizing elite, is premised on precisely that deception.

THE DEMOCRATIC PARTY AND SOCIALISM

The notion that Obama is a socialist—that he never abandoned his early radicalism but only learned to promote it in piecemeal fashion—

makes better sense of his overall record than the claim that he is a pragmatist. Obama's college socialism, the influence of socialist conferences
on his career, his choice of a profession dominated by socialists, and his
extensive alliances with the most influential stealth-socialist community
organizers in the country give the game away. Obama has adopted the
gradualist socialist strategy of his mentors, seeking to combine comprehensive government regulation of private businesses with a steadily
enlarging public sector. Eventually, this will transform American capitalism into something resembling a socialist-inspired Scandinavian
welfare state. Accumulating differences of degree will add up to a fundamental difference in kind. Wealth will be substantially redirected
away from individuals, local communities, and businesses, toward the
state and public-employee unions instead. Power will shift decisively
toward government and away from the private sector.

So the president is carrying out the ideals of his community-
organizer past from a new position. The socialist organizers who taught
and inspired Obama favored plans to quietly transform America's economic system with "non-reformist reforms"—programs that appear as
minor adjustments to capitalism but in fact undermine the system itself.
This strategy was favored by Obama's socialist mentors and associates
at New York's Socialist Scholars Conferences, the Midwest Academy,
and ACORN. To believe that Obama is a socialist merely assumes his
continued commitment to a world he has long described as his lodestar.
Now that we understand the hidden socialist underpinnings of community organizing, as well as the fact that organizers in general—and
Obama in particular—have done everything in their power to hide that
socialist subtext, it's tough to take the president's self-representation as
a pragmatist at face value.

Yet even if we grant that Obama was once a socialist—and remains
one in his heart of hearts today—would that commitment necessarily
have policy consequences? Would Obama's socialism affect the way
he governed, or would political necessity force him to act the part of
a standard-issue liberal Democrat instead? This is a false choice. It is

perfectly possible for socialists to work within the Democratic Party. That was Michael Harrington's strategy, after all. Here is how Harrington outlined the relationship between his Democratic Socialist Organizing Committee and the Democratic Party in 1974:

> As socialists of the democratic left, we stand for fundamental change, for socialism, and for every immediate gain which can be achieved by the largely non-socialist mass movements in which we loyally and enthusiastically participate: the unions, minority and women's organizations, the student movement, the liberal wing of the Democratic party among them . . . It is precisely because we are socialists that we feel we have a unique contribution to make to the democratic left, showing how increments of change must be turned toward structural transformation of the society itself . . . Perhaps the fullness of [our socialist] vision will never come to pass; perhaps it will. But whether it does or not, we believe that this dream is relevant to the increments of reform we can win in the next few years.[1]

Harrington understood that full socialism in America would never be achieved in his lifetime. Yet he was convinced that Democratic policy battles could be productively guided by a long-term socialist vision. The key was to focus on those changes most likely to transform the structure of American society—health care being a premiere example. In the statement quoted above, for instance, Harrington endorses Senator Edward Kennedy's latest health-care reform bill as a transitional step toward a single-payer system.[2] In other words, America's greatest modern socialist was in agreement with those conservatives who see government-controlled health-care reform as one giant step away from capitalism. A willingness to prioritize health-care reform—to risk substantial political capital for its sake—virtually defines Michael Harrington's incrementalist vision of an effectively socialist strategy for the Democratic Party.

Barack Obama's insistence on pressing an ambitious program of health-care reform during an economic downturn—in the face of intense opposition by a majority of Americans—has solidified for many the image of a president blinkered by socialist ideology. At a minimum, it's clear by now that, given the president's history and the incremental vision of socialist politics held by his associates in community organizing, the notion that Barack Obama is a socialist is anything but a fringe conjecture.

Considering what we know about modern American socialism, it's possible to offer a more general interpretation of Obama's plans. Obama's devotion to health-care reform may have less to do with ideologically driven political suicide than with a risky—but canny and plausible—long-term strategy for the political transformation of the United States. To develop a sense of the president's strategic goals, we'll need to review his actions in light of his socialist and organizing past. Let's return to square one, then. What exactly does a community organizer do, and how might that be related to the president's policies today?

WHAT DO COMMUNITY ORGANIZERS DO?

Community organizers in the tradition of Saul Alinsky keep their political beliefs to themselves.[3] They make a point of presenting themselves as pragmatists in search of "commonsense solutions for working families." Organizers trained by Obama's mentor Greg Galluzzo have perfected this stance—consciously suppressing radical jargon (which they freely use among themselves), clothing their leftist programs in the language of traditional American democracy, and making sure to present themselves in both dress and demeanor as average citizens, rather than as the sixties-style radicals many of them once were.

Alinskyites work to steer popular dissatisfactions in the direction of their leftist goals. Organizers spend months conducting "one-on-ones," interviews that reveal the patterns of self-interest in a given community.

If the neighborhood is worried about construction of a nearby expressway, for example, an Alinskyite organizer will use a campaign to block that expressway to build and motivate the membership of his group. Eventually, that organizer will work to turn the community's "populist" wrath against local banks or energy companies, in pursuit of his long-term socialist goals. While some organizers may appeal to the good of the larger community as a rationale for these campaigns, that is mere icing on the cake. Hidden ideological motivations notwithstanding, Alinskyite organizers frame their campaigns as appeals to the self-interest of those they lead.

Though commonsense pragmatism unfettered by ideology is their public theme, Alinskyites use polarization as a tactic. Organizers search for "enemies"—businessmen and political leaders who can either offer the group something valuable or serve as "targets" for anger. Targets are sometimes baited to strike back, thus further enraging the group. So whether a bank gives in and offers mortgages on easy terms or refuses to lower its lending standards, the community organization wins. Either the loans go through, or the group gets mad—and membership grows. Best of all, targeting encourages the public to view the business community—and ultimately capitalism itself—as "the enemy."

The core precepts of Alinskyite organizing explain a lot about the conduct of Obama's presidency. Like a good organizer, Obama has carefully avoided ideological labels. He certainly hasn't offered anything close a broad philosophical rationale for his policies. On the contrary, the president has generally portrayed his stimulus package and health-care reform plans as pragmatic responses to the financial crisis.

Notwithstanding his periodic invocations of the plight of the uninsured, Obama has presented his health-care program chiefly as a way to save consumers money, while also getting entitlement spending under control. For the most part, then, Obama's health-care campaign has appealed to self-interest, rather than compassion for the poor. In classic Alinskyite fashion, the president has drawn on public dissatisfaction with rising health-insurance costs, as well as public fears of entitlement-driven deficits, to support a policy that is in fact motivated by a vision of redistributive rights. The reason Obama hasn't articulated the philosophical underpinnings of his policies is that the truth wouldn't work. Liberal and conservative observers alike have noted Obama's reluctance to openly sell health-care reform on grounds of compassion and "social justice." Yet that is why he backs it.

Rahm Emanuel's infamous quip: "You never want a serious crisis to go to waste," gave the game away.[4] We've seen the long tradition among community organizers of using fiscal crises as a lever for incremental socialist change. Having cut his political teeth at the Illinois Public Action Council—the quintessential socialist community organization of its day—Emanuel grasped the principles of Alinskyite crisis management early on. Although sophisticated theorists like Cloward, Piven, and Dreier enlarged on the idea of using crises to encourage socialist change, the principle was built into Alinskyite organizing from the start. Manipulating public fear and anger to create support for incremental socialist ends is what Alinskyite organizers do. Turning a national financial meltdown to socialist purposes simply applies Alinsky's local technique to the national level. Obviously, you can't be a merely pragmatic problem-solver if you're worried about "wasting" a crisis. So from the administration's point of view, Emanuel's unguarded remark was a stupid and damaging mistake.

HEALTH CARE

Obama's deeper problem is that an ambitious national program of health-care reform doesn't lend itself to manipulation. The level of scrutiny for such a change—with its immense implications for every American—makes rhetorical diversion and fiscal trickery difficult to sustain. It's no wonder the president originally wanted to pass the massive health-care bill quickly, with virtually no debate.

A reform that increases insurance coverage for tens of millions of people either costs more money, or leads to the rationing of care, or both. For some, the losses in money and quality are worth the gains for the uninsured—and point to a more just set of social arrangements for additional sectors of the economy as well. For others, the financial costs of reform and the inevitable constraints on care are not balanced out by redistributive gains. To these citizens, the reform endangers the very system upon which our freedom and prosperity depend. The choices are fairly clear. The president's presentation of those choices was not. It would be tough to find a public policy battle better able to benefit from a serious debate about underlying principles than health-care reform. Obama's reluctance to take the debate in this direction was true to his organizer training, yet rang false to the public's ear.

Presenting health-care reform as a financial benefit to the vast majority of Americans required some serious fiscal trickery. Six years of benefits had to be balanced against ten years of costs to make the numbers match. Medicare cuts were double-counted as both savings and spending. Payments to doctors were removed from the main health-care bill so as not to undermine the claim that the reforms were fully paid for. And so on. In short, false promises of fiscal responsibility were used to seduce the public into a costly and difficult-to-repeal scheme that would leave them holding the bag for massive costs.

We saw the dress rehearsal for this in attempts by Obama and his Democratic allies in the Illinois state legislature to use the windfall settlement of a tobacco lawsuit to prevent cuts to state programs during a budget crisis.[5] At the time, the *Chicago Tribune* and *St. Louis Post-Dispatch* excoriated Illinois Democrats for "chickening out," for making use of "tricked up numbers," for a "cowardly abdication of responsibility," and for sacrificing the state's bond rating to "short term political gains." The "trick" was balancing the budget with a one-time windfall instead of regular revenues. That kind of thinking led to the fiscal disaster Illinois faces today. Worse, Obama's original plan was to use the tobacco-settlement money to finance his state-wide single-payer health-care reform scheme. That was a fundamentally dishonest way of seducing voters into a huge regular expenditure, in perpetuity. Obama's plan didn't pass . . . then. But the strategy of deception is clear.

Originally President Obama pushed hard to include a "public option" in the health-care bill. A government-run health-care plan designed to "compete" with private insurers parallels proposals by the Citizen/Labor Energy Coalition to create a government-owned energy corporation.[6] The term "competition" in this context is a misnomer, since entities backed by the taxing, law-making, and regulatory power of the federal government can easily drive private companies out of business. That is exactly what the socialist sponsors of the Citizen/Labor Energy Coalition were hoping for. Congresswoman Jan Schakowsky, the one-time activist for the Democratic Socialists of America who worked at the heart of the C/LEC and Midwest Academy network, enthusiastically acknowledges the real purpose of the health-care public option. The public option thus emerges as a pure example of the sort of "non-reformist reform" favored by Midwest Academy organizers—a supposedly modest tweak to the free enterprise system, designed to undermine it.

While the president preferred a public option, he removed it to save the bill. This is sometimes cited as proof that Obama is a pragmatist rather than a socialist. I take it as evidence that the president is a pragmatic socialist. The socialism of President Obama and his organizing associates is incremental. A government-run single-payer health-care system may be best from the socialist point of view, but a public option that could lead to single-payer is second best. Government regulation that could incorporate a public option in time will do in a pinch. Although Congress did not pass a public option "trigger," future dissatisfactions with private insurance plans are sure to bring calls for a public option. When he thinks he has political room, the president will respond.

After Senate passage of health-care reform, Senator Tom Harkin (D-IA) addressed the disappointment of the left at the absence of the public option by comparing the bill to a starter home with a good foundation. "We can build additions as we go along in the future. . . . Think about it that way."[7] The president undoubtedly thinks in these terms. Harkin, by the way, wrote the foreword to *Citizen Action and the New Populism*.[8] That book laid out the Midwest Academy's populist strategy, without so much as mentioning the socialism of its authors, Harry Boyte, Heather Booth, and Steve Max. In his foreword, Harkin praises the political pragmatism of the authors, and distinguishes their stance from "pie-in-the-sky ideology." Harkin also credits the Midwest Academy's Citizen Action coalition with helping to elect him to the Senate in 1984. The Midwest Academy's brand of progressivism is in the driver's seat today—with powerful alumni or supporters like Jan Schakowsky in the House, Harkin in the Senate, and Obama in the White House. Midwest Academy strategy is indeed pragmatic and patient. Yet behind the scenes, it's hard not to suspect that "pie-in-the-sky" Marxist ideology remains a motivating force for its former associates, just as it was for Boyte, Booth, and Max.

Even without the public option, the health-care bill places a sixth of the American economy under extensive regulatory control. The precedent-setting universal mandate to purchase a commercial product has sparked a series of legal challenges from the states. The novelty and scale of this reform suggests that something other than pragmatic tinkering is at work. When you juxtapose an undertaking this extensive with knowledge of the president's radical past, it's reasonable to account for it by something deeper than an effort to cut health-care costs during a fiscal crisis—especially when you consider that costs will actually rise. Would one-time Midwest Academy leaders like Jan Schakowsky and Robert Creamer be fighting for this change with everything they've got if it weren't about advancing socialism? It's reasonable to see a link between Obama's extensive ties to the Midwest Academy and his relentless pursuit of its leadership's highest priority.

STRATEGIC PATIENCE

What about the stimulus bill of 2009? Obama was criticized even by supporters for allowing congressional leaders to draw up this bill. Congress loaded the stimulus package with spending for projects Democrats had been unable to fund for a decade. Does this mean the president was derelict in his responsibilities? I doubt that's how he sees it. Under Republican rule in Illinois, Obama himself was a frustrated Democratic legislator with unfunded program ideas. One man's pork is another man's social justice. Given Obama's passionate defense of the use of tobacco-settlement money to evade budget cuts during a fiscal crisis, he undoubtedly saw turning the stimulus bill over to Congress as something more than logrolling. Obama views just about all social welfare spending as a principled good. Laid against his internal social-ist template, these expenditures seem like tiny steps toward a more just and comprehensive form of government largesse.

Ostensibly, the huge spending in the stimulus bill was designed to jump-start the economy with "shovel-ready" programs. The relative absence of Franklin Roosevelt–style public works programs from the actual bill has been cited as proof that the president is not a socialist.[9] Yet the real focus of stimulus spending does more to move us toward socialism than temporary public works projects ever could. Obama's public-employee-union allies directed stimulus spending to bailouts for state governments that had gotten themselves into the same fiscal mess as Illinois.[10] Was this a one-time affair or a difficult-to-undo prec-edent for federal bail-outs of profligate states?

For Obama's critics, the president's programs and proposals con-stitute an effort to fundamentally alter the contours of America's free enterprise system. Some of the president's supporters are more than happy to agree, while others take Obama on his own terms, as a center-left pragmatist merely tinkering with the system to keep it in working order. Whatever your view, it's critical to keep in mind that we are only at the beginning of this story. Community organizers in the Midwest Academy tradition are, above all, strategic. They do not lay out comprehensive wish lists, much less the ideological rationale behind their demands. That would scare people away. Whatever a Midwest Academy–style organizer lays on the table is only the partial revelation of a long-term strategic plan.

Organizers are patient. Obama took months to conduct his one-on-ones before beginning his protest campaigns. Obama's mentors Greg Galluzzo and Jerry Kellman devoted years of effort to increasing attendance and collections at local Catholic churches before moving to co-opt those institutions to their political purposes.[11] Obama's mentors at the Midwest Academy labored for years to shape America's energy policy, all along intending to form a national network of multi-issue organizations.[12] Years down the road, that happened. When Obama was a freshman in the Illinois State Senate, he complained that most legislators were more interested in cutting deals for their district than in developing a comprehensive legislative strategy.[13] Obama surely has such a long-term vision for his presidency, and we've seen only a part of it.

This strategic patience may be the most important implication of Obama's socialist organizing background. Whatever we see now is merely the opening gambit of what is sure to be an escalating program of structural economic change. It isn't just a question of health-care reform, but of the public option after that, and eventually single-payer. Obama's past statements show that he *wants* to make these transitions on health care.[14] Likewise, Obama's socialist background strongly suggests the existence of a long-term intention to expand the reach of the government so as to constrain the market and redistribute wealth on other issues as well.

Obama may not be able to turn the United States into Sweden in four, or even eight, years, but he can certainly move us vastly further in that direction than we are now. Whatever the president's stated tax and regulatory plans are, they are but the beginning. Equally important, how the president will exercise his regulatory authority has everything to do with his ultimate goals and intentions. You're never going to get a Reaganesque declaration of principles out of Obama. But you don't have to see into the future to know that having a socialist president is a problem. This president's past should be enough to sound the warning bell. Electing and re-electing a president is in significant measure a question of trust. By withholding the truth about his radical past, the president has broken that trust.

FOREIGN POLICY AND SOCIAL ISSUES

The left scoffs at the idea that Obama is a socialist, pointing to his escalation in Afghanistan, and his reluctance to push social causes like abortion and same-sex marriage. Even the Congressional Black Caucus complains about Obama's hesitance to direct benefits to blacks.[15] Yet this misses the strategic patience and incrementalism typical of socialist community organizers. Heather Booth made her reputation as a socialist-feminist, yet downplayed hot-button feminist demands for the sake of building her Citizen Action coalition around economic issues. Over time, Booth's Citizen Action groups experimented with open leftism on foreign policy—with Obama's mentors Ken Rolling and Alice Palmer leading the charge.[16] But Citizen Action never emphasized foreign policy. Economic populism was its focus.

Obama is following this course. The president is focused on health, energy, and banking regulation—classic organizer preoccupations, and the foundation of any successful populist/socialist movement. Obama's stance toward foreign policy and cultural issues combines quick and easy progressive changes with a still stronger desire to hold political conflict at bay. The point is to keep side issues stable enough to permit Obama to focus on structural changes to the economy.

I take the president's lengthy decision-making process on the surge in Afghanistan to have been an effort to explore every conceivable alternative to escalation. That Obama finally decided to expand that war means that failure to do so would have spelled disaster. If there was a practical way out the war, Obama would have taken it. The last thing Obama needs is blame for a military and national security disaster in the Middle East. In the end, he was more likely to put the issue to rest by escalating than by allowing the Taliban to retake the country.

On gay issues, Obama has done the minimum necessary to keep that restive constituency relatively quiet. Obama favors race-neutral programs that happen to disproportionately benefit minorities as the most politically viable way to promote racial equality. For Obama, slow-motion economic transformation (in a socialist direction) is the key to every other change.

Rather than disproving the claim that Obama is a socialist, these deviations from leftist orthodoxy reveal a president clever enough to preserve his political capital for the structural changes that matter most. Harrington himself could not have done better. Some claim that Obama's decision to bring advisors known and trusted by Wall Street into his administration—like Lawrence Summers and Timothy Geithner—is further proof that the socialism charge is nonsense.[17] Yet incremental socialists aren't interested in destroying the system at a blow. Why spook the markets and provoke a national political showdown by appointing a hard-left economic team? That would discredit socialism before it got its foot in the door. Health-care reform is the priority. So that is where the showdown must be. We saw prominent stealth-socialist organizers like Steve Max and Harry Boyte privately confess to justifying their socialist plans in capitalist terms.[18] So, too, a clever socialist president would keep the economy productive, even as he slowly reshaped it from within.

Americans expect to read a politician's plans and convictions from his speeches and decisions. It's a reasonable expectation, but it doesn't apply to the stealth-socialist Alinskyite organizers Obama spent a lifetime working with. Recall S. M. Miller's comment, also quoted in Chapter Three, on community organizing:

The left agenda is more profound and more disturbing than it is usually wise to tell those whom radical activists wish to help organize, at least at the beginning. This situation leads organizers not infrequently to be in the situation of keeping back, if not disguising, some of their ultimate objectives. . . . This raises issues of manipulation. . . . Such organizers are not fully representing themselves to others.

COMMUNITARIAN POPULISM

Harry Boyte and the leaders of the Midwest Academy favored a blending of communitarian and populist language to whip up a movement controlled by socialists from behind.[19] The communitarian language seems harmless—highlighting themes of civic responsibility and public stewardship. Yet it's a cover for socialism.

Does Obama use the same sort of language? He does. At the height of the 2008 presidential campaign, Mark Schmitt, executive editor of the liberal *American Prospect*, published a piece describing Obama's "communitarian populism."[20] Schmitt was talking about Obama's calls for shared sacrifice. When it comes to national challenges, says Obama, "We're all in this together." Schmitt continues:

Forced by Tom Brokaw to define health care as either a right or a responsibility, Obama called it, "a right," and said his health plan would make it one. But on his own, that's rarely how he talks about health care or economic fairness—both are wrapped up in a sense of national purpose, not individual rights. . . . Obama doesn't talk about "responsibility" in McCain's sense—you're responsible for your health and if you get sick and can't afford it, tough—but a deeper responsibility to engage and build the kind of system or order that achieves these goals.

So Obama's communitarian language works to disguise and soften his controversial extension of "rights" into the economic realm. At the same time, Obama's warm and fuzzy communitarian pitch would be suited to building a movement receptive to openly socialist goals at some future time. If it were only a question of Obama's communitarian-populist language, we couldn't say much about his underlying ideology. It's the confluence of Obama's language with his extensive ties to the Midwest Academy that gives pause.

Obama wants to seize and shape America's populist impulses. In a July 2009 interview with *Business Week*, Obama said: "Ordinary Americans right now, they feel at least as cynical about business as they are about government. And part of my motivation here is to channel what is going to be, I think, a lot of populist energy in a constructive way that does not end up preventing us from continuing to be the most dynamic, innovative economy."[21] Obama wants to channel populist anger at Wall Street toward his expansive vision of the regulatory state. A cynic might also see in this remark a warning to America's businesses: How I choose to "channel" populism depends on how strongly you oppose me.

OBAMA'S CHARISMA

Communitarian populism adds to Obama's appeal, but personal charisma was the key to his success. That is a problem for the president, and a complication in the classic community-organizer game plan. As far back as the Cooper Union Socialist Scholars Conference of 1983, Obama encountered the emerging socialist strategy of synergy between grassroots populism and electoral politics—the strategy outlined in Peter Dreier's 1980 "Socialist Incubators" article.[22] In this model, community organizers enter politics, riding on the enthusiasm and shoe leather of their grassroots constituencies. Once in office, these politicians continue to act as organizers: channeling resources to the com-

munity groups that supported them and crafting legislation designed
to energize populist movements, which they can lead in an ever-more-
socialist direction.

This describes Obama's career. His history of cooperation with
ACORN provided a ready source of campaign volunteers. At Project
Vote and in Springfield, Obama worked closely with ACORN and the
Midwest Academy. So Obama's career embodied the strategic vision
outlined by socialist organizers like Peter Dreier, Harry Boyte, and
Heather Booth. When Obama ran for president, however, the charismatic tail started wagging the communitarian-populist dog. Obama's
celebrity status became a force unto itself, and even from Obama's
point of view, that was not an unmixed good.

The problem was that Obama's charisma was independent of—and
even in tension with—his left-wing populist politics. Much of Obama's
appeal rested on the excitement of participating in the election of
America's first black president. In an era of polarization, the election
of the first black president seemed to portend a broader unification of
opposites. Obama highlighted this theme by promising a post-partisan
presidency. To some, the "we're all in this together" communitarian
themes—originally designed as code for progressive politics—sounded
instead like a promise of centrist compromise and consensus. Obama
encouraged this ambiguity during the campaign, until the breadth of
his ambition as president forced the contradiction into the open.

This conflict between pragmatic reconciliation and polarizing partisanship is familiar to community organizers. Obama experienced the
shift himself during his early organizing. Recall the fiasco of Obama's
big asbestos meeting, at which Chicago Housing Authority head Zirl
Smith refused to be "pinned" into a yes-or-no answer and ended up
being chased to his car as a result. This had more to do with intentionally polarizing tactics than Obama was willing to admit in *Dreams from
My Father*. After the meeting, Obama lost some supporters, several of
whom questioned his methods and motives. This is a common experience for Gamaliel organizers—the result of the contradiction between

their appealing pragmatic veneer, on the one hand, and their radical and intentionally polarizing goals and tactics, on the other.[23]

ENEMIES LIST

The early history of the Obama administration played out the usual conflict between the Alinskyite organizer's soothing and pragmatic initial self-presentation and his polarizing tactics. Actually, the problem emerged during the 2008 campaign, although not everyone noticed. When the Obama campaign deployed classic Alinskyite "targeting" tactics—attempting to keep critics like myself and David Freddoso off the radio—McCain supporters were up in arms.[24] These attempts to block the speech of critics were widely publicized in conservative media outlets, yet were virtually ignored by the mainstream press. They would hardly have been compatible with the image of Obama as a force for fairness and reconciliation.

Thus, early on, conservatives began to look upon Obama's benign self-presentation with suspicion, while the rest of the country remained caught up in his charisma. The lesson the Obama camp drew at the time was that, even at the national level, Alinskyite targeting tactics work. The truth is more complicated. In a compliant media environment, Alinskyite targeting works. Yet once the country as a whole witnessed an avowedly post-partisan president repeatedly resorting to polarizing Alinskyite tactics, Obama paid a political price.

The trouble started at the opening of the health-care campaign. When that video montage showed Obama and Jan Schakowsky confessing plans to use apparently limited health-care reforms as a path to single-payer, the White House struck back with its own videos, dismissing the offending clips as "out of context" and providing a website where "fishy" rumors about the president's plans could be reported.[25] The president's case was weak. His representatives never explained why the video clips were unfair or inaccurate, and the call to report neighbors with uncongenial political views to a government website provoked a wave of criticism. At the time, the White House explicitly pointed to their aggressive rumor-fighting operations during the 2008 campaign as a model for the health-care push. Now, however, Alinsky-ite tactics were backfiring.

Targeting operations continued. Rush Limbaugh was singled out and attacked, to polarize the country around a powerful enemy whom the White House believed would emerge from the battle with less support than the president.[26] FOX News was the next big target.[27] Yet the White House "war on FOX News," like its campaign against Limbaugh, only undermined the president's standing as a figure of reconciliation. When the Tea Party movement received similar treatment, the country was well and truly polarized.

A particularly interesting bit of Alinskyite targeting came when the president took the unusual step of denouncing a Supreme Court decision in his State of the Union Address—with the justices present, yet unable to respond. Although Chief Justice Roberts called the setting of the president's attack "very troubling," the administration in no way backed off, or even tried to soften what many considered a breach of decorum.[28] On the contrary, the justices who ruled that campaign finance laws improperly limited free speech had been targeted to serve as the "enemy" in a populist battle against corporations. In classic community organizer fashion, the administration has tossed aside its facade of pragmatism in favor of populist polarization. If this has had a political cost, community organizers willingly and regularly pay the price.

So it's no coincidence that a president who won on a promise of post-partisan reconciliation has polarized the country at least as sharply as his predecessors—arguably more so. That is how community organizers operate. The real challenge is to make out the larger plan behind Obama's targeting operations. For socialist organizers, polarization isn't just a tactic—it's a strategy. That a former organizer like Obama is polarizing the country is unsurprising. Yet his goal is not simply to heighten existing divisions, but to reshape the divisions themselves.

Before we consider the president's plans, however, let's complete our review of the Obama administration's early moves in light of the president's past.

STILL AN ORGANIZER

During his first run for public office, Obama articulated his community-organizer theory of politics:

> What if a politician were to see his job as that of an organizer . . . as part teacher and part advocate, one who does not sell voters short but who educates them about the real choices before them? . . . We must form grassroots structures that would hold me and other elected officials more accountable.[29]

Here Obama suggests something more ambitious than either pragmatic problem-solving or brokering compromises among competing groups. Obama hopes to change the way voters think, shifting the frame of public debate into terms he would set. Necessarily, Obama's voter "education" drive would have to flow from some ideological matrix, and in this 1995 profile—which highlights the future president's ACORN ties—that ideology is obviously far to the left.

Perhaps to distance Obama from his radical roots, friendly biographers have argued that he eventually abandoned his vision of the politician-as-organizer. In a widely noticed profile, for example, *New Yorker* reporter Ryan Lizza emphasized that the local "issue committees" Obama hoped to form when he first entered the Illinois state legislature never actually got off the ground.[30] For Lizza, this shows Obama abandoning the link between grassroots organizing and politics. Yet Obama never abandoned his original vision. Under Obama's guidance, the Woods Fund encouraged grassroots support for his legislative agenda. ACORN and the Midwest Academy were prominent among the groups Obama funded (with Bill Ayers's help) while in office.[31] Obama worked closely with these radical (actually, socialist) groups throughout his career. If there was any reason Obama took pains not to leave a paper trail during his time in the Illinois State Senate, his continued cooperation with these radical organizers was almost certainly it.

In 2008, Obama captured the nomination through grassroots organizing in the caucus states. Obama's organizer training camp was run by his buddies from the Gamaliel Foundation and Midwest Academy. Since he became president, Obama's allies have converted his campaign group, Organizing for Obama, into Organizing for America, with the intention of building a grassroots movement to support his legislative program. Midwest Academy co-founder Robert Creamer, in his continuing commentary on the Obama administration at the Huffington Post, rightly highlights this aspect of the president's strategy.[32] Creamer himself conducted training at Camp Obama, while the president's grassroots strategy was crafted by the Midwest Academy's favorite theorist, Harry Boyte. It's true that the deflation of Obama's charisma in the aftermath of his polarizing first year or so in office has reduced the effectiveness of Organizing for America. Yet the president still hopes to jump-start a grassroots movement that will support his program from below, while he presses his legislation from above.

As part of that project, the president included an extraordinary $1.4 billion in his 2011 budget to create a massive force of government-funded community organizers. Supposedly, these AmeriCorps recruits would be volunteers. In fact, they are to receive the equivalent of more than ten thousand dollars apiece in benefits.[33] Congressional Democrats managed to turn back Republican efforts to prohibit the flow of taxpayer dollars to groups "engaged in political or legislative advocacy."[34] So Obama has been pouring massive government funding into an array of left-wing pressure groups. The aim is to boost his political program while creating an army of young adherents in the process. In the meantime, the Obama administration fired AmeriCorps Inspector General Gerald Walpin for trying to rein in funding abuses.[35] It is as if the leaders of ACORN and the Midwest Academy had again been handed the keys to the VISTA program—but with a guarantee of freedom from charges of politicized abuse, not to mention vastly more funding than even they could have imagined. So the grassroots component of Obama's strategy remains.

SOCIALISM FROM BELOW

What about other elements of late-twentieth-century strategies for socialization of the economy "from below," like worker ownership of businesses and the transformation of corporate structures through public representation on boards of directors? This question brings us around to the Obama administration's auto bailout.

Peter Dreier's 1980 piece "Socialist Incubators" featured an illustration depicting a socialist utopia in which a "U.S. Motors" corporation would be controlled by a combination of auto workers and representatives from community organizations.[36] Obama's organizing mentor in *Dreams from My Father*, "Marty Kaufman," hoped to save a dying steel mill by transferring ownership to workers acting in coalition with community groups. Kaufman yearned for a battle in which he would force reluctant banks to finance the deal.[37] President Obama has bailed out two auto companies, General Motors and Chrysler, not only by taking control, but by granting ownership stakes on favorable terms to the United Auto Workers Union (to the great disadvantage of private bondholders). No community organizations were involved in the takeover. Yet through pull with the administration, environmental groups now exercise considerable de facto influence over the auto companies.

Is this socialist nationalization or, as the president's defenders argue, a temporary measure designed to return two wounded titans of free enterprise to sound footing? I do think the GM and Chrysler bailouts reveal the president's socialist inclinations. Yet the program of American socialism has changed. In the post-sixties era, America's democratic socialists de-emphasized nationalization and focused instead on controlling businesses from the ground up. The Corporate Democracy Act, supported by both the Midwest Academy and the Democratic Socialists of America, would have left America's corporate structure in place, while handing practical control to citizen-representatives charged with taking factors like environmental protection into at least as much account as profit.[38] The stealthily socialist New Party favored similar legislation, as well as a "demanding federal code of social responsibility" designed to reward corporations that hew to government guidelines with "most-favored-company" status.[39]

Without a Corporate Democracy Act, and without a formal corporate code of "social responsibility," the Obama administration is nonetheless well on its way toward modifying America's capitalist system in the direction outlined by the president's socialist mentors. Although the federal government will likely surrender direct control of General Motors and Chrysler, all three big auto companies—and many other businesses besides—are increasingly subject to de facto control by unions and environmental groups through a combination of government pressure, federal loans, and implicit promises of future bailouts. Companies willing to toe the administration line are being lured in with what could be described as "most-favored-company" treatment. Commentators on both the right and the left have noticed the systemic shift this represents. What few understand is that, even without formal nationalization, this *is* the program of modern American socialism.

In fact, the financial reform bill passed by the president in July of 2010 contains a controversial "proxy access" provision that embodies the program of the socialist-inspired Corporate Democracy Act of 1980. That provision grants unions, environmental groups, and other activists added power to place their own representatives on the boards of directors of every corporation in the United States.[40] Here President Obama is actively carrying out the incremental, grassroots socialist strategy of his Midwest Academy mentors. The connection is direct.

Midwest Academy founder Heather Booth who now leads the leftist group Americans for Financial Reform, has lobbied heavily for the proxy access provision.[41]

What, exactly, would a "democratic socialist" America look like? You're never going to get a straight answer to that question. Michael Harrington used to say that his group had vision and strategy, but no "finished blueprint" for society.[42] Harrington's vagueness had multiple sources. As leader of competing socialist factions, defining an end-point would have invited in-fighting. A fully articulated socialist vision might also have alienated moderate sympathizers. Some socialists were more enamored than others of the shift away from nationalization and central planning. Labor leader William Winpisinger allied with Heather Booth of the Midwest Academy to push an organizer-based grass-roots socialist strategy, yet we know that Winpisinger's ultimate vision was heavily statist. The Midwest Academy's favorite theorist, Harry Boyte, was more serious about developing a socialism reliant on community organizations as an alternative to the classic model.[43]

These differences aside, there is a statist dynamic built into even the most grassroots version of socialism. ACORN drove the rise of subprime lending, yet had to combine street-level demonstrations with pressure from Congress and the Clinton administration to get its way.[44] For years, banks incorporated ACORN's local housing arms into their subprime lending programs as a regrettable but necessary cost of doing business. With the subprime collapse, the federal government took Fannie Mae and Freddie Mac into "conservatorship." What began as a series of informal restrictions on capitalism engineered by a grassroots socialist front group ended up as an extraordinarily expensive act of nationalization.

Many of the socialist organizers who supported the Corporate Democracy Act and rigorous "social responsibility" mandates likely conceived of these proposals as "non-reformist reforms." While purporting to leave the core structures of capitalism in place, changes of this sort carry the seeds of the system's destruction. Businesses forced to downplay the profit motive in favor of an expansively defined "public interest" will fail, yielding still more government intervention, and eventually formal or de facto state control.

AUTO BAILOUTS

That dynamic is at work in the auto company bailouts. The editors of the conservative *National Review* magazine have argued that through a combination of bailouts, billions of dollars in "green loans," implicit threats of further interference, and implicit promises of future bailouts, the Obama administration is exercising effective control of all three big automakers, with or without formal ownership. (I am a contributing editor at National Review Online, but had no role in the writing of this editorial.) The real analogy to the auto bailouts, argues *National Review,* is the government's longstanding relationship to Fannie Mae and Freddie Mac.[45] These "government-sponsored enterprises" are privately owned, yet carry out a publicly mandated mission, and enjoy implicit financial guarantees as well. Just as the federal government was able to force Fannie and Freddie to meet subprime lending quotas, even without a formal ownership stake, federal pressure is now forcing Detroit to maintain expensive union benefits, while manufacturing "green cars" of questionable commercial appeal. If these public purposes undercut the automakers' bottom line, the federal government is implicitly on the hook for more bailouts—continuing the cycle of control. So even apparently temporary bailouts function as nationalization-by-other-means.

Other conservative observers have characterized the Obama administration's use of rewards and punishments to push corporations toward preferred behavior as a shift in the character of capitalism. Matthew Continetti at the conservative *Weekly Standard* calls the administration's affinity for bailouts "the birth of a new social system."[46] Representative Paul Ryan (R-WI), says that companies "increasingly compete for government favoritism, not for consumer choice or preference."[47] The president's cap-and-trade energy plan would increase the effect, by allowing the administration to hand out the vast bulk of emission allowances or credits. That would create huge benefits for politically favored companies and major problems for any corporation foolhardy enough to buck the administration line on unions, the environment, or anything else. What is this if not de facto "most-favored-company" status?[48]

The shift toward a grassroots socialist strategy in the eighties was largely a response to the loss of traction for leftist ideas at the federal level during the Reagan years. Once community organizing became American leftism's last redoubt (along with the nation's colleges and universities, of course), it made sense to work for socialist ends through new means. With a community organizer as president, socialist strategy is free to resume a somewhat more statist character. Even so, the administration prefers to transform the system indirectly, without formal nationalization, when possible. That helps deflect politically explosive charges of socialism, although socialism is emerging by degrees in any case.

It's hardly surprising that conservatives see the administration's aggressive regulatory stance as a disturbing shift in the character of the free enterprise system. What about liberals? While the verdict is mixed, there is a surprising willingness on the part of some to acknowledge that the Obama administration is transforming the capitalist system in fundamental ways—perhaps into something resembling Scandinavian-style socialism or "social democracy."

NUDGE-OCRACY

In a May 2009 article entitled, "Nudge-ocracy: Barack Obama's new theory of the state," Franklin Foer and Noam Scheiber, editors of the liberal *New Republic*, make the case that Obama's economic policy is nothing more than a gentle shift leftward.[49] "Obama has no intention of changing the nature of American capitalism," Foer and Scheiber assure us. The authors highlight Obama's avoidance of ideological labels, as well as his campaign stance as a budget-balancing "green-eye-shade pragmatist." Rather than controlling the economy through heavy-handed regulation, Foer and Scheiber say, Obama plans to "inculcate desirable habits like saving and philanthropy through a series of gentle "nudges." If, for example, seniors are too confused to enroll in one of many available prescription drug plans, the federal government will automatically enroll them in the plan that seems right for them, based on their drug-buying histories. Seniors will still be free to switch plans, but the government will step in to make sure that confusion doesn't keep seniors from taking advantage of any plan at all.

Seemingly harmless as described, the "nudge" theory is more intrusive than advertised. The trouble begins when Foer and Scheiber try to explain Obama's most ambitious economic plans as a "massively" scaled-up version of the relatively unintrusive incentives they use as examples. So according to Foer and Scheiber, the health-care public option merely gives private insurance companies a gentle, competitive "nudge." Similarly, say Foer and Scheiber, cap and trade non-intrusively arranges corporate incentives in such a way as to reflect unacknowledged "social costs" of fossil fuels. There is, however, an uncomfortable resemblance between the "social cost" calculations of cap and trade and the New Party's "demanding federal code of social responsibility" enforced through "most-favored-company" status. Similarly, if one-time socialist activist, Midwest Academy associate, and current Congresswoman Jan Schakowsky is to be believed, the health-care public option is a device designed, not to gently "nudge" private insurance companies, but to put them out of business.[50] And already, the seemingly modest nudge principle is giving way to sweeping and intrusive changes. In April of 2010, a New York assemblyman proposed a law presuming consent for organ donation from all New Yorkers unless they explicitly opt out.

One begins to suspect that even Foer and Scheiber don't quite believe their own gauzy portrait of the Obama administration's moderation. This is how they conclude:

> The political point is, in the end, difficult to overstate. Obama has groped toward a form of liberal activism that is eminently saleable in this country—both with the average voter, easily spooked by charges of creeping statism, and the constellation of political interests in Washington.

Foer and Scheiber's article is sufficiently filled with insightful qualifications that they barely seem to convince even themselves that Obama's ambitious economic policies are nothing but a series of gentle, capitalist-friendly nudges. Yet the *political* importance of Obama's preference for undermining the market by indirect means is indeed "difficult to overstate." The nudge-ocracy theory is really about political cover for an ambitious statist program.

In a courteous rejoinder to his colleagues Foer and Scheiber, *New Republic* senior editor John B. Judis does an excellent job of unveiling the real import of Obama's economic policies.[51] Recall that Judis is a character in our story, a former editor of *Socialist Revolution* who helped lead a faction out of the revolutionary New American Movement to produce a periodical, *In These Times*, designed to build support for an explicitly socialist electoral movement in the United States.[52] Judis argues that, whatever Obama's intention, the actual effect of his policies will be to "change American capitalism in fundamental ways." As for Obama's supposed "nudges," says Judis:

> They are an effort at national planning. And it doesn't matter, incidentally, whether the administration tries to get its way through manipulating the market or through outright control of investment; what matters is that it is using its government power to change the American economy in basic ways.

Judis goes on to highlight the growth of the public sector under Obama's budgets, arguing: "The American relationship of state to economy will begin to look more like that of France and Sweden, whose non-crisis budgets total over 45 percent of GDP."

In an August 2009 follow-up piece, Judis goes on to analyze Obama's health-care-reform proposals, his limits on executive compensation, and financial regulations as policies designed to fundamentally alter the capitalist system.[53] For Judis, all of these policies are implicitly driven by a politics of "class struggle." Without venturing a guess as to how much Judis's early socialist convictions have changed over the years, his analytical framework clearly borrows heavily from his past Marxism. Judis, who emerges from the same post-sixties socialist setting that shaped Obama, readily identifies the president's economic policies as transformational and, implicitly, incrementally socialist in character.

THE OBAMA COALITION

The most important clue of all to what the Obama administration may be up to comes from a fascinating analysis by Huffington Post political editor Thomas B. Edsall. Published in April 2010 by *The Atlantic*, Edsall's article, "The Obama Coalition," argues that the electorate is shifting toward a form of class-based political conflict unseen in America for decades.[54] As a rule, says Edsall, economic growth reduces competition between America's "haves" and "have-nots." Yet, as the economic downturn lingers, spending battles have increasingly turned into zero-sum struggles between taxpayers and tax beneficiaries. Edsall adds that the rapid rise in the proportion of relatively less-well-off blacks and Hispanics in the voting population accentuates this class division, by increasing the electoral power of the have-nots.

Edsall argues that as a result of these changes, a substantial political constituency for a European-style socialism, or "social democracy," is now developing in the United States. He points to the recent Gallup poll in which surprisingly large proportions of Democrats, liberals, and minorities took a positive view of socialism. These socialist-friendly voters, says Edsall, will transform the Democratic Party of the future—and already constitute the core of Obama's coalition. Edsall adds that the huge expansion of public-sector unions means that for the first time, a majority of the American labor movement is now directly dependent on taxpayer dollars. Ideologically motivated and relatively well-to-do college-educated professionals, Edsall says, make up the last critical segment of the Obama coalition. (Although Edsall doesn't make the point himself, it's worth noting that this last group emerges from America socialist-friendly elite universities.)

Back in 1983, when Harold Washington swept Chicago's machine aside, inspired America's socialists, and drew a young Barack Obama into community organizing, his urban coalition was made up of the same combination of blacks, Hispanics, and leftist whites that Edsall now identifies as a force to be reckoned with nationally.[55] America's socialists were far too optimistic in 1983 about the potential for Harold Washington–style coalitions to draw socialist-friendly candidates into the mainstream of American politics. Yet as the nation's demography has shifted and its economic circumstances have declined, it has become possible to imagine a Harold Washington–style, socialist-tinged political coalition taking power nationally. This has been Obama's aim all along.

REALIGNMENT STRATEGY

How can Obama best help push America in the direction outlined by Edsall? Here is where the political strategy outlined by Richard Cloward and Frances Fox Piven comes into play—less their infamous "break the bank" strategy than their plan to polarize and realign the American electorate along class lines.[56] Obama has already made a good run at breaking the bank. I don't believe his aim in enlarging America's deficit is to provoke an economic crisis, however. Another economic meltdown would only be blamed on him. Yet I do think President Obama is at least flirting with the financial dangers of a huge deficit so as to stampede the country into a value added tax—and the permanently enlarged European-style welfare state that goes with it. There is real risk to this strategy, even though the president surely wants to avoid a full-scale economic crisis on his watch. In any case, this part of Obama's long-term vision is already understood by many. The accompanying realignment strategy, however, has not been widely remarked upon. Yet a risky but winnable bid for fundamental political realignment would explain the chances Obama has been taking.

A play to polarize and realign the electorate along class lines, thus radicalizing the Democratic Party and pushing it toward "social democracy," fits nicely with Obama's entitlement-based strategy. Not coincidentally, this was the ambitious rationale behind Cloward and Piven's original voter registration drive. Their aim was not simply to register voters. The real hope was that by encouraging openly anti-Reagan efforts by government employees to register voters on welfare lines, the left might provoke an intense Republican reaction. According to the plan, Republicans would be goaded by intentionally politicized tactics into restricting voter registration at welfare offices, thus kicking off an angry movement of the poor. In Cloward and Piven's mind, this second coming of the civil rights movement would send low-income and minority voter registration through the roof, thus energizing and radicalizing the Democratic Party. The Cloward-Piven registration strategy dovetailed nicely with Michael Harrington's plan to provoke a class-based realignment of the parties by moving economic policy left, thus driving business interests toward the Republicans, while more than making up for the Democrats' losses with an inflow of radicalized unionists and the poor. Obama's funneling of stimulus money toward public employee unions can easily be seen as part of this larger plan.

These are the ideas Obama would have drunk in at those early Socialist Scholars Conferences. They also constitute the strategy behind

Project Vote, which maintained a close working relationship with the Cloward and Piven for years. Obama was deeply tied to this socialist network, and devoted himself to an in-depth study of its theoretical underpinnings. In fact, his statements as head of Illinois Project vote came directly out of this framework.

GO FOR IT!

All of this suggests that when President Obama says, "Go for it" to Republicans who hope to repeal his health-care-reform law, he means it. Those who already see Obama as a socialist tend to think of his insistence on backing health-care reform in the face of collapsing political support as the suicidal impulse of a true ideologue. It's more likely that Obama has a long-term class-based realignment strategy in mind. Obama would love the Republicans to try to take away the health care he's offered to millions of uninsured. Taking a leaf from the Cloward-Piven handbook, Obama hopes that a Republican campaign for repeal will ignite a political movement of the poor that will energize and radicalize the Democratic Party. If the president loses a segment of the business interests that initially supported him as a moderate pragmatist, so be it. To a degree, the president's ambitious regulatory projects have already pushed the business community away. In Edsall's telling, however, Obama has the demographic makings of a class-based strategy that would allow him to ride out that storm.

In short, President Obama's long-term political plan is a replay of Michael Harrington's socialist realignment strategy. Obama's goal is to polarize the country along class lines, with Republicans marked out as the aggressors. Harrington's bet was that, once the have-nots began to act as a unified class, they would naturally gravitate to socialism. Whatever the short-term political risks of this strategy, the potential long-term gains would be worth it, in Obama's mind. If the Republicans take power in the mid-term congressional elections, that only sets up the ultimate battle during the presidential race of 2012. With repeal of health-care reform and the rest of the Obama agenda on the line, the president hopes that a newly energized base of public employee unions, minorities, and the poor will overmatch the coalition of "haves" trying to take their new benefits away. At this point, the relatively dormant legions of Organizing for America and the vast new government-funded army of AmeriCorps volunteers would spring into action. America's budding social-democratic movement would come to life.

Ultimately, the success of this strategy depends upon blue-collar workers voting according to what the left considers to be their economic interests, rather than on cultural issues. The hope is that this can be accomplished in a country increasingly polarized along class lines—with a newly expansive government allied with labor.

Does this mean Republicans ought to abandon their efforts to repeal and roll back the Obama agenda? Not at all. But it does help explain the political thinking behind the risks the president is taking.

Here, Peter Dreier's transformational strategy based on the irreversible expansion of entitlements converges with the political realignment plans of Harrington, Cloward, and Piven. All of these socialist strategists worked together to refine and coordinate their ideas at the Socialist Scholars Conferences of the eighties.[57] (Dreier was an advisor to Obama's 2008 presidential campaign.) In the end, all the plans in question depend in some way upon riling up the have-nots by provoking the haves into taking something away from them (usually taxes pocketed from the haves to begin with).

On reflection, Greg Galluzzo's Alinsky-inspired polarizing tactics are a variation on the same strategic theme. Targeted politicians and businessmen are compelled to either fork over expensive goodies, or openly refuse to do so—thus enraging the community group and giving it the force of a movement. So President Obama's politically "suicidal" push for health care may actually have been crazy like a fox. At any rate, I'd wager that's how he sees it.

Conclusion

From his teenage years under the mentorship of Frank Marshall Davis, to his socialist days at Occidental College, to his life-transforming encounters at New York's Socialist Scholars Conferences, to his immersion in the stealthily socialist community-organizer networks of Chicago, Barack Obama has lived in a thoroughly socialist world.

That is why he downplayed and disguised the impact of the Socialist Scholars Conferences on his life. That is why he remained mum about his relationship to the crypto-socialist Midwest Academy. That is why he lied about his ties to ACORN during the 2008 presidential campaign, as a wealth of documentary evidence now establishes beyond doubt. That is why he has so thoroughly misled the public about the nature of his relationship to Bill Ayers and Jeremiah Wright—and a host of other radicals as well. That is why he was reluctant to be questioned about his past, even by a campaign research director tasked with defending him.

The evidence speaks for itself. The simplest and most obvious interpretation of all we have found is that Obama never abandoned his early socialist convictions but instead discreetly retained them, on the model of his colleagues and mentors in the world of community organizing. From the moment Obama attended that first Socialist Scholars Conference in 1983, he would have understood the socialist secret of modern community organizing. The fact that the president has spent his career offering political and financial support to socialist community organizers speaks volumes about his true political sympathies. More broadly, we've seen that the strategies offered at those early Socialist Scholars Conferences provided Obama with a roadmap to his entire career.

Obama's political rise depended at every turn on support from Chicago's socialist world. The early funding for his community organizing, his selection as head of Illinois Project Vote, his elevation to the boards of Public Allies, the Woods Fund, and the Chicago Annenberg Challenge, as well as his status as Alice Palmer's hand-picked successor in the Illinois State Senate, all depended upon the approval and support of Chicago's most powerful socialists. At every stage, his socialist sponsors had access to detailed information concerning Obama's political convictions. Looking at matters from their point of view, would all of these savvy socialist operators have supported Obama if he wasn't "one of them"?

Obama's writings emphasize the sincerity and consistency of his political convictions. Had Obama quietly turned away from socialism during his later political career in Illinois, surely he would have distanced himself from his community-organizer past—and from Jeremiah Wright, whose socialist convictions he well understood. Instead, Obama did the opposite. He placed community organizing and his ties to Reverend Wright at the center of his public persona. In true organizer "good-cop" fashion, Obama sought to put an appealing public face on his stealthily socialist circle.

At every turn, Obama has disguised his socialist past, sometimes through grievous sins of omission, sometimes through opaque and misleading pseudo-confessions, and at other times through outright lies. To say that Obama has lied about his past doesn't quite do justice to what's been going on, however. Never mind a discreet lie or two (or more). We're looking at a thoroughgoing pattern of deception. While Obama's stealthy practices certainly include lies, the president's portrayal of his past ultimately adds up to something larger and more disturbing than lies alone. By hiding his core political convictions, the president has systematically deceived the American people.

As politicians trim their positions to fit shifting political winds, they bend the truth from time to time. The public may even expect a bit of mild fibbing about their records from political leaders. Obama's way of presenting his own political past is far bolder and disturbing than this. Obama has made concerted efforts to hide his socialist convictions from the voters who put him in office. Had the American public known the truth, Obama would never have risen to the U.S. Senate, much less the presidency. That sort of systematic deception corrodes democracy itself.

Obama's pursuit of an expensive universal health-care plan in the teeth of majority public opposition has already kicked off a national debate over the president's alleged socialism. Yet after one learns how community organizing actually works, as well as what contemporary socialism has become, the socialist character of the Obama administration becomes far clearer still.

It could be argued that Obama's past no longer matters. After all, now we can judge Obama by what his administration does, rather than by whatever he did or did not believe in the past. I argue that the truth is the opposite. When it comes to Obama, the past, in a sense, matters more than the present. Only the president's socialist past reveals the full meaning of his plans for our future. The president himself won't honestly tell you his ultimate intentions. Judging Obama strictly on his conduct in office assumes a degree of ideological transparency that simply does not exist in this case.

We've seen that the favorite strategies of community organizers are designed to push the country into socialism well before the public can figure out what's happened. Stealth-socialist community organizers habitually disguise their long-term goals. That is why we must turn to Obama's past to discover the hidden ideological underpinnings of his policies.

Eight years is a long time. While a strong Democratic majority in Congress has emboldened Obama from the start, we're still in the early stages of the president's long-term program of change. Since Obama has not revealed the truth about where this change is headed, his past remains an essential source of guidance for the American people.

In sum, the fears of Obama's harshest critics are justified. The president of the United States is a socialist.

ACKNOWLEDGMENTS

The idea for this book grew out of a series of investigative articles on Barack Obama's political background, all published during the 2008 presidential campaign. I'm grateful to Robert Pollock for opening the pages of the *Wall Street Journal* to me at the height of the Ayers controversy. Over the years, the *Weekly Standard* has graciously allowed me to explore a variety of issues in depth. My thanks goes out to Bill Kristol, Richard Starr, and Claudia Anderson of the *Standard* for welcoming and encouraging my efforts during the 2008 campaign. Advice from *National Review* editor Rich Lowry during the controversies of 2008 is greatly appreciated. Thanks also to Rich and to Jason Steorts for publishing my pieces in *National Review* throughout the campaign.

National Review Online has been my home base for a decade. I'll always be grateful to NRO's Kathryn Jean Lopez for bringing me into the fold and giving me the run of the place. NRO's matchless speed and flexibility makes it the ideal venue for planting and defending a flag of opinion in the Internet Age. I took full advantage in 2008.

My boss, Ed Whelan, of the Ethics and Public Policy Center in Washington, D.C., offered invaluable advice and support during the campaign. Joseph Morris was my tireless guide and defender during the Ayers adventure in Chicago. When things got hectic, Chris Robling was kind enough to help with media.

I am very grateful to the redoubtable Milt Rosenberg for sticking with me and pressing on so unflappably in the face of considerable pressure. Zack Christenson and Guy Benson did yeoman service that night.

I am especially grateful to three friends and readers who were essential to this project. Peter Wood's detective instincts helped me as I followed the trail of clues. His considerable editorial insights, leavened by political savvy, have improved the text at every stage. Peter Berkowitz offered a mixture of hard-nosed criticism and support only a true friend could risk. His strategic suggestions and editorial comments have all been vindicated. I somehow tricked Mary Eberstadt, who has edited me professionally, into doing this job for free. Serious editing has every bit as much to do with human sympathy and worldly wisdom as with command of the language. That is what makes Mary's help worth asking for.

My agent, Alexander Hoyt, has been the sparkplug and defender of this project from the start. I'm grateful as well to the team at Threshold Editions, Mary Matalin, Louise Burke, Anthony Ziccardi, and Mitchell Ivers, for their help and advice, and for putting their faith in this work.

Thanks also to Velma Montoya and Marc Johnson, for forwarding helpful documents.

The archivist and librarian's profession is unsung, yet essential to our collective memory and self-understanding as a country. Despite one notable bump, I was the beneficiary of considerable help from librarians and archivists. My gratitude goes out to those who assisted me at the following collections:

Abraham Lincoln Presidential Library, Manuscript Collections; Bender Library, American University; Boston Public Library, Periodical Room; Brookens Library, Archives and Special Collections, University of Illinois at Springfield; Chicago Historical Society Research Center; Charles Deering McCormick Library of Special Collections, Northwestern University Library; Chicago Public Library Municipal Reference Collection; Columbia University Rare Book and Manuscripts Library; Cudahy Library, Loyola University Chicago; Donors Forum Library, Chicago; Drew Library, Special Collections, Drew University; DePaul University Library, Lincoln Park; Emerson Library, Webster University; Harold Washington Archives and Collections at the Harold Washington Library Center; Illinois State Library; Lauinger Library, Georgetown University; Library of Congress; Luhr Library, Eden Theological Seminary; New York Public Library Microforms Reading Room; Richard J. Daley Library Special Collections and University Archives, University of Illinois at Chicago; Ruth Lilly Special Collections and Archives at Indiana University–Purdue University Indianapolis; Schomburg Center for Research in Black Culture, New York; Shields Library, Special Collections, University of California, Davis; Sophia Smith Collection Women's History Archives at Smith College; Tamiment Library and Robert F. Wagner Labor Archives at New York University; University of Chicago Library, Special Collections Research Center; University of Wisconsin, Madison Library; Vivian G. Harsh Research Collection of Afro-American History and Literature at the Woodson Regional Library, Chicago; Widener and Lamont Libraries, Periodical Room and Newspaper and Microfilm Reading Rooms, Harvard University; Wisconsin Historical Society.

NOTES

Chapter 1: The Socialism Puzzle

1. Barack Obama, *Dreams from My Father: A Story of Race and Inheritance* (New York: Crown, 2004 [1995]), p. 122. Evidence for Obama's attendance at New York's Socialist Scholars Conferences is discussed in detail in Chapters Two and Three.

2. William J. Broad and David E. Sanger, "Youthful Ideals Shaped Obama Goal of Nuclear Disarmament," *New York Times*, July 5, 2009. A version can be found at http://www.nytimes.com/2009/07/05/world/05nuclear.html.

3. Associated Press, "Old friends recall Obama's college years," Politico, May 16, 2008, at http://www.politico.com/news/stories/0508/10402.html.

4. David Mendell, *Obama: From Promise to Power* (New York: Harper Collins, 2007), p. 59.

5. Broad and Sanger, "Youthful Ideals."

6. Barack Obama, "Breaking the War Mentality," *Sundial*, March 10, 1983, at http://documents.nytimes.com/obama-s-1983-college-magazine-article#p=1.

7. Broad and Sanger, "Youthful Ideals."

8. A conference flier can be found in the Frances Fox Piven Papers, Sophia Smith Collection, Smith College, Northampton, Mass., Box 84, Folder 7. A conference advertisement can be found at *In These Times*, March 23–29, 1983, p. 8.

9. A feature entitled "Marx Centennial: 'His name and work will endure forever' " appeared in the American Marxist newspaper *Guardian*, March 16, 1983, p. 21. This feature adapted material from Philip Sheldon Foner, editor, *Karl Marx Remembered: Comments at the Time of His Death, 100th Anniversary Edition* (San Francisco: Synthesis Publications, 1983).

10. Ibid.

11. An early flier for the 1983 Socialist Scholars Conference attached to Piven's hand notes for her Welcoming Remarks can be found in the Piven Papers, Box 84, folder 7. A later and more detailed conference program listing Piven's Welcoming Remarks can be found in the Democratic Socialists of America Records, Tamiment Library & Robert F. Wagner Labor Archives at New York University, Box 66, Folder: "Socialist Scholars Conference 4/1/83-4/2/83 NY." Note that the DSA Records have not been fully processed. Many box and folder numbers and names will charge after final processing.

12. Material pertaining to Piven's service on the DSA National Executive Committee can be found in series IV of the Piven Papers. Officially, as indicated by the brochure and advertising, the conference was cosponsored by the Institute for Democratic Socialism, an associated entity of the Democratic Socialists of America. In practical terms, although a wide variety of Marxists attended the event, the conference itself was clearly run by the DSA. For more, see Chapter Two.

13. Piven's writings and activities will be discussed in Chapter Two.

14. Piven Papers, Box 84, Folder 7.

15. Frances Fox Piven and Richard A. Cloward, *Poor People's Movements: Why They Succeed, How They Fail* (New York: Random House, 1977 [1979]).

16. Marc Kaufman and Rob Stein, "Record Share of Economy Spent on Health Care," *Washington Post*, January 10, 2006, http://www.washingtonpost.com/wp-dyn/content/article/2006/01/09/AR200601090 1932.html.

17. Jon Meacham and Evan Thomas, "We Are All Socialists Now," *Newsweek*, February 7, 2009, http://www.newsweek.com/id/183663.

18. See my interview with Lou Dobbs, October 30, 2008 "Stanley Kurtz on Obama's radicalism," http://www.youtube.com/watch?v=3dX9x XX1XiO; See also Stanley Kurtz, "Something New Here," *National*

Review Online, October 20, 2008, http://article.nationalreview.com/375696/something-new-here/stanley-kurtz.

19. With the assistance of librarians, I first discovered revealing programs from the 1984 and 1985 Socialist Scholars Conferences in the uncatalogued vertical files of the New York University's Tamiment Library. Additional documentation on these conferences will be discussed in Chapter Three.

20. For Cone's influence on Wright, see Stanley Kurtz, "Context You Say? A Guide to the Radical Theology of Rev. Jeremiah Wright," *National Review*, May 19, 2008, pp. 28–36.

21. Particularly helpful background on these matters can be found in Jerrold Seigel, *Marx's Fate: The Shape of a Life* (University Park: The Pennsylvania State University Press, 1993), pp. 217–52 (first edition Princeton University Press, 1978).

22. Obama, *Dreams from My Father*, p. 100.

23. "College Acquaintance: Young Obama Was 'Pure Marxist Socialist,'" February 16, 2010, Breitbart TV, http://www.breitbart.tv/college-acquaintance-young-obama-was-pure-marxist-socialist/.

24. David Remnick, *The Bridge: The Life and Rise of Barack Obama* (New York: Alfred A. Knopf, 2010).

25. Stanley Kurtz, "Senator Stealth: How to advance radical causes when no one's looking," *National Review Online*, November 1, 2008, http://article.nationalreview.com/?q=YjdjY2Y2YWU5YjQ1Y2Y5Mzg0MGRINDQ4YTkwYmI2ZDE=.

26. Broad and Sanger, "Youthful Ideals." The Internet version of this piece was published a day earlier than the front-page piece, with the title "Obama's Youth Shaped His Nuclear-Free Vision," http://www.nytimes.com/2009/07/05/world/05nuclear.html.

27. Consider controversies over administration figures like Van Jones, Patrick Gaspard, and Kevin Jennings. On Gaspard and Obama, see Stanley Kurtz, "Patrick Gaspard, ACORN, and Obama," The Corner, September 28, 2009, http://corner.nationalreview.com/post/?q=NjljYzYyMDhlY2Y4MTRhZTI4NGQ5OGVIMGE5YmIzYTI=.

28. NakedEmporerNews1, "Shock Uncovered: Obama IN HIS OWN WORDS saying his health care plan will ELIMINATE private insurance," August 2, 2009, http://www.youtube.com/watch?v=p-bY92mcOdk.

29. White House, "The Truth About Health Care Insurance Reform," August 3, 2009, http://www.youtube.com/watch?v=U0XC16OHgiM &feature=related.

30. Young, McKnight, and Schakowsky are discussed in the body of the book. See especially Chapters Four, Five, and Seven.

31. Stanley Kurtz, "Chicago Annenberg Challenge Shutdown," *National Review Online*, August 18, 2008, http://article.nationalreview.com/? q=MTgwZTVmN2QyNzk2MmUxMzA5OTg0ODZIM2Y2OGI0 NDM=; Stanley Kurtz, "Obama and Ayers Pushed Radicalism on Schools, *Wall Street Journal*, September 23, 2008, http://online.wsj .com/article/SB122212856075765367.html.

32. Stanley Kurtz, "Inside Obama's Acorn: By their fruits ye shall know them," *National Review Online*, May 29, 2008, http://article.national review.com/?q=NDZiMjkwMDczZWI5ODdjOWYxZTIzZGIyNzEyMj E0ODI=; Stanley Kurtz, "Jeremiah Wright's 'Trumpet': The content of the magazine produced by Barack Obama's pastor reveals the content of his character," *Weekly Standard,* May 19, 2008, pp. 32–36, http:// www.weeklystandard.com/Content/Public/Articles/000/000/015/082 ktdyi.asp.

33. "Barack Obama, Aspiring Commissar," *National Review Online*, August 28, 2008, http://article.nationalreview.com/?q=MmUwOTll NmMzZDN1MT1jMGFmY2JkZT11YmQyOTY0ODY=&w=MA==; Guy Benson, "Stanley Kurtz's Fairness Doctrine Preview," *National Review Online*'s Media Blog, August 28, 2008, http://media.national review.com/post/?q=ZmRhYmE3NzF1MT1jNTdmZGQ3MjhkYTVj NzdmMjVhMzE.

34. Stanley Kurtz, "Something New Here: Radical? Check. Tied to ACORN? Check. Redistributionist? Check," *National Review Online*, October 20, 2008, http://article.nationalreview.com/?q=OTc3NzZ kZDYxODZiZjE2OTg5Y WRmNDkzM2U0YTIwZGQ=; Stanley Kurtz, "Life of the New Party: A redistributionist success story," *National Review Online*, October 30, 2008, http://article.national review.com/?q=MmV1OTk1MzkwYmM2YTQzZmIxOTR1MjY3ZjZ kMTg0OTM=; "The Truth About Barack Obama and the New Party," Fight the Smears, http://fightthesmears.com/articles/28/KurtzSmears .html.

35. Kurtz, "Obama and Ayers Pushed Radicalism on Schools."

36. Kurtz, "Senator Stealth: How to advance radical causes when no one's looking."

Chapter 2: A Conference for Marx

1. Obama, *Dreams from My Father*, p. 133.
2. Ibid., pp. 134–35.
3. Ibid., p. 135.
4. Ibid., p. 133.
5. Ibid., pp. 135–36, 139–40.
6. Ibid., p. 133.
7. Ibid.
8. Ibid., p. 135.
9. Janny Scott, "Obama's Account of New York Years Often Differs From What Others Say," *New York Times*, October 30, 2007, http://www.nytimes.com/2007/10/30/us/politics/30obama.html; Ross Goldberg, "Obama's Years at Columbia Are a Mystery," *New York Sun*, September 2, 2008, http://www.nysun.com/new-york/obamas-years-at-columbia-are-a-mystery/85015/.
10. Scott, "Obama's Account of New York."
11. Broad and Sanger, "Youthful Ideals."
12. Scott, "Obama's Account of New York."
13. Goldberg, "Obama's Years at Columbia."
14. Broad and Sanger, "Youthful Ideals."
15. Ibid.
16. Colleen Sharkey, "Friends of Barry," *Occidental*, Winter 2009, pp. 12–17.
17. Linda Matchan, "A Law Review Breakthrough," *Boston Globe*, February 15, 1990, Metro/Region, p. 29.
18. Scott, "Obama's Account of New York."
19. Obama, *Dreams from My Father*, p. 122.
20. Associated Press, "Old friends recall."
21. *New York Democratic Socialist*, March 1983, p. 1.
22. *Democratic Left*, January 1983, p.11; February 1983, p. 7; March 1983, p. 11.
23. *In These Times*, March 23–29, 1983, p. 8.
24. *The Stony Brook Press*, March 24, 1983, p. 6.
25. *In These Times*, April 11–17, 1984, p. 7.

26. *Democratic Left*, January–February 1985, p. 16.

27. *Democratic Left*, February 1983, p. 7.

28. DSA Records, Box 66, Folder: Socialist Scholars Conference 4/1/83–4/2/83 NY.

29. Of course, if Obama had attended multiple socialist conferences at Cooper Union, but not the April 1983 Socialist Scholars Conference in honor of Marx, that would only represent further involvement with organized socialism in New York. And in Chapter Three I explain that all the key themes of the 1983 Cooper Union Socialist Scholars Conference were repeated at the 1984 Socialist Scholars Conference (often presented by the same speakers), where we have very strong documentary evidence of Obama's attendance. Any way you slice it, Obama absorbed the worldview of 1980s socialism in New York.

30. Piven Papers, Box 84, Folder 7.

31. John Trinkl, "Survivors In Search of a Revival," *Guardian*, April 20, 1983, p. 9.

32. Alice Widener, "Lonely Weekend, A Report on the Third Conference of Socialist Scholars," *Barron's National Business and Financial Weekly*, September, 25, 1967, p. 1.

33. Michael Harrington, *The Other America: Poverty in the United States* (New York: Macmillan, 1962).

34. Gary J. Dorrien, *The Democratic Socialist Vision* (New Jersey: Roman and Littlefield, 1986), pp. 101–2.

35. Ibid.

36. Widener, "Lonely Weekend."

37. Ibid.

38. Ibid.

39. A DSA file containing information on several of the revived Socialist Scholars Conferences includes planning materials from the 1983 conference. A chart assigns responsibility for various panels to individual members of the conference planning committee. Both the "Social Movements" and "Race & Class in Marxism" panels (which, I argue in this chapter, Obama likely attended) were assigned to "Stanley." This is almost surely Stanley Aronowitz. Aronowitz was one of the few DSA members with the stature and connections to arrange the main panels. With conference organizer Bogdan Denitch representing the "Harrington wing" of the DSA, Aronowitz would

have been an obvious balancing representative of DSA's ex-NAMers. Aronowitz is listed as a member of the 1984 Socialist Scholars Conference planning committee, so it seems very likely that he is the Stanley referred to on the charts from the 1983 conference. For the chart, see DSA Records, Box 72, Folder: Socialist Scholars Conf. For Aronowitz's name on the 1984 conference planning committee, see the program for the 2nd Annual Socialist Scholars Conference in the uncatalogued vertical files at the Tamiment Library at New York University.

40. Ibid.
41. Piven Papers, Box 84, Folder 7; DSA Records, Box 66, Folder: Socialist Scholars Conference 4/1/83-4/2/83 NY. The latter folder contains not only a detailed conference program, but other material, including a news report on the conference by Sharon McDonnell entitled "Lively Discussion and Marx Fete Mark U.S. Socialist Conference." Unfortunately, the newspaper in which this article appeared is neither identified nor dated. This piece contains the reference to Harrington's introduction, and much else of interest.
42. McDonnell, "Lively Discussion."
43. Michael Harrington, "Standing Up for Marx," *Democratic Left*, March 1983, pp. 3–4.
44. Dorrien, *The Democratic Socialist Vision*, pp. 112–21.
45. Ibid.
46. Ibid., pp. 121–25.
47. McDonnell, "Lively Discussion."
48. Trinkl, "Survivors."
49. Ibid.
50. McDonnell, "Lively Discussion."
51. John Atlas and Peter Dreier, "Tenant Power Is Growing," *Democratic Left*, March 1981, pp. 8–11.
52. Wright's role in the Harold Washington campaign will be discussed in Chapter Eight.
53. John Cameron and Steve Askin, "Socialists and Electoral Politics," *NAM Discussion Bulletin*, No. 21, Winter 1978, pp. 88–92.
54. Arnold James Oliver, Jr., "American Socialist Strategy in Transition: The New American Movement and Electoral Politics, 1972–1982," Ph.D. University of Colorado at Boulder, 1983.

55. Cameron and Askin, "Electoral Politics."

56. Oliver, "Socialist Strategy."

57. Robert A. Gorman, *Michael Harrington: Speaking American* (New York: Routledge, 1995), pp. 138–43.

58. John Cameron, "DSA Mobilizes for Harold Washington," *Chicago Socialist*, February/March 1983, pp. 1–2, in DSA Records, Box 17, Folder: Illinois, Chicago.

59. John Cameron, "Washington Campaign Brings Chicago Hope," *Democratic Left*, April 1983, pp. 4–6.

60. Bill Perkins, "Washington's Victory Will Change Much," *Chicago Socialist*, April/May 1983, p. 8, in DSA Records, Box 17, Folder: Illinois Chicago.

61. This information is contained in the responses to a detailed survey of individual chapters returned to the national DSA office by the Chicago local in DSA Records, Box 17, Folder: Illinois, Chicago.

62. Perkins, "Washington's Victory."

63. Advertisement in *Democratic Left*, April 1983, p. 7.

64. David Moberg, "Blacks, Left Spark Washington Win," *In These Times*, March 2–8, 1983, pp. 3–6.

65. "Washington Victory Ushers in a New Era of Coalition Politics," *In These Times*, April 20–26, 1983, p. 11.

66. John Trinkl, "Socialists Confer and Differ," *Guardian*, May 2, 1984, p. 2.

67. DSA Records, Box 72, Folder: Socialist Scholars Conf.

68. David James Smith, "The ascent of Mr. Charisma," *Sunday Times* (London), March 23, 2008, http://www.timesonline.co.uk/tol/news/world/us_and_americas/us_elections/article3582291.ece.

69. For conference programs, see note 30.

70. John Atlas and Peter Dreier, "Tenant Power Is Growing," *Democratic Left*, March 1981, pp. 8–11; Peter Dreier and Jim Schoch, "Electoral Politics Primer," *Democratic Left*, Sept.–Oct. 1982, pp. 14–15. For *Social Policy* articles, see below.

71. Peter Dreier, "Socialist Incubators," *Social Policy*, May/June 1980, pp. 29–34.

72. Peter Dreier, "The Case for Transitional Reform," *Social Policy*, January/February 1979, pp. 5–16.

73. McDonnell, "Lively Discussion."

74. John Atlas, Peter Dreier, and John Stephens, "Progressive Politics in 1984," July 23–30, 1983, pp. 1, 82–84.

75. Peter Dreier and Marshall Ganz, "We Have the Hope. Now Where's the Audacity?" *Washington Post*, August 30, 2009, http://www.washington post.com/wp-dyn/content/article/2009/08/28/AR2009082801817.html? sid=ST2009090403398.

76. Peter Dreier, "DSA Endorses Voter Registration Effort," *Socialist Forum A Discussion Bulletin*, No. 3, 1983, pp. 69–70; Richard Cloward and Frances Fox Piven, "Toward a Class-Based Realignment of American Politics: A Movement Strategy," *Social Policy*, Winter 1983.

77. Cloward and Piven, "Class-Based Realignment."

78. Ibid.

79. DSA Records, Box 66, Folder: Socialist Scholars Conference, 1983.

80. Ibid.

81. Obama, *Dreams from My Father*, p. 135.

82. "Democratic Socialists of America: DSOC and NAM United!" *Turn Left*, March 30, 1982, pp. 1–2, in DSA Records, Box 17, Folder: Illinois, Chicago.

83. DSA Records, Box 66, Folder: Socialist Scholars Conference, 1983.

84. Cornel West, "Review of *How Capitalism Underdeveloped Black America*," *Guardian Book Supplement*, Summer 1984, p. 5.

85. Manning Marable, *How Capitalism Underdeveloped Black America* (Boston: South End Press, 1983), Preface.

86. Ibid.

87. Ibid., p. 1.

88. Ibid., p. 2.

89. Ibid., p. 11.

90. Ibid.

91. Ibid., pp. 11–12.

92. Ibid., p. 18.

93. Ibid., p. 12.

94. Ibid., p. 18.

95. Ibid., p. 16.

96. Ibid.

97. Ibid., p. 133.

98. Ibid., p. 170.

99. Ibid., Chapters Four and Nine.

100. Ibid., p. 176.

101. Ibid., p. 177.

102. Ibid., p. 194.

103. Ibid., p. 257.

104. Ibid., p. 258.

105. Manning Marable, "Many Messages for Marxists from Chicago Mayoral Race," *Guardian*, March 16, 1983, p. 23.

106. Akinshiju C. Ola, "Blacks and '84: Focus Is Campaign, Not Candidate," *Guardian*, April 6, 1983, pp. 5–6.

107. James H. Cone, with comments by Michael Harrington, *The Black Church and Marxism: What Do They Have to Say to Each Other?* (New York: Institute for Democratic Socialism, 1980).

108. Cornel West, *Prophesy Deliverance! An Afro-American Revolutionary Christianity* (Louisville, Ky.: Westminster John Knox Press, 1982 [2002]), p. 169.

109. Ibid., pp. 95–127.

110. DSA Records, Harrington Correspondence, Box 6A, Folder: March–April 1982.

111. West, *Prophesy*, pp. 5, 136–137.

112. Ibid., p. 104.

113. Ibid., p. 105.

114. "Jeremiah A. Wright, Jr., Dr., Corinthian Baptist Church's Revivalist, April 21st to April 23rd, 2003, Biographical Summary," http://www.corinthianbaptistchurch.org/jeremiah_a_wright_jr.htm.

115. Bogdan Denitch, "Confronting Coalition Contradictions," *Social Policy*, Spring 1983, pp. 54–55.

Chapter 3: From New York to Havana

1. DSA Records, Box 81, folder: Socialist Scholars Conference.

2. Obama, *Dreams from My Father*, p. 122.

3. Minutes of the DSA governing board from an April 15, 1983, meeting quote Bogdan Denitch reporting 1,400 registered participants and a total attendance of 1,500. See Records of the Springfield, Illinois, Democratic Socialists of America, University of Illinois, Springfield, Box 1, Folder 10; Bogdan Denitch, "Marx Conference Is Big Success," *New York Democratic Socialist*, May 1983, p. 1; John Trinkl, "Survivors in search of a revival," *Guardian*, April 20, 1983, p. 9.

4. Programs for the 1984 Socialist Scholars Conference can be found in the uncatalogued DSA section of the vertical files of the Tamiment Library and Robert F. Wagner Labor Archives, New York University.

5. Jennifer B. Lee, "Where Obama Lived in 1980's New York," *New York Times*, City Room Blog, January 30, 2008, http://cityroom.blogs.ny times.com/2008/01/30/where-obama-lived-in-1980s-new-york/.

6. Associated Press, "Old friends recall Obama's college years," at Politico, May 16, 2008.

7. Ibid.; Lee, "Where Obama Lived."

8. Lee, "Where Obama Lived."

9. DSA Records, Harrington Correspondence, Box 6A, folder: March–April 1982 (Anita Snitow letter to Harrington, March 1, 1982).

10. Piven Papers, Box 45, folder 2.

11. John Trinkl, "DSA Embarks on a Long March, but Where To?" *Guardian*, October 26, 1983.

12. Ibid.

13. Ibid.

14. Ads for a wide range of classes at a "School for Democratic Socialism" can be found in various issues of *New York Democratic Socialist* during the mid-1980s. The ads were sponsored by the C.U.N.Y. Democratic Socialist Student Club, and the School for Democratic Socialism. Classes were often held at the CUNY Graduate Center, 33 West Forty-second Street, and sometimes featured prominent figures from the Socialist Scholars Conferences, such as Stanley Aronowitz, as instructors.

15. Jon Hillson, *A Socialist View of the Chicago Election: Forging a Black-Latino-Labor Alliance* (New York: Pathfinder Press, 1983), p. 26, in the Walter Goldwater Radical Pamphlet Collection at U.C. Davis Library.

16. Ibid.

17. Akinshiju C. Ola, "New Dawn Coming for the Rainbow Coalition?" *Guardian*, August 8, 1984, p. 3.

18. Paulette Pierce, "A New Direction and Democratic Alternative," *Socialist Forum*, Number 10, Early Winter 1986, p. 11, Piven Papers Box 45, folder 5.

19. Akinshiju C. Ola, "All Out for Jackson . . . Almost," *Guardian*, April 4, 1984, p. 6.

20. Ibid.

21. John Trinkl, "Jackson Campaign Sparks Broad Community Support," *Guardian*, January 18, 1984, p. 3.

22. Akinshiju C. Ola, "Jackson Has Already Won More Than a Nomination," *Guardian*, April 25, 1984, p. 7.

23. Jack Colhoun, "What Foreign Policy Would President Jackson Pursue?" *Guardian*, March 7, 1984, p. 7.

24. Ibid.

25. Guardian Viewpoint, "It's Rainbow Time," *Guardian*, November 23, 1983, p. 18.

26. Jim Shoch, "DSA, Jesse Jackson and the Rainbow Coalition: Some Cautious Considerations," *Socialist Forum*, Number 10, Early Winter 1986, pp. 29–29a, Piven Papers, Box 45, folder 5.

27. Pierce, "New Direction."

28. Kevin Kelley, "Little Support for Jackson Among White Left Liberals," *Guardian*, April 18, 1984, p. 3.

29. Guardian Viewpoint, "No Way to Make a Rainbow," *Guardian*, March 7, 1984, p. 18.

30. Obama, *Dreams from My Father*, p. 121.

31. Akinshiju C. Ola, "History Was Happening in Harlem," *Guardian*, April 1984.

32. "Second Annual Socialist Scholars Conference: The Encounter With America, April 19–21," Program, Piven Papers, Box 85, Folder 2.

33. West's presentation at the "Marxism and the Religious Left" panel, a panel sponsored by *Monthly Review*, probably appeared in reworked form in his July–August 1984 *Monthly Review* essay "Religion and the Left." West's presentation at the "New Developments in Racial Politics and Theory" panel was quite possibly published in reworked form in the DSA's *Third World Socialist* in the summer of 1984. Both of these pieces are reprinted in Cornel West, *Prophetic Fragments* (Grand Rapids, Mich.: Eerdmans, 1988).

34. This pamphlet was published in both New York and Los Angeles. I happen to have the Los Angeles version, which appears to add some material to the basic packet with Pierce's introduction and Garrow's essay. David Garrow's personal bibliography lists his pamphlet as: David Garrow, *Martin Luther King, Jr.: From Reformer to Revolutionary* (New York: Democratic Socialists of America, 1983, 1984.) I obtained a copy of the 1983 Los Angeles edition from the Walter Goldwater Radical Pamphlet Collection at U.C. Davis University Library. A May 17, 1983, letter from Michael Harrington to Bill Lucy appears to be a

first effort to find someone to produce such a pamphlet. See DSA Records, Harrington Correspondence, Box 6A, folder: May–August, 1983.

35. "Second Annual Socialist Scholars Conference," Program, Piven Papers, Box 85, Folder 2.

36. Obama, *Dreams from My Father*, p. 134.

37. Tim Harper, "The making of a president: Chicago helped shape Obama's outlook as he connected with mentors and honed his political elbows," *Toronto Star*, August 16, 2008.

38. Garrow pamphlet, Los Angeles edition, 1983, p. 3.

39. Ibid., p. 5.

40. Ibid.

41. Ibid.

42. Ibid.

43. Ibid., p. 29.

44. Ibid., p. 35.

45. David Garrow, "Don't Fall for Media Madness," *Democratic Left*, May–June 1985, p. 15.

46. James H. Cone, *Risks of Faith: The Emergence of a Black Theology of Liberation, 1968–1998* (Boston: Beacon Press: 1999), pp. 153–54.

47. Cone, "Black Church and Marxism," 1980.

48. Ibid., p. 8.

49. Ibid.

50. Ibid., p. 9.

51. Medell, "Promise," p. 59.

52. In this section, I draw on material from the Black Theology Project Records, 1976–87, at the Schomburg Center for Research in Black Culture of the New York Public Library. To a lesser degree, I also refer to the Theology in the Americas Records, 1951–88, also at the Schomburg Center. A members list of the BTP delegation to Cuba is contained in the "Black Theology Project of Theology in the Americas Bulletin," October 1984, p. 8. This can be found in BTP Records, Box 3, folder 8.

53. "Black Theology Project of Theology in the Americas Bulletin," October 1984, p. 2.

54. Ibid., pp. 1–8.

55. Glenn C. Loury, "The New American Dilemma: Racial Politics, Black and White," *New Republic*, December 31, 1984, p. 17.

56. Diego A. Abich, "Fidel Castro's Role Behind Jesse Jackson's Cuba Tour," *Wall Street Journal*, Friday, November 2, 1984, p. 29.

57. BTP Records, Box 4, Folder 13.

58. "BTP Minutes, 9/12/86," BTP Records, Box 1, Folder 40.

59. BTP Bulletin, October 1984, BTP Records, Box 3, Folder 8.

60. BTP Records, Box 4, Folder 13.

61. BTP Bulletin, October 1984, p. 3, BTP Records, Box 3, Folder 8.

62. Ibid., p. 4.

63. Ibid.

64. Ibid.

65. Milagros Oliva, "U.S. And Caribbean Christians Condemn Reagan's Central America Policy," *Granma*, July 20, 1986, BTP Records, Box 4, Folder 13.

66. Ibid.

67. BTP Board of Directors Meeting, February 5 and 6, 1986, Minutes, BTP Records Box 1, folder 35; "Memorandum Re: Suggested Class Assignments for Board of Directors," BTP Records Box 1, Folder 37.

68. "Jeremiah A. Wright, Jr., Dr., Corinthian Baptist Church Revivalist, April 21st to April 23rd, 2003, Biographical Summary."

69. See Theology in the America's Records finding aid.

70. "Rev. Wright Praises Magazine's 'No Nonsense Marxism,' " Breitbart TV, http://www.breitbart.tv/new-video-rev-wright-praises-magazines-no -nonsense-marxism/.

71. Mendell, *Obama: From Promise to Power*, p. 62.

72. Obama, *Dreams from My Father*, p. 135.

73. Ibid., pp. 120–21.

74. Ibid., p. 123.

75. Ibid.

76. Tom Bottomore, Editor, *A Dictionary of Marxist Thought* (Cambridge: Harvard University Press, 1983), pp. 115–16.

77. NYPIRG has posted a web page entitled "President Barack Obama's Work History as an Organizer with the New York Public Interest Research Group," http://www.nypirg.org/goodgov/obama.html.

78. The DSA tie with Ralph Nader's PIRGs is less public than the other connections. I found a folder in the DSA archives, however, with information on PIRGs, and a 1984 letter that indicated a working relation-

ship between the PIRGs and DSA organizers. DSA Records, Box 75, folder "PIRGS."

79. Harry Boyte, *The Backyard Revolution: Understanding the New Citizen Movement* (Philadelphia: Temple University Press, 1980).

80. Ibid., pp. 75–76.

81. Ibid., p. 60.

82. Ibid., p. 89.

83. Ben Whitford, "Coal and clear skies: Obama's balancing act," *Plenty*, December 2008, http://www.mnn.com/earth-matters/politics/stories/coal-and-clear-skies-obama%E2%80%99s-balancing-act.

84. Patrick Whelan, "The Catholic Case for Obama," Catholic Democrats, 2008, p. 51, http://www.catholicdemocrats.org/cfo/pdf/CatholicCase_for_Obama_booklet.pdf.

85. Robert Fisher, *Let the People Decide: Neighborhood Organizing in America* (Boston: G. K. Hall & Company, 1984).

86. Harry C. Boyte, *Community Is Possible: Repairing America's Roots* (New York: Harper & Row, 1984).

87. Another book on community organizing by an experienced practitioner that appeared in 1984 is: Gregory F. Augustine Pierce, *Activism That Makes Sense: Congregations and Community Organizing* (Chicago: ACTA Publications, 1984). This book is somewhat less known than the others, and slightly more specialized, since it specifically applies to church-based organizing. The book is influential, however, and is still assigned as a text to first-year organizers for the Gamaliel Foundation, Obama's original organizing sponsor. If Obama didn't read Pierce in New York, he very likely read it sometime after his arrival in Chicago.

88. Fisher, *Let the People Decide*, p. xiv.

89. Ibid., p. xv.

90. Ibid.

91. Ibid., p. 163.

92. Ibid., p. 25.

93. S. M. Miller, "Challenges for Populism," *Social Policy*, Summer 1985, pp. 3–6; Frank Riessman, Harry Boyte, S. M. Miller, "Populist Exchange," *Social Policy*, Fall 1985, pp. 38–41.

94. Miller, "Challenges for Populism," p. 4.

95. Ryan Lizza, "The Agitator: Barack Obama's Unlikely Political

Education," *New Republic*, March 19, 2007, http://www.tnr.com/article/the-agitator-barack-obamas-unlikely-political-education.

96. David Von Drehle, "The Five Faces of Barack Obama," *Time*, August 21, 2008, http://www.time.com/time/politics/article/0,8599,1834623-3,00.html.

97. "National Journal's 2007 Vote Ratings," National Journal, http://www.nationaljournal.com/voteratings/sen/lib_cons.htm?o1=lib_composite&o2=desc#results.

98. Davis's ongoing socialist sympathies are evident from his memoir, written late in life: Frank Marshall Davis, *Livin' the Blues* (Madison: University of Wisconsin, 1992). For more on Davis's politics, see Kathryn Wadell Takara, "The Fire and the Phoenix," Ph.D. University of Hawaii, 1993; John Edgar Tidwell, "Introduction: Weaving Jagged Words into Song," in Frank Marshall Davis, *Black Moods* (Urbana and Chicago: University of Illinois, 2002).

99. "College Acquaintance: Obama was 'pure Marxist socialist,'" Breitbart.tv, February 16, 2010, http://www.breitbart.tv/college-acquaintance-young-obama-was-pure-marxist-socialist/; "The B-Cast Interview: Was Obama a Committed Marxist in College?" Breitbart.tv, February 12, 2010, http://www.breitbart.tv/the-b-cast-interview-was-obama-a-committed-marxist-in-college/.

100. Remnick, *The Bridge*, p. 104.

101. Ibid.

102. Ibid.

103. Obama, *Dreams from My Father*, pp. 105–12.

104. Remnick, *The Bridge*, p. 109.

105. Ibid., pp. 107–9.

106. Ibid., p. 109.

107. Sam Stein, "Obama Mocks Socialist Attacks: "I Shared My Toys," The Huffington Post, October 29, 2008, http://www.huffingtonpost.com/2008/10/29/obama-sharpens-tone-agagain_n_138915.html.

108. Corsi, *Nation*, pp. 110–12; Remnick, *The Bridge*, pp. 62–68.

109. Obama, *Dreams from My Father*, p. 200.

110. Ibid.

111. Remnick, *The Bridge*, p. 109.

112. Ibid.

Chapter 4: Obama's Organizing: The Hidden Story

1. Helena Sundman, "UNO: Taking Organizing to a New Level, or Leaving the Community Behind," *Chicago Reporter*, May/June 1994, p. 9; Wilfredo Cruz, "The Nature of Alinksy-Style Community Organizing in the Mexican-American Community of Chicago: United Neighborhood Organization," Ph.D., University of Chicago, 1987, p. 117; R. Bruce Dold, "Mayor Keeps Jabbing at Percy," *Chicago Tribune*, October 25, 1984, Section 2, p. 3.

2. Sundman, "UNO," p. 8.

3. Gregory A. Galluzzo, "Gamaliel and the Barack Obama Connection," http://www.gamaliel.org/Obama%20Gamalie%201Connection.htm.

4. Obama, *Dreams from My Father*, p. xvii.

5. Galluzzo waited until after the 2008 election to publish an online account of his connection with Obama, "Gamaliel and the Barack Obama Connection" (see note 3). Galluzzo's account is roughly similar to what Obama says on pp. 226–29 of *Dreams*, with one major exception. In *Dreams*, Obama speaks of making an arrangement to pay "Marty" for weekly face-to-face consultations, after Marty moves out to Gary, Indiana. In Galluzzo's post-election account, when Jerry Kellman (Marty) moves out to Gary, he asks Galluzzo to become Obama's consultant. It's at least possible that Kellman drove back weekly from Gary to consult with Gary, to supplement the new weekly consulting from Galluzzo. In that case, Obama has simply left out the Galluzzo character altogether. Yet it also seems quite possible that this is a case of Obama creating a composite character (Marty) who combines elements of Kellman and Galluzzo. It's interesting that Galluzzo seems to have waited until after Obama was safely elected to post his version of events.

6. Remnick, *The Bridge*, p. 234.

7. Lynn Sweet, "Obama's Book: What's Real, What's Not," *Chicago Sun-Times*, August 8, 2004, p. 32.

8. Sunderman, "UNO"; Cazey Sanchez, "Building Power: One of the city's most powerful Latino organizations has figured out how to get a seat at the table," *Chicago Reporter*, January/February 2006.

9. Obama, *Dreams from My Father*, p. 141.

10. Ibid., p. 289.

11. Letta Tayler and Keith Herbert, "Chicago's Streets Obama's Teacher," *Newsday*, March 2, 2008, p. A6.

12. Harold Washington Archives and Collections (HWAC), Schedules and Evaluations Series, Box 2, Folder 10, "Vision 87" pamphlet.

13. Patrick T. Reardon, "Obama's Chicago: Take our unauthorized tour of the candidate's stomping grounds," *Chicago Tribune*, June 25, 2008, Tempo, Zone C, p. 1.

14. Ibid.

15. Cruz, "Alinsky-Style," p. 113; HWAC, Schedules and Evaluations, Box 2, Folder 10, "Vision 87" pamphlet.

16. Cruz, "Alinsky-Style," p. 56.

17. Ibid., p. 57.

18. Ibid., p. 59.

19. Ibid., p. 27.

20. Ibid., pp. 118–19.

21. Ibid., pp. 144–45; HWAC, Schedules and Evaluations Series, 5/21/87, Box 14, Folder 9.

22. Cruz, "Alinsky-Style," p. 37.

23. Ibid., p. 38.

24. Ibid., p. 39.

25. Ibid., pp. 76, 108, 128; Jean Davidson, "Hispanics Demand Job Training," *Chicago Tribune*, April 10, 1984, Section 2, p. 3.

26. Cruz, "Alinsky-Style," p. 123.

27. HWAC, Schedules and Evaluations Series, 2/19/87, Box 9, Folder 12.

28. Cruz, "Alinsky-Style," p. 76.

29. Ibid., p. 77.

30. Ibid., p. 44.

31. Ibid., pp. 51, 78–79.

32. Ibid., p. 74.

33. Ibid., pp. 48–49.

34. Ibid., pp. 45, 81.

35. Ibid., p. 68.

36. Ibid., pp. 19, 64–97.

37. Ibid., p. 81.

38. Ibid., p. 91; Patricia Zapor, "Obama cites influence of Cardinal Bernardin, prepares to meet Pope," Catholic News Service, July 2, 2009, http://www.catholicnews.com/data/stories/cns/0903039.htm.

39. Cruz, "Alinsky-Style," pp. 83–94.

40. Ibid., p. 95.

41. Obama, *Dreams from My Father*, p. 161.
42. Ibid.
43. Obama, *Dreams from My Father*, pp. 184–86.
44. Ibid., p. 196.
45. Ibid., pp. 223–26.
46. Peter Wallsten, "Obama defined by contrasts: He has cultivated associations with disaffected figures while keeping his own views on race issues," *Los Angeles Times*, March 24, 2008, p. 1.
47. The Loretta Augustine–Herron connection has been widely reported. The fact that Will in *Dreams* is Deacon Dan Lee is not well known, but the link was made in Bob Secter and John McCormick, "Obama Hits Chicago During Council Wars," *Chicago Tribune*, March 30, 2007.
48. HWAC, Schedules and Evaluations Series, 3/23/87, Box 11, Folder 9.
49. Ibid.
50. For conservative views, see James Bovard, "The Failure of Federal Job Training," CATO Institute, Policy Analysis No. 77, August 28, 1986, http://www.cato.org/pub_display.php?pub_id=943, and David Muhlhausen, Ph.D., and Paul Kersey, "In the Dark on Job Training: Federal Job-Training Programs Have a Record of Failure," Heritage Foundation, Backgrounder No. 1774, July 6, 2004, http://www.heritage.org/research/labor/bg1774.cfm. For a view from the left, see Gordon Lafer, *The Job Training Charade* (Ithaca: Cornell University Press, 2002).
51. Lafer, *The Job Training Charade*, p. 158.
52. Ibid., pp. 165, 169.
53. Ibid., p. 157.
54. Obama, *Dreams from My Father*, p. 150.
55. Ibid., p. 168.
56. Remnick, *The Bridge*, p. 179.
57. Lafer, *The Job Training Charade*, pp. 163–66.
58. Ibid., p. 170.
59. Muhlhausen and Kersey, "In the Dark."
60. Lafer, *The Job Training Charade*, pp. 172–77.
61. HWAC, Schedules and Evaluations Series, 3/23/87, Box 11, Folder 9.
62. Obama, *Dreams from My Father*, pp. 195–204.
63. Ibid., pp. 202–3.
64. Ibid., p. 196.

65. Peter Wallsten, "Fellow Activists Say Obama's Memoir Has Too Many I's," *Los Angeles Times*, February 19, 2007.

66. Wallsten, "Obama defined by contrasts."

67. Obama, *Dreams from My Father*, pp. 234–48.

68. HWAC, Mayoral Records Development Series, General Subject Files, Asbestos, etc., CHA 1986, Box 1, Folder 10.

69. HWAC, Chief of Staff Series, CHA Asbestos Report, June 1986, Box 22, Folder 9.

70. A number of news reports in the CHA Asbestos Report refer to Callie Smith as spokeswoman for the protesters, which at least suggests that this is the Sadie of *Dreams*.

71. Obama, *Dreams from My Father*, pp. 243–45.

72. Heidi J. Swarts, *Organizing Urban America: Secular and Faith-Based Progressive Movements* (Minneapolis: University of Minnesota Press, 2008), pp. 21–22.

73. Ibid., p. 23.

74. Obama, *Dreams from My Father*, pp. 185, 244–45. Obama does speak of working with his group leaders "preparing a script for the meeting" (p. 184), but without specialized knowledge of Galluzzo's techniques, it's almost impossible for ordinary readers of *Dreams* to understand the nature and purpose of the "pinning" process, or even to connect the yes-or-no demands Obama describes in passing to the idea of a meeting script.

75. Cheryl Devall, "CHA Director Leaves Hot Asbestos Session," *Chicago Tribune*, June 10, 1986, Chicagoland, p. 2; HWAC, Chief of Staff Series, CHA Asbestos Report, June 1986, Box 22, Folder 9.

76. Obama, *Dreams from My Father*, pp. 245–47.

77. HWAC, Development Sub-Cabinet Series, UNO 1984–1987, Box 16, Folder 3; HWAC, Schedules and Evaluations Series, 5/21/87, Box 14, Folder 9.

78. Cruz, "Alinsky-Style," pp. 119–21.

79. Obama, *Dreams from My Father*, p. 161.

80. Serge Kovalesky, "Obama's Organizing Years, Guiding Others and Finding Himself," *New York Times*, July 7, 2008, http://www.nytimes.com/2008/07/07/us/politics/07community.html?_r=1&pagewanted=1.

81. Jennifer Liberto, "Origin of Obama's Run Is on South Side," *St. Petersburg Times* (Florida), October 26, 2008, p. 1A.

82. Peter Slevin, "For Clinton and Obama, a Common Ideological Touchstone," *Washington Post*, March 25, 2007, A-Section, p. 1.

83. Sharon Cohen, "Barack Obama: Finding common bonds in different worlds," Associated Press, June 3, 2008.

84. Abdon M. Pallasch, "Taught residents to lobby; Mobilized people to fight for job training, school reform," *Chicago Sun-Times*, August 24, 2008, p. A15.

85. Tayler and Herbert, "Chicago's Streets."

86. Cruz, "Alinsky-Style," pp. 34, 51, 108–10; Wilfredo Cruz, "UNO: Organizing at the Grass Roots," *Illinois Issues*, April 1988, p. 22.

87. Ben Joravsky, "Dumpers Swamp City's Southeast Side With Noxious, Toxic Waste," *Chicago Reporter*, August 1983, pp. 1–5.

88. Steve Kerch, "Home-Grown Experts Crusade Against Waste Dumps," *Chicago Tribune*, April 15, 1984, Section 3, p. 2.

89. Casey Burko, "80 Southeast Side Residents Reject Firm's Offer On Landfill Use," *Chicago Tribune*, February 9, 1988, Chicagoland, p. 3.

90. Ibid.; Cruz, "UNO," p. 21; Tayler and Herbert, "Chicago's Streets."

91. Casey Sanchez, "Building Power: One of the city's most powerful Latino organizations has figured out how to get a seat at the table," *Chicago Reporter*, January/February 2006, pp. 14–15.

92. Obama, *Dreams from My Father*, p. 289.

93. Ibid., pp. 251–61.

94. Ibid., pp. 256–57.

95. Ibid., pp. 257–61.

96. HWAC, Developing Communities Project (Obama), 1987, Box 10, Folder 17.

97. HWAC, Central Files, DET, Box 27, Folder 27.

98. William S. McKersie, "Strategic Philanthropy and Local Public Policy Lessons from Chicago School Reform, 1987–1993," Ph.D. University of Chicago, 1998, pp. 330–77.

99. Had Harold Washington backed Obama's plans, we almost certainly would have heard about that fact. Also, a check of the Schedule and Evaluations Series of the HWAC lists no visits to Obama's Developing Communities Project beyond the ribbon-cutting ceremony.

100. HWAC, Central Files, DET, Box 27, Folder 27.

101. John Judis, "Creation Myth: What Barack Obama won't tell you about

his community organizing past," *New Republic*, September 10, 2008, http://www.tnr.com/article/creation-myth.

102. Tayler and Herbert, "Chicago's Streets."

103. Constanza Montana, "Meeting On School Reform Halted," *Chicago Tribune*, February 19, 1988, Chicagoland, p. 3.

104. The Midwest Academy's use of Alinskyite tactics comes out of the experience of many Academy personnel in Chicago's Citizen's Action Program (CAP). The tactical manufacture of anger by CAP is discussed in Emmons, "Community Organizing and Urban Policy," pp. 60, 322, 343–44. For a similar action by ACORN, see Stanley Kurtz, "Inside Obama's Acorn: By their fruits ye shall know them," *National Review Online*, May 29, 2008.

105. Ben Joravsky, "The Chicago School Mess," *Illinois Issues*, April 1988, p. 15.

106. O'Connell, "School Reform," p. 16.

107. Pallasch, "Taught Residents."

108. Ibid.

109. O'Connell, "School Reform," p. 16.

110. Tom Maguire, "The Obama-Ayers Connection—Follow the Bouncing Ball," JustOneMinute, October 15, 2008, http://justoneminute.typepad .com/main/2008/10/the-obama-ayers.h tml; Larry Johnson, "Obama, We Are Smarter; We Follow the Money and It Links You to Bill Ayers in the 1980's," No Quarter, June 2, 2008, http://www.noquarterusa .net/blog/2008/06/02/obama-we-are-smarter-we-follow-the-money-and -it-links-you-to-bill-ayers-in-the-1980s/.

111. Galluzzo, "Gamaliel and the Barack Obama Connection."

112. Barack Obama, *The Audacity of Hope: Thoughts on Reclaiming the American Dream* (New York: Crown Publishers, 2006), pp. 360–61.

113. John McKnight, *The Careless Society: Community and Its Counterfeits* (New York: Basic Books, 1995), pp. 153–60.

114. Sasha Abramsky, *Inside Obama's Brain* (New York: Penguin, 2009), p. 148.

115. DSA Records, Box 19, Folder LD: Chicago.

116. Tom Carlson, "Chicago's Health Care Dollar: What's the Community's Share?" *Health & Medicine*, Winter 1985, p. 34.

117. "Illinois: Legislators Press for Universal Care," American Health Line, November 17, 1997; "Dr. Quentin Young, Longtime Obama Confidante

and Physician to MLK Criticizes Admin's Rejection of Single-Payer Healthcare," Democracy Now, March 11, 2009, at http://www.democracy now.org/2009/3/11/dr_quentin_young_obama_confidante_and.

118. Ben Smith, "Obama once visited 60's radicals," Politico, February 22, 2008, at http://www.politico.com/news/stories/0208/8630.html.

119. "Red Emma: Excerpts from *Living My Life*, the autobiography of Emma Goldman," *Health & Medicine*, Spring 1987, pp. 5–6; "While Passing Through," *Health & Medicine*, Spring 1987, pp. 11–13.

120. Nancy Worcester, "Nicaragua's Health Revolution," *Health & Medicine*, Winter 1985, pp. 20, 22–25.

121. Carlson, "Chicago's Health Care Dollar."

122. "Sweden at the Crossroads," *Health & Medicine*, Winter 1985, pp. 9–12.

123. Swarts, *Organizing Urban America*, p. 51.

124. Ibid., pp. 52, 59.

125. Obama, *Dreams from My Father*, p. 169.

126. Dennis A. Jacobsen, *Doing Justice: Congregations and Community Organizing* (Minneapolis: Fortress Press, 2001).

127. Ibid., p. 18.

128. Ibid., p. 79.

129. Ibid., pp. 87–88.

130. Ibid., p. 78.

131. DSA Records, Box 17, Folder: Illinois-Chicago.

132. Kevin Fagan, "Transformations: A lifetime of evolving and adapting his identity has helped propel Barack Obama near the pinnacle of U. S. Politics," *San Francisco Chronicle*, September 14, 2008, p. A1.

Chapter 5: The Midwest Academy

1. This pamphlet can be found under the heading "What To Do" in the Midwest Academy Records, Box 291, Folder 16. In the Midwest Academy Records, this pamphlet is without a cover and the "What To Do" heading is on the first page of text, along with a listing of six authors: Heather Booth, Paul Booth, Harry Boyte, Sara Boyte, Steve Max, and Roger Robinson. The words "Labor Day 1969" appear at the bottom of the last page of the pamphlet. A curriculum vitae for Harry Chatten Boyte in Midwest Academy Records, Box 18. Folder: Boyte 1980 lists a 1969 pamphlet by the same six authors as a publication in

1969 under the title "Socialism and the Coming Decade." Presumably, therefore, the missing cover/title of the manuscript pamphlet in the Midwest Academy Records is "Socialism and the Coming Decade."

2. Lizza, "Agitator."

3. Booth et al., "Decade," pp. 3, 5.

4. Ibid., p. 2.

5. Ibid., pp. 1, 8.

6. Ibid., p. 4.

7. Ibid.

8. Midwest Academy Records, Box 251, Folder 12.

9. Horwitt, *Rebel*, pp. 529–34.

10. David Emmons, "Community Organizing and Urban Policy: Saul Alinsky and Chicago's Citizen's Action Program," Ph.D. University of Chicago, 1986, p. ii.

11. Ibid., p. 301.

12. Ibid., pp. 343–44.

13. See resumes for Heather Booth and Day Creamer in Midwest Academy Records, Box 3, Folder: Historical 1972–73.

14. Heather Booth, Day Creamer, Susan Davis, Deb Dobbin, Robin Kaufman, Tobey Klass, "Socialist Feminism: A Strategy for the Women's Movement," written in 1971, reprinted by the Midwest Academy, n.d., in Midwest Academy Records, Box 48, Folder 27.

15. Sanford D. Horwitt, *Let Them Call Me Rebel: Saul Alinsky—His Life and Legacy* (New York: Random House, 1989).

16. Booth et al., "Socialist Feminism," Ibid., p. 7.

17. Ibid., pp. 8–9.

18. Ibid., p. 12.

19. Ibid., p. 4.

20. Ibid., p. 15.

21. Oliver, "American Socialist Strategy," p. 69. Other than official sources like NAM's newsletters and the NAM Discussion Bulletin, Oliver's dissertation is probably the most important source on the topic. Beyond the detailed page references below, Oliver should be consulted for a in-depth understanding of the political processes discussed here. Paul Booth's founding role in NAM is confirmed in his resume in Midwest Academy Records, Box 3, Folder: History 1972–73.

22. Ibid., pp. 135–38.

23. Oliver, "American Socialist Strategy," pp. 70, 78.

24. Ibid., p. 143.

25. Northwestern University, Special Collections (Deering Library), Paul Rosenstein, "Organizers' Workshop," *New American Movement*, April 1972, p. 4.

26. Midwest Academy Records, Box 80, Folder 2: NAM Training School, 4/7–9/72.

27. This undated letter from "Steve" to Paul and Heather Booth begins, "I got your packet of stuff on the cadre school." See Midwest Academy Records, Box 80, Folder 2, NAM Training School, 4/7–9/72.

28. "Memo from Kat, Re: Academy Board of Directors," November 25, 1980, Midwest Academy Records, Box 1, Folder: Board of Directors 1981.

29. Steve Max, "Summer Session, June 1973," Manuscript in Midwest Academy Records, Box 27, Folder: Max 1973–74.

30. Ibid.

31. Midwest Academy Summer Session, June 17–June 29, 1973, in Midwest Academy Records, Box 3, Folder: History 1972–73.

32. Steve Max, "Academy History & Goals," March 1979, in Midwest Academy Records, Box 3, Folder: History and Goals 1979–80.

33. Midwest Academy Records, Box 27, Folder: Max 1973–74.

34. James Miller, *Democracy Is in the Streets: From Port Huron to the Siege of Chicago* (Cambridge, Mass.: Harvard University Press, [1987] 1994), pp. 73–74.

35. "Director's Report, June 5," in Midwest Academy Records, Box 2, Folder: Board 6-6-74; "Director's Report, August 12," in Midwest Academy Records, Box 2, Folder: Board 8-12-74.

36. "Director's Report, June 5," in Midwest Academy Records, Box 2, Folder: Board 6-6-74.

37. "Director's Activity: February 14–March 18, 1974," in Midwest Academy Records, Box 2, Folder: Board Notes 3-18-74; listing of groups Academy did training for, in Midwest Academy Records, Box 2, Folder: Board 8-12-74.

38. "Student List—Fall Session, 1974," in Midwest Academy Records, Box 2, Folder: Board 10-8-74.

39. This undated letter to Heather Booth begins, "If this looks better typed . . ." and is found in Midwest Academy Records, Box 27, Folder: Max 1973–74.

40. Oliver, "American Socialist Strategy," pp. 131–58.

41. Ibid., p. 134; "Announcing the Formation of a NAM Marxist-Leninist Organizing Caucus," *NAM Discussion Bulletin #11*, September 1975, pp. 8–12.

42. For NAM's involvement with the Cambridge Homeowners and Tenants Association, see "Where We're Working—And Why," Middlesex NAM, Cambridge Collective, in New American Movement Records, Tamiment Library/Robert F. Wagner Labor Archives, New York University, Box 13, Folder: Middlesex 1974–75. For the internal splits within NAM, see Frank Ackerman, "On Putting Ourselves Together," *NAM Discussion Bulletin #9*, March 1975, pp. 61–63; a caucus of twelve members of Middlesex NAM, "An Evaluation of Struggle and Growth in Middlesex NAM," *NAM Discussion Bulletin #10*, June/July 1975, pp. 41–48; Phil Woodbury et al., "Notes on the Political Debate Within Middlesex NAM," *NAM Discussion Bulletin #10*, June/July 1975, pp. 49–53.

43. Oliver, "American Socialist Strategy," p. 135.

44. Ibid., p. 265.

45. Ibid., p. 135. Judis's role within NAM is treated in detail throughout Oliver.

46. John Judis, "Our New Party: Poised Between the Bolsheviks and the Democrats," *NAM Discussion Bulletin #6*, March–April 1974, p. 8.

47. Ibid., p. 9.

48. Flier for Socialist Feminist Conference, Summer 1975, and Heather Booth, "Outline for Presentation to Community Organizing Workshop," in Midwest Academy Records, Box 253, Folder 6.

49. Ibid.

50. Letter from Harry Boyte to Michael Harrington, January 10, 1974, begins, "We talked several years ago," DSA Records, Harrington Correspondence, Box 5A, Folder 1973.

51. The most important letter is an undated item to Heather Booth that begins, "I am not at the moment clear . . ." This letter is in a folder dated 1976, but given events discussed, probably dates from an earlier period. See Midwest Academy Records, Box 284, Folder: Correspondence Steve Max 1976. Another letter to Booth in the same folder beginning, "I had a long talk with Elizabeth . . ." is also of interest. The other key undated letter to Booth begins, "Here is the Committee of Correspondence stuff." This letter, also probably earlier than the date

of the folder that contains it, can be found in Midwest Academy Records, Box 27, Folder: Max 1977–78.

52. Midwest Academy Records, Box 3, Folder: Committee of Correspondence 1977.

53. Letter from John Musick to Heather Booth, May 4, 1977 in Midwest Academy Records, Box 3, Folder: Committee of Correspondence 1977.

54. A correspondent in Washington, D.C., "Committee of Correspondence #2," p. 5, in Midwest Academy Records, Box 3, Folder: Committee of Correspondence 1977.

55. Steve Max, "Perspectives on our Organizational Work," pp. 6–7, and Harry Boyte, "Committee of Correspondence #2," p. 1, both in Midwest Academy Records, Box 3, Folder: Committee of Correspondence 1977.

56. Oliver, "American Socialist Strategy," pp. 173–96; Dorothy Healy, "Debate on Electoral Tactics," *NAM Discussion Bulletin #14*, May 1976, pp. 54–59; Max Gordon, "Reform and Revolution," *NAM Discussion Bulletin #20*, Autumn 1977, pp. 20–24; Max Gordon, "Sectarianism and NAM's Electoral Tactics: A Discussion," *NAM Discussion Bulletin #27*, Summer 1979, pp. 40–45.

57. Harry Boyte and Miles Moguleson, "Draft: Revolution, Strategy and Organization," January 1975, pp. 22–23, manuscript in Midwest Academy Records, Box 18, Folder: Boyte 1975.

58. Ibid., p. 25.

59. Frank Ackerman, "The Melting Snowball: Limits of the 'New Populism' in Practice," *NAM Discussion Bulletin #18*, 1977, p. 19.

60. Harry C. Boyte, "After the Snow Melts, Spring Time Begins: A Defense of Fair Share and Strategic Thoughts on the New Populism," *NAM Discussion Bulletin #19*, p. 26.

61. Partial and unidentified article reprint from February 1981 in Midwest Academy Records, Box 18, Folder: Boyte 1980.

62. Harry Boyte, September 4, 1980, letter to Rick Kunnes, NAM, in Midwest Academy Records, Box 18, Folder: Boyte 1980. See also material regarding "Commonwealth" statement in Midwest Academy Records, Box 18, Folder: Boyte 1981.

63. Citizen/Labor Energy Coalition, "A History of the Citizen/Labor Energy Coalition," n.d., in Midwest Academy Records, Box 236, Folder: C/LEC Histories 1978–83; Applied Political and Social Science Re-

search, Inc., "Report on the Citizen/Labor Energy Coalition," 1983, in Midwest Academy Records, Box 236, Folder: C/LEC Histories 1978–83; Milton R. Copulos, "CLEC: Hidden Agenda, Hidden Danger," Heritage Foundation Reports, February 9, 1984; James T. Bennett and Thomas J. DiLorenzo, *Destroying Democracy: How Government Funds Partisan Politics* (Washington: CATO Institute, 1985) pp. 11–135; Andrew Battista, *The Revival of Labor Liberalism* (Urbana and Chicago: University of Illinois Press, 2008) pp. 103–21.

64. Applied Political and Social Science Research, "Report on the Citizen/Labor," pp. 22–24.

65. Applied Political and Social Science Research, "Report on the Citizen/Labor;" Copulos, "Hidden Agenda," Bennett and DiLorenzo, *Destroying.*

66. The exception here was the early anonymous report by Applied Political and Social Science Research, Inc. This report did mention that Winpisinger was a vice chairman of the DSOC, but the other think-tank accounts appear to have missed this.

67. A number of letters to Winpisinger regarding contributions from the International Association of Machinists are scattered throughout the Harrington correspondence. See especially DSA Records, Harrington Correspondence, Letter of January 22, 1982, Harrington to Winpisinger, Box 6A, Folder: 1–2 1982; Letter of May 20, 1982, Harrington to Winpisinger, Box 6A, Folder: 5–8 1982; Letter of March 31, 1987, Harrington to Winpisinger, Box 6A, Folder: 1987; Letter of June 22, 1987, Harrington to Winpisinger, Box 6A, Folder: 1987.

68. William W. Winpisinger, "System Slips: Change Gears," *Democratic Left*, September 1979, pp. 1–4.

69. Midwest Academy Records, Box 220, Folder: Harry Boyte 1977–1979.

70. Copulos, "Hidden Agenda," p. 10.

71. Eugene J. McAllister and William T. Poole, "The Corporate Democracy Act and Big Business Day: Rhetoric vs. Reality," *Heritage Foundation Reports*, March 11, 1980.

72. William T. Poole, "The New Left in Government: Part II, The VISTA Program as Institution-Building," *Heritage Foundation Reports*, February 1982.

73. Gary Delgado, *Organizing the Movement: The Roots and Growth of ACORN* (Philadelphia: Temple University Press, 1986), p. 23.

74. Poole, "New Left in Government."

75. Thomas W. Pauken, "VISTA attacks on proposed phase-out self-serving move," *Dallas Times Herald*, n.d., in Midwest Academy Records, Box 233, Folder: VISTA Investigation 1981.

76. Midwest Academy Records, Box 233, Folder: VISTA Investigation 1981.

77. Memo from Kat to Heather Booth, et al. Re: Academy Board of Directors, November 25, 1980, Midwest Academy Records, Box 1, Folder: Board of Directors 1981.

78. Heather Booth, "Left With the Ballot Box," *Working Papers*, May/June 1981, in Midwest Academy Records, Box 292, Folder 5.

79. A history of Citizen Action by its leaders can be found in Harry C. Boyte, Heather Booth, and Steve Max, *Citizen Action and the New American Populism* (Philadelphia: Temple University Press, 1986), pp. 47–68.

80. Ibid., p. 146.

81. Ibid.

82. Boyte, Booth, and Max, *Citizen Action*, p. 147; Bob Creamer, "Illinois Public Action Council," *Social Policy*, Spring 1983, pp. 23–25.

83. Boyte, Booth, and Max, *Citizen Action*, p. 147.

84. David Moberg, "Evans Runs Again on Populist Agenda," *In These Times*, October 17–23, 1984, p. 6. See also Harry Boyte, "Put the Community Into Organizing," *Democratic Left*, January 1983, pp. 8–9.

85. "New Directions Initiators List (Partial Listing), Midwest Academy Records, Box 272, Folder 2. The congressmen on this list include George Crockett, Ron Dellums, Don Edwards, Lane Evans, Barney Frank, Charles Hays, Robert Kastenmeier, Parren J. Mitchell, and Esteban Torres; *Chicago Socialist*, October/November 1982, p. 4, in DSA Records, Box 17, Folder: Illinois, Chicago.

86. Ibid.

87. George Wood, "Citizen's Group in Anticorporate Mood," *Democratic Left*, February 1981, pp. 6–7.

88. Ibid.

89. John Herbers, "Grass-Roots Groups Go National," *New York Times*, September 4, 1983, Magazine Desk, p. 22.

90. Donald C. Reitzes and Dietrich C. Reitzes, "Alinsky in the 1980's: Two Contemporary Chicago Community Organizations," *Sociological Quarterly*, vol. 28, no. 2, p. 271.

91. Midwest Academy Records, Box 2, Folder: Citizen Action Development 1980–81.

92. Herbers, "Grass-Roots Groups Go National."

93. "Obama Invited Lane Evans to Election Night Suite," Progress Illinois, November 10, 2008, at http://www.progressillinois.com/2008/11/09/obama-hosts-lane-evans.

94. Midwest Academy Records, Box 283, Folder: Correspondence 1977–1988.

95. Ibid.

96. "About (Jan Schakowsky)," Janschakowsky.org, at http://www.jan schakowsky.org/about; "Administrative & Management Training Session: Application," Midwest Academy Records, Box 74, Folder: Schakowsky 1976–79.

97. Midwest Academy Records, Box 74, Folder: Schakowsky 1976–79.

98. Ibid.

99. "Building Democratic Populism: Midwest Academy Retreat," August 2–4, 1985, pamphlet in Midwest Academy Records Box 55, Folder 3; "Toward a Progressive Majority: Midwest Academy Retreat," July 25–27, 1986, pamphlet in Midwest Academy Records, Box 56, Folder 1; "It's Up to Us: Midwest Academy Retreat," June 17–19, 1988, pamphlet in Midwest Academy Records, Box 56, Folder 8.

100. "Questionnaire," Midwest Academy Records, Box 74, Folder: Scha-kowsky 1976–79.

101. Jan Schakowsky, "Hopes and Fears Dominate IPAC Conference," *Chicago Socialist*, February/March 1983, pp. 4–5.

102. "DSAers on the Move," *DSA News*, June 9, 1986, p. 2.

103. John Cameron, "A Socialist's Guide to Citizen Action," *Socialist Forum*, no. 1, undated, c. 1982, pp. 30–35.

104. Leo Casey, "Citizen Action: A Report and a Proposal," *Socialist Forum*, no. 4, part 1, Focus on DSA 1983 Convention, pp. 34–38.

105. Ibid., p. 37.

106. Ibid.

107. Ibid., p. 38.

108. Cameron, "A Socialist's Guide," p. 35.

109. Boyte, Booth, and Max, *Citizen Action*.

110. Ibid., p. 34.

111. Ibid., p. 37.

112. Sasha Abramsky, *Inside Obama's Brain* (New York: Penguin, 2009), p. 33.

113. Event Transcript, "Mr. Obama's Neighborhood," Hudson Institute's Bradley Center for Philanthropy and Civic Renewal, p. 3, http://www .hudson.org/files/documents/BradleyCenter/Transcript; sf2008_10_01 .pdf.

114. Abramsky, *Inside Obama's Brain*, pp. 72, 261.

115. Ibid., pp. 89–90, 93.

116. Tom Fitton, "Obama's Records Problem," Judicial Watch, March 14, 2008, at http://www.judicialwatch.org/jwnews/2008/03142008.pdf.

117. David Moberg, "Obama's Third Way," Shelterforce Online, Spring 2007, at http://www.nhi.org/online/issues/149/obama.html; Trevor Loudon, "Obama File 26: William McNary, Yet Another Obama Radical?" September 2, 2008, at http://newzeal.blogspot.com/2008/09/ obama-file-26-william-mcnary-yet.html; Abramsky, *Inside Obama's Brain*, p. 31.

118. Steve Max, undated letter to Heather Booth beginning, "I am not at the moment clear on how to proceed with the NYPIRG," in Midwest Academy Records, Box 284, Folder: Correspondence Steve Max 1976; Steve Max, Letter to Heather Booth, December 8, 1976, in Midwest Academy Records, Box 27, Max 1977–78.

119. "Observers invited to founding Citizen Action conference," Midwest Academy Records, Box 128, Folder: Advisory Committee 1980.

120. Midwest Academy Records, Box 22, Folder 36.

121. Dreier and Ganz, "We Have the Hope. Now Where's the Audacity?"

122. Casey, "Report and a Proposal," p. 34.

123. Midwest Academy Records, Box 55, Folder 6; Box 138, Folder: International Affairs 1984–86 #1; Box 139, Folder: International Affairs Central America 1985 #1; Box 139, Folder: International Affairs Central America 1985 #2; Box 139, Folder: International Affairs Project Proposals 1983–85; Box 140, Folder: Central American Peace Campaign 1989.

124. "Central America Project: Proposal Submitted to the Philadelphia Foundation," in Midwest Academy Records, Box 139, Folder: International Affairs Project Proposals 1983–85.

125. "Nicaragua: A Look at the Reality," pamphlet in Midwest Academy Records, Box 140, Folder: International Affairs: Citizen Action 1984.

126. Midwest Academy Records, Box 55, Folder 6.

127. "Building Democratic Populism: Midwest Academy Retreat," August 2–4, 1985, pamphlet in Midwest Academy Records Box 55, Folder 3; "Toward a Progressive Majority: Midwest Academy Retreat," July 25–27, 1986, pamphlet in Midwest Academy Records, Box 56, Folder 1; "It's Up to Us: Midwest Academy Retreat," June 17–19, 1988, pamphlet in Midwest Academy Records, Box 56, Folder 8.

128. Jack W. Germond and Jules Witcover, "Protectionism May Backfire as Campaign Issue," *National Journal*, September 21, 1985, p. 2150; Mitchell Locin, "Democrats Bandy Harsh Talk Right and Left but Find Common Ground," *Chicago Tribune*, August 2, 1987, p. 8.

129. Bill Peterson, "Activists of the 60's Meet, With Optimism, Under a New Banner," *Washington Post*, January 11, 1982, p. A9; William K. Stevens, "Activists Meeting to Plan a New U.S. Agenda," *New York Times*, August 2, 1987, p. 30.

130. See biography of Ken Rolling in John Simmons, "School Reform in Chicago: Lessons and Opportunities," A Report for the Chicago Community Trust, Donors Forum of Chicago, August 200, p. 95. Available from Donors Forum Library, Chicago, IL.

131. Midwest Academy Records, Box 2, Folder: Board 12-16-88.

132. William T. Poole and Thomas W. Pauken, *The Campaign for Human Development: Christian Charity or Political Activism?* (Washington, D.C.: Capital Research Center, 1988); Kathryn Jean Lopez, "Catholic Campaign for Human Development: Still Entranced by Leftist Activism, Despite Growing Unrest," *Foundation Watch*, October 2000; Louis Delgado, "Lessons from Philanthropy: A Case Study Approach (A Report to the Ford Foundation)," 2007, pp. 66–92, at http://www.luc.edu/curl/pdfs/report_ford_case_studies.pdf.

133. "CHD Contributes Experience to CHRISTIANITY AND CAPITALISM," *Thirsting for Justice*, Spring 1982, p. 1, in Midwest Academy Records, Box 227, Folder: CHD 1981–82.

134. "Three Priority Principles," *Thirsting for Justice*, Spring 1982, p. 2, in Midwest Academy Records, Box 227, Folder: CHD 1981–82.

135. "Educational Materials," CHD Report 1981, pamphlet in Midwest Academy Records, Box 227, Folder: CHD 1981–82.

136. "What in the World Are We To Do?" Keynote Address at 1982 CHD

Regional Meetings by Rev. Marvin Mottet, in Midwest Academy Records, Box 227, Folder: CHD 1981–82.

137. "CHD Contributes Experience to CHRISTIANITY AND CAPITALISM," *Thirsting for Justice*, Spring 1982, p. 2, in Midwest Academy Records, Box 227, Folder: CHD 1981–82.

138. Mitchell Locin, "Her School Trains Organizers," *Chicago Tribune*, July 1, 1982, Metro/North p. 1.

139. Moberg, "Obama's Third Way."

140. Midwest Academy Records, Box 2, Folder: Board 7-31-87.

141. Abramsky, *Inside Obama's Brain*, p. 2.

142. Midwest Academy Records, Box 2, Folder: Board 7-31-87.

143. In *Dreams* (p. 279), Obama speaks of his successor taking over the day-to-day activities of the Developing Communities Project. On p. 290 he writes of setting dates for a training retreat. A fellow Gamaliel Foundation organizer, David Kindler, recounts a training session led by Obama in Sharon Cohen, "A political journey at warp speed," Associated Press Online, January 17, 2009. In the piece about his organizing experiences Obama published in 1988, the byline lists him as a "consultant and instructor" for the Gamaliel Foundation. See Barack Obama, "Why Organize? Problems and Promise in the Inner City," *Illinois Issues*, August & September 1988, p. 42.

144. Midwest Academy Records, Box 27, Folder 28.

145. Records of ACORN New York, Box 6, Folder 2. Contains two pamphlets: "Public Allies: An Action Plan By Young People" and "Public Allies: The National Center for Careers in Public Life Honors Tomorrow's Leaders Today."

146. Ibid.

147. Ibid.

148. "Young Leaders Honored, Recruited," *The Neighborhood Works*, October/November 1992, p. 4.

149. Mark S. Allen, "My Personal Relationship With Obama's (1): From Adversary to Longtime Ally: Veteran Activist/Journalist Mark S. Allen and President Barack Obama," text begins, "At no time in our relationship of over 20 years has Barack Obama said nothing but nice things about me . . ." at http://www.blackvoices.com/boards/welcome/welcome/by-welcome-forum/my-personal- . . .

150. File on Public Allies at Donor's Forum Library, Chicago, Ill.

151. "Public Allies Congratulates . . . the 1995–96 Partner Organizations," *Check-In* (Public Allies Chicago Newsletter), Fall 1995, p. 3. Even the Girl Scout project had a bit of a "non-traditional" edge: "Non-Traditional G-Scouts," *Check-In*, Winter 1995, p. 1; "1994–95 Allies Partner Organizations," *Check-In*, Winter 1995, p. 2, see also File on Public Allies at Donor's Forum Library, Chicago, IL.

152. "Wanted: Allies and Partners!" *Check In*, Spring 1997, p. 4.

153. "Team Service Projects . . . Allies Take Action," *Check-In*, Winter 1995, p. 3; "1995–96 Ally Team Service Projects," *Check-In*, Fall 1996, p. 4.

154. "Tomorrow's Leaders Today," *Check-In*, Spring 1997, p. 5. This issue of *Check-In* dates from just after Michelle Obama left the program, but indicates the structure already in place. The Tomorrow's Leaders Today awards go back to the origins of the national program. See the Records of ACORN New York at the Wisconsin Historical Society, Box 6, Folder 2.

155. "Tomorrow's Leaders Today," *Check-In*, Summer 1997, p. 4.

156. Records of ACORN New York, Box 6, Folder 2.

157. Liza Mundy, *Michelle: A Biography* (New York: Simon & Schuster, 2008) p. 114.

158. The Public Allies Chicago Advisory Board is listed in several issues of *Check-In*. See, for example, "Public Allies Chicago Advisory Board," *Check-In*, Fall 1993, p. 3.

159. Boyte, Booth, and Max, *Citizen Action*, p. 59.

160. Carl Shier, "The 41st Annual Debs-Thomas-Harrington Dinner," New Ground, May–June 1999, at http://www.chicagodsa.org/ngarchive/ng64.html#anchor713759.

161. "Board of Directors," Midwest Academy, http://www.midwestacademy.com/board-directors.

162. "Fact Sheet About Public Allies and the Obamas," at http://www.publicallies.org/site/c.liKUL3PNLvF/b.3960231/.

163. "Board of Directors, Midwest Academy," at http://www.midwestacademy.com/board-directors.

164. Abramsky, *Inside Obama's Brain*, pp. 60, 63, 91, 95–96.

165. "Fact Sheet About Public Allies and the Obamas," at http://www.publicallies.org/site/c.liKUL3PNLvF/b.3960231/; "Public Allies Speakers Series Launched," *Check-In*, Winter 1995, p. 3; "1996 TLT Workshops and Day of Service," Fall 1996, p. 3.

166. "Norman Thomas–Eugene V. Debs Dinner (Program)," May 9, 1987 (See award citations to Grimshaw and Booth), and text of Heather Booth's award acceptance speech, Midwest Academy Records, Box 273, Folder 11.

167. "New Directions for the Democratic Party: A Public Forum with Heather Booth, Miguel Del Valle, Jackie Grimshaw, and David Orr, sponsored by the Chicago Democratic Socialists of America" flier in Midwest Academy Records, Box 272, Folder 3; "Heather Booth, Jackie Grimshaw and Michael Dyson Wow Crowd at U. of Chicago," *New Ground,* Spring 1992, p. 9.

168. Remnick, *Bridge*, p. 221.

169. Strategic Consulting Group, "A Partial List of SCG Clients," at http://www.stratcongroup.com/clients.php.

170. Michael Higgins and Laurie Cohen, "Democrat Consultant Sentenced to Prison," *Chicago Tribune*, April 6, 2006, Metro Section, p. 1.

171. Glenn Beck, "Robert Creamer's Book Is a Hit With Progressives," FoxNews.com, December 8, 2009, at http://www.foxnews.com/story/0.2933.579761.00.html; Aaron Klein, "Alinsky trainer developed 1st Obama volunteers," WorldNet Daily, March 25, 2010, at http://www.wnd.com/index.php?fa=PAGE.printable&pageId=131465; Biography of Robert Creamer at Discover the Networks: A Guide to the Political Left, at http://www.discoverthenetworks.org/individualProfile.asp?indid=2438; Joel B. Pollack, "Was Democrats' Health Care Strategy Written in Federal Prison?" Big Government, December 7, 2009, at http://biggovernment.com/jpollak/2009/12/07/was-democrats-health-care-strategy-written-in-federal-prison/.

172. Strategic Consulting Group, "Testimonials" (for *Stand Up Straight!*) at http://www.stratcongroup.com/publication/testimonials.php.

173. Ibid.

174. Higgins and Cohen, "Democrat Consultant Sentenced to Prison."

175. Robert Creamer, "Republicans Want to Vote Against Health Care Reform? Go Ahead, Make My Day," Huffington Post, March 8, 2010, at http://www.huffingtonpost.com/robert-creamer/memo-to-republicans-want_b_489832.html.

176. Jackie Kendall, "Midwest Academy Retreat Introduction," July 31, 1987, Midwest Academy Records, Box 56, Folder 7.

177. See Chapter Nine.

178. Remnick, *Bridge,* p. 278.

179. Ben Smith, "Obama once visited 60's radicals," Politico, February 22, 2008, http://www.politico.com/news/stories/0208/8630.html.

180. Basil Talbott, " 'Outsider' Helps Lead Machine to Victory," *Chicago Sun-Times,* November 11, 1996, p. 12.

181. Heather Booth, "Victories and Lessons," *The Neighborhood Works,* December 1993/January 1994, p. 8.

Chapter 6: ACORN

1. Robert Fisher, ed., *The People Shall Rule* (Nashville: Vanderbilt University Press, 2009), pp. 5, 12, 251, 252.

2. Swarts, *Organizing Urban America,* pp. 41, 44.

3. Piven and Cloward, *Poor People's Movements*; Richard Poe, "The Cloward-Piven Strategy," DiscoverTheNetworks.org, 2005, http://www.discoverthenetworks.org/Articles/theclowardpivenstrategypoe.html.

4. Dreier, "Socialist Incubators."

5. Piven and Cloward, *Poor People's Movements,* pp. 264–361.

6. Richard A. Cloward and Frances Fox Piven, "The Weight of the Poor: A Strategy to End Poverty," *Nation,* May 2, 1966, http://www.commondreams.org/headline/2010/03/24-4.

7. For more on Cloward's and Piven's relationship to ACORN, see below and Ann Withorn, "Socialist Analysis and Organizing: An Interview with Richard A. Cloward and Frances Fox Piven," *Radical America,* vol. 21, no. 1, January–February 1987, pp. 21–29.

8. "Party Time: An Interview with Dan Cantor of the New York Working Families Party," *Social Policy,* Summer 2001, p. 19.

9. I say "apparently" because I am working from a portion of Cantor's memo quoted in Gary Delgado's book *Organizing the Movement.* So it's possible that this spelling error is Delgado's, rather than Cantor's.

10. For Dreier's work with ACORN on its banking campaign, see below. For an example of Dreier's many recent pieces in defense of ACORN, see Peter Dreier, "First They Came for ACORN," Huffington Post, September 26, 2009, http://www.huffingtonpost.com/peter-dreier/first-they-came-for-acorn_b_300941.html.

11. For the story of ACORN's People's Platform, see Delgado, *Organizing the Movement,* pp. 123–61.

12. Ibid., pp. 125–26.
13. Carey Rogers, "Neighborhood Organizing Leads to Nat'l Platform," *Democratic Left,* January 1980, p. 9.
14. Webb Smedley, "Report on the ACORN Convention," *NAM Discussion Bulletin,* #26, Spring 1979, p. 107.
15. Delgado, *Organizing the Movement,* p. 144.
16. ACORN Records, M2005-121, Box 1, Folder 3, Wade Rathke, "H. L. Mitchell, Organizer Southern Tenant Farmer's Union," Community Organizing: Handbook #1, pp. 12–18.
17. "Follow the Money: ACORN, SEIU and their Political Allies," Staff Report, U.S. House of Representatives, 111th Congress, Committee on Oversight and Government Reform, Darrell Issa (CA-49), Ranking Member, February 18, 2010, at http://republicans.oversight.house .gov/images/stories/Reports/20100218followthemoneyacornseiuandt heirpoliticalallies.pdf.
18. Ibid., p. 3.
19. Ibid., p. 4.
20. Ibid., p. 3.
21. Ibid.
22. "Chicago ACORN Board Meeting, November 27, 1984," Illinois ACORN Records, Box 1, Folder 11.
23. "January '84, Regional Report, Great Lakes region," Illinois ACORN Records, Box 1, Folder 9.
24. "Great Lakes Regional Report, Feb. 1984, from: MT," Illinois ACORN Records, Box 1, Folder 9.
25. "Year End/Year Begin Report and Plan, Jan. 1/1985," Illinois ACORN Records, Box 2, Folder 63.
26. "Chicago ACORN YE/YB Report & Plan, 1988–89, Dec. 30–31, 1988," p. 4, Illinois ACORN Records, Box 2, Folder 62.
27. See, for example, various papers and notes related to arrests in Illinois ACORN Records, Box 2, Folder 71.
28. Madeline Talbott's spiral notebook, handwritten notes from 8/10/85 (about one-third of the way through the notebook covering that date).
29. Keith Kelleher, "Growth of a Modern Union Local: A People's History of SEIU Local 880," *Just Labor,* vol. 12, Spring 2008, p. 5, at http:// www.justlabour.yorku.ca/volume12/pdfs/01_kelleher_press.pdf.
30. Ibid.
31. Ibid., p. 7.

32. Ibid.

33. Ibid., p. 10.

34. "Group breaks into foreclosed home," *Chicago Tribune*, April 8, 1989, section 1, p. 5.

35. Clem Richardson, " 'Squatters' Begin Repairs," *Chicago Sun-Times*, May 15, 1985.

36. Stanley Ziemba and Jerry Thornton, "Squatters Pledge to Give Houses Life," *Chicago Tribune*, May 15, 1985.

37. TNW Roundtable, "Activist Women Explore Shelter Issues," *The Neighborhood Works*, October 1986, p. 11.

38. Delgado, *Organizing the Movement*, p. 157.

39. "Great Lakes/Prairie Regions, Year End/Year Begins Report and Plan, Dec. '91," Illinois ACORN Records, Box 1, Folder 9.

40. Tayler and Herbert, "Chicago's streets Obama's teacher."

41. See "Summary of Grant Application" and attached "Proposal from the Institute for Social Justice to the Discount Foundation for the Chicago ACORN Southside Toxics Organizing Project," Illinois ACORN Records, Box 3, Folder 47.

42. ACORN/Union Internal Evaluation, December 7, 1985, p. 2, Illinois ACORN Records, Box 2, Folder 72; "Chicago Board Meeting, May 21, 1985, Agenda," Illinois ACORN Records, Box 1, Folder 11; "Notes on March 26 Board Meeting, Chair: Irma Sherman," Illinois ACORN Records, Box 1, Folder 11.

43. The Montes-led action against Waste Management, which Obama helped plan, is described in Chapter Four.

44. Steuart Pittman, "Status Report, 12/17/84, Altgeld Tenants United," Illinois ACORN Records, Box 2, Folder 62; "Altgeld Tenants United (ATU)/ACORN, Second Organizing Committee Meeting," October 4, 1984, Illinois ACORN Records Box 3, Folder 58; "Year End/Year Begin Report and Plan, Jan. 1/1985, Illinois ACORN Records," Box 2, Folder 63.

45. "Organizing Plan, Chicago ACORN, 11/1/86–6/30/87," p. 2, Illinois ACORN Records, Box 2, Folder 32.

46. "Great Lakes Regional Report/Plan, Jan. '88," Illinois ACORN Records, Box 1, Folder 9.F

47. "Chicago ACORN YE/YB Report & Plan, 1988–89, Dec. 30–31, 1988," p. 3, Illinois ACORN Records, Box 2, Folder 62.

48. Bill Rumbler, "Help for Home Buyers; Putting Loans Within Reach," *Chicago Sun-Times*, April 28, 1995, Homelife, p. 16.

49. Aaron Pressman, "Community Reinvestment Act had nothing to do with subprime crisis," *Bloomberg Businessweek*, September 29, 2008, at http://www.businessweek.com/investing/insights/blog/archives/2008/09/community_reinvestment_act_had_nothing_to_do_with_subprime_crisis.html.

50. Kim Nauer, "CRA," *The Neighborhood Works*, December 1993/January 1994, pp. 15–19.

51. Memo from Mike Shea to HO's Board, regarding "Information to Request from Banks," ACORN New York Records, Box 4, Folder 20.

52. Ibid.

53. Accounts of the 1989 housing battle can be found in various documents in New York ACORN Records, Box 5, Folder 30. See, for example, "Financial Democracy Campaign Victories"; Memorandum, August 8, 1989, from Steven Kest to Friends of the Financial Democracy Campaign, regarding "Victories in the S&L Bailout Campaign"; Memorandum, June 28, 1989, from Phil Wheeler to Owen Bieber, regarding "Contacting Senator Reigle Regarding the Bailout Bill For the Savings and Loan Industry"; Memorandum, August 8, 1989, from Steven Kest to Staff and Board, regarding "Final Victory in the S&L Bailout Campaign."

54. Letter from Phil Gramm to "Dear Colleague," August 3, 1989, New York ACORN Records, Box 5, Folder 30.

55. See, for example, the July 5, 1989, letter of thanks, with a continued request for help, from Mildred Brown to Nancy Pelosi, and a list of others to be thanked, New York ACORN, Box 5, Folder 30.

56. Memorandum, December 19, 1990, from Dreier to Atlas, Kendall, Kest, Max, and Morrissey, regarding "Next steps for housing campaign; outreach to unions"; Memorandum from Jackie Kendall and Steve Max to Atlas, Dreier, Kest, and Morrissey, regarding "Housing Strategy, Tactics, Peter's Memorandum of 12/20/90, And the Possibility of Recession and War"; Memorandum, January 10, 1991, from Peter Dreier to Steering Committee, regarding Housing Justice Campaign 1991–1993.

57. The crisis in this case was the tendency of S&L scandals at this time to discredit federal housing programs. The opportunity was for new

federal housing programs with greater participation from community organizations, and more "progressive" banking policy generally: Memorandum, January 10, 1991, from Peter Dreier to Steering Committee, regarding "Housing Justice Campaign 1991–93."

58. "Great Lakes Region Report/Plan, 12/30/89," p. 3, Illinois ACORN Records, Box 1, Folder 9.

59. "Great Lakes/Prairie Regions, Year End/Year Begins Report and Plan, Dec. '91," Illinois ACORN, Box 1, Folder 9.

60. "YE/YB Report 1992–93, Chicago ACORN, 1-1-93," Illinois ACORN Records, Box 2, Folder 62.

61. Jim Allen, "Six Protesters Charged After Attempt to Storm City Council Chambers," *Chicago Daily Herald*, July 31, 1997, p. 10; Madeline Talbott, "Where Do We Begin?" *Boston Review,* Summer 1996, http://bostonreview.net/BR21.3/Talbott.html.

62. Ted Cornwell, "Housing Group Challenges Ill. Thrift Merger," *National Mortgage News,* February 19, 1990, p. 21.

63. Mike Dorning, "Avondale Under Fire for Record On Minority, Low-Income Loans," *Chicago Tribune*, April 1, 1992, Business, p. 3.

64. Monica Copeland, "Minorities Hope Banks Lend a Hand," *Chicago Tribune*, May 12, 1992, Chicagoland, p. 2.

65. J. Linn Allen, "Study Cites Racial Gap In Reinvestment," *Chicago Tribune*, June 5, 1992, Business, p. 1.

66. J. Linn Allen, "Banks, Activists Tailor Loans to Communities, *Chicago Tribune*, September 1, 1992, p. 1.

67. Memorandum, 10/28/91, from Madeline Talbott to all ACORN offices, regarding "follow up to HMDA report and press," ACORN Records, 1973–1997, Box 4, Folder: Bank Campaign 1991 (Second Folder).

68. Madeleine Adamson, "The ACORN Housing Agenda," *Shelterforce,* March/April 1993, pp. 8–11, ACORN Records, M2005-121, Box 1, Folder 4.

69. Ibid.

70. Jamie Gottula Buelt, "Pressure on Lenders 'a New Experience,' " *Business Record*, April 20, 1987, p. 1; Jay Rosenstein, "Community Groups Ask More Housing Loans," *American Banker*, September 21, 1987.

71. ACORN Records, 1973–1997, Box 4, Folder: Bank Campaign 1991 (second of two folders), ACORN Alert, July 12, 1991, ACORN's Fannie Mae & Freddie Mac Affordable Housing Proposal.

72. Edward Pinto, "Acorn and the Housing Bubble," *Wall Street Journal*, November 12, 2009, http://online.wsj.com/article/SB1000142405274 8703298004574459763052141456.html.

73. "YE/YB Report 1992–93, Chicago ACORN, 1-1-93," Illinois ACORN Records, Box 2.

74. Michelle Malkin, "Finally: New McCain ad on ACORN," Michelle Malkin blog, October 10, 2008, http://michellemalkin.com/2008/10/10/finally-new-mccain-ad-on-acorn/.

75. "Project Vote not 'an arm of ACORN,' " PolitFact, October 10, 2008, http://www.politifact.com/truth-o-meter/statements/2008/oct/17/john-mccain/project-vote-not-an-arm-of-acorn/; Albert Milliron, "McCain Internal memo Blasts Obama's Involvement with ACORN," Now Public blog, October 11, 2008, http://www.nowpublic.com/world/mccain-internal-memo-blasts-obamas-involvement-acorn.

76. Stanley Kurtz, "Inside Obama's Acorn," *National Review Online*, May 29, 2008, http://article.nationalreview.com/358910/inside-obamas-acorn/stanley-kurtz; Stanley Kurtz, "O's Dangerous Pals," *New York Post*, September 29, 2008, http://www.nypost.com/p/news/opinion/opedcolumnists/item_cvq7rDCHftKwJyLaecfPQK; Stanley Kurtz, "Planting the Seeds of Disaster," *National Review Online*, October 7, 2008, http://article.nationalreview.com/374045/planting-seeds-of-disaster/stanley-kurtz; Stanley Kurtz, "Spreading the Virus," *New York Post*, October 13, 2008, http://www.nypost.com/p/news/opinion/opedcolumnists/item_2apJAuC2tslB4no8AK15iO.

77. Jim Hoft, "The Obama campaign privately updated . . ." Gateway Pundit blog, October 12, 2008, http://gatewaypundit.firstthings.com/2008/10/oops-obama-camp-caught-scrubbing-its-fight-the-smears-web page-on-acorn/.

78. John McCormick, "Barack Obama Talks About ACORN," The Swamp, October 14, 2008, http://www.swamppolitics.com/news politics/blog/2008/10/obama_talks_about_his_acorn.html; Jim Hoft, "The brazen dishonesty . . ." Gateway Pundit, February 20, 2010, http://gatewaypundit.firstthings.com/2010/02/oh-me-oh-my-obama-caught-in-a-major-acorn-lie-video/.

79. "Third Presidential Debate" *New York Times*, October 15, 2008, http://elections.nytimes.com/2008/president/debates/transcripts/third-presidential-debate.html.

80. "Project Vote not 'an arm of ACORN.' "

81. "ACORN Accusations," FactCheck.org, October 18, 2008, http:/www .factcheck.org/elections-2008/acorn_accusations.html.

82. Stephanie Strom, "On Obama, Acorn and Voter Registration," *New York Times*, October 11, 2008, http://www.nytimes.com/2008/10/11/ us/politics/11acorn.html.

83. Sam Graham-Felsen, "ACORN Political Action Committee Endorses Obama," Obama '08, Community Blogs, Sam Graham Felsen's Blog, February 21, 2008, http://my.barackobama.com/page/communitypost/ samgrahamfelsen/gGC7zm.

84. Clark Hoyt, "The Tip That Didn't Pan Out," *New York Times*, May 16, 2009, http://www.nytimes.com/2009/05/17/opinion/17pubed.html? _r=2; John Hinderaker, "Killing A Story: How It's Done," Power Line Blog, May 17, 2009, http://www.powerlineblog.com/archives/2009/05/ 023580.php.

85. Sean Hannity, "Did Obama Lie About Relationship With ACORN?" Fox News, February 23, 2010, http://www.foxnews.com/story/0,29 33,587239,00.html?CFID=25138835&CFTOKEN=383c30279b85 66cc-2476617F-1D09-2FD4-733809CAD99D4172.

86. "ACORN Accusations."

87. Peter Slevin, "For Clinton and Obama, a Common Ideological Touchstone," *Washington Post*, March 25, 2007, http://www.washington post.com/wp-dyn/content/article/2007/03/24/AR2007032401152.html.

88. "Project Vote not an 'arm of ACORN.' "

89. See the link to Graham-Felsen's blog post on Obama's endorsement pitch to ACORN in Kurtz, "Inside Obama's Acorn."

90. Kelleher, "Growth of a Modern Union Local," p. 10.

91. Memorandum, n.d., from Myra to "all organizing staff, ACORN and Local 880," Illinois ACORN Records, Box 2, Folder 72.

92. Kelleher put in a proposal for voter registration funding on behalf of both SEIU Local 880 and ACORN, for example: Memo from Keith Kelleher to Robin Leeds, regarding "Voter Registration, GOTV, Election Day Proposal for SEIU Local 880 and ACORN in Chicago and Southwest Illinois."

93. "Coalition Pledges to Increase Minority Voter Registration By Over 100,000," Press Release dated Monday, June 1, 1992, SEIU Local 880 Records, Box 6, Folder 28.

94. Wikipedia, "1992 Los Angeles riots," at http://en.wikipedia.org/wiki/1992_Los_Angeles_riots.

95. Letter from Yvonne V. Delk, Joseph Gardner, and Barack Obama to Keith Kelleher, April 28, 1992, SEIU Local 880 Records, Box 6, Folder 28.

96. BTP Records, Box 1, Folder 37, Undated Memorandum From J. Dodson to Executive Committee "Re: Suggested Class Assignments for Board of Directors"; Box 6, Folder 10, Letter of August 2, 1986 from Yvonne Delk and William Watley to Chicago Area BTP Members, beginning: "For some time the Board . . ."

97. A brief biography of Gardner can be found in Midwest Academy Records, Box 274, Folder 13.

98. Columbia University Rare Book and Manuscript Library, Human SERVE Records, Box 45, Folder 2034, Joseph Eugene Gardner Resume.

99. Mark S. Allen, "My Personal Relationship With Obama's (1): From Adversary to Longtime Ally: Veteran Activist/Journalist Mark S. Allen and President Barack Obama," Text begins, "At no time in our relationship of over 20 years has Barack Obama said nothing but nice things about me . . . ," at http://www.blackvoices.com/boards/welcome/welcome/by-welcome-forum/my-personal . . .

100. Human SERVE Records, Box 45, Folder 2034, Joseph Eugene Gardner Resume.

101. "Press Conference: Lakefront Citizens for Joseph E. Gardner, January 22, 1988," Midwest Academy Records, Box 274, Folder 13.

102. Human SERVE Records, Box 45, Folder 2034.

103. For the steering committee members, I am drawing on a May 11, 1992, list of twenty-two individuals, representing twenty-two organizations, who attended the founding meeting of the Project VOTE Chicago Coalition, or were added to the list within days after that initial meeting. Since the April 28 invitation calling on Keith Kelleher to join the Project Vote steering committee refers to a May 5 meeting, I presume that the list in question (which includes Kelleher) is the Project Vote steering committee. The list contains a note indicating that while all or most of the names listed are expected to join the coalition, a final commitment to join will not be requested until the following meeting: "Project VOTE! Chicago Coalition," SEIU Local 880 Records, Box 6, Folder 28.

104. Vernon Jarrett, "Voter Registration Is Key to Respect," *Chicago Sun-Times,* August 4, 1992.

105. "Heather Booth," DiscoverTheNetworks.org, http://www.discoverthe networks.org/individualProfile.asp?indid=1641.

106. Letter from Keith Kelleher to Heather Booth, May 29, 1992 and handwritten notes of 5/20/92 meeting with Heather Booth, SEIU Local 880 Records, Box 6, Folder 28.

107. Piven Papers, Box 50, Folder 12, "ACORN's Perspective on Voter Registration."

108. Dee Gill, "ACORN Storms Citicorp Over Low-Income Lending," *Houston Chronicle,* July 14, 1992, p. 2C, ACORN Records 1973–1997, Box 4, Folder: Banking Campaign 1991 (First Folder).

109. Memorandum, 7/18/92, from Wade to Madeline and Steve, regarding "Followup on Banking Actions," ACORN Records 1973–1997, Box 4, Folder: Banking Campaign 1991 (First Folder).

110. Ibid.; Memorandum, August 2 1992, from Wade Rathke to Steuart Pittman, regarding "Banking Loose Ends and General Campaigns," ACORN Records 1973–1997, Box 4, Bank Campaign 1991 (First Folder).

111. Rathke's comment prefaced his concern that ACORN might actually be being "bribed" too "cheaply" by the banks. The memo on bankers who see ACORN as an extortion ring notes that at least a few bankers had praise for ACORN. One wonders how sincere this praise was, given the pressure from ACORN: Memorandum, 7/22/92, from Deepak to Steve, Mike, Interested Parties, regarding "Bank Campaign, Summit Follow-Up," ACORN Records 1973–1997, Box 4, Folder: Bank Campaign 1991 (First Folder).

112. Memorandum, 8/31/92, from Mike Shea to Wade, Steve, Madeline, Keith, Jon, Deepac, Steuart, regarding "Citibank Negotiations results & status," ACORN Records 1973–1997, Box 4, Folder: Bank Campaign 1991 (First Folder); Memorandum, 9/23/92, from Steuart to HO's, regarding "Citicorp," ACORN Records 1973–1997, Box 4, Folder: Bank Campaign 1991 (First Folder).

113. "Buycks-Roberson v. Citibank Fed. Sav. Bank," http://www.clearing house.net/detail.php?id=10112.

114. Memorandum, October 21, 1992, from Steve to Deepak, Mike, Bruce, Steuart, Brian, Madeline, and Wade, regarding "Clinton Housing/

Banking Transition," ACORN Records 1973–1997, Box 3, Folders: Memos 1992 (Second Folder).

115. The memo that mentions the Waters legislation is one of three attached memos. The top of the packet is a 9/23/92 memo from Steuart to HO's, regarding Citicorp. The memo in question is a 9/23/92 memo from Steuart to HO's, regarding "HMDA Data Release," ACORN Records 1973–1997, Box 4, Folder: Bank Campaign 1991 (First Folder).

116. Bob Ringham, "The Loan Rangers," *Chicago Sun-Times*, September 23, 1993, Financial, p. 57.

117. Letter from Maud Hurd to Mack McLarty, February 5, 1993, ACORN Records, 1973–1997, Box 3, Folder: Memos 1993; Memorandum, April 13, 1993, from Steve to Mike, Deepak, Steuart, Madeline, Zach, Wade, regarding "Webb Hubbell Meeting," ACORN Records 1973–1997, Box 3, Folder: Memos 1993; Legislative Update, March 29, 1993, ACORN Records, M2005-121, Box 1, Folder 9.

118. Legislative Update, March 29, 1993, ACORN Records, M2005-121, Box 1, Folder 9.

119. An account of ACORN's first meeting with Cisneros can be found in a special addendum to a "Legislative Report" of May 4, 1993. The addition is titled "Legislative Report: Addendum—Report on Meeting with Cisneros, May 3, 1993," ACORN Records, M2005-121, Box 1, Folder 9.

120. Mark R. Warren, *Dry Bones Rattling* (Princeton: Princeton University Press, 2001).

121. Cruz, "The Nature of Alinsky-Style Community Organizing."

122. Memo from SRB to WR, DLR, SK, MS, DB, 5-7-93, regarding "money from Cisneros from HUD," ACORN Records 1973–1997, Box 3, Folder: Memos 1993; Memorandum, 5/8/93, from Zach to Steve/Madeline/Mike/Wade/Jon/Steuart/Deepak/Jerry, regarding "Thoughts on Cisneros & HUD Funding Community Organizations," ACORN Records, 1973–1997, Box 3, Folder: Memos 1993.

123. Memorandum, May 6, 1993, from Wade Rathke to Steve Kest, regarding "Cisneros, HUD, and Funding Organizing," ACORN Records, 1973–1997, Box 3, Folder: Memos 1993.

124. "Legislative Report, June 7, 1993," ACORN Records, M2005-121, Box 1, Folder 9; "Legislative Report, July 12, 1993," ACORN Records, M2005-121, Box 1, Folder 9.

125. "Legislative Report, June 21, 1993," ACORN Records, M2005-121, Box 1, Folder 9.

126. Dennis Sewell, "Clinton Democrats are to Blame for the Credit Crunch," Spectator.co.uk, October 1, 2008, http://www.spectator.co .uk/essays/all/2189196/clinton-democrats-are-to-blame-for-the-credit -crunch.thtml.

127. Achtenberg is referred to at numerous points in ACORN's various legislative reports. Some of the key documents are the "Report on Meeting with Cisneros," referred to above, and "Legislative Report, May 18, 1993," ACORN Records 2005-121, Box 1, Folder 9; "Legislative Report, June 7, 1993," ACORN Records, M2005-121, Box 1, Folder 9; "Legislative Report, June 21, 1993," ACORN Records, M2005-121, Box 1, Folder 9.

128. ACORN Records 1973–1997, Box 4, Folder: USA 1993–1997; "Chicago ACORN Unites Behind School Reform," *United States of ACORN*, May/June 1993, p. 6.

129. Stanley Kurtz, "Something New Here," *National Review Online*, October 20, 2008, http://article.nationalreview.com/375696/something -new-here/stanley-kurtz; Stanley Kurtz, "Life of the New Party," *National Review Online*, October 30, 2008, http://article.national review.com/376951/life-of-the-new-party/stanley-kurtz.

130. "The Truth About Barack Obama and the New Party," Fight the Smears, http://www.fightthesmears.com/articles/28/KurtzSmears.html.

131. Ben Smith, "The Dread New Party," Politico, October 25, 2008, http:// www.politico.com/blogs/bensmith/1008/The_dread_New_Party.html; Ben Smith, "Choosing Corsi," Politico, October 26, 2008, http:// www.politico.com/blogs/bensmith/1008/Choosing_Corsi.html; Stanley Kurtz, "A Party Without Members?" The Corner, October 26, 2008, http://corner.nationalreview.com/post/?q=NjdmMGU4NTBkMTZhN WU0MDk1NjU2ODAzNzM5YTkzM2Y=; Stanley Kurtz, "Bias Un-masked," The Corner, October 26, 2008, http://corner.nationalreview .com/post/?q=MzM4Mzc2ZmJiYzE0MzRkNTc0NGRkN2F1NzkzMG Q4NTE=.

132. Smith "The Dread New Party."

133. Michelle Malkin, "Look what Scozzafava's favorite ACORN front group is up to now," Michelle Malkin Blog, October 27, 2008, http:// michellemalkin.com/2009/10/27/look-what-scozzafavas-favorite-acorn -front-group-is-up-to-now/.

134. Joshua Cohen and Joel Rogers, "Associative Democracy," in Pranab K. Bardhan and John E. Roemer, eds., *Market Socialism* (New York: Oxford University Press, 1993), pp. 236–52.

135. The Cantor/Rogers proposal is quoted in a letter/memo from Jim Lardner titled "MORE THAN A PARTY," ACORN Records, 1973–1997, Box 1, Folder: New Party (one of several similarly titled folders).

136. Ibid.

137. SEIU 880 Records, Box 6, Folder 46, "Questions and Answers About the New Party: April 1992."

138. SEIU 880 Records, Box 6, Folder 48, "General Points of Vision Statement," Dan Swinney, June 4, 1993.

139. Geoff Kurtz, "Happy Birthday, Party! What 'The Party-That's Not-A-Party' Is Doing As It Turns Five," *The Activist*, 1998, p. 7. *The Activist* was a short-lived supplement to the Democratic Socialists of America Newsletter, *Democratic Left*, published by DSA's Youth Section. It can be found on the same microfilm reel as *Democratic Left*, as part of vol. 26, no. 3, at Harvard's Lamont Library Microfilm Stacks.

140. While the New Party had no official platform, a pamphlet authored by New Party supporter Juliet Schor was widely taken to represent the New Party's position on the issues. The pamphlet was developed out of an article by the same title Schor published in a collection of essays by New Party supporters: Juliet Schor, "A Sustainable Economy for the Twenty-first Century," in Greg Ruggiero and Stuart Sahulka, eds., *The New American Crisis: Radical Analyses of the Problems Facing America Today* (New York: W. W. Norton & Company, 1995), pp. 266–87.

141. Geoff Kurtz, "Happy Birthday," p. 8.

142. Schor, "Sustainable Economy."

143. Kurtz, "Life of the New Party."

144. Ibid.

145. Piven Papers, Box 88, Folder 4, April 1, 1993, Memo from Daniel Cantor to Shakoor Aljuwani et al. Re: "PHOTO OPPORTUNITY at the SOCIALIST SCHOLARS CONFERENCE."

146. Kurtz, "Something New Here", Kurtz, "Life of the New Party."

147. Kurtz, "Something New Here."

148. Micah Sifry, *Spoiling for a Fight* (London: Routledge, 2002), p. 236.

149. Talbott is described as the local New Party "convener" in a the template for a form letter from Dan Sweeney, April 27, 1993, SEIU Local 880

Records, Box 6, Folder 49. Talbott even represented the national New Party at a meeting with Canadians: Memorandum, December 30, 1992, from Carolyn to Wade, regarding "CND $ For Chicago NP in DECEMBER and JANUARY," SEIU Local 880 Records, Box 6, Folder 46. A 1993 chart lists the most active groups and participants in the Chicago New Party, with ACORN and SEIU Local 880 leading the way: "Chicago New Party Chapter Report, 6/11/93," SEIU Local 880 Records, Box 6, Folder 46.

150. Geoff Kurtz, "Happy Birthday," p. 8.

151. These two memos are stapled together. On top is a memo, dated July 13, 1993, from Wade to Zach, regarding "Reactions to Your Thoughts," below that is a Memorandum, dated July 8, 1993, from Zach to Wade, regarding "Thoughts on Party Building," ACORN Records 1973–1997, Box 3, Folder: Memos 1993.

152. Fax from Commissioner Joseph Gardner to Keith Kelliher [*sic*], July 27, 1993, SEIU Local 880 Records, Box 6, Folder 49.

153. Memorandum, May 19, 1992, from Madeline and Carolyn to Wade, regarding "May plan on voter reg & third party for CND $."

154. "NP Mailing List," SEIU Local 880, Box 6, Folder 49. This is not a full mailing list, but a much shorter list of names mean to be added to the larger list.

155. Handwritten note from MT to Keith, dated 6/4, SEIU Local 880 Records, Box 6, Folder 48.

156. "Minutes of Chicago New Party (CNP) Meeting, June 15, 1993," June 18, 1993, SEIU Local 880 Records, Box 6, Folder 48.

157. "Report from the Chicago New Party, August 12, 1992, Submitted by: Madeline Talbott," Chicago ACORN, SEIU Local 880, Box 6, Folder 43.

158. Memorandum, March 31, 1993, from Steve to Zach, regarding "Meeting with Fran Piven/Richard Cloward," ACORN Records 1973–1997, Box 3, Folder: Memos 1993.

159. "Chicago New Party Organizing Report," June 2, 1993, SEIU Local 880, Box 6, Folder 47; "New Party Interim Executive Council Meeting Report," June 11–13, 1993, SEIU Local 880 Records, Box 6, Folder 48.

160. "What is Progressive Chicago?" SEIU Local 880 Records, Box 6, Folder 48.

161. "Chicago New Party Organizing Report," June 2, 1993, SEIU Local 880 Records, Box 6, Folder 47.

162. Keith Kelleher's handwritten notes of meeting with Jacky Grimshaw, 5/12/93, SEIU Local 880 Records, Box Six, Folder 49.

163. Remnick, *The Bridge*, p. 221.

164. Handwritten notes from Keith Kelleher's meeting with Barack Obama, 7/27/93, SEIU Local 880 Records, Box 6, Folder 49.

165. Letter from Sarah E. Siskind to Mr. Wade Rathke, May 7, 1992, ACORN Records 1973–1997, Box 1, Folder: New Party (one of several similarly labeled New Party folders).

166. Letter from Daniel Cantor to Barack Obama, August 12, 1993, beginning "Sarah Siskind asked that I send along . . ." SEIU Local 880 Records, Box 6, Folder 48.

167. Memorandum, September 30, 1993, from Keith Kelleher to Danny Cantor, regarding "New Party Progress and Plans Since June IEC," ACORN Records, Box 1, Folder: New Party 1993.

168. Memorandum, November 2, 1993, from Keith to MT, MG, CB, and Sam, regarding "Conversations with Steve Saltsman," SEIU Local 880 Records, Box 6, Folder 47. See also Kelleher's handwritten note of November 2, 1993, to M.T./Cindy, SEIU Local 880 Records, Box 6, Folder 47.

169. See the top two pages of a three-page packet, Memorandum, November 10, 1993, from Steve Bachman to Keith Kelleher, Steve Saltsman, Zak [*sic*] Polett, Dale Rathke, regarding "attached, and letter from Steven Saltsman to Steve Bachman," November 15, 1993, SEIU Local 880 Records, Box 6, Folder 47.

170. Letter from Joe Gardner and Ron Sable to Barack Obama on Progressive Chicago letterhead, December 31, 1993, beginning, "We are writing to invite you . . ." SEIU Local 880 Records, Box 6, Folder 49.

171. As noted, the packet of materials in question (hereafter referred to in these notes as "June 1994 Memo Packet") is contained in a small, gray archive box with late-arriving material from 1994, as opposed to the bulk of the SEIU Local 880 Records, which are contained in large record center cartons. The folder is labeled "Correspondence File." The four memos in question, consisting of nine pages, are stapled together. I will list them from the top to the bottom of the packet: Memorandum from KK to WR, regarding "Structure of Progressive

Chicago," June 17, 1994; Memorandum from Keith to MT, Zach, Marvin, Leslie, regarding "Conversations with Carol Harwell, June 17, 1994"; Project Vote Fax Memorandum from Leslie Watson-Davis to Marvin Randolf, Zach Polett, Subject: "Chicago Trip—For Your Information," 6/13/1994; Memorandum from Keith Kelleher to Carol Harwell, regarding "List of Positions that Need Resolution," June 8, 1994.

172. "Chicago Trip" Memorandum, SEIU Local 880 Records, June 1994 Memo Packet.

173. See also Gretchen Reynolds, "Vote of Confidence," *Chicago Magazine*, January 1993, http://www.chicagomag.com/Chicago-Magazine/January -1993/Vote-of-Confidence/.

174. "Conversations with Carol Harwell," SEIU Local 880 Records, June 1994 Memo Packet.

175. "Structure of Progressive Chicago," SEIU Local 880 Records, June 1994 Memo Packet.

176. "The Truth About Barack Obama and the New Party," Fight the Smears.

177. Memorandum, October 23, 1994, to ACORN Offices from Zach Polett, regarding "National Voter Registration Act (NVRA) Implementation Campaign: Report and Follow-Up on NVRA Implementation Conference," ACORN New York Records, Box 5, Folder 42.

178. Mike Robinson, "Obama Got Start in Civil Rights Practice," *Washington Post*, February 20, 2007, http://www.washingtonpost .com/wp-dyn/content/article/2007/02/20/AR2007022000045.html.

179. Human SERVE Records, Box 16, Folder 747, Memorandum, December 2, 1994, from David to "All Re: Illinois Implementation (or lack thereof)"; Box 16, Folder 747, unsigned letter of November 14, 1994, on ACORN letterhead to Ronald D. Michaelson beginning, "As the chief elections officer . . ." Box 35, Folder 1495, Memorandum, February 1, 1995, from Juan Cartagena to NVRA Implementation Attorney Network.

180. Human SERVE Records, Box 16, Folder 747, Memorandum, December 2, 1994, from David to "All Re: Illinois Implementation (or lack thereof)"; Box 16, Folder 747, Fax, September 30, 1994, from Susan Locke to David Plotkin; Box 16, Folder 748, Fax, March 29, 1995, from Barack H. Obama to David R. Melton; Piven Papers, Box 50, Folder 12, "ACORN's Perspective on Voter Registration"; Piven Accession 993–

50, Box 1, Memorandum of August 14, 1995 from David Plotkin to Frances and Richard "Re: ACORN."

181. Memorandum, July 23, 1994, from Zach Polett and Maude Hurd to ACORN Delegation for White House Meeting, regarding "Preparations & Assignments for White House Meeting," ACORN Records 1973–1997, M2003-006, Box 4, Folder: White House Meeting 1994. See also numerous other items regarding preparations for the White House meeting in this folder.

182. "ACORN Agenda for President Clinton," ACORN Records 1973–1997, M2003-066, Box 4, Folder: White House Meeting 1994. See item 4 on Cisneros and item 4d, an implicit reference to Achtenberg, as well.

183. Memorandum, July 25, 1994, from Zach Polett to All Offices, regarding "Taking It to the Top—The Meeting with the President," ACORN Records 1973–1997, M2003-066, Box 4, Folder: White House Meeting 1994; "Agenda Items, ACORN Meeting at the White House, July 25, 1994," ACORN Records, Box 4, Folder: White House Meeting 1994.

184. Memorandum, July 25, 1994, from Zach Polett to All Offices, regarding "Taking It to the Top—The Meeting with the President," ACORN Records 1973–1997, M2003-066, Box 4, Folder: White House Meeting 1994.

185. Ibid.

186. Peter J. Wallison, "Cause and Effect: Government Policies and the Financial Crisis," American Enterprise Institute, November 2008, http://www.aei.org/outlook/29015; Peter J. Wallison, "Not a Failure of Capitalism—A Failure of Government," American Enterprise Institute, December 2, 2009, http://www.aei.org/paper/100080.

187. Toni Foulkes, "Case Study: Chicago—The Barack Obama Campaign," *Social Policy*, Winter 2003/Spring 2004, pp. 49–52; Kurtz "Inside Obama's Acorn."

188. See Chapter Seven.

189. Foulkes, "Case Study."

190. Smith, "The Dread New Party"; Kurtz, "A Party Without Members."

191. Bruce Bentley, "Chicago New Party Update," *New Ground*, #42, September–October 1995, at http://www.chicagodsa.org/ngarchive/ng42.html#anchor792932.

192. "New Party Member Heads for the Hill," *New Party News*, Spring

1996, pp. 1–2. A copy of this issue can be found at the library of the University of Wisconsin, Madison. A picture of the text can also be found at Trevor Loudon, "Obama File 41 Obama Was a New Party Member—Documentary Evidence," New Zeal Blog, October 23, 2008, http://newzeal.blogspot.com/2008/10/obama-file-41-obama-was-new -party.html.

193. "The Truth About Barack Obama and the New Party," Fight the Smears.

194. Bruce Bentley, "Chicago New Party Update."

195. Jim Cullen, Editorial, *Progressive Populist*, November 1996, http:// www.populist.com/11.96.Edit.html

196. Bruce Bentley, "New Party Update," *New Ground*, #47, July–August 1996, at http://www.chicagodsa.org/ngarchive/ng47.html#anchor78 1435.

197. John Nichols, "How to Push Obama," *The Progressive*, January 2009, p. 21.

198. Hoft, "The Obama campaign privately updated . . ."

199. Toni Foulkes, "Case Study."

200. Stanley Kurtz, "Obama Acorn Cover-up?" The Corner, October 8, 2008, http://corner.nationalreview.com/post/?q=MTNiN2YwMmQ4 Njc2MzE4ZDUxYWV1YTA1NzZlMmY3YmM=.

201. Hank De Zutter, "What Makes Obama Run?" *Chicago Reader*, December 8, 1995, http://www1.chicagoreader.com/obama/951208/.

202. Ibid.

Chapter 7: Ayers and the Foundations

1. Stanley Kurtz, "Chicago Annenberg Challenge Shutdown," National Review Online, August 18, 2008, http://article.nationalreview.com/ 366637/chicago-annenberg-challenge-shutdown/stanley-kurtz; Milt Rosenberg, "Extension 720 Audio Archives, August 2008," wgnradio .com, http://www.wgnradio.com/shows/ext720/wgnam-ext720-audio -archives-aug2008,0,3288472.story; John Kass, "When Daley says shhh, library is quiet on Obama," *Chicago Tribune*, August 21, 2008, http://www.chicagotribune.com/news/columnists/chi-kass-ayers-thurs -21-aug21-archive,0,3528940.column; Guy Benson, "Stanley Kurtz's Fairness Doctrine Preview," Media Blog, *National Review Online*,

August 28, 2008, http://www.nationalreview.com/media-blog/32766/
stanley-kurtzs-fairness-doctrine-preview/guy-benson; National Review,
"Barack Obama, Aspiring Commissar," *National Review Online*,
August 28, 2008, http://article.nationalreview.com/368298/barack
-obama-aspiring-commissar/the-editors; Ben Smith, "Obama camp
blasts National Review writer as "slimy character assassin," Politico,
http://www.politico.com/blogs/bensmith/0808/Obama_camp_blasts_
National_Review_writer_as_slimy_character_assassin.html; Stanley
Kurtz, "Obama and Ayers Pushed Radicalism on Schools," *Wall Street
Journal*, September 23, 2008, http://online.wsi.com/article/SB1222
12856075765367.html; Stanley Kurtz, "Obama's Challenge," National
Review Online, September 23, 2008, http://article.nationalreview.com/
372023/obamas-challenge/stanley-kurtz; Stanley Kurtz, "Founding
Brothers," *National Review Online*, September 24, 2008, http://article
.nationalreview.com/372137/founding-brothers/stanley-kurtz; Stanley
Kurtz, "NYT's Ayers-Obama Whitewash," The Corner, *National
Review Online*, http://corner.nationalreview.com/post/?q=ZWI0MjY3
NzMyODgxZGM2ZjUwNTE1MmEzOGRiZmFkNWE=.

2. Lynn Sweet, "Mayor Daley defends Obama, vouching for William
Ayers," Lynn Sweet's blog, *Chicago Sun-Times*, April 18, 2008, http://
blogs.suntimes.com/sweet/2008/04/mayor_daley_defends _obama_
vouc.html; Kass, "When Daley says shhh."

3. Ron Chepesiuk, *Sixties Radicals Then and Now* (Jefferson, N.C.:
McFarland & Co., 1995), p. 102.

4. Bill Ayers, *Fugitive Days* (Boston: Beacon Press, [2001] 2009); Bernardine Dohrn, Bill Ayers, and Jeff Jones, eds., *Sing a Battle Song* (New
York: Seven Stories Press, 2006); Bill Ayers and Bernardine Dohrn,
Race Course Against White Supremacy (Chicago: Third World Press,
2009).

5. Peter Collier and David Horowitz, *Destructive Generation* (New York:
Free Press, 1996), p. 119.

6. Ayers, *Fugitive Days*, p. 286.

7. Ayers and Dohrn, *Race Course Against White Supremacy*, p. 108.

8. Miller, *Democracy Is in the Streets*, p. 207.

9. Ibid., p. 6.

10. Dohrn, Ayers, and Jones, *Sing a Battle Song*, p. 352.

11. Ayers, *Fugitive Days*, pp. 82–94.

12. David Barber, *A Hard Rain Fell* (Jackson: University Press of Mississippi, 2008), pp. 148–49.

13. Bill Ayers and Jim Mellen, "Hot town: Summer in the City," *New Left Notes*, April 4, 1969, pp. 8–9.

14. Todd Gitlin, *The Sixties* (New York: Bantam Books, 1987), pp. 377–408; Collier and Horowitz, *Destructive Generation*, pp. 67–119; Barber, *Hard Rain*, pp. 145–87.

15. "SDS Convention Documents," FRED, the Socialist Press Service, Vol. 1, #23, July 21, 1969, p. 10b.

16. Collier and Horowitz, *Destructive Generation*, p. 84; Barber, *A Hard Rain Fell*, pp. 173–74.

17. Barber, *A Hard Rain Fell*, pp. 174–75.

18. Ayers, *Fugitive Days*, p. 159.

19. Collier and Horowitz, *Destructive Generation*, p. 83; Barber, *A Hard Rain Fell*, pp. 176–77.

20. Ayers, *Fugitive Days*, p. 111.

21. Dohrn, Ayers, and Jones, *Sing a Battle Song*, pp. 352–53.

22. Ibid., p. 255.

23. Ibid., p. 355.

24. Ayers, *Fugitive Days*, pp. 281–82.

25. Ibid., p. 264.

26. Ibid., p. 295.

27. Dohrn, Ayers, and Jones, *Sing a Battle Song*, p. 36.

28. Ibid., pp. vii, x.

29. Chepesiuk, *Sixties Radicals Then and Now*, pp. 99, 102.

30. Ayers, *Fugitive Days*, p. 296; Ayers and Dohrn, *Race Course Against White Supremecy*, pp. 83–91.

31. Ibid., p. 95.

32. Sandra O'Donnell, Yvonne Jeffries, Frank Sanchez, and Pat Selmi, "Evaluation of the Fund's Community Organizing Grant Programs," Woods Fund of Chicago, April 1995, pp. 7–8.

33. Wieboldt Foundation, "1987 Annual Report," pp. 15, 16; Wieboldt Foundation, "1988 Annual Report," p. 15.

34. Chicago Annenberg Challenge (CAC) Records, University of Illinois, Chicago Library, Box 130, Folder 919, Letter of September 10, 1995, Anne C. Hallett to Walter Annenberg, beginning "Gail Levin said you heard Bill Ayers and me . . ."

35. See, for example, front matter listing foundation officials from Wieboldt's 1981, 1982, and 1983 annual reports.

36. Wieboldt Foundation, "1984 and 1985 Annual Reports," front matter, p. 2; Wieboldt Foundation, "1986 Annual Report," p. 2.

37. William Upski Wimsatt, "Anonymous Benefactor," *Chicago Reader*, March 26, 1998, http://www.chicagoreader.com/chicago/anonymous -benefactor/Content?oid=895912.

38. "Stanley Hallett," Wikipedia, http://en.wikipedia.org/wiki/Stanley_ Hallett.

39. Malcolm Bush and Daniel Immergluck, "Research, Advocacy, and Community Reinvestment," in Gregory D. Squires, ed., *Organizing Access to Capital* (Philadelphia: Temple University Press, 2003), pp. 163–64.

40. See Chapter Four.

41. DSA Records, Box 17, Folder: Illinois-Chicago, "Organizer's Report," *New Ground*, vol. 2, no. 1, January 1988, p. 4.

42. Note that the instances of support for a given group referenced here and below are meant to be illustrative rather than exhaustive. Woods Charitable Fund, "A Report for the Years 1979 and 1980," pp. 2–6; Woods Charitable Fund, "A Report for the Year 1984," p. 3; Woods Charitable Fund, "A Report for the Year 1985," pp. 2–4; Woods Charitable Fund, "A Report for the Year 1986," pp. 1–3.

43. Woods Fund, "1986," pp. 2, 11; Woods Charitable Fund, "A Report for the Year 1988," p. 26.

44. Woods Fund, "1985," pp. 15, 27; Woods Fund, "1986," p. 22; Woods Charitable Fund, "A Report for the Year 1987," pp. 23, 24.

45. Woods Fund, "1985," pp. 4, 14; Woods Fund, "1986," p. 20; Woods Fund, "1987," p. 20; Todd Swanstrom and Laura Barrett, "The Road to Jobs: The Fight for Transportation Equity (Gamaliel Foundation)," Fulfilling the Dream Fund, http://www.fulfillingthedreamfund.org/ news/the-road-to-jobs-the-fight-for-transportation-equi.

46. Woods Fund, "1988" pp. 27, 28; Woods Charitable Fund, "A Report for the Year 1989," p. 22.

47. Woods Fund, "1985," p. 22.

48. Woods Charitable Fund, "A Report for the Year 1993," pp. 3–4.

49. "Woods Fund of Chicago," Wikipedia, http://en.wikipedia.org/wiki/ Woods_Fund_of_Chicago.

50. Woods Charitable Fund, "A Report for the Year 1992," p. 24.

51. Woods Fund, "1993," p. 3; Woods Fund of Chicago, "1994 Annual Report," p. 1.

52. Woods Fund, "1994," pp. 3, 4, 6–8.

53. Ibid.

54. Woods Fund, "Evaluation," p. 39.

55. Sandy O'Donnell, Jane Beckett, and Jean Rudd, "Promising Practices in Revenue Generation for Community Organizing," Center for Community Change, Washington, D.C., pp. 76–79, 91–94, http://comm -org.wisc.edu/papers2005/beckett.htm.

56. Woods Fund, "Evaluation," p. 8.

57. Woods Fund, "1994," p. 18; Woods Fund of Chicago, "1995 Annual Report," p. 18.

58. Foulkes, "Case Study."

59. Acorn Records 1973–1997, Box 4, Folder: Acorn Community Schools 1992, Memorandum, July 23, 1993, from Madeline to "Head Organizers Re: Schools Campaign."

60. Ibid., Memorandum, April 7, 1994, from Madeline Talbott to "Head Organizers, Interested Parties Re: Report on ACORN School Development."

61. Woods Fund, "1993," p. 35.

62. CAC Records, Box 131, Folder 937, Memorandum, March 10, 1995, from Anne Hallett to "Annenberg Challenge Board of Directors Re: Chicago School Reform Collaborative."

63. Dorothy Shipps and Karin Sconzert with Holly Swyers, "The Chicago Annenberg Challenge: The First Three Years," Consortium on Chicago School Research, 1999, pp. 15, 26–27, http://ccsr.uchicago .edu/publications/p0b06.pdf; Alexander Russo, "From Frontline Leader to Rearguard Action: The Chicago Annenberg Challenge," in Thomas B. Fordham Foundation, "Can Philanthropy Fix Our Schools? Appraising Walter Annenberg's $500 Million Gift to Public Education," p. 42, at http://www.edexcellence.net/doc/annenberg.pdf.

64. Remnick, *The Bridge*, p. 280.

65. Ayers, *Fugitive Days*, pp. 264–65, 294; Dinitia Smith, "No Regrets for a Love of Explosives; In a Memoir of Sorts, A War Protester Talks of Life With the Weathermen," *New York Times*, September 11, 2001, http://www.nytimes.com/2001/09/11/books/no-regrets-for-love-explo sive-memoir-sorts-war-protester-talks-life-with.html.

66. Ibid.
67. *Anderson Cooper 360°*, "Transcripts: Dow Drops; Presidential Campaign Turns Negative," October 6, 2008, http://transcripts.cnn .com/TRANSCRIPTS/0810/06/acd.01.html.
68. Remnick, *The Bridge*, p. 281.
69. Mark A. Smylie et al., "The Chicago Annenberg Challenge: Successes, Failures, and Lessons for the Future," Consortium on Chicago School Research, August 2003, pp. 98, 104.
70. Ibid.
71. See the extensive files on grants to ACORN and the Developing Communities Project in the CAC Records.
72. Kurtz, "Ayers and Obama Pushed Radicalism."
73. CAC Records, Box 50, Folder 250: Vision, Strategy, Goals; Box 51, Folder 253: Peace School; Box 51, Folder 254: Peace School Narrative Report; Box 51, Folder 256: Peace School Newsletter; Box 51, Folder 256: Peace School Pamphlet.
74. Marcia Froelke Coburn, "No Regrets," *Chicago Magazine*, August 2001, http://www.chicagomag.com/Chicago-Magazine/August-2001/ No-Regrets.
75. Chris Carger, section in: "An Activist Forum IV: Pledging to the World," in William Ayers, Jean Ann Hunt, and Therese Quinn, eds., *Teaching for Social Justice* (New York: The New Press, 1998), pp. 241–44.
76. Gabrielle H. Lyon, "When *Jamas* is Enough," in William Ayers, Michael Klonsky, and Gabrielle Lyon, eds., *A Simple Justice* (New York: Teachers College Press, 2000), pp. 125–135.
77. John Kass and Karen Thomas, "Firing Principals not Top Goal of Group: UNO Is Using Schools to Build Political Muscle," *Chicago Tribune*, March 1, 1990; "Telpochcalli Community Arts Elementary School," http://cct2.edc.org/SCIP_II/schools/telpoch.htm: CAC Records, Box 51, Folder 256, "The Teacher Leadership Academy Directory of Network Schools," p. 19.
78. William Ayers, *To Teach* (New York: Teachers College Press, 2001), p. 114.
79. William Ayers, *Summerhill Revisited* (New York: Teachers College Press, 2003), pp. 3–15, 37–60; William Ayers, *Teaching Toward Freedom* (Boston: Beacon Press, 2004), p. 18; William Ayers, *Teaching the Personal and the Political* (New York: Teachers College Press, 2004), p. 79.

80. Shipps and Sconzert, "Three Years," pp. 20, 21, 27, 28, 47; Russo, "Frontline," pp. 41–43, 49; Smylie et al., "Successes, Failures," pp. 111–12.

81. Smylie et al., "Successes, Failures," pp. 112–14.

82. Steve Diamond, "Behind the Annenberg Gate," Global Labor and Politics Blog, August 20, 2008, http://webcache.googleusercontent.com/search?q=cache:FhwHUTiGv3AJ:globallabor.blogspot.com/2008/08/behind-annenberg-gate-inside-chicago.html+%22Steve+Diamond%22+Annenberg+%22Arnold+Weber%22+principals&cd=1&hl=en&ct=clnk&gl=us.

83. Ibid., pp. 108–9.

84. See Chapter Four.

85. Ayers, Klonsky, and Lyon, *A Simple Justice*.

86. "Barack Obama and the Committees of Correspondence," Key Wiki, http://keywiki.org/index.php/Barack_Obama_and_CoC.

87. "Carl Davidson," DiscoverTheNetworks.org, http://www.discoverthenetworks.org/individualProfile.asp?indid=2322; Trevor Loudon, "Obama File 36, 'How Socialist Was Obama's "New Party"?'" New Zeal Blog, October 11, 2008, http://newzeal.blogspot.com/2008/10/obama-file-36-how-socialist-was-obamas.html.

88. Remnick, *The Bridge*, pp. 343–48.

89. Woods Fund, "1995," pp. 4, 27.

90. Woods Fund of Chicago, "1996 Annual Report," pp. 30, 31; Woods Fund of Chicago, "2001 Annual Report," p. 30.

91. Woods Fund, "1996," pp. 1, 13, 29.

92. Ayers and Dohrn, *Race Course Against White Supremacy*, pp. 53–66.

93. Woods Fund, "1996," p. 13.

94. Woods Fund of Chicago, "1999 Annual Report," pp. 2, 5–6.

95. See Chapter Nine.

96. Woods Fund of Chicago, "1997 Annual Report," p. 29; Woods Fund of Chicago, "Form 990-PF," p. 8.

97. Woods Fund, "1997," p. 1.

98. Woods Fund of Chicago, "2001 Annual Report," p. 3.

99. Woods Fund, "2001," pp. 20, 21, 24, 29; Woods Fund of Chicago, "2002 Annual Report," pp. 12, 31, 35, 37.

100. Woods Fund, "2001," pp. 8–13.

101. Kurtz, "Chicago Annenberg Challenge Shutdown."

102. Kurtz, "Founding Brothers."
103. Rosenberg "Archives"; Benson, "Stanley Kurtz's Fairness Doctrine Preview"; National Review, "Barack Obama: Aspiring Commissar"; Smith, "Obama camp blasts national review writer."
104. Benson, "Stanley Kurtz's Fairness Doctrine Preview."
105. Kurtz, "Obama and Ayers Pushed Radicalism."
106. Kurtz, "Obama's Challenge."
107. Scott Shane, "Obama and 60's Bomber: A Look Into Crossed Paths," *New York Times*, October 3, 2008, http://www.nytimes.com/2008/10/04/us/politics/04ayers.html?_r=1&hp&oref=slogin.
108. Kurtz, "NYT Ayers-Obama Whitewash"; Diamond's writings on the Ayers-Obama issue were posted at his Global Labor and Politics Blog.

Chapter 8: Jeremiah Wright

1. See Chapter Nine.
2. John Bentley, "Obama's Church Says Pastor's Comments Taken Out of Context," cbsnews.com, March 16, 2008, http://www.cbsnews.com/8301-502443_162-3942187-502443.html; Remnick, *The Bridge*, p. 520.
3. "Obama's Pastor: Rev. Jeremiah Wright," FOX News Interview Archive, foxnews.com, March 2, 2007, http://www.foxnews.com/story/0,2933,256078,00.html.
4. James H. Cone, *Black Theology and Black Power* (Maryknoll, N.Y.: Orbis, [1969] 2006).
5. Jeremiah Wright, "An Underground Theology," in Dwight N. Hopkins, ed., *Black Faith and Public Talk* (Waco, Tex., Baylor University Press, 2007), p. 98; Iva Carruthers and Gayraud Wilmore, "The Black Church in the Age of False Prophets: An Interview with Gayraud Wilmore," in Iva E. Carruthers, Frederick D. Haynes III, and Jeremiah A. Wright Jr., eds., *Blow the Trumpet in Zion* (Minneapolis: Fortress Press, 2005), pp. 167–68.
6. Margaret Talev, "Obama's Church Pushes Controversial Doctrines," McClatchy Newspapers, March 20, 2008, http://www.mcclatchydc.com/2008/03/20/31079/obamas-church-pushes-controversial.html.
7. Cone, *Black Theology and Black Power*, pp. 2–3.
8. Ibid., p. 3.

9. Ibid.

10. Ibid.

11. Ibid., p. 6.

12. Ibid., pp. 7–8.

13. Ibid., p. 23.

14. Ibid.

15. Ibid., p. 40.

16. Ibid., pp. 131, 135.

17. "Obama: Stealth Socialist?" *Investor's Business Daily*, IBDeditorials .com, May 16, 2008.

18. Talev "Controversial Doctrines."

19. Transcript, "Obama's Remarks on Wright," *New York Times*, April 29, 2008, http://www.nytimes.com/2008/04/30/world/americas/30iht-29 textobama.12450754.html.

20. Abramsky, *Inside Obama's Brain*, p. 264.

21. For the history of Wright's church, see Jeremiah A. Wright, Jr., "Doing Theology in the Black Church," in Linda E. Thomas, ed., *Living Stones in the Household of God* (Minneapolis: Fortress Press, 2004), pp. 13–23; Julia Speller, *Walkin' the Talk: Keepin' the Faith in Africentric Congregations* (Cleveland: The Pilgrim Press, 2005), pp. 72–103; Jeremiah A. Wright, Jr., "Growing the African American Church through Worship and Preaching," in Carlyle Fielding Stewart III, ed., *Growing the African American Church* (Nashville: Abingdon Press, 2006), pp. 63–81.

22. Stanley Kurtz, "Jeremiah Wright's Trumpet," *Weekly Standard*, May 19, 2008, http://www.weeklystandard.com/Content/Public/Articles/000/ 000/015/082ktdyi.asp.

23. Obama, *Dreams from My Father*, p. 280.

24. James H. Cone, *My Soul Looks Back* (Maryknoll, New York: Orbis Books, [1986] 2005), pp. 123, 130.

25. Ibid., p. 138.

26. Jeremiah A. Wright, Jr., *What Makes You So Strong?* (Valley Forge, Pa.: Judson Press, 1993), p. 98; Kurtz, "Trumpet."

27. Obama, *Dreams from My Father*, p. 293.

28. Remnick, *The Bridge*, p. 470.

29. Jeremiah A. Wright, Jr., "Another Year, Another Chance," *Trumpet Newsmagazine*, January 2007, p. 12.

30. Obasi A. Kitambi, "The Value of Black Life," *Trumpet Newsmagazine*, January 2007, p. 24.

31. Remnick, *The Bridge*, 169.

32. Ibid.

33. Ibid., p. 174.

34. Ibid., p. 175.

35. Ibid.

36. See Chapter Three.

37. Obama, *Dreams from My Father*, p. 283.

38. Mendell, *Obama: From Promise to Power*, p. 76.

39. Lynn Sweet, "Obama on NBC's 'Meet the Press' pressed by Russert with Wright questions; Transcript May 4, 2008 show," Lynn Sweet's *Chicago Sun-Times*, http://blogs.suntimes.com/sweet/2008/05/obama _on_nbcs_meet_the_press_p.html.

40. In addition to the account of sympathetic biographer David Mendell, cited above, see, for example, Cathleen Falsani, "I Have A Deep Faith," *Chicago Sun-Times*, April 5, 2004, p. 14. Here Falsani reports on a lengthy interview with Obama about his religious beliefs and describes Wright as Obama's "close confidant."

41. "History," Centers for New Horizons, http://cnh.org/?id=about& pageid=55.

42. Woods Charitable Fund, Inc., "A Report for the Year 1986," pp. 1, 2.

43. See Chapter Six.

44. Beverly Reed, "Senator Obama's Bronzeville Connection," *South Street Journal*, January 17, 2008, p. 14, at http://ccnmtl.columbia.edu/broad cast/hs/journalism/southside_archive/2008/SSJ-2008-01-17.pdf.

45. Ayana I. Karanja, Ph.D., Resume, pp. 10, 11, at http://www.luc.edu/ curl/pdfs/cv-ayana_karanja.pdf.

46. Woods Fund of Chicago, "1997 Annual Report," p. 21; Woods Fund of Chicago, "Form 990-PF," p. 6; Woods Fund of Chicago, "1999 Annual Report," p. 30; Woods Fund of Chicago, "2000 Annual Report," p. 18.

47. Trinity United Church of Christ, *Perspectives, a View from Within: A Compendium Text for Churchwide Study*, Chicago, Ill., 1982.

48. Ibid., p. 138.

49. Ibid., p. 140.

50. Ibid., pp. 141, 142.

51. Ibid., p. 143.

52. Ibid., pp. 80, 83.

53. Ibid., pp. 120, 122.

54. Jeremiah A. Wright, Jr., "What Are We Teaching Our Children?" *Trumpet Newsmagazine*, March 2006, p. 16.

55. *Perspectives*, p. 38.

56. Jeremiah Wright, "Church Growth and Political Empowerment," in Henry J. Young, ed., *The Black Church and the Harold Washington Story* (Bristol, Ind.: Wyndham Hall Press, 1988), p. 1.

57. Jeremiah A. Wright, Jr., "Looking Back, Looking Around, Looking Ahead!" *Trumpet Newsmagazine*, May 2006, p. 12.

58. HWAC, Series from Harold Washington's Congressional Office, Files of the District Administration Education Task Force, 1982, Box 28, Folder 37, Jeremiah A. Wright, Jr., Resume and Application for School Board Appointment.

59. Wright, "Church Growth," pp. 1–9.

60. Brookins is identified as a member of Wright's church in briefing notes for a Harold Washington visit to Trinity United Church of Christ on February 15, 1987. HWAC, Schedules and Evaluations Series, Box 9, Folder 8.

61. Abraham Lincoln Presidential Library, Howard B. Brookins Papers 1975–1992, Box 2, Folder: Misc. Letters, 1985, letter of June 25 1995 from Jeremiah A. Wright, Jr., to Howard Brookins, beginning "I'm writing to urge you . . ."

62. Abraham Lincoln Presidential Library, Howard B. Brookins Papers 1975–1992, Box 5, Folder: Misc. Correspondence, 1989–91, letter of August 8, 1990 from Jeremiah A. Wright, Jr., to Howard Brookins.

63. Abraham Lincoln Presidential Library, Howard B. Brookins Papers 1975–1992, Box 1, Folder: Centers for New Horizons, letter of July 27, 1983, Gregory F. Washington to Howard Brookins, beginning "Enclosed are copies of letters clients . . ."; letter of August 2, 1983, Howard Brookins to Gregory Coler, beginning "The letter comes to requests . . ."; letter of September 19, 1983, Mauriece L. Graham to Sokoni Karanja, beginning "As we discussed during the meeting"; letter of October 24, 1983, Howard Brookins to Mauriece L. Graham, beginning "I am in receipt of your letter . . ."

64. Abraham Lincoln Presidential Library, Howard B. Brookins Papers

1975–1992, Box 3, Folder: State Board of Education Vacancies, letter of February 25, 1983, Howard Brookins to Jeremiah Wright, Jr., beginning "I appreciate your recent letter"; letter of March 29, 1983, Jeremiah A. Wright, Jr., to Howard Brookins, beginning "Pursuant to your letter of March 18"; letter of April 11, 1983, Howard Brookins to Iva Carruthers, beginning, "As you may be aware . . ."; see similar letters on the same date from Brookins to the other three potential nominees, Vallmer E. Jordan, Randall Davenport, and Frances Holliday; Box 3, Folder: Resumes, letter of April 28, Howard Brookins to Governor James R. Thompson, beginning "I am enclosing resumes."

65. Medell, *Obama: From Promise to Power*, p. 76.
66. Ibid., pp. 159–60.
67. "Obama: Wright Was Never My Political Counsel," FOXNews.com, May 4, 2008, http://elections.foxnews.com/2008/05/04/obama-wright -was-never-my-political-counsel/; Reuters, "Obama renounces fiery pastor's comments," Reuters.com, March 15, 2008, http://www.reuters .com/article/idUSN1453951820080315.
68. Sherry Stone, "Ministers Set for '94: Violence Issue On Agenda," *Philadelphia Tribune*, January 28, 1994, p. 1-A.
69. Remnick, *The Bridge*, pp. 468–72.
70. Ibid., p. 518.
71. Jeremiah A. Wright, Jr., "Before This Time Another Year . . ." *Trumpet Newsmagazine*, January 2005, p. 6. Wright's columns from *Trumpet* going back to late 2004 remained available on the Internet even after the main Trinity United Church of Christ website had been scrubbed in 2008 (shortly after the Obama-Wright controversy broke). By 2010, however, these Wright columns seem to have been removed from the Internet as well.
72. Ibid., pp. 6–7.
73. Falsani, "Deep Faith."
74. Andrew Malcolm, "Why Oprah quit Jeremiah Wright's church and Barack Obama didn't," Top of the Ticket blog, May 4, 2008, http:// latimesblogs.latimes.com/washington/2008/05/obamaoprah.html.
75. De Zutter, "What Makes Obama Run?"
76. Kurtz, "Trumpet."
77. Obama, "Why Organize?" p. 42.
78. Ibid.

79. Stanley Kurtz, "Wright 101," *National Review Online*, October 14, 2008, http://article.nationalreview.com/374927/wright-101/stanley-kurtz.

80. Sweet, "Meet the Press"; Anderson Cooper, "Interview With Illinois Senator Barack Obama"; "Severe Storms Strike Atlanta," cnn.com, March 14, 2008, http://transcripts.cnn.com/TRANSCRIPTS/0803/14/acd.01.html; Hannity & Colmes, "Obama Talks to Major Garrett on 'Hannity & Colmes,'" RealClearPolitics.com, March 14, 2008, at http://www.realclearpolitics.com/articles/2008/03/obama_talks_to_major_garrett_o.html; transcript, "Obama's Remarks on Wright," *New York Times*, April 29, 2008, http://www.nytimes.com/2008/04/29/us/politics/29text-obama.html.

81. David Plouffe, *The Audacity to Win* (New York: Viking, 2009), p. 207.

82. Peter Wallsten, "Fellow Activists Say Obama's Memoir Has Too Many I's," *Los Angeles Times*, February 19, 2007, http://www.latimes.com/news/politics/la-na-obamaorganize19-2007feb19,0,6545664.story.

83. Lynn Sweet, "Did Obama take too much credit?" Lynn Sweet's blog, February 20, 2007, *Chicago Sun-Times*, http://www.suntimes.com/news/politics/obamacommentary/264478.CST-NWS-sweet20.stng.

Chapter 9: State Senate Years

1. Jodi Kantor, "Teaching Law, Testing Ideas, Obama Stood Slightly Apart," *New York Times*, July 30, 2008, http://www.nytimes.com/2008/07/30/us/politics/30law.html.

2. Ibid.

3. Ibid.

4. Ibid.

5. Remnick, *The Bridge*, p. 265.

6. Ibid., pp. 265–66.

7. Obama, *The Audacity of Hope*, p. 247.

8. Ibid.

9. Jason Zengerle, "Con Law," *New Republic*, July 30, 2008, http://www.tnr.com/article/con-law?id=86dd0277-c6ee-4e3c-83e9-0bb468c5c40d&p=2; Remnick, *The Bridge*, pp. 265–66, 385.

10. Kantor, "Teaching Law"; Zengerle, "Con Law"; Remnick, *The Bridge*, p. 264.

11. "Chicago DSA Endorsements in the March 19 Primary Election," *New Ground* #45, March–April 1996, http://www.chicagodsa.orgngarchive/ng45.html#anchor1078925.

12. Ibid.

13. "New Party Member Heads for the Hill," *New Party News*, Spring 1996, p. 1; Trevor Loudon, "Obama File 41: Obama Was a New Party Member—Documentary Evidence," New Zeal Blog, October 23, 2008, http://newzeal.blogspot.com/2008/10/obama-file-41-obama-was-new-party.html.

14. The hard-copy edition of *New Ground* and Chicago DSA Executive Committee Meeting Minutes in the DSA Records present a more detailed account of Chicago DSA's 1996 endorsement of Obama than the online version of *New Ground*: "Chicago DSA Executive Committee Meeting Synopsis, January 20, 1996," *New Ground*, March–April 1996, p. 2; DSA Records, Box 116, Folder: Chicago DSA, "Chicago DSA Executive Committee Meeting Minutes," January 20, 1996.

15. Bob Roman, "A Town Meeting on Economic Insecurity," *New Ground* #45, March–April 1996, http://www.chicagodsa.org/ngarchive/ng45.html.

16. Robert Roman, "Chicago DSA Recommendations for the March Primary Election," *New Ground* #69, March–April 2000, http://www.chicagodsa.org/ngarchive/ng69.html#anchor535144.

17. Nancy Ryan and Thomas Hardy, "Sen. Palmer Ends Bid for Re-Election," *Chicago Tribune*, January 18, 1996, http://pqasb.pqarchiver.com/chicagotribune/access/17170536.html?dids=17170536:17170536&FMT=ABS&FMTS=ABS:FTF.

18. Remnick, *The Bridge*, pp. 288–93.

19. Copies of *New Deliberations* can be found in the Alice Palmer Papers at the Vivian G. Harsh Research Collection of Afro-American History and Literature, Woodson Regional Library, Chicago Illinois, Boxes 1 and 2. This is an unprocessed collection, without folders; Jan Carew, "Socialism Is the Only Way Forward," *New Deliberations*, Spring/Summer 1986, p. 8, Alice Palmer Papers, Box 2.

20. David Freddoso, *The Case Against Barack Obama* (Washington, D.C.: Regnery, 2008), pp. 128–29.

21. Alice Palmer Papers, Box 1.

22. Remnick, *The Bridge*, 278.

23. DSA Records, Box 116, Folder: Chicago DSA, "Chicago DSA Executive Committee Meeting Minutes," January 20, 1996.

24. DSA Records, Box 116, Folder: Chicago DSA, "Chicago DSA Membership Convention Minutes," June 8, 1996 (see Addendum: Bob Roman, "State of the Chapter Report").

25. Remnick, *The Bridge*, 399.

26. For a more detailed account, see Stanley Kurtz, "Barack Obama's Lost Years," *Weekly Standard*, August 11–August 18, 2008, http://www.weeklystandard.com/Content/Public/Articles/000/000/015/386abhgm.asp.

27. Chinta Strausberg, "Obama: Illinois Black Caucus is Broken," *Chicago Defender*, June 1, 1999, p. 1.

28. Peter S. Canellos, "Just Don't Call Barack Obama Liberal, Okey Doke?" *Boston Globe*, February 26, 2008, http://www.boston.com/news/nation/articles/2008/02/26/just_dont_call_barack_obama_liberal_okey_doke/; Peter Wehner, "Obama and the 'L' Word," *Wall Street Journal*, April 2, 2008, http://online.wsj.com/article/SB120709783253682035.html?mod=opinion_main_commentaries.

29. Greg Downs, "Candidates Spar Over Health Care," *Hyde Park Herald*, November 17, 1999, p. 1.

30. David Hawkings and Brian Nutting, eds., *CQ's Politics in America: 2004* (Washington, D.C.: CQ Press, 2003), p. 320.

31. Down, "Candidates Spar."

32. Karen Shields, "Congress Campaign Moves Into Home Stretch," *Hyde Park Herald*, March 15, 2000, pp. 1, 8.

33. "Our Endorsements," Editorial, *Chicago Defender*, March 13, 2004.

34. Chinta Strausberg, "Fitzgerald's Backing Out, Pushes Obama In Front," *Chicago Defender*, April 16, 2003, p. 3.

35. Barack Obama, "Bye George, Gore and Bush Are Different," *Hyde Park Herald*, November 1, 2000, p. 4.

36. "Who Hyde Parkers Voted For In the National Election," *Hyde Park Herald*, November 22, 2000, p. 6. Figures were obtained by combining votes in both Hyde Park wards.

37. William Ayers, *A Kind and Just Parent* (Boston: Beacon Press, 1997).

38. Ibid., p. xv.

39. Mary Wisniewski Holden, "The Juvenile Justice Reform Act," *Chicago Lawyer*, June 1998.

40. Jo Becker and Christopher Drew, "Pragmatic Politics, Forged on the South Side," *New York Times*, May 11, 2008, http://www.nytimes.com/2008/05/11/us/politics/11chicago.html?pagewanted=all; "Mark My Word," *Chicago Tribune*, December 21, 1997, Section 14, p. 5.

41. Ayers, *A Kind and Just Parent*, xviii.

42. Hope Reeves, "The Way We Live Now: 9-16-01: Questions for Bill Ayers; Forever Rad," *New York Times Magazine*, September 16, 2001, p. 21.

43. Ayers, *A Kind and Just Parent*, p. 45.

44. Ibid., p. 8.

45. Ibid., p. xiii.

46. Ibid., pp. 168–74.

47. Ibid., pp. 165–67, 178, 183.

48. Shields, "Congress Campaign."

49. Pam Belluck, "Fighting Youth Crime, Some States Blend Adult and Juvenile Justice," *New York Times*, February 11, 1998, Section A, p. 1.

50. Holden, "Juvenile Justice Reform Act."

51. Lorraine Forte, "Legislators Divided On 'Get Tough' Reforms," *Chicago Sun-Times*, September 28, 1997.

52. Chinta Strausberg, "Obama Seeks Tougher Youth Crime Bill," *Chicago Defender*, June 25, 1997, p. 5.

53. Chinta Strausberg, "Obama: Juvenile Justice System Flawed," *Chicago Defender*, December 3, 1997, p. 3.

54. "Should a child ever be called a 'super predator'?" The University of Chicago News Office, November 4, 1997, http://www-news.uchicago.edu/releases/97/971104.juvenile.justice.shtml.

55. Chinta Strausberg, "Juvenile Justice Bill In Jeopardy?" *Chicago Defender*, January 12, 1998, p. 1.

56. Holdern, "Juvenile Justice Reform Act"; Ray Serati, "Senate sends juvenile justice legislation to Gov. Edgar's desk," Copley News Service, January 29, 1998; Jason Piscia, "Senate approves Edgar's changes to juvenile justice bill," Copley News Service, May 5, 1998; Kurt Erickson and Mike Wiser, "Senate oks juvenile justice reforms," The Pantagraph, May 6, 1998, p. A5; The Associated Press, "Toughened Illinois Juvenile Crime Law Wins Final OK; Dual Sentence Provision Could Keep Youths In Jail," *St. Louis Post-Dispatch*, May 19, 1998, p. B2.

57. Sam Youngman and Aaron Blake, "Obama's crime votes are fodder for

rivals," *The Hill*, March 13, 2007, http://thehill.com/homenews/news/ 11316-obamas-crime-votes-are-fodder-for-rivals.

58. Ayers, *Fugitive Days*, pp. 289–90.

59. Remnick, *The Bridge*, p. 280.

60. Martin Kramer, "Khalidi of the PLO," Sandbox blog, October 30, 2008, http://sandbox.blog-city.com/khalidi_of_the_plo.htm; Martin Kramer, "In praise of the LA Times," Sandbox blog, November 2, 2008, http://sandbox.blog-city.com/in_praise_of_the_los_angelestimes.htm.

61. Peter Wallsten, "Allies of Palestinians see a friend in Obama," *Los Angeles Times*, April 10, 2008, http://articles.latimes.com/2008/apr/ 10/nation/na-obamamideast10.

62. Ayers, *Kind*, pp. ix–x; Ayers, *Fugitive Days*, p. 305; Rashid Khalidi, *Resurrecting Empire* (Boston: Beacon Press, 2004, 2005), pp. 212–13.

63. Remnick, *The Bridge*, p. 281. See also Chapter Seven.

64. Edward McClelland, "The crazy uncles in Obama's attic," Salon, March 18, 2008, http://www.salon.com/news/opinion/feature/2008/ 03/18/hyde_park.

65. Woods Fund of Chicago, "2001 Annual Report," p. 19; Freddoso, *The Case Against Barack Obama*, p. 149.

66. Joe Ruklick, "Fund-Raising Success Gives Obama Momentum," *Chicago Defender*, July 26, 2003, p. 5.

67. Todd Spivak, "Racial Profiling Bill Blocked by Senate Leader, Again," *Hyde Park Herald*, May 9, 2001, p. 1.

68. Ruklick, "Fund-Raising Success."

69. Joe Ruklick, "Hail Passage of Anti-Crime Bills," *Chicago Defender*, July 19, 2003, p. 1.

70. Heather Mac Donald, "The Myth of Racial Profiling," *City Journal*, Spring 2001, http://www.city-journal.org/html/11_2_the_myth.html.

71. Barack Obama, "Putting a Stop to Racial Profiling," *Hyde Park Herald*, February 16, 2000, p. 4.

72. Heather Mac Donald, "Is the Criminal-Justice System Racist?" *City Journal*, Spring 2008, http://www.city-journal.org/2008/18_2criminal _justice_system.html.

73. Todd Spivak, "Obama Lobbies for State Racial Profiling Legislation," *Hyde Park Herald*, February 28, 2001, pp. 1–2.

74. Jonann Brady, "Controversial Priest Returns to the Pulpit," ABC News, June 26, 2008, http://abcnews.go.com/GMA/story?id=5247464&

page=1; "Michael Pfleger," Discover the Networks, http://www
.discoverthenetworks.org/individualProfile.asp?indid=2313; "James
Meeks," Discover the Networks, http://www.discoverthenetworks.org/
individualProfile.asp?indid=2329.

75. Obama, *The Audacity of Hope*, pp. 230, 255, 258, 259.

76. Chinta Strausberg, "Illinois Black Caucus Bills Pass," *Chicago Defender*, May 23, 2001, p. 10.

77. Randolph Burnside and Kami Whitehurst, "From the Statehouse to the White House?" *Journal of Black Studies*, July 31, 2007, pp. 77–91.

78. Ibid., p. 85.

79. Ibid., p. 84.

80. Charles N. Wheeler III, "Grim Prognosis," Illinois Issues, April 2007, http://illinoisissues.uis.edu/features/2007apr/health.html.

81. John O'Connor, "Few clear winners in austere state budget," Associated Press, June 3, 2002; Adam Kovac, "Lawmakers Generally Play It Safe," *Chicago Tribune*, June 4, 2002, Metro p. 1.

82. John O'Connor, "Legislators will have to cut more than they thought," Associated Press, June 9, 2002.

83. "Passing the Buck," Editorial, *St. Louis Post-Dispatch*, June 4, 2002, p. B6; "Get out the knife, Governor," Editorial, *Chicago Tribune*, June 4, 2002, p. 18.

84. O'Connor, "Legislators will have to cut more."

85. Barack Obama, "Special Session Brings Some Hard Choices," *Hyde Park Herald*, July 3, 2002, p. 4; Chinta Strausberg, "Budget Cuts Severe to State's HIV/AIDS Program," *Chicago Defender*, June 11, 2002, p. 1.

86. Doug Finke, "Ryan leaves vetoes in lawmakers' hands," Copley News Service, June 10, 2002.

87. Charles N. Wheeler III, "The Hot Rod Express Speeds Toward a Budget Deficit Behemoth," *Illinois Issues*, February 2003, http://illinoisissues-archive.uis.edu/politics/budget2003.html.

88. On Obama's work with Quentin Young, see Chapter Four. On Bernardin Amendment, see Barack Obama, "State Health Plan on the Table, *Hyde Park Herald*, November 10, 1999, p. 4; Burnside and Whitehurst, "From the Statehouse," p. 90.

89. Barack Obama, "State-Wide Meetings Focus On Uninsured," *Hyde Park Herald*, October 2, 2002, p. 4.

90. Chinta Strausberg, "Democrats Urge Congress to Help Seniors, Patients, Meet Rx Costs," *Chicago Defender*, January 19, 2000; Obama, "State Health Plan;" Obama, "State-Wide Meetings."

91. Todd Spivak, "Obama Bill Increases Rights for Rape Victims," *Hyde Park Herald*, August 15, 2001, p. 2.

92. Freddoso, *The Case Against Barack Obama*, pp. 191–210.

93. Todd Spivak, "Sen. Obama Helps Defeat a Concealed Firearm Bill," *Hyde Park Herald*, April 11, 2001, p. 3.

Chapter 10: The Obama Administration

1. Michael Harrington and the Democratic Socialist Organizing Committee, "Toward a Socialist Presence in America," *Social Policy*, January/February 1974, pp. 5, 10.

2. Ibid., pp. 8–9.

3. This chapter freely draws upon all that has been established earlier in the book. When I am discussing material from a particular chapter, I'll indicate it in these notes, although the links to earlier sections of the book are not meant to be exhaustive. This section on community organizing draws particularly on Chapter Four.

4. Gerald F. Seib, "In Crisis, Opportunity for Obama," *Wall Street Journal*, November 21, 2008, http://online.wsj.com/article/SB1227212780 56345271.html.

5. See Chapter Nine.

6. See Chapter Five.

7. Lynda Waddington, "Harkin: Think of Health Care Reform as a Starter Home," *Iowa Independent*, December 17, 2009.

8. Boyte, Booth, Max, *Citizen*, pp. ix–x.

9. Norman J. Ornstein, "Obama: A Pragmatic Moderate Faces the 'Socialist' Smear," *Washington Post*, April 14, 2010, http://www .washingtonpost.com/wp-dyn/content/article/2010/04/13/AR20100 41303686.html.

10. Stephen Spruiell, "Unholy Union," *National Review*, November 23, 2009, http://nrd.nationalreview.com/article/?q=ZGFmMDY4NzdkM mIwZTQ1MzU2ZDA4NGZhNzJINGU2MTE=.

11. See Chapter Four.

12. See Chapter Five.

13. Jennifer Davis, "Freshmen Ponder Spring Lessons as They Return for the Fall Session," *Illinois Issues*, October 1997, pp. 6–7.

14. See Chapter One.

15. Sheryl Gay Stolberg, "For Obama, Nuance on Race Invites Questions," *New York Times*, February 8, 2010, http://www.nytimes.com/2010/02/09/us/politics/09race.html.

16. See Chapter Five.

17. Robert Jensen, "Is Obama a Socialist?" Counterpunch.org, September 25–27, 2009, http://www.counterpunch.org/jensen09252009.html.

18. See Chapter Five.

19. See Chapter Five.

20. Mark Schmitt, "Populism Without Pitchforks," *American Prospect*, October 20, 2008, http://www.prospect.org/cs/articles?article=populism_without_pitchforks.

21. "Obama Tells BW He's Not Antibusiness," *BusinessWeek*, July 29, 2009, http://www.businessweek.com/magazine/content/09_32/b4142000676096.htm.

22. See Chapter Two.

23. See Chapter Four.

24. Ed Morrissey, "Obama's character assassins target another National Review journalist," Hotair.com, September 16, 2008, http://hotair.com/archives/2008/09/16/obamas-character-assassins-target-another-national-review-journalist.

25. "White House Launches Web Site to Battle Health Care 'Rumors,' " Foxnews.com, August 10, 2009, http://www.foxnews.com/politics/2009/08/10/white-house-launches-web-site-battle-health-care-rumors. Also see Chapter One.

26. Karl Rove, "The President is 'Keeping Score,' " *Wall Street Journal*, April 2, 2009, http://online.wsj.com/article/SB123862834153780427.html.

27. Jim Rutenberg, "Behind the War Between White House and Fox," *New York Times*, October 22, 2009, http://www.nytimes.com/2009/10/23/us/politics/23fox.html.

28. Robert Barnes and Anne E. Kornblut, "It's Obama vs. the Supreme Court, Round 2, Over Campaign Finance Ruling," *Washington Post*, March 11, 2010, http://www.washingtonpost.com/wp-dyn/content/article/2010/03/09/AR2010030903040.html.

29. De Zutter, "What Makes Obama Run?"

30. Ryan Lizza, "Making It: How Chicago Shaped Obama," *New Yorker*, July 21, 2008, http://www.newyorker.com/reporting/2008/07/21/080721fa_fact_lizza?currentPage=all.

31. See Chapter Seven.

32. Robert Creamer, "Obama's Secret Weapon: OFA," Huffington Post, January 5, 2010, http://www.huffingtonpost.com/robert-creamer/obamas-secret-weapon-ofa_b_411605.html.

33. "Editorial: Rotten to the AmeriCorps," *Washington Times*, February 10, 2010, http://www.washingtontimes.com/news/2010/feb/10/rotten-to-the-americorps/.

34. Ibid.

35. Ibid.

36. See Chapter Two.

37. Obama, *Dreams from My Father*, pp. 169–70.

38. See Chapter Five.

39. See Chapter Six.

40. Patrice Hill, "Finance Bill Favors Interests of Unions, Activists," *Washington Times*, July 14, 2010, http://www.washingtontimes.com/news/2010/jul/14/finance-bill-favors-interests-of-unions-activists/.

41. "Comments of H. Booth on S7-10-09," August 10, 2009, Securities Exchange Commission, http://www.sec.gov/comments/s7-10-09s71009-91.htm; Americans for Financial Reform, "Here's what's on deck today, June 17, in the financial reform Conference Committee," at http://ourfinancialsecurity.org/2009/06/call-congress-toll-free-at-866-544-7573-2/.

42. Michael Harrington, "Serious About Socialism," *Democratic Left*, November 1979, p. 4.

43. See Chapter Five.

44. See Chapter Six.

45. "Fannie Motors," *National Review Online*, June 2, 2009, http://article.nationalreview.com/395777/fannie-motors/the-editors.

46. Matthew Continetti, "The Bailout State," *Weekly Standard*, June 15, 2009, http://www.weeklystandard.com/Content/Public/Articles/000/000/016/586sjvrv.asp.

47. Fred Barnes, "The Triumph of Crony Capitalism," *Weekly Standard*, July 13, 2009, http://www.weeklystandard.com/Content/Public/Articles/000/000/016/695beqni.asp.

48. Ibid.
49. Franklin Foer, Noam Scheiber, "Nudge-ocracy," *New Republic*, May 6, 2009, http://www.tnr.com/article/politics/nudge-ocracy
50. See Chapter One.
51. John Judis, "Fundamentally Different," *New Republic*, April 23, 2009, http://www.tnr.com/article/politics/fundamentally-different.
52. See Chapter Five.
53. John Judis, "Classless," *New Republic*, August 6, 2009, http://www.tnr.com/article/politics/classless.
54. Thomas B. Edsall, "The Obama Coalition," *Atlantic*, April 2010, http://www.theatlantic.com/politics/archive/2010/04/the-obama-coalition/38266/.
55. See Chapter Two.
56. See Chapter Two.
57. See Chapter Two.

INDEX